Stephan Schmidt-Wulffen, German A. Duarte (eds.)
The Object as a Process

Culture & Theory | Volume 264

The editors would like to extend their gratitude to the volume's language editor, Taylor Breckles, for her invaluable contribution.

Stephan Schmidt-Wulffen (Prof. Dr.) is a philosopher, art theorist, curator and currently professor of art theory and curatorial studies at Freie Universität Bozen. He was visiting professor at Columbia University in New York, he became *Rektor* of Akademie der bildenden Künste Wien (2001-2011). His research focuses on art theory, philosophy, artistic practices and contemporary art.
German A. Duarte (Dr.) is a media theorist, film scholar, film editor and currently assistant professor of film and media studies at Freie Universität Bozen. His research interests include the history of media, film history, cognitive cultural economy and philosophy.

Stephan Schmidt-Wulffen, German A. Duarte (eds.)

The Object as a Process

Essays Situating Artistic Practice

[transcript]

Bibliographic information published by the Deutsche Nationalbibliothek
The Deutsche Nationalbibliothek lists this publication in the Deutsche Nationalbibliografie; detailed bibliographic data are available in the Internet at http://dnb.d-nb.de

https://www.transcript-verlag.de/

Cover layout: Kordula Röckenhaus, Bielefeld
Cover illustration: El Anatsui, *Flower Garden* (2012), detail from the installation at the Kunstmuseum Bern, March 2020. Photo: Karen van den Berg.
Proofread: Taylor Breckles

https://doi.org/10.14361/9783839461143
Print-ISBN 978-3-8376-6114-9
PDF-ISBN 978-3-8394-6114-3
ISSN of series: 2702-8968
eISSN of series: 2702-8976

Contents

Foreword ... 7

Speaking of Things - An Introduction
Stephan Schmidt-Wulffen ... 9

The Autonomous Aesthetic of Allure: Mary Bauermeister's *Needless Needles* and Graham Harman's Object Philosophy
Hauke Ohls ... 17

Simply things
A phenomenological interpretation from technology to poetry
Martina Olivero ... 33

Origins and Ends: Understanding the Medium of Painting According to Heidegger's Truth
Tom Palin ... 47

Object as Symbol: Baudrillard's Thanatopoietic Form
Georgios Tsagdis ... 65

Co-Production: Towards a Relational Ontology of Aesthetic Objects
Olga Moskatova ... 85

Correspondences: Exploring the Echoes of Jack Spicer's Poetics in the Paintings of Matt Connors
Job Boot ... 101

The Object of Non-Aesthetics
Jonathan Fardy ... 113

Solid Gifts
Seven Lessons from the Fossil
Luca Trevisani ... 125

Massimo Bartolini's *Untitled Untitled* (2001)
The Strategy for Visualizing the Hyperspace
German A. Duarte ... 139

The Lure of Absence: Can there be Process without Artists?
Heidi C. Gearhart ... 155

A noisy love affair: The Language of Things in the Works of Mark Leckey and *Musa paradisiaca*
Miguel Ferrão ... 171

The photographic multiples of Joseph Beuys as an extension of himself
Pierre-Emmanuel Perrier de la Bâthie ... 185

Obsolescence and reinvention: the case study of João Maria Gusmão and Pedro Paiva
Filippo De Tomasi, Maura Grimaldi ... 197

A Two-Way Mirror: Narcissism and Surveillance from the Closed Circuit to the Network
Olivier Asselin ... 213

Shape of Things, Shapes of Time
Hans-Jörg Rheinberger ... 225

El Anatsui
"Triumphant Scale": Material Realism and the Logic of Things
Karen van den Berg ... 237

Authors ... 257

Foreword

The discussions concerning the need to dive deeper into the notion of the object and its influence on the creative process started to take place during our innumerous multidisciplinary research meetings, reading groups, and research projects dedicated to the general notion of artistic practice. During our discussions at the faculty of Design and Art at the Free University of Bozen-Bolzano, there appeared to be a recurring question: How does artistic practice lead to the production of knowledge?

This vast and complex question, as one might imagine, dragged our analysis to the empirical approach that the artistic field imposes as epistemic practice. Another inevitable question also became apparent during these discussions: How does, in turn, artistic knowledge relate to its material base? And, successively, how does contingent materiality guide the artist towards finding form and developing a statement?

Within a technological context in which both objects and subjects face the force of dematerialization exerted by digital technology, we considered it to be of extreme importance to inquire into the ways in which the object, its materiality, affordance, resistance, and digital dematerialization could influence – and maybe determine – creative processes and artistic practices.

The following chapters are consecrated to the object as a process; this is to say, to the features of the object, broadly constructed, that turn it into an active element in artistic practice. The following essays employ, from a multidisciplinary lens, notions such as object, thing, product, and form. In some texts, the reader will find the ways in which materiality – and sometimes immateriality – contribute to the creative process by resisting the artist's intentions and ideas.

The research project that allowed for the publication of this volume was fully sponsored by the Free University of Bozen-Bolzano. We thank very much the University for all of its support. We would also like to extend our gratitude to all of the authors that accepted to contribute to this volume. It would be impossible to mention and thank all of the colleagues and friends that directly and indirectly participated and enriched our discussions around the issue of the object. They all know our gratitude.

Stephan Schmidt-Wulffen and German A. Duarte, Bolzano, May 2022.

Speaking of Things – An Introduction

Stephan Schmidt-Wulffen

> "Y a-t-il une parole grandie de tout
> ce qui n'est pas l'humain,
> ô salines, roches et granites, puissants déserts?" [1]

In 1947, the painter Willi Baumeister introduced the concept of the "creative angle," which opens – as he explained – between the artist's intention and the final work. It is the materials of paint, brushes, and canvas that gradually changes the initial idea during production. In a lecture at MoMA some years later, Marcel Duchamp referred to this same phenomenon as the 'art coefficient': "a difference between the unexpressed but intended and the unintentionally expressed."[2]

The materials given play a crucial role in artistic practice, disturbing the smooth flow of thought and deviating from preconceived ideas. They introduce strangeness beyond individual imagination. Artists who would miss the wondering process would call the work an 'illustration,' indicating that it is only a voluntary transposition of an idea into reality. To allow the stubbornness of the material may also indicate a difference to other non-artistic practices. A mathematical operation should stay the same, independent of how it is performed.

Only a few scholars have strived for a more detailed view of this specific type of production. One was the art historian, Walter Sedlmayr.[3] According to Sedlmayr, the production process is continuous self-determination; self-expression of the later work. Like the artist Baumeister, he finds a vision at the beginning, a magnet and filter simultaneously: new ideas might show up during production, and results might be taken out of the process. The initial 'imaginative character' echoes in the details:

---

1 Éduard Glissant, *Philosophie de la Relation* (Paris: Gallimard, 2009), 98.

2 Willi Baumeister, *The Unknown in Art* (Willi Baumeister Stiftung: Berlin, 2014). Marcel Duchamp, *The creative Act*, (1961) http://www.fiammascura.com/Duchamp.pdf, cosnsulted 15–12-2021.

3 Hans Sedlmayr, *Kunst und Wahrheit. Zur Theorie und Methodik der Kunstgeschichte* (Mittenwald: Mäander, 1978).

a color spot, some lines, a figure. In each of these details, the complete 'organism' of the work seems potentially contained.

The relationship between the artist and the material – between the artist and the thing being processed – plays a central role in our book. It is one of the outcomes of a research group at the Free University Bozen-Bolzano which comprised of anthropologists, sociologists, art historians, and media theorists. We tried to define the specific quality of artistic production by asking ourselves, how do artists produce knowledge? This vast and complex question, as one might imagine, dragged our analysis to the empirical approach that the creative field imposes as epistemic practice. Another inevitable question also became apparent during these discussions: How does, in turn, artistic knowledge relate to its material base? And, successively, how does contingent materiality guide the artist towards finding form and developing a statement? Faced with complex problems like these, one tends to overlook a straightforward question: Can we perceive something beyond imagination, the 'Ding an sich'? Kant was quite clear: preconditioned forms of time and space shape every perception. Our senses transform everything we see; a perceiving subject turns perception into an 'object.' Graham Harman – introduced by Hauke Ohls in his essay on Mary Bauermeister – also stresses that the subject can never fully recognize the object – artwork. Therefore, he introduces a quadruple object structure, which distinguishes between real objects, natural qualities, and sensual objects/sensual qualities. The 'real' parts remain inaccessible.

How do we refer, then, to the material side of the artwork? If we habitually call it an 'object,' we are already establishing the authority of a subject and it's categorization of the real. By overlooking the quality of the very thing, thinking always generates, through the reflecting subject, an object instead. This is why many of the essays in this book try to overcome the subject:object divide. As the thing is left as something principally unrecognizable, a blank spot appears in the center of aesthetic thinking. In all the contributions of this book, we find different and, significantly, mostly performative templates organized around this blank. Harman for example introduces 'allure' to relate real qualities to sensual ones insofar as allure only alludes to the hidden real attributes. The viewer has to instigate what cannot be experienced.

But it is in Heidegger's philosophy where the ontology of the thing plays the center role. We, therefore, even invited two authors – Martina Olivero and Tom Palin – to confront his theories. Heidegger stresses the autonomy of things because they are autonomous from the subjects that think about them. He finds in Greek philosophy a model of how things could have meaning without a subject ascribing it. Olivero outlines Heidegger's concept of the 'thing' and what qualifies it as art. For that, he has to introduce Heidegger's terminology, which refers to Greek origins and the idea of poiesis. The process of poiesis in Greek thinking links to unveiling: the craftsman lets the truth appear. Objects are taken out of non-existence by a craftsman, and production makes truth apparent: Aletheia. The Greek temple demonstrates the function of art. In holding its place against a storm raging above it, it makes the storm visible in its violence. The temple does not represent God but allows for his presence. The work of art can only be understood based on itself, neither as product nor object. As such, it is manifestation and openness. It is therefore constructed to be looked at, to be experienced. Truth is called forth in the production and understanding of the work, says Tom Palin. He connects to Heidegger's interest in Hölderlin, who chooses the Danube River's continuous movement as a metaphor for this perpetual becoming. Heidegger opens up the distance between form and content through the concept of rumor. Rumor amounts to that which permits a continuous dislocation between an actual event and the language of an event (and so equals 'allure'). Rumor has no recognizable origin, and its repetition is always a repetition of repetition. Palin establishes repetition as a chain of transformation with his particular interest in painting: paint transforms from mere material to equipment, then is bound up in the work and later in discourse.

What, in Baumeister, was the impact of material resistance on the artist's imagination is the independent appearance of 'truth' in Heidegger. Even if the autonomy of matter has had a significant impact on thinking after Heidegger, the ontology of a metaphysical truth soon looked antiquated. Heidegger observes processes initiated by men but not entirely directed by them. Heidegger qualifies this excess as 'truth.' Later, philosophers tried to grasp the same 'excess' in different – pragmatic and performative – ways.

Georgios Tsagdis reminds us of Jean Baudrillard and his thanatopoetic form in the book on symbolic exchange and death. Baudrillard defines death not as an actual event that happens to a body or a subject, but rather as a form inherent to life. He imagines an energetic system that binds and unbinds energies. It is capitalism that divides life and death, subject and object. Through reversibility, Baudrillard tries to overcome divisions, to develop a new poetics. What becomes clear in Baudrillard's rhetoric is the fact that the 'object' is constituted in a semiotic dimension, while the 'thing' rests outside the semiotic. One has to use language in an elliptic, 'pointing' way to approach the thing. Roman Jakobson would define this pointing language as one which transposes the metaphoric dimension (Ähnlichkeit') onto the metonymic one ('Kontiguität'), indicating the prominent role of concatenation, sequence, and series in poetic practice.[4]

Sequences and series, which we will repeatedly meet in all of the essays, are not only interesting as structure and product. It is crucial for their ontology that they have to be continuously produced. They essentially structure aesthetic labor: they allow for the replacement of any essentialism – Heidegger's truth f.e. – by social prac-

4 Roman Jakobson, "Linguistik und Poetik", in: *Roman Jakobson. Poetik. Ausgewählte Aufsätze 1921–1971*, ed. Elmar Holenstein and Tarcisius Schelbert (Frankfurt: Suhrkamp, 1979), 83–121.

tice, first by experts (artists) and then by non-experts (audience). 'Making,' therefore, becomes even more prominent than semiotics. It is the process of production that allows for a rearrangement of subject and object. Hans Jörg Rheinberger introduces George Kubler's concept of temporal series or sequences of works as connected expressions. The work of art, pace Kubler, is an arrested happening, a "graph of activity now stilled."[5]

In her text, Olga Moskatova introduces the theories of Simondon, who designed making as a co-production between men and matter. The process of making is no longer described by 'active' (men) and 'passive' (matter), by 'immaterial' and 'material' (wherein the immaterial is supposed to be the leading force). Making, here, is described as a co-individuation in the between, which entails relational becoming for both the aesthetic object and the human subject. The aesthetic object becomes a multiplicity. We deal no longer with figure/ground, but rather with a metastable field as a relational process of pluralization, pervaded by multiple differences. Moskatova uses the films of Len Ley as a model. The artist scratches his motives frame by frame into the celluloid. Here, the singular frame is never a homogenous entity but rather a "multitude of functionally different zones." The artist's activity is relational, slowly harmonizing different processual factors and actors.

What holds for images on a filmstrip can also stand as a model for other artistic practices. As Job Boots analyses, the painter Matt Connors uses one picture to make another one, again constituting a series. Also, here the one painting does not stay autonomous, but instead becomes a tool for constructing a trajectory: it demonstrates what should be done in the next painting. A conversation takes place between the works. Things 'not working' become a guiding principle for Connors. A primary inspiration is the poet Jack Spicer, who treats poems as 'things among other things.' The observation of Connor's practice leads Boots to a conception of the image as neither representative nor defined by an equipmental kind of thingness à la Heidegger. Instead, the picture forges connections with other things (or images), transgressing our intentionality. Similarly, Hauke Ohls observes the cross-references in three early needleworks of Bauermeister. Using Harman's art-object philosophy, he understands the three pieces as one interconnected object and makes an invisible object the background of the experience of artworks.

We have to replace the simple dialectics at work in Baumeister or Sedlmayr through a forcefield of practices – always material, but only partly semiotic – which allow identities to articulate, may they be artworks, artists, or audiences. However, that opens an additional perspective: while the older dialectics were relatively mute, the new practices invite discussion. What is their principle of construction? Are there different aesthetic practices? I already mentioned Jakobson's observation on their metonymic character, yet Jonathan Fardy, in his essay, is more interested in

5 George Kubler, *The Shape of Time* (New Haven/London: Yale University Press, 2008), 17.

how philosophers constitute their objects. He looks at Adorno, who recommended that philosophy be composed like music; he looks at Benjamin, who took art as a model for a philosophical composition following surrealist techniques of juxtaposition and montage; and he looks at Derrida, who turned to the 'margins' of philosophical thought. All of his examples – and we could add others, easily – are inspired by the arts (remember that Derrida uses a visual artifice, replacing a letter in 'différence' that does not change pronunciation, to indexically denote a meaning that can perhaps be experienced but not articulated). Following François Laruelle's non-aesthetic, Fardy postulates a theory of art as an art of theory. The non-aesthetic treats philosophical work as a craft that makes concepts. As philosophy becomes, what he calls, an art of 'installation' – integrating a multiplicity of practices and processes – its practice becomes significant for understanding artistic practices 'as such.'

This is why we invited the artist, Luca Trevisani, a colleague from Bolzano, to contribute his ideas on materiality in his practice. His text is not just a theory, but also a strategic speech which elliptically tries to catch the void left by 'the thing.' Trevisani uses the fossil to qualify the artwork. Like Baumeister, he stresses the self-making component of the work but erases the part of the artist-producer nearly completely. He says that getting a hold of the fossil is a matter more of listening than of producing. We encounter, here, a widespread doubt concerning the role of the author. Instead, the fossil intrudes into the contemporary, creating a temporal delay. It is never fixed, and acquires new wrinkles and new meanings that are continuously changing. 'Metamorphosis' is the principle of a body born by itself. In the epistemology of the fossil, we have copies without an original, always returning as a simulacrum of itself. They are not copies but, as Trevisani says, "solid ghosts, neither positive nor negative." As the fossil continuously creates itself, we no longer know what is alive and what is dead. In a certain sense, it, therefore, combines body and mind.

Trevisani's metaphor of the fossil also refers to crucial topics which show up in the discourse around artworks today and their material existences. The artistic author is reduced to an element in a chain of production in which things play an active role. The object falls out of the dialogues with the subject; as a mere 'thing,' it loses its identity also in the sense that constant change replaces its former inertness. The thing becomes fluid and we can add metamorphosis to the governing principles of the sequence or series.

Still, the philosopher tends to *name* the object of his reflections, while the artist may *handle* material in a significant, explicatory way. His 'language' is one of decisions, gradually building up to a trajectory of actions, mirrored in the series of works. Oliver Asselin, therefore, calls the video work a 'philosophical model.' German Duarte shows us how a simple piece by Massimo Bartolini could change space and time. 'Untitled Untitled' (2001) is a sculpture only in a metaphorical sense, as it is also a performance: a golden pill held in the hand of a museum guard, never shown, never documented. Duarte demonstrates how a seemingly simple artistic gesture brings into play complicated philosophical reflections and forces us to think about non-Euclidean space. While Euclidean space implies three dimensions that 'contain' objects, philosophers like Bergson and Whitehead, and mathematicians like Gauss, Riemann, or Poincaré describe space as a product of relations between entities. Also, in Bartolini's piece, space is constituted as a relationship between subjects and objects, deriving from the potential presence of the pill. Duarte also demonstrates that entities that generate space in this way cannot be considered isolated entities, instead, they should be conceived through a series of states distributed in a duration. The object is in process.

The detailed study of artists' work in the second part of our book contributes to the question of different pragmatic aspects in artistic practices, while the theoretical first part pictures the larger scene. Heidi Gearhart enters a scriptorium of the Middle Ages. She observes how the copyists integrate holes in the parchment into the overall appearance of the handwritten and decorated page. Gearhart compares this old strategy with the performances of Marina Abramović and argues that the entire system (producer – material – work – viewer) is part of the process of the work. But she also hints at the transformative powers sustained by the working process. The defect of the parchment is not accepted as a given, but is treated in its contingency. It turns into an unexpected motor of production. A transformation is wandering through the chains of production. The hole turns into an animal's body; the bicycle saddle turns into a bull's head; a bottle dryer turns into a sculpture. In his chapter, Miguel Ferrão describes how the artist Mark Leckey confronted a statue by Henry Moore with his technical sculpture of today: a speaker-stack. One of the humorous images in this book is when the British artist tries through music and sounds to move the modernist sculpture "until it starts to speak." The production process takes up something to transform it into something else. Conceptual art introduced intermedia as a significant mode of such a transformation. Smithson's 'spiral Jetty' photographs are not supplementary documentation because the work is too far away. "Spiral Jetty", on the contrary, is far away in order to make documentation part of a 'work' that only exists in the play between media forms like photo, film, and text. The object has become 'fluent' because it is wandering through its prolonged translation. Duarte even argues that video is the medium of our time as, by its digital nature, it dissolves its objects and turns them into a continuum in a very literal way.

Processes of transformation in practice can also be translations like in intermedia. Pierre de La Bâthie describes the circulation of objects and how this characterizes the status of 'work.' For example, Josef Beuys was a target for photographers. He used these pictures, replicated them into multiples, and gave value by signing them. The signing turned the object into a relic, precious because it bears a trace of him. When circulation supplemented creation, the concept of appropriation got a prominent role. Appropriation changed the character of the artwork drastically: it reached the value of a palimpsest. You could always see a prior meaning, a second use, and social history through the work. It did not only get its meaning through the artistic author, but also by an earlier social use. Its allegorical structures made its trajectory through history co-present and readable.

Similar transformations take place when older technologies are introduced into new works. Filippo De Tomasi and Maura Grimaldi describe the reevaluation processes between obsolescence and reinvention in the installations of João Maria Gusmão and Pedro Paiva. They apply projector technology – old slide and film projectors – which is usually out of use. Following Rosalind Krauss, they define these media as a 'set of conventions.' To re-use them creates a critique of normative use and the (social) role of the beholder. This technique corresponds with appropriation (of found slides), and with DIY and hacking. The authors also propose a new order of time, a temporal inversion, resulting in a "reinvention of time", as argued by Elsaesser. All rethink the limits of the apparatus.

Even if the topic only shows up here in a marginal way, we should not forget that we can redefine 'identity' as we did with 'time' and 'space'. Baumeister learned from Kant, but also from Hegel, who developed a dialectic of objectification and internalization. Self-consciousness has to externalize itself; and in this externalization, it posits itself as an object or the object as itself. Then, self-consciousness has to supersede this externalization by sublation. The subject forms itself in its otherness through a continuous process of communication. The production of artworks for a long time parallels the production of the self. Transgressing the subject: object divide means overcoming a dialectic of thesis, antithesis, and synthesis in a complex network of terms, and in practices. It is, therefore, interesting to follow artistic experiments that simulate identity. As de la Bathie shows, Beuys used the circulation of pictures to produce a public persona.

The photographs compose a network, which constitutes Beuys' artistic public persona. Through the experiments to dissolve the antagonism of subject and object the role of the author became critical. Artists like Josef Beuys, but also Katharina Sieverding or Martin Kippenberger used a multiplied, circulating work to define with it a public persona. Asselin observes in his essay how closed-circuit video installations cause the social constitution of the subject. Video, he finds, is a specific way to establish relationships between subject and object. He shows the active role technology generally plays in the very constitution of both of them. The gaze in the video might even have a 'pre-identitarian' quality, equaling the partial look of the baby before the primal scene.

In observing the practices of scientists in labs, Hans-Jörg Rheinberger designs a complex production system which many of today's object strategies echo. It seems like a summary of many of our observations, and it proposes additional arguments for reading artistic production. He develops a model of 'bricolage' in which research tools can continuously change roles. A field of 'subduction' also opens, in which the unforeseen happens: a field opens in-between the agent of knowledge and his objects. In Rheinberger's theory, the series, the sequence becomes the 'epistemic thing' – more of a question than an answer – to be developed in the research project. The 'technical thing' would be the material surrounding of the lab, which enters into a complex relation with the epistemic one. The sequences of epistemic things form ensembles. They increase, exhaust themselves, ramify new series, and become focused, intertwined, and transposed. Rheinberger, in his essay, proposes five different trajectories of these series. Scientists and artists have to acquaint themselves with the micrological givens of particular systems, their materialities, and their temporalities. To have an idea means becoming aware of an option that such systems offer by either displacing elements, inserting new techniques, or pursuing signals that have surfaced in hidden corners of the system. Where Baumeister experienced a simple dialectic, Rheinberger established a complex structure of transformative actions of different degrees of 'objecthood.'

The African artist, El Anatsui, uses liquor-bottle caps for his huge 'tapestries.' When Karen van den Berg analyses this practice, she makes us aware that appropriation or hacking are being established as a paradigmatic form of artistic practice; as she says, a whole new 'materialistic realism.' We already noticed the political turn in the works of Mark Leckey, as Ferrão described it. Leckey appropriated DIY films of British nightclub culture and reassembled them in his famous 'Fiorucci Made Me Hardcore.' This appropriation shed light on the identity of working-class culture. Van den Berg also hints at the political coloring of this aesthetic practice. She highlights the connections between the work process, the material, and the studio as a social space. The history of African colonization is inscribed into the working circle and its material outcome. Here, the artistic transformation makes the object's historical, social, and even geopolitical scripts visible. The work paradigmatically revolves around a performative understanding of matter, reality, and thingness.

If we – like Èdouard Glissant – try to hear the language of things, salt pans, rocks, or deserts, we have to change position in a dance of agency constantly. The thing, which is what these essays teach us, remains an empty spot in the human imagination. We can only summon it by continuously creating 'objects' of many kinds. The quotation marks here are essential: 'Object' is not a term. It is part of a complex space wherein 'object', but also 'subject', 'product', 'producer' and 'recipient' float and are continuously redefined. One aspect of artistic practice today lies in redefining the standards of the field continuously, and you will experience this while reading.

The Autonomous Aesthetic of Allure: Mary Bauermeister's *Needless Needles* and Graham Harman's Object Philosophy

Hauke Ohls

> "The human is not primarily part of the artwork's situation, but is an ingredient of the work no less than paint or marble."[1]

In determining what an object can be and how it relates to its environment, the American philosopher Graham Harman takes an extreme position. For him, everything is an object – an assumption without exception. Moreover, every object is autonomous, consisting of uncountable other objects; even every human experience is a new temporary object, while humans are of course also objects. This philosophical approach is known as *Object Oriented Ontology* (OOO), a subcategory of *Speculative Realism*.[2] In his book *Art and Objects*, published in 2020, Harman attempts for the first time to systematically apply his object philosophy and interpretation of aesthetics to works of art; previously he had only written essays or short passages in books on the subject.[3] Nevertheless, his approaches have already struck a chord among artists,

1 Graham Harman, *Art and Objects* (Cambridge, Medford: Polity Press, 2020), 58.

2 Levi Bryant, Graham Harman, and Nick Srnicek, eds., *The Speculative Turn: Continental Materialism and Realism* (Melbourne: re.press, 2011); Avanessian, Armen, ed., *Realismus Jetzt. Spekulative Philosophie und Metaphysik für das 21. Jahrhundert* (Berlin: Merve, 2013).

3 The most important publications that refer to art are: Graham Harman, "Der dritte Tisch," in *DOCUMENTA (13). Das Buch der Bücher. Katalog 1/3*, ed. Carolyn Christov-Bakargiev and Chus Martinez (Ostfildern: Hatje Cantz, 2013), 577–580; Graham Harman, "Über stellvertretende Verursachung," in *Speculations III*, ed. Michael Austin, Paul J. Ennis, and Fabio Gironi (Brooklyn: punctum books, 2013), 210–240; Graham Harman, "Art Without Relations," *ArtReview* (September 2014): 144–147; Graham Harman, "Greenberg, Duchamp and the Next Avantgarde," in *Speculations V. Aesthetics in the 21st Century*, ed. Ridvan Askin, Paul J. Ennis, Andreas Hägler (Brooklyn: punctum books, 2014), 251–274; and Graham Harman, *Dante's Broken Hammer. The Ethics, Aesthetics, and Metaphysics of Love* (London: Repeater, 2016). An overview in: Hauke Ohls, *Objektorientierte Kunsttheorie. Graham Harmans spekulative Philosophie im Kontext einer (nicht-)relationalen Ästhetik* (Hamburg: Avinus, 2019).

art theorists, and curators in contemporary discourse. However, there is a lack of research into what new perspectives can be gained on works of art and their reception if it is actually assumed that everything is an object.[4]

In the following, these perspectives will be explored using a group of works by the German visual artist, Mary Bauermeister, entitled *Needless Needles*, which she created between 1963 and 2016. We can be sure that Bauermeister was not influenced by OOO in the development of her themes, as Harman's work had not yet seen the light of day at the time the artist started the group of works.[5] This study will also briefly discuss Bauermeister's influences and points of reference, but the focus will be on OOO. The aim is not to explain the philosophical model by means of works of art, but rather to attempt to expand the reception of those artworks by using Harman's theories as a key to a new interpretation. What new perspectives can be added to works of art when everything is considered as an object? The focus of this essay is on the initial pieces of the *Needless Needles* group of works, which initially consisted of a light sheet from 1963 along with a drawing and a lens box from 1964.[6] The term *Needless Needles* is a play on words and refers to the motif of needles and sewing, which occurs repeatedly in these three works. However, the title contains an inaccuracy in favor of alliteration, as Bauermeister wanted to use the expression "Nutzlose Nadeln," which would be translated literally into English as "Useless Needles." She used *Needless Needles* instead, as starting point for a constant play with words, for example the recipient can read "needless needless" or "needless noodles" in the works. It is evident that grammatical accuracy is not a priority in the artist's works and that the title is used as a conscious stylistic device to suggest both process and interconnectedness. These two aspects – process and interconnectedness – are reflected not only within the works but also between the works and can be grasped using OOO, even though the insistence of OOO on the autonomy of the object initially suggests the opposite.

Graham Harman's art-object philosophy and *Needless Needles*

In his latest monograph, *Art and Objects*, Harman turns increasingly to formalism in order to interpret works of art. This was not reflected to the same extent in his

4 Andrew Cole, "Those Obscure Objects of Desire," *Artforum* (Summer 2015): 319–323.

5 Mary Bauermeister was born in Frankfurt am Main in 1934, Graham Harman in Iowa City in 1968.

6 The group of works was constantly expanded by Mary Bauermeister and there is another light sheet called *Needless Needles Junior*. From the beginning of the 1970s, more lens boxes were created, with the last ones being created in 2016.

previous writings. His use of the term 'formalism' is based on the theories of Immanuel Kant, whom Harman describes as the "godfather of formalism in aesthetics and everywhere else."[7] He also refers to the art criticism of Clement Greenberg and Michael Fried and their reinterpretation of the notion of formalism for abstract expressionism.

The central element, for Harman, is that Kant's formalism describes an autonomy that must always be granted to the object. He refers in particular to Kant's "thing in itself," which, according to Harman, should form the focus of how artworks are described.[8] In Kant's view, since intellectual comprehension cannot fully absorb the sensual, we are not able to fully grasp things outside of our own consciousness.[9] Alongside the "thing in itself," Kant's concept of "beauty" from the *Critique of Judgement* is decisive for Harman: "Beauty" is independent of both the subject and personal pleasure.[10] Harman concludes from this that works of art cannot be described by their effects, but rather that "beauty" is the central reference point for works of art by which they should be judged or prioritized.[11] It is a common practice of Harman's to distill one aspect of a philosophical model and adapt it for his own interpretations, while also rejecting other constitutive aspects. Where he differs crucially from Kant is in his rejection of so-called "correlationism," which states that we "only [have] access to a correlation of thinking and being, and never separately to either of the two concepts."[12] The challenge of the "correlationist circle" is, on the one hand, to dissolve the dependence that arises from the fact we only have access to the world outside of our minds through our thinking – meaning that the world is always formed by our subjective insights – and, on the other hand, to avoid falling into a dichotomy of "subject" and "object," or "spirit" and "matter," which not only separates people from the outside world but also privileges them above it.

Further, Harman focuses on Clement Greenberg's and Michael Fried's art-based formalism, especially on the autonomy of the artwork both two art critics describe. The exclusion of biography, context, economy, and other factors from interpretation

7 Harman, *Art and Objects*, 31.

8 Harman, *Art and Objects*, 4.

9 Immanuel Kant, *Kritik der reinen Vernunft* 1, ed. Wilhelm Weischedel (Frankfurt am Main: Suhrkamp, 1974), 277–282. The Kantian "noumenon" is always transformed by our mind into a "phenomenon".

10 Immanuel Kant, *Kritik der Urteilskraft*, ed. Willhelm Weischedel (Frankfurt am Main: Suhrkamp, 1974), 239–241.

11 Harman, *Art and Objects*, 34, 166.

12 Quentin Meillassoux, *Nach der Endlichkeit. Versuch über die Notwendigkeit der Kontingenz* (Zürich, Berlin: diaphanes, 2013), 18. Own translation, original citation in German: "nur Zugang zu einer Korrelation von Denken und Sein haben, und nie gesondert zu einem der beiden Begriffe."

is not as fundamental to Harman as it is for the theoreticians of abstract expressionism. For Harman, these aspects are only an addition, the object remains largely autonomous.[13] He sees the decisive difference between the two American art critics and Kant as opposing views of formalism: while Kant starts from the subject and relates the determinations to the human mind and categories, Greenberg and Fried start with the object and try to interpret it independently of context and subject.[14]

At this point it becomes obvious why Harman bases his art theory on formalism and makes these generalizations: he primarily underlines the autonomy that the object has in formalism and the idea that it cannot be fully recognized by a subject. The formalist tradition, according to Harman, offers the most distant antithesis to a relational conception of art; he refers not only to interpretations such as relational aesthetics, but also generally to context-related "further banging of the anti-formalist political/ethnographical drum."[15]

Even if Harman's art theory is connected to Kant or Greenberg and Fried, the concept of the object is fundamentally different. Instead, it is similar to other philosophical borrowings that Harman uses to elaborate his object structure, be it Aristotle, Gottfried Wilhelm Leibniz, Edmund Husserl, Alfred North Whitehead, or Martin Heidegger – an approach for which he often has been criticized.[16] In the context examined here, it suffices to point out that the object structure that Harman develops from the various philosophical positions is a quadruple one. Each object consists of four parts: the "real object," the "real qualities," the "sensual object," and the "sensual qualities".[17] The parts with the word "real" are always "withdrawn" from other objects, which means they are not accessible to other objects and are essentially in a sealed-off sphere. Only the "sensual" components, i.e. the "sensual object" and the "sensual qualities," reveal themselves to another object, for example to me as an observer. All four parts of an object are connected among each other and with themselves. The term "object" is not to be understood as denoting a material entity; not only is an ocean an object, but also every drop of water in it. It is important to note that every object is a quadruple one and has autonomous parts that can never be reached by another object. It is furthermore impossible for the object's potential to be fully exhausted by relations to (parts of) other objects.

In *Art and Objects*, Harman simplifies his "perception of art" in comparison to his earlier writings. The viewer and the work of art remain essential, only the process is

---

13 Harman, *Art and Objects*, 32–33.

14 Harman, *Art and Objects*, 52–56.

15 Nicolas Bourriaud, *Relational Aesthetics* (Dijon: les presses du réel, 2002); Harman, *Art and Objects*, 166.

16 Dan Zahavi, "The end of what? Phenomenology vs. speculative realism," *International Journal of Philosophical Studies* 24, No. 3 (2016): 289–309.

17 Graham Harman, *Vierfaches Objekt* (Berlin: Merve, 2015). Harman describes his understanding of objects in detail in this publication.

different and seems highly relational. The viewers are necessary for a work of art to be created at all: "Clearly there is no art without a human ingredient."[18] This means that the "real object" of the quadruple recipient-object – the part always withdrawn into an autonomous sphere – connects with the "sensual qualities" of the artwork object. This situation of reception forms a "third and higher object," a union of parts of the viewer and parts of the artwork.[19] For Harman, the rejection of relationality is based on the fact that the artwork can never be completely absorbed in the reception situation, but rather only part of it. The core, the "real object" of the artwork, and thus countless other "sensual qualities" and countless other interpretations, withdraws into an underlying, unreachable, autonomous sphere.

The so-called "allure" plays a dominant role in this union that constitutes the work of art: "For the aesthetics of OOO, it is the allure of individual objects that lies at the center of the artwork."[20] Harman uses the term "allure" to describe the connection between the "real object" and the "sensual qualities." This connection exists, on the one hand, between the parts of the object that become a work of art and, on the other hand, between the object that is a hybrid of recipient and artwork. Harman has recently reframed the double function of the "allure," now defining it as existing when a work of art not only shows its "sensual qualities" but also alludes to its own hidden "real object."[21] This "allure" makes works of art interesting in the first place, because it permits the observer to speculate about what can never be seen or experienced; the autonomous and withdrawn object is addressed indirectly. In everyday experience, the "real object" of the observer only interacts with the "sensual object" and does not necessarily lead to a newly-formed object; works of art thus have a more specific situation of perception.[22] Here, it becomes clear why works of art are repeatedly given such a central position in Harman's ontology: the "real object" of a viewer creates an artwork by combining it with the "sensual qualities" of another object. In this connection, "allure" insinuates something objective – figuratively speaking – into Kant's "thing in itself." Works of art do this because they act as "metaphors" – i.e. they create objects that are not merely "literal," but offer illogical and counterintuitive alternatives to the everyday world that is "so often boring, depressing, and stupefyingly familiar."[23]

Harman's update of his art theory turns increasingly to Kant's aesthetics and describes the gap between the "real object" and the "sensual qualities" such as "beauty." Here, he refers to the "real object" of the painting, sculpture, or photograph and its

---

18 Harman, *Dante's Broken Hammer. The Ethics, Aesthetics, and Metaphysics of Love*, 222.

19 Harman, *Art and Objects*, 173.

20 Harman, *Dante's Broken Hammer. The Ethics, Aesthetics, and Metaphysics of Love*, 207.

21 Harman, *Art and Objects*, 47.

22 Harman, *Vierfaches Objekt*, 129.

23 Harman, *Art and Objects*, 177.

own "sensual qualities": "For OOO, the meaning of beauty is not some vague appeal to an ill-defined aestheticism, but is explicitly defined as the disappearance of a real object behind its sensual qualities."[24] The term "beauty" remains ill-defined in Harman's work because it cannot be precisely determined in discourse. To provide an expression for a speculative process but not offer further any evaluation criteria does not help with the dilemma that has accompanied the term "beauty" for centuries. This strategy can be observed repeatedly in Harman, his appropriation of terms and concepts being only a partial reinterpretation and not a clarification based on discourse. Another reevaluation is within Michael Fried's concept of "theatricality." While Fried as a formalist sees "theatricality" as a significant effect of minimal art and therefore rejects it, Harman evaluates the "theatrical" as thoroughly positive.[25] Artworks exist in a profoundly "theatrical" situation because they only become art through the ingredient of the recipient. Harman slightly changes his terms and the reference points for OOO with each publication, which can cause confusion; his ambiguity is a particular challenge. Looking at the work group *Needless Needles* with his current orientation, the recipient would enter into a "theatrical" connection with, for example, the drawing *Needless Needles*: the "real object" of the recipient connects with the "sensual qualities" of the artwork and this would form a new (quadruple) object. This tension between the "real object" of the drawing and its own "sensual qualities" is what Harman calls "beauty." If the "sensual qualities" of the drawing were to insinuate into its own "real object," this would be called "allure". As an example, we will now consider the drawing *Needless Needles* created completely in ink and pencil on paper (Fig. 1).

Since Harman describes objects as an "infinite regress," it is possible to create an infinite number of objects out of this artwork, which would all be works of art if they would connect with the viewer as highlighted above.[26] This means that the painted circular structure with the inverted 21 in the upper right corner would be a (new and autonomous) object going through the same process of art perception whilst being simultaneously included in the first object (the entire drawing).

---

24 Harman, *Art and Objects*, 24.

25 Harman, *Art and Objects*, 45–49.

26 Harman, *Vierfaches Objekt*, 139.

Figure 1: Mary Bauermeister, Needless Needless, 1964, pastel, ink on paper 49,8 x 60 cm

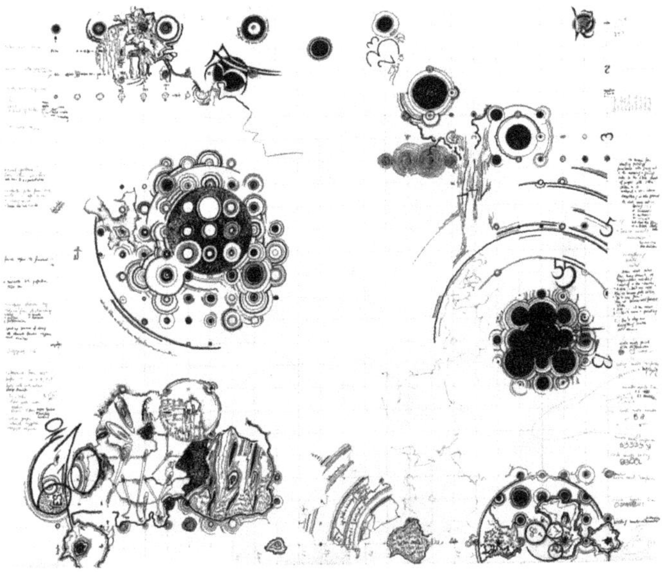

The sequence can go on *ad infinitum* and is likely to occur not only when observing the drawing in the museum, but also through various forms of reproduction. Thus, not only can each element within the drawing be connected to every other element to become a common object of art perception, but also contexts can be included – for example, the exhibition space or the situation in which the work was created – in this case by a young artist in New York in the early 1960s. According to Harman's approach to formalism, all possible contexts can be included, but they are only an almost marginal aspect of the work as a whole; its major part remains withdrawn and autonomous.

These remarks roughly summarize Harman's art analysis, but everything remains on a speculative level of the philosophical model. This cannot be described more precisely, in part due to the ontological approach, but nevertheless an attempt is made to explore what new perspectives can be gained for *Needless Needles*, at least.

Mary Bauermeister's *Needless Needles* in the mirror of OOO

Figure 2: Mary Bauermeister, Needless Needles, 1963–64, found linen sheet, fluorescent tubes, canvas, ink sewing needle, wooden objects and painted wood construction, 350 x 700 x 11 cm

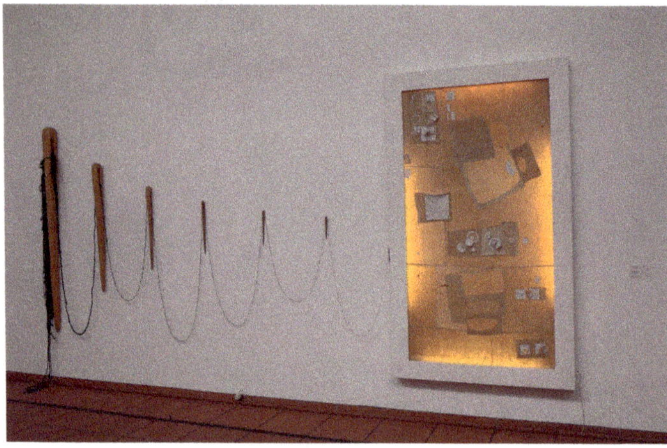

The group of works *Needless Needles* begins in 1963 with the light sheet (Fig. 2). Although titled *Linen Nähbild* in the first exhibition, its themes refer to the *Needless Needles* group of works. And ever since Bauermeister made the drawing in 1964, the light sheet has also been called *Needless Needles.*[27] Bauermeister found the material for the light sheets during a stay in Sicily in the winter of 1962–63 - used bed sheets that had been patched by the local population over generations. Bauermeister stretched the bed sheets in wooden boxes and illuminated them with neon tubes making the structure of the patches visible. Some light sheets have been altered by the artist and some are completely unedited. The core of the group includes the lens box *Needless Needles Vol. 5*, which was also produced in 1964 as the last of the three works (Fig. 3).

27 *Mary Bauermeister. Paintings and Constructions.* New York: Galeria Bonino, 1964. Exhibition catalogue.

Figure 3: Mary Bauermeister, Needless Needless, vol. 5, 1964, ink, offset print, glass, glass lens, wooden sphere, canvas, photographs, sewing needles and painted wood construction, 96 x 63,5 x 10,7 cm

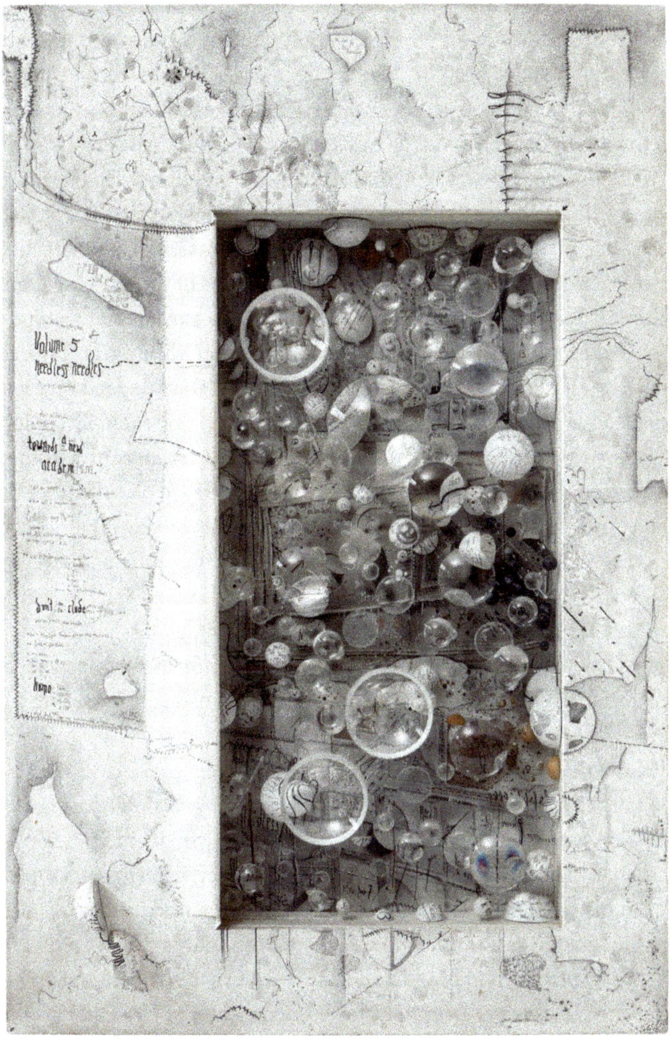

The term "lens boxes" refers to a technique that is the basis of Bauermeister's most famous works. It uses optical lenses and several layers of glass to combine writing, drawing, natural materials, and found objects into an assemblage-like hybrid of picture and sculpture. Today, the *Needless Needles* light sheet is in the Museum Ludwig in Cologne, the drawing in the Museum of Modern Art in New York, and the lens box in the artist's personal collection.

The common title, *Needless Needles,* creates a basic interconnectedness between the three works. Furthermore, the needle motif and its transformation, along with drawn, written, and partly embroidered comments by Bauermeister appear in all three works. The needles become "useless/needless," freed from their actual function of sewing. In the light sheet, the needle, which presumably produced the many seams in the work, now becomes as much a part of a wall installation as the drawings. In the lens box, physical sewing needles are glued into the work and there are drawn needles deformed by lenses and marked wooden spheres. In the drawing *Needless Needles,* "planted" needles are depicted with roots. This detail in the lower left corner corresponds to the written text on the right edge of the drawing: Bauermeister had a dream in which she is planting paintings in a garden that change over the seasons – needles grow out of the drawn roots. However, the motifs of the changing sewing needles are never the same in the works, but always depend on each particular medialization. In the lens box, the optical distortions created by the lenses and wooden spheres are used to achieve this. In the light sheet, in contrast, the needles have a distortion that leads to their un-usability as they are placed out of the work, next to each other on the wall, and in ascending order of size. The needles in the drawing show a kind of intrinsic transformation that depends on a drawn grid of small squares. Within this grid, the elements of the drawing can be distinguished from each other, sometimes through explicit labels such as "circle meets writing" or "circle meets number" and sometimes through unspecific instructions such as "finish before it's finished" and "shopping list" – not every instruction leads to a drawing or a word.

All three works contain references to the Fibonacci sequence. This is a mathematical sequence of natural numbers that creates a progression starting from 1 and adding the previous number: (0), 1, 1, 2, 3, 5, 8, 13. Known of since ancient times, it was described by Leonardo da Pisa, known as Fibonacci, in terms of natural growth principles in his book *Liber Abaci,* published in 1202 (revised in 1227).[28] It is closely related to the "golden ratio" – a division of a section that is considered to be a harmonic compositional principle and that has often been used in art and architecture. The further the series progresses, the closer the quotient of two Fibonacci numbers comes to the "golden ratio."[29]

In the *Needless Needles* drawing, the numbers which represent natural processes and aesthetic composition line up along the upper right of the grid. They are also

---

28 Huberta Lausch, *Fibonacci und die Folge(n)* (Berlin: De Gruyter, 2009), 1–3. Leonardo da Pisa used it to describe the growth of rabbit populations, but the sequence of numbers also pertains to other growth processes in nature, such as in flowers, mussels or fatty acids.

29 Lausch, *Fibonacci und die Folge(n)*, 119–132.

used inside the drawing, distorted and placed in all orientations, with 610 as the last identifiable number of the progression. The Fibonacci sequence is also part of the lens box. The title, *Vol. 5*, is not a reference to a numbering sequence since there is no "Vol. 4," but is instead referring to the "natural" growth of the *Needless Needles* series. To support this interpretation, the sequence of numbers is often listed inside the box; for example, it is written in the upper right corner on the middle layer of glass one below the other up to the number 13. In the light sheet, the wooden needles are kept in the Fibonacci sequence: the size of each needle is the product of the two preceding ones and the sequence of numbers is also written in the upper left corner on a piece of canvas. Another striking interconnectedness between the light sheet and the lens box is that a section of the bed sheet is embroidered with canvas and forms the background of the lens box as a photographic reproduction. The lenses, writings, and drawings thus "comment" on parts of the light sheet, mediated by the distortions of the *Needless Needles* drawing that are caused by the instructions at the edge of the grid.

The interconnectedness is expressed in many other aspects, all of which lead to a common basis of cross-references. Under Harman's object theory, these cross-references can be described as the production of an interconnected object. In *Needless Needles*, the Fibonacci sequence, just like every single stroke, has its own real and inaccessible object. Here, the Fibonacci sequence is incorporated in various ways in the three works and this creates a tension with the "alluring real object."[30] As a work of art, each individual work, the three works together, and their implementations of the Fibonacci sequence appear simultaneously in a "theatrical" connection with the recipient. Thus, each element of the works could be added by the viewers to this already existing multi-layered object connection.

In addition to the needle motif already mentioned, circles appear in all of the works as a basic form. In the light sheet, they appear as half-opened, painted front and back cutouts of canvas sewn onto the work. The lens box shows the circle motif in the photographic and drawn reproductions, as well as in the round convex or concave lenses or in the wooden spheres. Additionally, many different circles are part of the drawing *Needless Needles*; some of them spread out in proliferation and some of them reveal that underneath the carrier medium is another layer of drawing and of writing arranged in a circle. There are also circular drawings reminiscent of distorting lenses which are filled with the words "Needless Needles." As a connection to the Fibonacci sequence, it seems like the circular motifs are in a transformation induced by the "natural" processes described in the mathematical progression. In the *Needless Needles* works, "Fibonacci" and "circle" form an object and since all objects within the works are equal, the viewer can be the key to interpret the others and even explain the transformation of the objects.

30 Harman, *Art and Objects*, 47.

One aspect Bauermeister and Harman share is their rejection of the strict dichotomies of subject and object, thinking and being, spirit and matter, and culture and nature. Harman rejects this separation as "modernist" and it is his main point of criticism of Kant.[31] Bauermeister's recurring reference is the German philosopher Gotthard Günther, who sought to overcome this dichotomy in his 1959 publication, *Idee und Grundriß einer nicht-aristotelischen Logik*. For Günther, the dichotomy of being and thinking – or identity and non-identity – has shaped Western thinking since Plato and Aristotle, but this momentous simplification first became apparent with Georg Wilhelm Friedrich Hegel's transcendental logic.[32] According to Günther, every situation of reflection must be at least trivalent, since it contains an "I, non-I and object." A second subject, a "you," enables an expanded point of view, since it has its own process of reflection on an object, which is not necessarily congruent with "mine," as the first subject.[33] In the next step, Günther describes an excess of thinking with the terms "being identity" and "reflection identity." He creates the expression "self-reflection of self- and hetero-reflection" to describe Hegel's analysis of the reflection process. Hegel describes the process of thinking about an object as a process of reflection that will be reflected upon again.[34] According to Günther, this double reflection does not lead to mutual cancellation, but instead creates a general extension of the subject-object dichotomy up to a polyvalence that encompasses "the entire metaphysical world process itself."[35] What Bauermeister achieves with works is the possibility of making contradictory statements that have the same validity. A rudimentary example, which occurs again and again in her entire œuvre, is the use of the words "Yes, No, Perhaps." They are not mutually exclusive, but equally "true."[36] Günther would interpret this ambiguity in Bauermeister's work as still being a function of the subjects, but her work's tendency to overcome the (bivalent) implications of logic and to assume a (multivalent) speculation reflect Harman's model more closely.

---

31 Harman, *Art and Objects*, 142.

32 Gotthard Günther, *Idee und Grundriß einer nicht-Aristotelischen Logik. Die Idee und ihre philosophischen Voraussetzungen* (Hamburg: Meiner, 1991), 241–242.

33 Günther, *Idee und Grundriß einer nicht-Aristotelischen Logik. Die Idee und ihre philosophischen Voraussetzungen*, 64–72.

34 Georg Wilhelm Friedrich Hegel, *Wissenschaft der Logik. Erster Band, Die objektive Logik. Zweites Buch, Die Lehre vom Wesen. Hauptwerke in sechs Bänden, Band 3* (Hamburg: Meiner, 2018), #241-#260.

35 Günther, *Idee und Grundriß einer nicht-Aristotelischen Logik. Die Idee und ihre philosophischen Voraussetzungen*, 267. Own translation, original citation in German: "der gesamte metaphysische Weltprozeß selbst."

36 The words are written on and in the lens box *Needless Needles* several times. Many of Bauermeister's works include the written formula $1 + 1 = 3$, which also expresses a trivalence.

Object aesthetics of *Needless Needles*

Harman has repeatedly been accused of merely extending his own subjectivism to objects in his object theory and, therefore, of taking not a realistic but rather a deeply idealistic approach.[37] Whether everything is an object and accordingly humans are objects as well, or whether Harman's description of the impossibilities of establishing complete relations to objects is merely hypostasis will not be discussed here. With regard to *Needless Needles*, the conclusions are more important than the question of whether or not everything can be an object, with the object "human being" having the most sensory possibilities, according to Harman.[38] This also explains why the recipient is needed to create a work of art and it is this process that Harman calls "aesthetics." He considers it to be the "first philosophy" and uses the term in a very general sense and without reference to the philosophical discipline of aesthetics that begin with Alexander Gottlieb Baumgarten. For Harman, aesthetics is instead the description of perception or contemplation, deriving from the Greek word *aisthesis*. An aesthetic phenomenon occurs when the "real object" of a recipient absorbs the "sensual qualities" of an artwork, a process triggered by the artwork's "allure." Works of art, or more specifically the quadruple object structure that becomes an artwork, act as a metaphor:

> The minimal negative condition for something to count as an artwork is that it cannot primarily be a form of knowledge, whether of the undermining or the overmining sort. This does not exclude the possibility that artworks might also communicate certain literal truths, but it does entail that anything that solely communicates truths is not an artwork.[39]

This advantage of artworks – the fact that not all relations are translatable into knowledge – also applies to the attempt to describe art using a philosophical model, because artistic works are too complex in comparison to theory. At least, however, new thought-provoking stimuli emerge that do a little justice to the complexity of art.

In *Needless Needles*, Mary Bauermeister created a group of objects with a very close interconnectedness amongst themselves because of their shared elements. Further, the works challenge the classical logic of the subject-object dichotomy because she incorporated Gotthard Günther's multivalent logic as a central aspect.

---

37 Quentin Meillassoux, *Iteration, Reiteration, Repetition: A Speculative Analysis of the Meaningless Sign*, Lecture, Freie Universität Berlin, 20. April 2012. http://s3.amazonaws.com/arena-attachments/886529/539a4b4a8c213179c159eefc04a28947.pdf?1487320131.

38 Harman, *Vierfaches Objekt*, 60. Just because all objects are quadruple ones, it does not mean that all have the same capability to expand relations.

39 Harman, *Art and Objects*, 30.

Following Harman's theory, an increased concentration on individual elements in one work, and an examination of several works as one object, can happen simultaneously, in addition to constant reinterpretation since the works are never described by their relations. Furthermore, all aspects should be considered equal, which leads to challenging the object-concept; its structure is horizontal. Each circle and each needle has a fundamental autonomy, but through the connections between and the comments within the works there is also a process of mutual influence among the objects. For instance, when I focus my reception on one of the needles in the *Needless Needles* drawing on the lower left this leads to one new object because my "real object" is in a "theatrical" connection with the "sensual qualities" of the needle. When a painted or glued needle from the lens box *Needless Needles Vol. 5* is taken into this "theatrical" situation, together with maybe one of the wooden needles of the light sheet, the "sensual qualities" of the needle change drastically and the result is a new and equally autonomous object. According to Harman, we have a different mindset when we encounter art and this leads to the emergence of new objects and to allusions of the "real objects" in the series of artworks. This plurality of "real objects" is important, because every object inside one work and between the works can be a new artwork, as long as there is a "theatrical" connection with a viewer. During the process of perception, a never-ending manifold of new objects can be depicted, which means that the three artworks in question – the light sheet, the drawing, and the lens box – consist of countless artworks and they all have to be considered on the same level.

The additional meanings that artworks contain compared to theory and to everyday objects can lead to a metaphorical extension: a speculation on the non-perceptible. The many transformations of certain motifs in the *Needless Needles* group of works throw into disarray the status of the objects that appear as allusions to the withdrawn "real object." The patches on the *Needless Needles* light sheet, for example, are not compositional decisions intentionally made by the artist, but are instead determined by a double coincidence – firstly that exactly these parts of the bed sheet had to be repaired and secondly that Bauermeister found the sheet. In addition, there are patches that were added, partly from fabric and partly from canvas, and they mirror the existing ones, such as the combination of several larger patches in the upper right part of the work. As a next step, Bauermeister re-embroidered the outlines of the patches with sewing thread so that above and beside the patches there are "projections" of the outlines. These countered silhouettes only become visible on closer inspection. One object (the patch) is thus given additional objects (the re-embroidered silhouettes) and they have a double function: on the one hand they are new objects, but on the other hand they are also a projection of the first. All of them have an equivalent identity for Bauermeister, according to her interpretation of Günther's multivalent logic and according to Harman and his OOO. The countered outlines of the patches appear as the next layer of the "sensual qualities," which can be connected to the "sensual qualities" of the added patches. This object is reused in the background of the *Needless Needles* lens box as another representation, distorted by lenses, spheres, drawings, and comments. The *Needless Needles* group of works therefore evokes a multiplicity of objects through the process of reception and due to their own interconnectedness – an ongoing aesthetic "allure."

Simply things

A phenomenological interpretation from technology to poetry

Martina Olivero

Things and objects

In 1950, Martin Heidegger gave a lecture to the students of the Academy of Fine Arts in Bavaria. This speech (whereas slightly changed and with the previous title *Einblick in das was ist*) has opened one year before a series of four lectures given by the German philosopher in Bremen in December 1949, and then published in the volume 79 of the *Gesamtausgabe* as the *Bremer und Freiburger Vorträge*. Heidegger's Bavarian presentation was a reflection on artistic practice; however, surprisingly, the lesson had been entitled *Das Ding* (*The Thing*). To a novice reader, it is a text of high complexity, linguistically and conceptually (I wonder how many students could indeed comprehend its meaning). I argue that *Das Ding* can be fully understood only if compared to some of Heidegger's other works. Firstly, *Der Ursprung des Kunstwerkes* (1935–36) (*The Origin of the Work of Art*), initially published in *Holzwege, Off the Beaten Tracks* (first edition 1949; second ed. Klostermann, Frankfurt a. M., 1950), is an explicit study of the artifact. Secondly, *Die Frage nach der Technik* (*The Question Concerning Technology*, 1949, published in *Vorträge und Aufsätze*, 1954), approaches some of the questions previously developed in *Das Ding*. It is impossible, then, not to refer to his masterpiece, *Sein und Zeit* (*Being and Time*, 1927), as a background of some of the philosopher's main concepts about things and works. From this shortlist, we already have some compelling indications about the Heideggerian interpretation of objects, based on the attention given to their topological features. Hence, his theory insists on four dimensions of dwelling (the famous four-fold represented by earth, sky, mortals, and divinities), which, for Heidegger, are the very essence of (artistically) living. From this perspective, the true existence is the aesthetic existence.

All creative and artistic processes ultimately refer to the Greek notion of *poièsis*. In both the *Nichomachean Ethics* and the *Poetics*, Aristotle discusses the famous division between practical and poietic objects, with each of them presenting precise characteristics. If practical products are meant as ends, per se, poetic devices – built from that complex of knowledge, abilities, and *savoir-faire* named *techne* – are, rather, means to reach an intended end. Yet, this clear distinction manifests some ambiguities. First of all, it is only relatively late in history (from the XVII-XVIII century) that we have started to distinguish the poietic objects in artifacts and autonomous works of art. Secondly, one side of *techne* has become what we now call technology, the other what we refer to as art. It is indeed well known that, starting from the prologue of *Antigone* by Sophocles (vv. 332–333), human abilities are considered dreadful because they can deal with everything except for death. Also, they never completely exist without illness, labor, effort, or pain. In this way, technology, which is – in Aristotelian terms – the ability to make means through which one can reach a desired end, must be preceded by a determined prevision and anticipation. According to Massimo Donà (*Il fare perfetto: dalla tragedia della tecnica all'esperienza dell'arte*, 2000), the technological project is thus always concentrated around the *subject* of this prevision, and it contains, sometimes more sometimes less, an idea of domination relying upon self-affirmation. On the contrary, art has always existed in a process that rotates around the *object*, the work of art, and around the act of creation itself, so that any anthropocentrism here is removed. So, we will ask, does technology really have an egocentric nature?

Instruments and Devices

The text that emerged from the conference entirely dedicated to technology, *Die Frage nach der Technik*, was first published in 1954 and corresponds with the second lesson (out of four) held by Heidegger in Bremen in 1949. Here, Heidegger approaches some of the questions he would develop one year later in *Das Ding*. A few years after the end of the World War II, and after the recognition (although never official pronounced from the side of Heidegger himself) of the abominable horrors perpetrated by the National Socialist German Party, the philosopher warns against the neutral behavior concerning technology adopted by his contemporaries. According to him, ignorance perpetuates blindness about the essence of technology; while, whether accepted or denied, technology has had a huge impact on human freedom.

Since Antiquity, technology has been primarily understood as (1) a means to achieve anticipated ends, and (2) a human activity. These two explanations, however, are strictly linked because building and using means, as well as providing ends, are human actions. Tools, instruments, and machines are all things manufactured to satisfy needs and thus to obey specific ends, thereby constituting what is called technology. Consequently, technology is itself a device: *Einrichtung*, in German, *instrumentum*, in Latin. This is what Heidegger names the instrumental and anthropological conception of technology. However, according to his view, this instrumental conception only partially understand technology and does not access the essence of it. Indeed, the instrumental character (the verb *instruo* in Latin means to put together and, by extension, to dispose of, to order) derives from the adoption of a means to achieve a purpose. But one means, Heidegger remarks, is "something by which something is operated and thus obtained"[1]. Now, this "by which" that results in something (its finality) is otherwise called a cause.

Traditionally, in philosophy, starting from Aristotle, we find four distinct causes: *causa materialis*, the material through which an object is made; *causa formalis*, the form which represents the essence of the object; *causa finalis*, the finality that the object serves; and *causa efficiens*, the most dominant meaning today, which corresponds to the cause that concretely produces the object, for example, the craftsman. To understand the instrumental notion of technology, it is necessary to relate the production of means to these four causalities. However, among the causes mentioned, one seems decisive and another, the final cause, has been completely forgotten. The Heideggerian etymological research often contributes to the development of his thought, and this is also the case with the notion of causality. Cause derives from the Latin *causa* and refers more to the Aristotelian doctrine of four causes than to the Greek word αἰτία, which itself comes from the verb αἰτέω, to ask. Αἰτία translates to "the act for which one answers", and to *Verschulden* in German, something for which we are subject to account ; hence its meanings of responsibility and accusation. However, the only entity capable of resembling all of the definitions of cause seems to be the worker who, alone, can answer for the material (ὕλη), formal (εἶδος), and final (τέλος) cause. The craftsman (in Heidegger's text, represented by a goldsmith), in consideration of the three elements, makes the object emerge from its non-occultation; in other words, he makes it appear (ἀποφαίνεσθαι). This corresponds, more precisely, to the definition that Plato gives of ποίησις in the *Symposium* ("Take the following: you know that poetry [ποίησις] is more than a single thing. For of anything whatever that passes from not being into being the whole cause [205c] is composing or poetry; so that the productions of all arts are kinds of poetry, and their craftsmen are all poets.", 205 b-c). This passage from the interpretation of technology is associated with the truth implicit in the poietic act of bringing to the surface, of producing something from a hidden background. The Greeks called this operation ἀλήθεια, the Romans translated it into *veritas*, and today, *verità* in Italian, *verité* in French, and *Wahrheit* in German. Truth ended up designating the accuracy of representation (mimesis) more than a productive, artistic, artisanal, or technological operation (poièsis). Heidegger's thesis therefore proves that originally technology is essentially a matter of truth, conceived, both etymologically and conceptually, as an *unveiling*.

---

1 Martin Heidegger, "*The question concerning Technology*" in *Essais et conférences* (Paris: Gallimard, 1958), 12.

Poièsis and Technology

In *The Question Concerning Technology*, when Heidegger addresses its instrumental notion, he delivers an analysis of the quadruple causality which defines the *instrument* to conclude that all four of them can be reduced to one, that of the craftsman, *causa efficiens*. Now, the latter is responsible for the operation which takes objects out of non-existence and makes them emerge into existence. This approach is perfectly described by Plato in the known passage from *Symposium* (205 b-c) mentioned above: "ἡ γάρ τοι ἐκτοῦ μὴ ὄντος εἰς τὸ ὂν ἰόντι ὁτῳοῦν αἰτία πᾶσά ἐστι ποίηησις"[2], "All getting-in [*Veranlassung*] for that – whatever it is – which passes and advances from the non-present into the presence, is ποίησις, is pro-duction [*Hervor-bringen*]". Now, if Heidegger wants to understand the act of ποίησις not only in all its comprehensiveness but also in the sense that the Greeks gave to it, he cannot consider it only as a poetic and artistic achievement "which informs and makes the image appear"[3]. Heidegger supports the thesis for which nature, φύσις, is also a poietic work. Indeed, and according to Greek thought and then classical neo-scholastic, nature possesses *in itself* (ἐν ἑαυτῷ) the principle of its production – of its poietic act. On the other hand, the produced objects depend on the craftsman or the artist, thus the principle of their causality is external to them. In regard to nature and art, the poietic production is realized through the four causes in the form of bringing to the surface what was once hidden. The form of this revelation is what the Greeks called ἀλήθεια. Now, it is a question of proving that any production is an act of unveiling and therefore of truth. This thesis, supported by Heidegger during the conference, ends up rejecting the instrumental and current conception of technique: "thus technology is not only a means: it is a mode of unveiling"[4]. If instrumentality represents the fundamental feature of technology, it is in the unveiling of truth that resides the possibility of poièsis. Τέχνη, being part of ποίησις, does not only represent mechanical and artisanal doings, but also any act of artistic production, which is equivalent to the production of truth in beauty. Now, if, at the origin of Western culture and history, the word τέχνη has inhabited this polysemy, when dealing with technological questions (and for a comprehensive etymological-conceptual inquiry) we must also investigate art. With Heidegger, we would discover eventually that art is the secret essence of technology. The second part of the present article will thus be dedicated to the explanation of art's truthful fulfillment of technology.

Before proceeding further, however, we must acknowledge that there is a major difference between the classical, artisanal technological knowledge and the modern,

2 Heidegger, "*The question concerning Technology*", 16.

3 Heidegger, "*The question concerning Technology*", 16.

4 Heidegger, "*The question concerning Technology*", 18.

mechanized one, based on modern natural science. Heidegger states that modern technology also allows us to access the truth. Only, the unveiling of the truth does not take place as a production (poièsis), as in classical technology, but rather takes the form of a *provocation*. This expression, when we think about how the text dates back to 1950s', is particularly judicious and shows, after the nuclear disasters of Hiroshima and Nagasaki, a certain environmental sensitivity. According to modern technological thought, nature has become a reservoir of energy that can be exploited as desired and from which it is possible to accumulate materials as needed. The windmill, for example, harnesses natural forces when they are present and turns them directly into energy. It is not designed for the accumulation of resources but works with a now-forgotten relationship: need-satisfaction. Technological logic, on the contrary, leads to an interpretation of nature as a gigantic reservoir, and this is what Heidegger understands by provocation. So, "the earth's crust is revealed today as a coal basin, the soil as a storehouse of minerals"[5], and so on. Even an activity like that of the farmer passes from the mode of the confidence of seeds and the watching over the land's products to the provocation of the ground in the context of intensive motorized cultivations. The Heideggerian study manifests an environmental concern (today we would say ecological) and an infallible interest in the semantic field related to the earth and to the activities that concern it (agriculture, landscape, forestry but also simply dwelling). Like the craftsman becoming a worker in a system of automated factories, the peasant's work is radically transformed as a result of technological innovation. From a progressive perspective, any provocation seeks to make things advance positively while pushing them towards their extreme use (at lower cost) and infinite accumulation. The technological provocation takes place precisely when "the energy hidden in nature is released, what is thus obtained is transformed, the transformed is accumulated, the accumulated in turn distributed, and the distributed again commuted"[6]. However, here technology is, at the same time, a provocation but also, and more essentially, the unveiling of truth. This is possible through the *Gestell*, translated into English as *Enframing*.

To conclude the reasoning, Heidegger returns once again to the essence of technology, identified in the *Gestell*. This clarification concerns the use of the word *essence*, which here does not have its traditional meaning of *quidditas* (what something is, *quid* in Latin), of the universal common genus. *Gestell*, which we have identified for the moment as Enframing, does not correspond to an instrument or a device and is not their general concept. Admittedly, these elements are part of the *Gestell* as funds or principals, but do not constitute its essence. *Gestell*, on the one hand, and ποίησις, on the other, are both part of the truth (unveiling), which, by a destiny call which remains inexplicable to thought, manifests itself either as

5 Heidegger, "*The question concerning Technology*", 20.
6 Heidegger, "*The question concerning Technology*", 22.

a provocation (*Gestell*, modern technology) or as a production (ποίησις, arts and crafts). Now, while ποίησις is the historical origin of *Gestell*, *Gestell* makes ποίησις unrecognizable. However, to conceive *Gestell* as the essence of modern technology, it is imperative to adopt a new meaning of the word "essence": *Wesen*. *Wesen* shares the root of the verb *währen*, to last. Essence would then insist on the notion of duration, what endures and is maintained, what lives. Only, what endures cannot be reduced to the εἶδος or to the Platonic ἰδέα; to "τὸ τί ἦν εἶναι", "what everything was already", according to Aristotle; or to the *essentia* in traditional metaphysics. Rather, essence as that which lasts and endures from the beginning is, for Heidegger, what, in the sense of the verb *ge-währen* (to grant), is *Gewähr*, the guarantee for all things to be what they are. So, it is for men. The essence of technology guarantees men and women to be what they themselves, alone, cannot provide, "Because – a man who would be only a man, only of and by himself – such a thing does not exist"[7]. Human ex-sistence implies that men are assigned to the event (*Ereignis*) of truth through technology. This event is not only capable of saving them, but it also consigns and guarantees men their dignity.

Far from a catastrophist vision, here Heidegger shares a conception quite opposite to that which was to reign in public opinion after the nuclear catastrophes of 1945. However, to guarantee this possibility of being saved and, at the same time, *to remain human*, it is essential to perceive the true essence of technology and not to confuse it with technological objects, mechanical devices which nevertheless constitute it but are not essential to it. Like the truth, the essence of technology is ambiguous. If, on the one hand, it provokes and threatens our mission, on the other, it allows us to access a true existence. All human action is accomplished in between danger and salvation and can never resolve the antinomy. Antinomy and ambiguity belong to the essence of technology. If in antiquity τέχνή also included 'art', it is because it also designated ποίησις, the production of truth in beauty. Finally, and more recently, ποίησις ends up designating more specifically a single art form, to which Heidegger attributes excellence among all, and which is called poetry. Friedrich Hölderlin wrote that "man dwells in this land as a poet", a phrase much loved by Heidegger since poetry (as ποίησις and therefore τέχνή) would precisely allow access to the truth. This is why, even in ambiguity and uncertainty, technology can (and must!) be understood only as a reflection on art as a process.

Gifts and Sacrifices

With the essay on *The Thing* (1950), we approach the essence of art. Not only was this conference thought to have been given in a school of arts as a meditation on

7 Heidegger, "*The question concerning Technology*", 43.

the artistic process, but it is itself written in a poetical language. Poetry refuses to obey the traditional speculative language of metaphysics, which is guilty of the reification of things and people. The entire history of European metaphysics and science is responsible for hiding the true essence of things. Therefore, the essay intends to criticize traditional representative thought. Indeed, the simple operation of representing (*Vorstellen*) by putting something in front of itself consists of a subject (the *ego* or *cogito*) that handles the world as an ob-ject, *ob-jectum* (*Gegen-stand*). This means depriving the object of its dignity by claiming an anthropocentric superiority over it. Representative logic answers, from one side, with a form of subjectification (the reduction of things to ob-jects ready-to-hand) and, from the other, with reification (the reduction of people to things and of things to objects). In the first case, the sense of every-thing is reduced to the subject. Outside of this relation, things have no meaning anymore. This problem that we have observed has a twofold consequence. Firstly, things are objects of the representation, and secondly, in the modern era, they become objects of technological operations. The *modus operandi* of representation (*Vor-stellung*) and of production (*Her-stellung*) is fundamentally the same. Both traditional metaphysics and modern science contribute to reification processes wherein things are massively instrumentalized, merchandised, and consumed as objects and wherein subjects use objects (and sometimes people) at their complete disposal, as part of an economic system. If the entire meaning of things is reduced to the subject, then things are no-thing (a non-sense). Objectifying thinking denies the autonomy of things. Yet, properly speaking, in Heidegger's perspective, things are not completely autonomous. At their very essence, things stand in a fourfold relationship with earth, sky, people, and divinities. The long-standing objectifying Western thought has automatically confined the essence of things to eternal oblivion. As we have seen, according to Heidegger, technology is not a problem per se, but it nevertheless represents a great danger. In technology, men can lose their proximity to things, to that relation that binds them together, and that defines human dwelling. If we can resist the will to reify, possess, transform, and commodify objects, only then will we truly encounter things. However, what are things?

The first characteristic of a thing seems to be its autonomy. Let's say that things are autonomous from the subjects who think about them, but, at the same time, they are not autonomous in comparison to themselves. I argue that their ontological status obeys more of a heteronomous logic than one of pure autonomy. Nevertheless, for now, the autonomy of things exists in the impossibility of being re-presented (*vor uns stellen*) in front of a subject, in the refusal of being at their complete disposal. The jar remains a jar whether we represent it or not. Now, even if the jar is already produced by an artisan or an artist, it can still be a thing. Yet, the fact of being a thing (*das Dingliche*) is independent from the productive process. Both the object (*Gegenstand*) and the product (*Her-stand*) depend on someone who represents and produces them. This is not the case with the thing which is defined neither from an efficient cause nor a material. The essence of the jar (*Krugwesen*) rests in the void at its center. While physical science would say that the void is indeed filled with atoms of oxygen, phenomenology does not consider the jar from a scientific point of view. Therefore, it is precisely this void (when one is not scientifically speaking) that defines the jar-thing. The void hosts either the air or a liquid so that the jar can donate. Its essence is a gift (*das Geschenk*) which consists of first receiving something and then pouring it. Whatever the object of the gift is (water or wine), it always responds to these two gifts. That said, each liquid is the fruit of the combined action of earth, sky, mortals, and divinities which form the Four-fold (*das Geviert*). Coming from this quadruple relation, the jar offers an authentic gift which is, at the same time, an offer from the mortals and a sacrifice addressed to the divinities. The essence of the thing lives in the generous union of these four elements. I should remark here that while classical metaphysics leans on the Aristotelian theory of the four causes, phenomenology, in opposition to this tradition, suggests a new kind of causality. It is no longer a univocal connection from the cause to the effect, but rather a plural heteronomous relationship between each of the four elements. The thing is a thing (*das Ding dingt*) not in the sense of the Latin *res* or the medieval *ens* or the modern object; instead, the Thingness lies in its proximity to the people and the divinities. While in our globalized world, objects (*res, ens*) can be constantly present without any detachment, proximity saves the distance. Meaning that things in the proximity are not immediately available; we dwell in the proximity when we preserve each identity without any assimilation or reduction. Instead of proceeding towards greater domination, Heidegger suggests taking a step backward (*Schritt zurück*). In this stepping backward, we should renounce our speculative arrogance and embrace simple and trivial (*gering*) things. Compared to the unlimited number and excessive volume of serially produced objects, simple is the thing (the ring is the Thing, *ring ist das Ding*).

Works of Art

In *Der Ursprung des Kunstwerkes* (*The origin of the work of art*), which is a lecture given by Heidegger on November 13th, 1935 in Freiburg the notion of the world undergoes a profound revision with respect to the ontological-existential interpretation given in *Sein und Zeit* (*Being and time*, 1927). Now, how does this revolution happen? The implementation of the work of art is capable of combining the chronological dimension of duration to the topological expansion of the world. According to Heidegger, "the work itself is a rising in which a world is forced to open and, as it is opened in an inaugural way, planted"[8]. While the work of art is at work, it exhibits its world, a

8 Heidegger, *Dell'origine dell'opera d'arte e altri scritti*, ed. Adriano Ardovino (Palermo: Centro Internazionale Studi di Estetica, 2004), 37.

system of relationships constituting the life of a community, which creates simultaneously the space that surrounds it and the place on which it stands. Nevertheless, the artwork's world remains unfamiliar to those who look at it for the first time. When a work of art can exhibit the world in this way, it has reached its authentic essence; it is truly a work of art and not simply proof of artistic skills.

Ephemerality and Resistance

What is a work of art? Prior to addressing this question, I have cleared up how the processes of poièsis and technology are linked and are joined in the revelation of truth. I now focus on the notion of *work*. First of all, a distinction is imposed by the philosopher: on the one hand, we have the *animal laborans* which is enslaved to the work and, on the other, the *homo faber* whose task is to accomplish the *manufacturing*, from the Latin *facere*. The manufacturing describes working with wood – being a carpenter or a joiner – but Anatole Bailly also attests to the use of the substantivized participle ὁ τεκταινόμενος on the part of Plato in *Timaeus* (28c), meaning, more generally, the creator. It would be useful to recall that this same verb derives from the Greek τεκνόω, which is related to both to engender and to procreate. Indeed, since Aristotle and Plato, to manufacture means to create something from nothing, *ex nihilo*. Therefore, the origins of the fulfillment of *techné* in *ars* are already hidden in the polysemy of the Greek words which describe the double action of making something by hand but also of creating it. At the same time, these two terms testify to a familiarity that still endures, for manufacturing has never ceased, in the end, to be related to creation. Vice-versa, starting from artifacts' technological reproducibility, the question of their being manufactured, has returned to impose itself on aesthetic thinking. This polysemy, at the same time linguistic and conceptual, is added to the dimension of the gift associated with techné since Prometheus's theft of divine fire; a theft which, through myth, also expresses the generous nature of technological mastery that all humanity can enjoy. Τέκτων-ονος, just as much as the Latin *fabri*, signifies any person who, from a block of hard material (stone or wood), manages to produce an object. This person can be a worker, a craftsman, or a poet. According to Hannah Arendt, the notion of *work*, which is associated with *homo faber*, keeps the polysemy relevant in modern times, to both technique and art. Her definition maintains a very general spectrum by including any manufactured object, "the sum of which constitutes the human artifice"[9]. *Artifices* comprehend objects which not only provide "stability, without which men would not find a homeland", but also objects "which have strictly no use and which, moreover, because they are unique, are not exchangeable and therefore defy equalization by means of a common denominator

9 Hannah Arendt, *Condition de l'homme moderne* (Paris: Gallimard, 2012), 187.

such as money; if we put them on the market, we can only set their prices arbitrarily"[10]. We can consider this to be the definition of art elaborated upon by Arendt, at least as it is given in *The Human Condition* (1958).

Now, according to Arendt, a work of art, which shares the nature of work with a technical means, has certain identifiable characteristics. The first one relates directly to human nature and therefore guarantees that men can find their essence among the objects they manufacture. Individuals cannot be satisfied only by producing means (objects which have a function and are useful to satisfy a need, an interest, or a desire). Among the products of the ancestral technological manufacturing capacity, we must be able to contemplate perfectly useless and unique artifices. The uniqueness of the work, which is borrowed from the notions of aura and authenticity developed by Walter Benjamin in the 1930s, prevents this type of object from keeping the same predetermined and universally valid exchange value. Once again, Arendt recalls that the status of the work does not, in essence, belong to the ordinary experience[11]. Arendt finds in art the possibility for positive resistance against magical, mythical, and religious powers, a resistance which is due to its *durability*. Utility corrodes ordinary objects and leads them to their disappearances, while work, among all artifices, is the only one able to achieve, in its durability, "eminent permanence"[12].

Theodor Adorno, in his *Aesthetic Theory* (1970), also takes up the notion of duration, but with quite a different meaning. Since the *Querelle* between the Ancients and Moderns, formally begun in the second half of the 17th century (1667–1694), modern art has protested against duration through the notion of the *New*. In this context, the durability of works is explicitly banned because, according to the principles of critical theory, the work is temporally and socially situated and therefore cannot be understood as lasting eternally. Elsewhere, Adorno gives the example of Picasso's *Guernica* (1937) which not only changes the formal codes of representation, but also shows the unbearable violence of the Spanish Civil War. Art could therefore only speak at a time and in the context of a specific tradition[13]. The idea that art should show *resistance* against death is an illusion. "Even the beautiful must die!", says Schiller. If Adorno disputes the duration of artworks, it is because duration has always been claimed by traditional thought – the *prima philosophia*, "which takes refuge in isolated and absolutized derivatives, after having had to collapse as a total-

10 Arendt, *Condition de l'homme moderne*, 222.

11 "It must also be removed from the needs and demands of everyday life, with which it has as little contact as possible", Arendt, *Condition de l'homme moderne*, 193.

12 Arendt, *Condition de l'homme moderne*, 193.

13 "Whoever denounces a tradition can hardly count on another in which it would subsist.", Theodor Adorno, *Théorie Esthétique* (Paris: Klincksieck, 2011), 51.

ity"[14]. According to this conservative conceptual system, works of art are conceived as durable in line with the model of personal property. However, from the moment this fetishization of duration manifests, the work has already lost its inalienable character. According to Adorno, works would like to surrender to time, precisely to prevent them from being enslaved to it. In this sense, the image of fireworks, which is created only to shine for a single moment, is particularly striking and represents the true model of temporal artwork. The arts to which Adorno refers are theater and music, in particular. With the loss of durability – which for Walter Benjamin means a loss of the *aura* (namely, the authentic but also historical nature of the work, which allows for it to be located in a precise tradition) – the notion of work changes altogether. If modern art achieves the secularization of its transcendence, its existence is dialectical: it must live, accept, and affirm its death (that is to say its temporal nature) in order to be capable of truly existing. Nevertheless, if the fact that art subsists and resists time, on the one hand, means that the superstructure is struggling to evolve, it also, on the other hand, signifies the insubordination to a logic of profit that would end up winning by following purely materialistic interests. Rather than serving an ideological and subjective human need, art should only respond to an *objective* demand that belongs to the misery of the *world*.

Conclusions

By refusing the status of the product (of an artist) and of the object (belonging to an artistic-specific context), the work of art can only be understood based on itself. However, if we are to consider the work of art as a simple work (*Werke*), we quickly realize that (even from a Heideggerian perspective) the work is *manifestation* and *openness* (words which refer to Hölderlin's poetics). For this reason, it is constituted to be looked at, to be listened to, and to be experienced. Except that, here, contrary to what Benjamin and Adorno claim, the public opening of the work must be a call to eventually conceive its interiority. Prior to its ruin, then, the work must essentially accomplish a destruction[15]. So, the relationship, the only one to which the work opens to, is ultimately doomed to be destroyed because, once again, the only thing that matters is the work itself.

This disclosure on behalf of the work is also an implementation. For Heidegger, all great art could be reduced to architecture. The temple of Zeus and the statue of Apollo belong to it, and even a Greek tragedy is "the edifice of a poetic literary work

14 Adorno, *Théorie Esthétique*, 51.

15 "The *only* connection there is with the 'public' […] is that it destroys it. And it is by this force of destruction that the greatness of a work of art is measured", Heidegger, *De l'origine de l'œuvre d'art* (Paris: Éditions Payot et Rivages, 2014), 56.

in the language of a people"[16]. The work as a building implements a *consecration*, a celebration, and a sanctification so that the divine enters the disclosure of the work. The work opens a world which is, as already anticipated in 1927, not limited to an enumeration of present things, nor to a framework for what is present. Rather, *Welt weltet*: the world worldifies, the world becomes a world. Once again, Heidegger's thought inhabits the tautological circularity.

Nevertheless, the world can retreat or even get swept up in chaos and become a non-world. Indeed, somehow, we are always strangers to the world and it remains inhospitable (*Unheimisch*, the opposite of feeling at home) to us. The phenomenon of the fundamental strangeness of existence is already the subject of the 1927 study, but it is amplified by art. The work of art, in its truly being a work, sets up a world, opens it up, and, at the same time, rejects it, which results in the isolation and strangeness of each work.

It seems, then, that the work is made up of a double nature: on the one hand, openness, offering, and availability, and on the other, inhospitality and loneliness, as if art were always caught between publicity and incommunicability. According to Heidegger, art explains its essential strangeness to human nature, but it also retains a proper sacral and architectural character. This sacred, almost sacrificial element of the work of art therefore justifies a vision of human existence according to four dimensions (earth, sky, mortals, and divinities) wherein verticality lingers alongside horizontality.

On Poetry

In conclusion, from a phenomenological perspective, the question concerning technology, art and their objects must refuse two erroneous conceptions of the work. Firstly, the one which claims to assimilate artworks to a manufactured thing, namely a matter shaped into an artisanal product. To remedy its nature, one adds allegorical meanings or symbolic interpretations which have the sole function of making it acquire the status of a manufactured work of superior quality. Secondly, we are used to conceiving of the work as a representation (*Darstellung*) of something. Yet, what emerges from traditional dualism is always the inferiority of the matter that only makes accessible a nobler, formal element. The matter is deprived of any dignity and is always subordinate to the human senses able to reach it. In this way, from Plato onwards to Christian theology, the matter-form dualism has been associated with the polarity of sensitive (lower) and suprasensible (higher). Nevertheless, as Heidegger explains it: "the artwork is nothing; and that, for the good and simple reason that

16 Heidegger, *De l'origine de l'œuvre d'art*, 57.

it has nothing that it must represent"[17]. The fact that the work has nothing to represent does not mean that it must withdraw into itself, but rather that it does not refer to something independent from itself. Art manifests a relationship, although a conflicting relationship. The solution of the autonomy of the work of art is now definitively excluded. Unfortunately, from Plato, the dominant Western conception considers the work as an object made from an ideal model and that has no (or very little) reality. Yet the Heideggerian ontological claim is clear: nothing is more real than works of art, which are the very foundation of our historical existence. Art is real since it is the advent of truth. From ἀ-λήθεια, which he interprets as composed of privative α- and the verb λανθάνω, "to be hidden", truth is something that emerges from the shadows, but which always remains in a shadow-light dimension.

Amongst all art, poetry (ποίησις in ancient Greek, *Dichtung* in German) as a language is the place wherein truth manifests itself further. All art is a language because it expresses something. It is in this language of "poetry originating from a people"[18] that the truth is properly conveyed. Construction and figuration adopt a language just secondarily. Only poetry, which is the essence of art, knows how to bear witness to the "*establishment of Being*"[19]. To establish means three things: first, to offer freely; second, to found; and finally, to begin, in the sense of instituting something. Poetry, the essence of art and the act of establishing the Being, is at the same time gift, foundation, and beginning. As a gift, poetry offers something unusual compared to everyday life, but as a foundation, poetry is established as a historical event. Thus, art as poetry is the *origin* (the beginning) of truth. But poetry also constitutes the origin of the work. There is a true work of art to the extent that there is poetry. To the question, why must there be art? We answer, phenomenologically, because art puts truth to work. If there is truth, then there must be history, so too a work of art, which truly exists by establishing the Being. This establishment represents the beginning and inaugurates the origin. In an anti-metaphysical approach, Heidegger reviews not only the system of Western art but also of history since there is no history without art. Always and more than ever, it is a question of leaping, without which no artistic beginning would take place. However, the jump into the origin of the creative process remains secret because it only answers to an act of freedom. In truth, men and women may genuinely dwell in this land as poets.

17 Heidegger, *De l'origine de l'œuvre d'art*, 70.

18 Heidegger, *De l'origine de l'œuvre d'art*, 81.

19 Heidegger, *De l'origine de l'œuvre d'art*, 82.

Origins and Ends: Understanding the Medium of Painting According to Heidegger's Truth

Tom Palin

In philosophy, Martin Heidegger has done the most to shift our understanding of the world away from the static and deterministic and towards the fluid and experiential. In this paper, the idea of truth (*aletheia*) relies on that which was developed in Heidegger's essay "The origin of the work of art", published in 1936, and its implications for the material, the picture, and the medium of painting.[1] Although, outside of this essay, Heidegger's project pertains not to art (let alone to painting) but to *Dasein*, art nevertheless falls within the purview of his analysis of the structures of human existence.[2] To develop this, I will reconsider the essay's central themes. This will involve a clarification of Heidegger's understanding of *being*, to enable a specific understanding of the medium of painting. I will therefore position the paradoxes of Heidegger's argument and address his re-definition of truth to challenge the primacy of aesthetics, thereby answering metaphysical questions regarding the artwork's spatial, temporal, material, and linguistic constitution.

With Georg Wilhelm Friedrich Hegel's thesis regarding the *end of art* providing the backdrop to this inquiry (in the dual sense of it signalling the death of painting and thus the death of the medium of painting), I will engage with Heidegger's reading of Friedrich Hölderlin's river poems. I will reflect also on Eva Geulen's analysis of Heidegger's *Hölderlin Lectures* by addressing the idea of a preservational modality prior to providing an account of the necessity of poetising the end of art as a means

1 In Greek, *aletheia* approximates to *unconcealedness* or *disclosure*, and was revived by Heidegger. "The Origin of the Work of Art" was worked on between 1935 and 1937, and reworked for publication in 1950, and again in 1960. It was initially based on lectures he delivered in the early-mid 1930s in Frankfurt and Zurich.

2 As Peter Osborne pointed out in *Anywhere or Not at All*, 170. In *Being and Time*, the word *art* is never used. In *Being and Time*, 1927, the concept of *Dasein* (*existence*, sometimes translated as *being there* or *being the there/situation*) permitted Heidegger to sidestep prior philosophical assumptions as to the existence of objects and subjects, or bodies and minds. To Heidegger, *Dasein* operates against a background in which *encountering* takes place, and into which it is thrown. This *thrownness* (*Geworfenheit*) serves to connect *Dasein* with the present and the past, whilst pushing into the future.

of circumnavigating more literal approaches to the subject, with important implications for the beginning (of art/painting) too.

The point of this work is to permit the structural particularities of paintings to attain centrality in respect to the work's meaning. I will consider Hölderlin's reliance on rumour and double-directedness, as approached through his poem "The Ister", which signals in the direction of a new ontological model for painting.[3] The medium will be presented as *equipment*, with the stages of its operability revealed sequentially. The mechanism of the *caesura* will attain prominence as a holding bay in which picture and material are suspended. The result: the medium-aspect of a painting might, within a Heideggerian and Hölderlinean framework, become resurrected and re-situated—its functionality made visible through its embeddedness in both language and history.

1. Originating Origins

In "The Origin of the Work of Art", Heidegger refers to the notion of the hermeneutic circle (Table 1), which, in this case, is based on a paradox.[4] How, Heidegger contends, can one know of relations among things without knowing the identities of the entities that interrelate? Conversely, how can one know the identities of related entities in isolation from their relations to one another? For Heidegger, "[n]ot only is the main step from work to art, like the step from art to work, a circle, but every individual step that we attempt circles within this circle".[5] How is it, then, that a work becomes knowable as a work at all?

3 The ancient Greek name for the Danube.

4 This essay is a redirection of his thinking towards the ontological condition of the (art)work. Friedrich Daniel Ernst Schleirmacher (1768–1834), as one of the founders of modern hermeneutics, first employed the notion of a hermeneutic circle. Dilthey also used the circle in his work. Later, Hans-Georg Gadamer (1900–2002) and Paul de Man (1919–1993) extended Heidegger's application.

5 Martin Heidegger, "The Origin of the Work of Art", 1936, in *Off the Beaten Track*, ed. and trans. Julian Young and Kenneth Haynes (Frankfurt: Vittorio Klostermann GmbH, 1950), 2.

Table 1: The Hermeneutic Circle

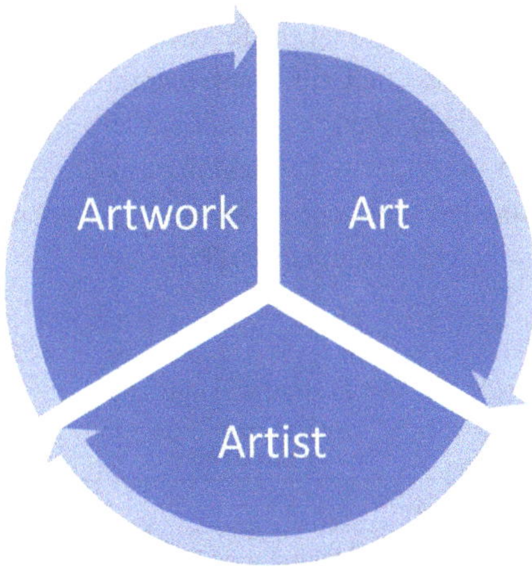

Distinguishing the work from other things involved a classification of states of being. Heidegger begins with a general observation: "(art)works are as naturally present as things. The picture hangs on the wall like a hunting weapon or a hat".[6] *Thinglyness*, in this sense, provides a form of experiential platform from which one can begin contemplating the work.

For Heidegger, things of all types can be classified into *mere* (*elemental, non-serviceable, non-manipulated* things / *Ding*), and *manipulated* things (things to which Heidegger assigns the label *equipment* (*Zeug*)). Equipment is serviceable in that it is the product of a process of making, and it is also *for* something.[7] Artworks, therefore, straddle two camps: being manipulated and therefore being equipmental, yet also being constructed of mere materials. Things can also be self-contained (complete within themselves) or otherwise (requiring completion). To use his example: whilst a pair of shoes has been fashioned and is therefore equipmental (their being resides in their usefulness), they share with the mere thing, once completed, the property of self-containment. This is further complicated by a presumption of self-sufficiency on the part of the art thing and the mere thing, but not the equipmental thing, whose being requires use. To clarify a subtle distinction: self-containment is to have maintained or else arrived at completeness, whereas self-sufficiency is simply the quality of being without the requirement of use.

6 Heidegger, "The Origin of the Work of Art", 2–3. To Heidegger, this *thingly character* is what a painting shares with a book of poems, a sculpture, a building, or a piece of sheet music.

7 Heidegger, "The Origin of the Work of Art", 10.

If both the art thing and the mere thing share the property of self-sufficiency, and both the equipmental thing and the art thing are shaped by human hands, one must conclude the following: that the mere thing is, in being mere, both self-contained and, in its mereness, self-sufficient; that the equipmental thing is mere, self-contained (once finished), though not self-sufficient, and is also serviceable; and that the art thing is mere (derived of base materials), self-contained (complete within itself), self-sufficient (able not to be used), serviceable (of making), and equipmental (a tool / that which is *in order to*) (Table 2).[8]

Table 2: Heidegger's Ontological Classification of Things

Mere Thing	Equipmental Thing	Art Thing / Truth (of)
Self-contained	Mere	Mere
Self-sufficient	Self-contained (once finished)	Self-contained
	Serviceable	Self-sufficient
		Serviceable
		Equipmental

To understand how it is that the painting *A Pair of Shoes* (1886), by Vincent van Gogh, functions differently from the shoes themselves, one must consider what it is that the shoes themselves do, and to whom. To the peasant who wears them, the being of the shoes – their usefulness as equipment – is known through wearing (*in actu*), "without observation or reflection".[9] The shoes are reliable: they wear and decay; in the process of this condition, they reveal their mode of being.[10] This *activity of shoes* does not serve, in this instance, Van Gogh in his painterly labours – as Hugh Silverman points out – but the peasant-wearer only.[11]

The truth of the shoes attains visibility in the painting of the shoes. Heidegger knows this not from living with peasants, nor from re-staging the wearing of the shoes, nor from scrutinising their decay.[12] What is known is known *through the work*,

8 Heidegger, "The Origin of the Work of Art", 4–12.

9 Heidegger, "The Origin of the Work of Art", 14.

10 Being is not necessarily seeing, though seeing is *of being*. In short: to the peasant, they are, for the most part, invisible.

11 Hugh J. Silverman, *Textualities: Between Hermeneutics and Deconstruction* (New York and London: Routledge, 1994), 136.

12 The painter's life veiled beneath the life of the subject of the painting.

and it could not be known (as it is known) otherwise.[13] The being of the shoes (which includes, but is not reduceable to, their equipmentality) has become visible.[14] To Heidegger, "[t]his painting spoke. In the vicinity of the work we were suddenly somewhere else than we usually tend to be, [and so the] artwork let us know what the shoes, in truth are".[15]

In disclosing the equipmental nature of the shoes, the painting's concealment is double-edged. Both process and object become subsumed in the process of disclosing the truth of the shoes. Though Heidegger claims that the thing-like substructure of the work does not *belong* to the work, the work has nevertheless become equipmental in its transition to being a manipulated thing.[16] As paint and canvas, the work is manipulated, having once been mere.[17] Furthermore, in operating as a visual language, the composition of the work is no longer merely a malleable, coloured substance able to adhere to other substances; it is now an activity, both a picture and a thing—in the world *as* meeting, and *in* surface. To Heidegger, the mere is something close to stopping short of the character of serviceability. To become operable, however, disclosure and concealment require what amounts to a form of uni-directional ontological weighting. The painting, then, as a work of art, can reveal the truth of the shoes, yet the shoes cannot reveal the truth of the painting.

Heidegger presents the paradox of a work of art opening up the space to which it will belong (the space of truth), and which will also serve to accommodate its varied relations to other things in the world. The shift in emphasis from the painting to the

---

13 Heidegger refutes the notion of self-projection, as this would require the formulation of a projection independent of that upon which one wished to project (presumably, subject to its own determination of being)—one would have to, in effect, conjure an origin outside of the work itself, then bring it to the work from whence it came.

14 Equipmentality is what it is that accompanies utility, and utility is that which we know about the shoes from bearing witness to them.

15 Martin Heidegger, "The Origin of the Work of Art", 15. For a detailed consideration of the relationship between aesthetics and truth, see: J. M. Bernstein, *The Fate of Art: Aesthetic Alienation from Kant to Derrida and Adorno* (Pennsylvania: Pennsylvania State University Press, 1992). Heidegger writes evocatively about the dark opening of the shoes, the stiff heaviness and the slow trudge (Laurie Schneider Adams, *The Methodologies of Art*, 170). There is a reflection of this in T. J. Clark's description of Courbet's *Stonebreakers*, in *Image of the People*, 79, where he employs the terms pressure, thickness, and gravity.

16 Paint is a composite of pigments (as granular solids), a binder (to allow the paint to cohere and to form a film), and usually an extender (to increase, dilute, and/or modify properties). In isolation, all are mere. Assembled, the paint occupies a position between mere and equipmental, as pre-equipmental (having the propensity to become equipmental *in the painting*). The individual substances in isolation (prior to becoming paint) have pre-equipmental potential, too, though of a non-painterly orientation. As the vehicle of painting (in/as painting) paint becomes fully equipmental, and ontologically capped.

17 Natural materials that become paint and canvas.

temple that occurs later in the essay appears designed to cement an understanding of how truth can show up and also provide what could be considered a *context* (a situation, or a space for truth to function). According to Michael Inwood, Heidegger attends to the temple so as "to distinguish his own view from the view that art is imitation; the temple is not representational".[18]

Moreover, in the case of Van Gogh's painting, this opening up evaded – in his earlier analysis – such a detailed consideration. In accounting for this shift, and to move things on, Heidegger writes that "[a]s long as we supposed the reality of the work to lie primarily in its thingly substructure, we went astray".[19] Heidegger's analysis of that which, in normal conditions, cannot move – namely, the Greek temple – functions to demonstrate how a work both produces and gathers truth to it.[20] For instance, the temple, in, "hold[ing] its place against the storm raging above it, [...] first makes the storm visible in its violence".[21] It is clear, here, that Heidegger is reversing the terms that we come to know. Thus, light is brought to light through reflecting stone, and air through the towering of the building. Heidegger calls this *earth*, and the process of *coming forth*, "lights up that on which Man bases his dwelling".[22]

In the case of the temple, as a work, it functions to make God visible—not to paint a portrait of God, but to allow for His presence. As such, the work of the temple and God become synonymous. God is not *in* the work, but the work *is* God.[23] To demonstrate his conception of what he terms *world*, Heidegger uses the example of the setting up of a painting for an exhibition.[24] Setting up, he contends, brings with it a "sense of dedication or praise".[25] This dedication or praise is what is earth, and, in the instance of the work, has been set forth by the *work-being* of the work. In so doing, the work sets up a world (wherein objects are never there merely to be looked

---

18 Michael Inwood, *Heidegger: A Very Short Introduction* (Oxford: Oxford University Press, 1997), 118.

19 Martin Heidegger, "The Origin of the Work of Art", 18. This is something close to material.

20 Heidegger, "The Origin of the Work of Art", 20.

21 Heidegger, "The Origin of the Work of Art", 21.

22 Heidegger, "The Origin of the Work of Art", 21.

23 In the sense that the meaning of God is framed by the conditions pertaining to God. More broadly, to invoke the magical is, in part, to subdue the rational impulse in favour of the irrational. In a post-industrial information age, that which opposes or seeks to short-circuit an over-determined, mechanistic message seems desirable. To seek out *unknowing* (to bring forth the supernatural) is not, in itself, a denial of Enlightenment thinking. In its appeal to possibility, process, and ritual, magic becomes a strategy with which to rethink anew one's connectedness to material, technology, language, and change.

24 World is not a collection of things that are-present-at-hand (within the purview of one's compass, to be examined).

25 Heidegger, "The Origin of the Work of Art" 22.

at), for world is, to Heidegger, "that always non-objectual to which we are subject".[26] With its self-referential structure, abstract painting, in particular, could be considered in light of this.

This, then, is, "what a work does".[27]The newly established world has thus been constituted through earth.[28] World encompasses all human relations and acts to circumvent an objectification (of things) to which earth alone would attest. Only when the work becomes dislocated from its surroundings – either by time, or misunderstanding, or neglect (or even relocation) – does it lose its power to disclose and thereby becomes passive, to be pointed at.[29] To point at earth without world could perhaps be likened to pointing at an object without a subject – a form without content – yet not because one happened to conceal the other, but because, in the instance of pointing, there wasn't *another* to conceal.

Heidegger establishes a situation whereby the work discloses the truth of what it is as a dual disclosure (it *sets forth* the earth and *sets up* a world). This disclosure is a form of knowing, and Heidegger's supposition points towards a complex notion of the medium that is bound-in to the work of art (as it is *in* and *of* the world), whilst at the same time foregrounding its identity as distinct from it. This, in painterly terms, would be akin to having a painting's surface become visible alone, without, or alongside its subject.[30] It is important to state that Heidegger did not use the term medium. Nevertheless, within Heidegger's artwork hypothesis, the notion of the medium becomes permissible as that which can be mapped onto the spaces or joins between a well-trodden series of dualisms: word and image; object and subject; means and message; conceptual and non-conceptual; drawing and painting; time and space, etc. Being neither an object nor a subject, neither form nor content, medium eludes position. Thus, in situating itself indeterminately between an object

---

26 Heidegger, "The Origin of the Work of Art", 23. Paskow (*The Paradoxes of Art*, 28) presents earth as unknowable, and world as a cultural and temporal term. Heidegger turns nouns into verbs.

27 Heidegger, "The Origin of the Work of Art" 22.

28 Michael Inwood, *Heidegger: A Very Short Introduction*, 119. This state of affairs resembles the relationship between the mere and equipmental in respect to the earlier example of Van Gogh's painting.

29 Consider this in relation to Rosalind Krauss's objection to Clement Greenberg's insistence on pointing (*Perpetual Inventory*, 195).

30 To show the surface as a distinct aspect *alongside* the subject is surely impossible in any practical sense (regarding brush marks that do or do not depict). But the look of separation between them can be brought off by a clever manipulation of effects and the right choice of subject, so as to have the appearance of a tactile surface floating above the subject – as if looking at a screen – leaving the subject to appear surface-less, i.e., photographic. See: "Depiction and the Golden Calf", 1987, by Michael Podro (1931–2008), wherein he examines the painting *The Adoration of the Golden Calf*, 1633/4, by Nicolas Poussin (1594–1665), and also the work of Frank Auerbach (born 1931).

and a subject, a form and content, the medium draws from both sides. In its *inbetweeness* it establishes the being of that which positions it on either side. Its equipmental being is, therefore, to be inferred from that which becomes positioned, through the particularity of the form of its disclosure.

To Heidegger, "[b]y the opening of a world, all things gain their lingering and hastening, their distance and proximity, their breadth and their limits".[31] Worlding is, then, the finding of space within the already spacious, and the work is that which "holds open the open of the world".[32] Worlding denotes dwelling, or the ways in which inhabiting the world takes shape. It is a human world of houses, tools, and things of all manner of particularity; of all that permits living.[33] Stephen Melville has drawn attention to Heidegger's use of light and shadow as a metaphor for concealment.[34] In respect to painting, this can be understood as akin to the dwelling of a subject within a surface, or else a surface within a subject.[35]

2. Forestalling Ends

> But he seems almost
> Reversing and
> Must come, I think,
> From the East
> And much
> Might be said about that. And why
> Does he cling to the hills so? The other,
> The Rhine, went off
> Sideways. Never for nothing
> Do rivers run in the drylands. [...][36]

In *The End of Art: Readings in a Rumour after Hegel*, Eva Geulen pays close attention, in the last two chapters of the book, to Heidegger's understanding of the form and language of Hölderlin's verse in respect to what is, more often than not, taken to be

31 Martin Heidegger, "The Origin of the Work of Art", 19.

32 Heidegger, "The Origin of the Work of Art", 19.

33 Michael Inwood, *Heidegger: A Very Short Introduction*, 119.

34 Stephen Melville, *Becoming Medium*, 2013. That, in a sense, the visible is present as an absence.

35 The implications of worlding are explored in greater detail in the third section of Heidegger's essay.

36 Friedrich Hölderlin, "The Ister", lines 41–50, trans., David Constantine, in *Friedrich Hölderlin: Selected Poems* (Newcastle upon Tyne: Bloodaxe Books, 1997), 63.

its content.[37] In Heidegger's analysis, this poetic form, as Geulen argues, functions to compel a method of knowing that *arises from* rather than being *imposed upon* the work. Heidegger lectured extensively on Hölderlin in the middle period of his career, at a time of ultimate strife, and Geulen addresses the impact of his encounters with the German poet on the course on his thinking.[38] The Hölderlin lectures come either side of "The Origin of the Work of Art". Having learned the lessons of Hölderlin's *inspired unreason*, the lectures demarcate the period at which "philosophy abdicates in favour of poetry".[39]

With Heidegger's poetising of philosophy comes the "demotion of the production of art [...] in favour of its preservation".[40] Demotion amounts, in fact, to an extension of the possibility of art—a form of insurance that, to borrow a phrase from Robert Browning, its, "reach will exceed its grasp".[41] In *Hölderlin's Hymn: The Ister,* Heidegger attends to what is a rather short poem.[42] To David Nichols, these lectures mark a shift in the orientation of his thought from a Nietzschean interest in the will to power to a consideration of how it is that poets provide dwellings.[43] Nichols writes:

> In the Ister lectures, Heidegger focuses upon the different ways in which *Dasein* takes residence within its historical situation. Greek tragedy demonstrates how human beings are always trying to make themselves at home without ever fully

---

37 Ezra Pound (1885–1972) considered *content* and *music* to be to two roads of poetry—to subject matter and versification, respectively.

38 Friedrich Hölderlin (1770–1850) was born in the same year as William Wordsworth (1770–1850). Hölderlin studiedtheology at the Tübinger Stift. His fellow students included fellow Swabians, Georg Wilhelm Friedrich Hegel (1770–1831) and Schelling (Schelling he had known from school). It has been suggested that it was Hölderlin who brought to Hegel's attention the work of Heraclitus (c. 535 – c. 475 BC), and the union of opposites, which would form the basis of the dialectic. Heidegger lectured on Hölderlin in 1934/5, 1941/2, and 1942. The first series was titled *Hölderlin's Hymns Germania and the Rhine*. Hölderlin offers Heidegger a means for displaying his ontological hypothesis (almost of seeing it in action), and, from the mid-1930s, Heidegger's understanding of poetry becomes the primary route to a fuller understanding of being.

39 Eva Geulen. *The End of Art: Readings in a Rumour After Hegel*, (California: Stanford University Press, 2006), 136. Paskow (*The Paradoxes of Art: A Phenomenological Investigation*, 31) sees Heidegger's later writing as akin to the poetic essays of Rainer Maria Rilke (1975–1926). *Inspired Unreason* is a phrase used by George Steiner, *Heidegger*, 142.

40 Eva Geulen, *The End of Art: Readings in a Rumour After Hegel*, 124.

41 Robert Browning, *Andrea del Sarto (The Faultless Painter)*, from *Men and Women*, 1855.

42 Seventy-two lines. Heidegger also addresses Sophocles' *Antigone* and the mechanisms of Greek tragedy. *Hölderlin's Hymn* was the second of Heidegger's Hölderlin lecture series.

43 For being to occupy. *The will to power* first appeared in *The Wanderer in his Shadow* (1880) and then in *Daybreak* (1881).

> accomplishing this goal. They occupy the uncanny (*unheimlich*) status of extraordinary beings among ordinary appearances, always estranged from the larger framework of beings, never able to completely fit into its structure.[44]

To be German, for both Hölderlin and Heidegger, meant to be rooted in what it meant (from a western European perspective) to be Greek, and against this backdrop Nichols points to Hölderlin's understanding of poetry as a process of uncovering truth. To poetise is to challenge the prevailing gods, and to seek to create unity with them through a tragic alignment—to maintain the particularities of difference (conflictedness) within the very fabric of that which permits its visibility.[45]

Heidegger opens this analysis with an etymological scrutiny of the word *hymn*, which he derives from the Greek *hýmnos* (from *hydeō*), meaning song of praise *for the gods*. By praise, Heidegger is referring to something akin to *a calling forth* rather than *a calling to*, and that which is called forth – the work/poem/temple – remains, in its openness, to be attended to. The lecture proceeds to attend to Hölderlin's poem "The Ister" and also, by attending, to preserve its being. In determining the conditions into which the work becomes operable as a work (countering the scientific, deterministic implications of production), the work serves to inaugurate the means of its own form of preservation, for, to Heidegger, "a work is only a work when held in preserving".[46]

Preserving, in this context, means to take note of – *noticing in attending* – rather than *to look after*. What Geulen appears to imply is that Heidegger's origin – in all its layered complexity – is designed to point not to the truth of the work of art, but to the truth of the preservation of the work of art (the work's truth, as outlined in Part 1, is a second-order effect realised alongside a more fundamental preservational primacy). Preservation, here, can be thought of as that which is operable through the medium of art (though not necessarily through the particular art form's medium), which functions to perpetuate works and thereby reveal truth. Modes of preservation, however, vary as they take on different forms, to the point in which even neglect is able to be couched in the affirmative.[47] All that attests to the work is, to Heidegger,

44 David Nichols, "Antigone's Autochthonous Voice: Echoes in Sophocles, Hölderlin, and Heidegger", 2009, accessed September 29, 2016, http://www.iwm.at/publications/5-junior-visiting-fellows-conferences/vol-xxv/antigones-autochthonous-voice/#_edn 4.

45 Heidegger sometimes uses the terms *gods* to represent what he refers to as macro-paradigmatic works of art. To him, fundamentally transformative works, like the Greek temple or tragic drama, would reside in this category. Paintings or poems would constitute paradigmatic works. The micro-paradigmatic classification denotes something approximating a coming to awareness of things that matter to us.

46 Eva Geulen, *The End of Art: Readings in a Rumour After Hegel*, 124.

47 Modes of preservation that arrive as a result of the disclosure of the truth of the work, Heidegger considers as *ownmost*. Neglect, too, derives its understanding from (in relation to) the being of the work.

in the service of preservation. Aside from the more obvious forms of institutional *enframing*, language offers a means whereby the work's truth might be conserved and held.[48] Why, then, it seems appropriate to ask, does Heidegger go to such lengths to foreground the preservational aspect of the work? Following Geulen's analysis, it is likely that he hopes to expose modernity's ontological modality; something that modernism does in contrast to the past, from which the work can be seen to draw, and to which it returns.[49]

The central paradox of the artwork essay, says Geulen, is that whenever there is a commitment to a beginning, there is an invocation of an end. To counter this, Heidegger must conceive of an origin as something that is retained, in action. Preservation, here, implies maintenance (to keep something alive in the process of dealing with it). Not to preserve would therefore amount to neglect (to the relinquishing of being). Moreover, to attend to the work would be to bring about and to preserve the work. However, there are difficulties to overcome, and Heidegger, in the *Hölderlin Lectures*, sets out to demonstrate the means whereby the truth of the ancient Greeks might become visible in Hölderlin's poetry, and in so doing he posits a form of kinship. Hölderlin's understanding of the river is key.

Geulen writes that Heidegger's interest in the river in Hölderlin's poem stems from its double-directedness. Importantly, Hölderlin's account of the Ister does not signal a directedness that would point to the meaning of the river as being determined solely by its final resting place.[50] Instead, the meaning/being of the river in/as the present draws from both its source (far away) and its destination (seaward), which, in turn (assisted by its tributaries), establishes it as a/the river.[51] In drawing from both source and destination, Hölderlin maintains the river as a thing in perpetual flux—the river can never reach its end, nor can we witness its beginning. To Geulen, the river parallels history, but in reverse—"he (the river) seems

48 Heidegger developed the concept of *enframing* (*Gestell*) in *The Question Concerning Technology* (1954) to denote a framework or structure that lies beneath technology. Heidegger's use differs from the more common use of *framing*, in that *Gestell* implies an active component that is integral and perpetual to technology's being.

49 Geulen, *The End of Art: Readings in a Rumour After Hegel*, 126. The detail of this modality is outlined more fully in Heidegger's "The Age of World Picture" (1938).

50 Geulen, *The End of Art: Readings in a Rumour After Hegel*, 126.

51 Including: the Indus, the East, the Alphaeus, the other side, down there, and the Isthmus.

almost reversing".[52] To Hölderlin, events seem to be held between and defined by the particularities of their destination and their origin.[53]

It is important to keep in mind the distinction between subject and surface (or content and form) within modernist criticism, which assigned an autonomous, atemporal identity to both language and material, and which served to confine each to a position of periodic absence through a posited engagement with the other. And yet, following W. J. T. Mitchell, to know a painting is to know something of the artifice of painting, within whose confines both language and material subsist. In following Heidegger's logic, the medium's equipmentality amounts to its propensity to act as a horizon of being—a meeting place wherein surface and subject rendezvous. Both are maintained in situ—as the work. In the work's subsequent disclosure, the medium is concealed *as the work*.[54]

But how is this accomplished? In respect to both the end of art thesis and the medium of painting, the intrusion of language generates an added layer of complexity—the end of art is a written thesis, and painting, too, operates within linguistic structures. Geulen comments on the language-aspect, and she alludes to a problem that arises out of a sense of distance between *event* and *language of event*. The assumption that language *refers to* or *arises out of* permits language to follow or trail, and to trace what will become – in language – a series of sequential, ordered events; in short: language plots history. To see it another way, history serves to structure the language that follows it and establishes it *as* history. Thus, the relationship is clearly reciprocal. Language comports itself *in* and *as* history, and vice versa. However, in respect of painting, if language is *of* or *with* the medium, then where does the imbrication lie?

Hegel naturalised the linkage between language and event. Moreover, Hegel's notion of *totality* amounts to a vast composite of regulating moments, which in respect of the medium would play out – one thing after another – with discrete mediums driving the shape that the individual arts came to assume.[55] And yet, the end of art thesis is not a moment as such (in that it amounts to something that has happened, in the world), and it attests to a theoretical possibility; thus appearing in a performative guise, as language of a non-existent event: one that cannot exist if the

52 Friedrich Hölderlin, "The Ister", lines 41–41.

53 This alignment or double projection appears close to Heidegger's *clearing* (*lichtung*) and it also illuminates the being of the medium. After all, medium is but a thing in flux, positioned as *equipment* between its source as thing (formerly mere material) and its destination as work—between object and image; means and message; form and content; subject and surface.

54 Peter Osborne, *Anywhere or Not At All*, 204.

55 Hegel, in *Becoming Medium* (Stephen Melville, 2013). Event produces language that, in turn, situates event *in* language *as* thesis. The partiality of times is only partial in respect to what is to come, not in the sense of something being missing.

thesis is to maintain its meaning as end of art thesis.[56] This paradox relieves language of historicism and points to Hölderlin's employment of rumour.[57] To Heidegger, rumour amounts to that which permits a dislocation between an actual event and the language of an event. As Michael Belshaw puts it: "a rumour is reliant on a simulacrum—it has no recognisable origin, and its repetition is always a repetition of a repetition; which is to say it is always *out of joint*".[58]

It is useful, here, to distinguish between the medium as material and the medium as perhaps something else. As material, the medium's meaning is *as paint* – a designation that takes into account various material extensions to the material (including the inclusion of other forms of material object) that serve with/as paint to establish the work's structural particularities, – providing a means of location: the work can be pointed to as *of the material of paint*.[59] In painting, too, language appears to trail behind the paint, which it follows and establishes as the medium. Paint assembles and is assembled by the image-material that shadows it. As a medium, the paint of a painting can be seen to have re-deployed its material properties in the process of becoming a work (a painting).

The medium's concealment behind the work's *subject* (by/through the *surface* of the work) is partial; it amounts to one half of the dual course of disclosure. For the framework to attain equilibrium, the medium's equipmentality must also become visible, and through the reciprocity of the process—that of the medium's concealment behind the work's surface (by/through the subject of the work). By this, I mean to suggest that the subject, thus construed from out of the painting's surface and

---

56 J. L. Austin (1911–1960), in *How to do things with Words* (1962) distinguishes between performative and constative utterances. Performative utterances can be neither true nor false. Constative utterances describe an action, object, or event, and can be true or false, as there is the possibility of disproving them. For example, Emily says, "I promise to do my homework" and, in so doing, *performs* the promise irrespective of whether Emily in fact completes her homework. This is, therefore, a performative utterance, as even the non-completion of the homework will not contradict the utterance itself. Austin uses the example, "I now pronounce you man and wife", spoken in the course of a wedding ceremony, as a common example of a performative utterance.

57 Geulen reminds us that Hegel's lectures were transcribed by his students, and thus from the offset they were determined by rumour.

58 Michael Belshaw, *Readings in a Rumour of the End of Art* (Leeds: Workshop Press, 2012), 11. Jacques Derrida, *Specters of Marx: The state of the debt, the work of mourning and the new international* (New York and London: Routledge, 1993). Derrida invented the term *hauntology* to describe a lack of origin or presence (and of an end, too), as a state of perpetual ontological disjunction—a ghost, neither present or absent, neither dead nor alive. Serving as a response to Francis Fukuyama's assertion of the end of history and the triumph of capitalism, Derrida redeploys a line from *Hamlet* (William Shakespeare, 1564–1616): "the time is out of joint".

59 Common extenders include wax, plaster, sawdust, sand, cement, glass, ceramic, and paper.

having been disclosed through the work, acts to disclose the hidden hemisphere of being from which its disclosure has been constituted (initially, this is concealed within its primary act of disclosure—that of the equipmentality of the shoes, to return to Heidegger's painterly example).[60] Thus, the disclosure of the equipmentality of the shoes is also the disclosure of the equipmentality of the material of paint, in accordance with the established ontological structuring of the work (Table 3). If, *in the artwork, the truth of what is has set itself to work*, then it might seem fitting to suggest that, in painting, truth is both the work and the medium of the work setting themselves to work.

Table 3: Disclosure of Medium's Equipmentality

Disclosed as surface through subject—**MEDIUM**—Disclosed as subject through surface

The dual disclosure of the work's truth and also the equipmentality of the paint amounts to *being at work in the service of truth*—doing what it is that work and paint do. What it is that *paint as medium* does, however, comprises little more than being a painting. I don't mean to suggest partiality or lack thereof, but merely that paint, as medium's vehicle, is also a limitation.[61] Paint is neither worn nor eaten. It provides neither warmth nor sustenance.[62] Its usefulness is to be found in its malleability and movability; in its mercurial fittedness for transformation; in its vehicular characteristics and chimeric potentialities. Medium becomes operable as/through paint in its move from the mere to the equipmental, and again in its move from the equipmental to becoming bound up in/as a work. The medium of painting, as Matt Saunders's has

60 The truth of the equimentality of the shoes takes precedence over the truth of the equipmentality of the medium. As work, and to stay with Heidegger's example, it bears on both the equipmentality of the shoes and the equipmentality of the medium in its transformation from mere material. Unburdened of the weight of the shoes, it must divest itself of the medium in order to retain a neutral charge—a prerequisite if one is to present an active ontological model free of the presumption of presence.

61 As with Heidegger's example of the peasant – who simply knows of the usefulness of the shoes from wearing them – an equivalent must be found for the truth of the medium (a specificity particular to the medium's form of equipmentality) in order to legitimise the truth/knowledge to which the *subject* of the work's disclosure attests.

62 In painting, that is. And, if/when it is, then the possibility of painting is extended to include such situatedness, and new limits might be drawn up. However, novelty alone is not an extender of painting's possibilities.

suggested, arises out of the redeployment or mobilisation of material.[63] If language speaks, then painting paints.

To clarify: the equipmentality of the shoes is disclosed through the painting (the work). However, to assert that the equipmentality of the paint is disclosed through the work of painting feels like a tautology and an assertion of the painting's autonomy, in that a painting seems, here, not to require an outside or a context for seeing. Nevertheless, this would be inaccurate, and such a supposition fails to take into account a fundamental division within the work. For *A Pair of Shoes*, there is clearly an outside – the peasant working in the field – an aspect of whose truth is authored, anchored, and enacted by the work of art.[64] As for the painting itself, a division also exists, but it is a division between the fluid processes of painting and the stasis of its settled object. The stasis of the work's object belies its processes, serving, in the process, to activate the paint's latent equipmentality. Once activated, the paint (as material) in effect sublimates itself through the work and becomes invisible (concealed) over the course of positioning the work as a work. The equipmentality of the material of paint is then disclosed through/as the painting for the simple reason that there is nowhere else for it to become disclosed.

3. Caesura: The End of the End—Painting in the Contracted Field

> This one contents himself;
> But rock needs gashes
> And the earth furrows
> Or how should we plant and dwell?[65]

Transformation and malleability comprise the more materially-manifest facets of the medium's equipmentality, of interest chiefly to the maker of the work, or to one concerned with the work's construction. There is something more. What of the receiver of the work? In Latin, the term caesura denotes a pause or break between words in musical or poetic composition; marked by written notation or evident in performance.[66] Integral to the work, the caesura structures the line and so provides the verse with its formal particularities. Hölderlin employs this device in his poetry, as did the Greeks, which serves to invest metric and rhythmic cadence

63 Matt Saunders, "Thread, Pixel, Grain", in *Painting Beyond Itself*, 174.
64 That which is outside, and whose truth the work services.
65 Friedrich Hölderlin, "The Ister", lines 67–70.
66 Meaning *to cut*.

with its specificity and sense, in order to, "name[...] what is holy".[67] The caesura also has an additional role by serving as an enabler, as, within the structure of a Greek tragedy, it functions to redirect the narrative at key junctures and to remind the audience of what has taken place.[68] Thus, it occupies an odd position within writing and speech—being both absent and passive (a gap) and present and active (integral to what has been and to what is to come). In permitting the positivising of nothingness (a *holding open*), the caesura negates the possibility both of absence and of resolution (of unification).

In Hölderlin's work, as with Greek tragedy, the caesura, by suspending the action, also suspends the abyssal void. On the necessity of the retention of disruption in tragic poetry, Nichols writes,

> Tragic poetry houses and sustains the essential negation of human experience in a way that funnels that emptiness, as a tragic transport, toward the direction of a particular fate. Poetry serves as the measure of an encompassing whole—the place where the poet envisages the entirety of an experience.[69]

And so, Hölderlin, in both his theoretical work and in his verse, seeks to maintain the prospect of wholeness, though in contradiction to Hegel. Hegel's wholeness arises from the restorative resolution of differences, through the synthesis of thesis and antithesis.[70] Hölderlin, on the other hand, seeks to preserve difference – the discrete graininess of things – through the formal mechanism of the caesura—*in* the work, built into its very structure. Such maintenance serves to ensure the sense and particularity of occurrence.

What, then, of the notion of an end of art, and also of medium? If an event – in Hölderlin's case, the course of the Ister – requires an origin and a destination (the Black Forest and the Black Sea) to establish it as a river, then the end of art thesis, too, requires an origin and a destination, which it must maintain if it is to retain its meaning as the end of art thesis.[71] Within German metaphysics (and art historical

67 George Steiner, *Heidegger*, 146. One example of which is the chorus in *Antigone*. The chorus acts as narrator, determining how the audience can/should react. Additionally, the chorus can interact with the players and assist in the determination of occurrences.

68 The chorus also functions to underscore past events and to point to those still to come.

69 David Nichols, "Antigone's Autochthonous Voice: Echoes in Sophocles, Hölderlin, and Heidegger", 2009.

70 This formulation of the dialectic in fact came from Johann Fichte (1762–1814).

71 *The Ister*, directed by David Barrison and Daniel Ross, 2004. The film journeys upstream to the source of the river. Bernhard Stiegler (1952–2020), Jean-Luc Nancy (1940–2021), Philippe Lacoue-Labarthe (1940–2007) and others reflect on time, war, poetry, home, technology, and National Socialism. Stiegler argues that Man and technics are indissociable (*hominization*: technical living), and that for most of what amounts to human time there was no awareness or sense of the technicisation of being (2004).

discourse), the end of art draws from Hegel as its source, and the prophesied end of art as its destination. With both ends buffered by rumour (of pronouncement and expectancy), the thesis is, in effect, uncoupled from the *events* it is ordinarily taken to chart. Here, rumour acts as caesura. In so doing, the end of art can attain both freedom and endlessness (through its bondedness to that which frames it) and, in the process, become a rumour of itself.

Within this formulation, the medium of painting carefully cushions its captives: at one end, the mere thing (as origin: paint) and, at the other, the work's functionality in language (as destination: work). In disclosing the equipmentality of paint as medium, the medium further discloses a second tier of equipmentality—as a double caesura.[72]

The caesura's equipmentality functions as a partition, connecting the work's mereness to its station *as work*, and does the same with its language, with what Heidegger calls its allegory and symbol.[73] Harnessed against the backdrop of a reversal of history (a history that Stephen Melville has likened to a stirring up of sediment), the medium harnesses its harnessers – the mere thing and language – in a three-fold embrace as *artwork*.[74] As caesura, the medium is retained as two absent presences: neither wholly material nor wholly linguistic. As the *gashes and furrows* of painting, the medium repudiates assimilation (into language or material) and permits *planting* and *dwelling* (as language and material).[75] By resisting resolution, the medium – in the stasis of its mobilisation – acts to safeguard nothing less than the perpetual preservation of painting (Table 4).

---

72 To be thought of as two positively-charged suspensions or gaps.

73 This gets around the false differentiation, identified by Richard Wollheim (1923–2003) in *On formalism and its Kinds* (1995), between the syntactic (formal) structure of a painting and any linguistic counterpart (a vocabulary of language that refers to the world). Wollheim, here, deals with Yve-Alain Bois's comment, at a seminar organised by The Museum of Modern Art in New York in 1989 (in the aftermath of the Picasso-Braque exhibition), that painting sometimes functions like a language and sometimes functions not like a language.

74 Stephen Melville, *Becoming Medium*, 2013. In this, he follows the lead of Heinrich Wölfflin (1864–1945). Remember, to Heidegger, the past becomes knowable as/through the artwork, not in advance of it.

75 Friedrich Hölderlin, "The Ister", from lines 68–69.

Table 4: Ontological Positioning of Medium as Caesura

<table>
<tr><td>Thing / Origin</td><td>Medium
Caesura
Equipment</td><td>Artwork</td><td>Medium
Caesura
Equipment</td><td>Language / Destination</td></tr>
<tr><td colspan="2">Mere</td><td>Equipment</td><td colspan="2">Work</td></tr>
<tr><td colspan="2">Black Forest</td><td>River Ister</td><td colspan="2">Black Sea</td></tr>
<tr><td>Hegel</td><td>Rumour
Caesura
Equipment</td><td>End of Art Thesis</td><td>Rumour
Caesura
Equipment</td><td>End of Art</td></tr>
<tr><td colspan="5">PAINTING</td></tr>
<tr><td colspan="5">YROTSIH</td></tr>
</table>

Object as Symbol: Baudrillard's Thanatopoietic Form

Georgios Tsagdis

'Death must be played against death.'[1]

Prelude: On the Paradoxical Logic of Life

A very old scheme divides being into subject and object, and all that belongs in neither position it classifies as process. A hierarchy that places the subject above the object and relegates the process to a tertiary position soon ensues. Much of 20th century thought can be read as the attempt to reverse or recast this hierarchy, but the century's most audacious efforts were expended in questioning the structure and presuppositions of this configuration, in its totality. Art has been complicit in this effort, more often than not foregrounding the work over the artist and the practice over both, while occasionally suspending the scheme altogether. For reasons that will become immediately apparent, life, and with it, death – or perhaps death, and with it, life – present a privileged vantage point for making the subject-object-process triangle tremble.

Starting with life, as one does, demands a brief mention of what cannot be discussed in brief, is imperative. Hegel's placing of life at the close of the 'Logic of the Concept', latter being itself the last moment of his magnum opus, *Science of Logic*, signals something particularly important for the history of philosophy. Life is, here, the first element of the Idea, which follows upon and completes the stages of subjectivity and objectivity within the 'Logic of the Concept'. Hegel begins the section on life by admitting that the idea of life concerns a subject matter or object (*Gegenstand*) so concrete, that it seems to overstep the traditional domain of logic.[2] Undoubtedly, then, in the process of showing that life in all its manifestation is integral to logic, Hegel will have to expand the concept of logic. The three manifestations he identifies

1 Jean Baudrillard, *Symbolic Exchange and Death*, translated by Ian Hamilton Grant (London: Verso, 2017), 26.

2 Georg Wilhelm Friedrich Hegel, *Science of Logic*, translated by George di Giovanni (Cambridge: Cambridge University Press, 2010), 676.

are the living individual, the life-process, and the genus-process, which correspond accordingly to the subjective, objective, and dialectically sublated-conceptual, moments of life.[3] Life, as such, comes after the subject and the object, because it is subject, object, and process at once. Thinking this calls for a new logic.

It is beyond the present scope to pursue the exigencies, resolutions, and limits of this new logic. Importantly, however, in framing life – and death, which is dialectically conquered within the concept of life – as subjective, objective, and processual *at once*, Hegel clearly recognised that the singular character of life confronted classical logic with an onto-epistemological paradox, summed up in this simultaneity, this '*at once*' of life.

This paradox does not diminish with the advance of modern life sciences. Thus, for example, Jacques Monod – who shared the Nobel prize in biology with François Jacob and André Michel Lwoff in 1965 – opens his *Chance and Necessity*, with the chapter 'Strange Objects'. Monod sets the stage with a thought experiment, which soon concedes that it is only because of the human projective perspective of creating, that this distinction between natural and artificial objects appears unquestionably intuitive.[4] It is only because of the perspective that human *poiesis* imposes, that the distinction between the natural and the man-made object can appear objective. Moreover, this distinction is only meaningful at the macroscopic level, completely vanishing at microscopic scales. Monod's conclusion of the thought experiment on the elusive, perspectival difference between natural and artificial objects is the postulation of the notion of 'teleonomy'. Teleonomy qualifies living beings as "*objects endowed with a purpose or project*, which at the same time they exhibit in their structure and carry out through their performances (such as, for instance, the making of artifacts)".[5] "Living creatures are strange objects"[6] in that they manifest themselves '*at once*' as structures (and thus as objects of scientific objectivity) and as projective performances (and thus as purposive subjects of agentic subjectivity).[7] Importantly, Monod admits, living beings share teleonomy with the artifacts they create: works of art exhibit the logic of their existence both in their objective structure and in their subjective performance. Works of art share in the onto-epistemic paradox of their creator's lives and press the limits of logic.

3 Hegel, *Science of Logic*, 678ff. In typical Neoplatonist manner, triads in the *Science of Logic* redouble by vesting themselves within homologous structures. Life is the first element of the Idea which sublates subjectivity and objectivity, but life also sublates subjectivity and objectivity within itself. The function of life in Neoplatonism and specifically its place in the Soul, is a further parallel calling for research.

4 Jacques Monod, *Chance and Necessity*, translated by Austryn Wainhouse (New York: Alfred A. Knopf, 1971), 4.

5 Monod, *Chance and Necessity*, 9.

6 Monod, *Chance and Necessity*, 17.

7 Monod, *Chance and Necessity*, 21–2.

A fuller account of the triangular refraction of life into subject, object, and process must be deferred, not least because it resurfaces in a protean manner at every turn of the theoretical landscape.[8] This essay turns, instead, to Jean Baudrillard's attempt to explicate and exploit the paradoxical logic of life by establishing a new 'form', thereby placing the emphasis on its obverse: death.

Baudrillard's Thanatopoietic Form

The resonant publication, in 1970, of Jacques Monod's *Chance and Necessity* and François Jacob's *The Logic of Life* (1973),[9] appears to have converged with the involvement of Georges Canguilhem in the *agrégation* committee towards the adoption of 'Life and Death' as the 1975–76 examination theme. Whereas Derrida's *Life Death* lectures that attempted to think beyond the (op)positionality of life and death were a direct fruit of this curricular decision,[10] the emergence of Foucault's seminal notion of biopolitics from the same year was not. Whether a direct product of the *agrégation* or an indirect product of its milieu, Baudrillard's *Symbolic Exchange and Death* appeared in 1976, to offer a novel understanding of the logic of life under the heading of death.

Baudrillard understands his early works,[11] leading up to *Symbolic Exchange and Death*, as having approached his three main influences (semiotics, psychanalysis, and Marxism) from the perspective of their object, rather than from that of the discipline that mastered this object.[12] Although this is reminiscent of Adorno's critique of Hegel and Marx in *Negative Dialectics*, Baudrillard reserves some irony for his not 'particularly philosophical approach,' his 'pataphysics' or 'situationism,' which sought to expose itself to the 'self-evidence' of the world, to discover a radical

8 Another recasting: "What we call life is neither a thing apart from matter, nor merely 'living matter,' but an informational and energetic process at Earth's surface." Schneider, Eric D. and Dorion Sagan, *Into the Cool: Energy Flow, Thermodynamics, and Life* (Chicago: The University of Chicago Press, 2005), 145. Figurations proliferate.

9 François Jacob, *The Logic of Life: A History of Heredity*, translated by Betty E. Spillmann (New York: Pantheon Books, 1973). The French title, *La Logique du Vivant*, is more accurately rendered as *The Logic of the Living*. The odd translation appears much more palatable if life is understood as subject, object, and process at once.

10 Jacques Derrida, *Life Death*, translated by Pascale-Anne Brault and Michael Naas (Chicago: The University of Chicago Press, 2020).

11 Not least, his doctoral thesis, published in 1968, *The System of Objects*. See: Jean Baudrillard, *The System of Objects*, translated by James Benedict (London: Verso, 2002).

12 Roy Boyne and Scott Lash, "Symbolic Exchange: Taking Theory Seriously. An Interview with Jean Baudrillard," *Theory, Culture and Society* 12, no. 4 (Autumn, 1995): 81.

objectivity, rather than a radical subjectivity. This no longer meant producing or mastering the object, but rather seducing and being seduced by it.[13]

When Baudrillard decided to make his subject the strange object of death in 1976, a particularly novel and interesting scheme emerged, coalescing around the notion of the *symbolic exchange of death*. This scheme would not be developed further and would be overshadowed, especially in art theory and media studies, by his later work on seduction and simulation.[14] Only radical social theorists seemed to register the development, while philosophers for the most part ignored both what came before and what came after. Accordingly, both at the time of publication and to this day, this chapter of Baudrillard's thought remains largely overlooked and under-theorised. The present essay aims to supplement what constitutes a deficit for both theory and artistic practice.

There is a performative dimension to Baudrillard's analysis of the symbolic exchange of death, as his own analysis effects and, in turn, must be read as an act of symbolic exchange. It is thus most conducive to consider symbolic exchange reflexively, from the perspective of theory, the task of which is, for Baudrillard, to 'complicate' the object in order to give back *more*, in order to offer the surplus-value that characterises symbolic exchange.[15]

The following sections will flesh out the logic of symbolic exchange, or what Baudrillard calls its 'form'. Before proceeding however, a note on this form is necessary. Reflecting on *Symbolic Exchange and Death*, Baudrillard remarks that values are perishable; indeed, values are dying away and "there is nothing more to be had from a system of values".[16] At the height of capitalism, value-based morality is bankrupt. His gesture can be seen accordingly as the countering of 'values' with 'forms': unlike values, forms are imperishable. A form is a rule of play, a rule of the game "at the level of illusion".[17] It is a rule created immanently *from* play; ultimately in the case of life and death, the play of the world. For Baudrillard, this turn to forms expresses neither optimism nor pessimism and has nothing to do with nihilism – the play and its pleasure are unto themselves.[18]

The immanence of forms – their emergence out of play – is important to prevent them from assuming the status of universal principles, the status of 'laws' or 'metanarratives'. More so perhaps than seduction, "reversibility in particular is a form".[19]

---

13 Boyne and Lash, "Symbolic Exchange," 81.
14 Boyne and Lash, "Symbolic Exchange," 79.
15 Boyne and Lash, "Symbolic Exchange," 82.
16 Boyne and Lash, "Symbolic Exchange," 89.
17 Boyne and Lash, "Symbolic Exchange," 89.
18 Boyne and Lash, "Symbolic Exchange," 89.
19 Boyne and Lash, "Symbolic Exchange," 89.

Accordingly, Baudrillard's aim is to engage in a symbolic exchange that will complicate the object of reversibility: if the most irreversible of processes is the passage from life to death, a certain *poiesis* will have to fashion a different death, one that can be exchanged for life or any other sign.

Framing Symbolic Exchange

'Symbolic exchange' is already operative in Baudrillard's *The Mirror of Production*, published in 1973, and provides one of the main threads of continuity between the earlier and later phases of his thought. The concept is clearly indebted to French sociology from Mauss to Levi-Strauss, but this debt is – deliberately – unthematised and unexplicated. As Robert Hefner suggests, Baudrillard employs the term in order to move beyond the Marxian framing of value,[20] and indeed, as is already clear, of value altogether. Baudrillard is attempting to shape a 'form' that will exceed the valuations of psychology, anthropology, and political economy: 'symbolic exchange' undertakes a radical transvaluation of values, probing the other side of value and non-value.

This project is carried forth in *Symbolic Exchange and Death* by confronting death in late capitalism with ritual sacrifice, but in the *Mirror of Production* the focus is restrained to the economy of the gift in juxtaposition with capitalism's value-creation.[21] For Marx, 'primitive' societies are predominantly acquainted with use-value: in conditions of generalised scarcity, things are consumed to satisfy direct, concrete needs, rarely being produced in such excess as to warrant trade. It is only within developed capitalist structures – in which unified exchange markets and quantified values are established – that exchange value begins to predominate and antagonise use-value.[22] This is an infrastructural as much as an ideological development; in order for exchange to become the foundation of production, exchange value must first become a value.

Baudrillard exploits this ambivalence in order to occlude the 'reality' and thus the historico-logical priority of use-value. For him, both use- and exchange-values are constructs of the capitalist code.[23] Baudrillard does not challenge Marx on anthropological grounds to point out the numerous documented occasions in which the circulation of goods (occasionally at fixed relative values) is entrenched in pre-capitalist societies.[24] Baudrillard's concern is not anthropological veracity, but the

20 Robert Hefner, "Baudrillard's Noble Anthropology: The Image of Symbolic Exchange in Political Economy," *SubStance* 6/7, no. 17 (Autumn, 1977): 105.

21 The theory of the gift is however further developed in *Symbolic Exchange and Death*, along with an examination of the anagram and a foray into simulation as figures of reversibility.

22 Hefner, "Baudrillard's Noble Anthropology," 107.

23 Hefner, "Baudrillard's Noble Anthropology," 108.

24 Hefner, "Baudrillard's Noble Anthropology," 108.

creation of a 'form' through which to oppose capitalist logic; this form is precisely the *symbolic*. Accordingly, for Baudrillard, the circulation of objects within the symbolic fashions a primordial sphere from which things of functional use are appropriated. This sphere does not care about residues because it does not have survival as its principle: "For the primitives, eating, drinking, and living are first of all acts that are exchanged: if they are not exchanged, they do not occur."[25] For Baudrillard, nature must first be 'objectified' before one submits to its law; a law that is philosophically formulated as scarcity. Thus, scarcity only emerges within the market economy as the foundation of the production and reproduction of economic exchange.[26] It is his reading of Marshall Sahlins,[27] that drives the casting of the 'objective' dimension of scarcity as a capitalist *product*, but Baudrillard takes this line of thought to its inescapable conclusion, which will be pursued below: the ultimate scarcity is that of time, and its ultimate form is death.[28]

Prima facie, the cases that counter Baudrillard's audacious strokes, abound. Not only are many pre-capitalist societies mired in scarcity – being barely familiar with any kind of circulation of objects – but cases such as the Polynesian Tykopia, who temporarily suspend circulation in the face of scarcity,[29] make clear that 'primitive' valuation breaks with Baudrillard's 'form'. Perhaps, as Clifford Geertz writes, "every man has a right to create his own savage for his own purposes. Perhaps every man does."[30] Whether exercising a right or not, Baudrillard is with little doubt after the footprints of Rousseau's noble figment; the question is not whether this tracing constitutes a matter of fact, or enough of a matter of concern in Latour's sense,[31] but rather whither the path leads.

In order to follow along the path, that much must be made clear: Baudrillard establishes a notion of 'symbolism' that eschews not only the art-historical meaning of the term, but also its received anthropological employment. A more archaic understanding is needed: the symbol must be explicated as *sym-bolon*, a token broken into two fragments and then put (*ballein*) together (*syn*), con-nected, anew. 'Symbolic exchange,' accordingly, means connective exchange, an assembly. And this, as Heidegger and Latour remind us, is nothing but the meaning of the *thing*: "in all the European languages, including Russian, there is a strong connection between

25 Jean Baudrillard, *The Mirror of Production*, translated by Mark Poster (St Louis: Telos Press, 1975), 79.

26 Baudrillard, *The Mirror of Production*, 59.

27 Marshall Sahlins, Stone Age Economics (New York: Atherton, Inc, 1972).

28 Baudrillard, *Symbolic Exchange*, 167.

29 Hefner, "Baudrillard's Noble Anthropology," 110.

30 Clifford Geertz, "The Cerebral Savage: On the Work of Claude Lévi-Strauss," in *The Interpretation of Cultures: Selected Essays* (New York: Basic Books, 1973), 347.

31 Bruno Latour, "Why Has Critique Run out of Steam? From Matters of Fact to Matters of Concern," *Critical Inquiry* 30, no. 2 (Winter, 2004).

the words for thing and a quasi-judiciary assembly."[32] 'Symbolic exchange' emerges thus as the exchange in which the thing that one calls community – which means at the same time, community for itself, recognizing itself as such – assembles, *even if* only in part, in segments through individual acts of exchange.

In *Symbolic Exchange and Death,* this form is further honed. Using the Lacanian threefold symbolic-real-imaginary, that, according to his own admission, led to significant misinterpretations,[33] Baudrillard overlays the symbolic upon the real and the imaginary as what resolves their opposition. The symbolic is here determined not as a concept, agency, category, or structure, but as "an act of exchange and *a social relation which puts an end to the real*".[34] As such, the symbolic constitutes the limit of the real. Baudrillard continues,

> The symbolic is what puts an end to this distinctive code and to separated terms. It is the u-topia that puts an end to the topologies of the soul and the body, man and nature, the real and the non-real, birth and death. In the symbolic operation, the two terms lose their reality.[35]

Reality and objectivity (of nature or the body) are accordingly the result of separation, of a distinction between the human and nature or the soul and the body. The original object, the object before objectivity, is *symbolic.*

Symbolic Exchange at Work

We must undertake a final excursion, a diversion, on the path to death in order to appreciate why for Baudrillard, *contra* Marx and Freud, the understanding of labour as a diversion of death remains blind to a radically different possibility, the symbolic exchange of death.

The *Mirror of Production* offers the groundwork of this possibility by countering Julia Kristeva's reading of the body in Marx as the locus of "discharge, play, anti-value, non-utility, non-finality, etc".[36] For Baudrillard, Marx's notion of discharge, unlike that of Bataille, is not one of 'pure waste' ('pulsating, libidinal'), but remains economic. By coupling the 'labor-father' with the 'earth-mother', it establishes a scheme that generates wealth and only produces waste as a necessary by-product. The 'normality' of this productive frame rests on traditional reproductive practices

---

32 Latour, "Why Has Critique Run out of Steam?," 232–3; Cf. Yan Thomas, "Res, Chose et Patrimoine (Note sur le Rapport Sujet-Objet en Droit Romain)," *Archives de philosophie du droit* 25, (1980).

33 Boyne and Lash, "Symbolic Exchange," 85.

34 Baudrillard, *Symbolic Exchange*, 153.

35 Baudrillard, *Symbolic Exchange*, 154.

36 Baudrillard, *The System of Objects*, 42.

which know enjoyment only as a filthy by-product. For Baudrillard, the issue is not, however, pleasure – it is putting labour into value, rather than putting labour into play. Whereas Marx knows of discharge only as investment, with Bataille, a gratuitous and festive expenditure of the body's energies is established – this is clearly a "game with death", which echoes in other bodies and nature at large, for it is nature at large for Baudrillard that plays and discharges.[37] As for humans, not only the sphere of sexuality, but also the sphere of artistic practice, is open to them, to play out the festive discharge of life, to touch death.

Symbolic Exchange and Death elaborates on this picture by casting labour as slow death. As slow death however, labour is not so much set against life, a fulfilled or good life, a life that has taken its course, spent its energies gracefully, before reaching death; rather – more truly – labour as slow death is set against violent, that is, sacrificial or symbolic death. Accordingly, much more decisive and forceful than the physical exploitation of the worker, becomes their symbolic annihilation, that is, the expropriation of the worker's symbolic death through the establishment of an equivalence of wage and death at the level of signs. Once salary is understood – represented and circulated as the sign of a fragment of death – the worker has been deprived of their symbolic death. Unsurprisingly, what transpires for the subject transpires also, in parallel, for the object: the transformation of everything into a commodity annihilates symbolically, albeit not physically, the object. Nothing *is*, but rather everything subsists in exchange limbo, waiting to be passed on as capital flow. In terms of life, this subsistence in which life and death enter into an indifferent equivalence and are gradually consumed defers death and is, as such, to be understood as *survival*.[38]

It becomes then clear that Baudrillard casts Marx and, as evidenced below, Freud as thinkers of *survival* rather than thinkers of *death*. To think death is to experience the rhythm of symbolic exchange which demands that something be given back *in the same movement*, lest reciprocity collapse. In contrast, capitalism strives to "displace the time of the exchange, substituting continuity and mortal linearity for the immediate retaliation of death", thus establishing a "*différance* of death", which no amount of the worker's giving of life is capable of recuperating: "violent death changes everything, slow death changes nothing".[39]

The capitalist "*différance* of death" ensures the reproducibility of power by replacing the logic of reversibility through sacrificial death (of the king), or through ritual inversion (through feasts and rites) with the logic that animates the master-slave dialectic.[40] Baudrillard interprets the latter as a demonstration of the origina-

---

37 Baudrillard, *The System of Objects*, 43–4.

38 Baudrillard, *Symbolic Exchange*, 60.

39 Baudrillard, *Symbolic Exchange*, 62.

40 Baudrillard, *Symbolic Exchange*, 63.

tion of the power of the master from the suspension, or 'confiscation', of the slave's death. The slave is no longer free to give their death, to risk their life; this life is rather granted to them little by little, economically, by the master. Thus, "by removing death, the master removes the slave from the circulation of symbolic goods".[41] The slave – that is, ultimately in capitalism, everyone – is a subject without death, a subject without object, a subject without symbol.

A Lost Object: Death

The loss of death constitutes for Baudrillard an 'irreversible evolution from savage societies to our own".[42] Excluded from symbolic circulation, the dead are assembled in the ghetto of the cemetery, initially at the heart of the community, then extradited to its periphery. Eventually, tombs become temporary, the dead become socially mobile. In tandem, death becomes 'extraterritorial', one no longer dies among family, but in hospitals.[43] For the first time, a society is formed in which the majority do not have the opportunity to experience the death of the other.[44]

Yet, very much like Victorian sexuality, the total censure of death makes it omnipresent:[45]

> By dint of being washed and sponged, cleaned and scoured, denied and warded off, death rubs off onto every aspect of life. [...] To sterilise death at all costs, to varnish it, cryogenically freeze it, air-condition it, put make-up on it, 'design' it, to pursue it with the same relentlessness as grime, sex, bacteriological or radioactive waste.[46]

This obsession qualifies life as natural and death as against nature, countering the naturalisation of death as a simulacrum of life. Whereas the 'primitive' "showers the dead with signs" in order to expedite the transition, to cross the threshold of death as fast as possible into the realm of difference, whence the dead can exchange their signs, modern 'thanatopraxis' is guided by "the will to ward off this sudden loss of signs that befalls the dead, to prevent there remaining, in the *asocial* flesh of the dead, something which signifies nothing."[47] To signify nothing: the horror of horrors for a system premised on utility.

41 Baudrillard, *Symbolic Exchange*, 61.
42 Baudrillard, *Symbolic Exchange*, 147.
43 Baudrillard, *Symbolic Exchange*, 202.
44 Baudrillard, *Symbolic Exchange*, 203.
45 Baudrillard, *Symbolic Exchange*, 205.
46 Baudrillard, *Symbolic Exchange*, 200–1.
47 Baudrillard, *Symbolic Exchange*, 201.

The intimation that a novel thanatopoietics must be opposed to this thanatopraxis is in the air, but Baudrilliard expends his efforts on an ever more elaborate diagnosis, suspending the question of a cure. This diagnosis incorporates for Baudrillard Foucault's claim that "medicine becomes modern with the corpse",[48] but also grows bolder: modernity's total emergence is premised on the construction of the corpse as detritus, waste, an object of no significance. As society rationalises, the dead become increasingly purposeless, of less value than delinquents and misfits who can still be put to some marginal use: "only the death-function cannot be programmed and localised".[49] Death, for the first time, becomes an 'unthinkable anomaly'.[50]

The church plays a pivotal role in this development by establishing a "political economy of individual salvation" through faith and the accumulation of goods works.[51] The ultimate sense and value of this economy, which presupposes and glorifies the individual, is immortality. The invention and distribution of immortality coincides, over the *longue durée*, with the process of the segregation of the dead. Once conceived as a possibility, eternal survival is democratised, conferred from the few to the many, while at the same time the many, who are always the dead, are hidden from sight.[52] The transformation of death into sempiternal survival amounts to a voiding of its experience; the economy expands into a new space of life (life after death), making death into an insignificant occurrence and turning the corpse from a symbol – an object that assembles the collective – into a nugatory cipher left behind by a transmigrating individual.

Baudrillard observes that even at the end of the Middle Ages the "*collective theatre* of death" was not completely individualised into a private projection on the screen of consciousness. The "great messianic and egalitarian festival of the Dance of Death" of the 15th century that made kings and fools equal in the face of death was the last moment in which death exercised a collective force, before social revolutionary movements relegated it to the reactionary margins of bourgeois individualism.[53] Unsurprisingly, socialism was no more able than capitalism to look death in the eye. As for the latter, its strategy would be to assume equality before death as a form of general equivalence within transaction networks, in the face of which everyone stands alone.[54] Only on the basis of this individuation was capitalism able to entwine the

48 Baudrillard, *Symbolic Exchange*, 147.

49 Baudrillard, *Symbolic Exchange*, 147.

50 Baudrillard, *Symbolic Exchange*, 147.

51 Baudrillard, *Symbolic Exchange*, 166.

52 Baudrillard, *Symbolic Exchange*, 149. Baudrillard identifies a parallel logic in the increasing removal of the elderly from view, as their life expectancy grows. The causal underpinnings of this development remain similarly unclear.

53 Baudrillard, *Symbolic Exchange*, 166.

54 Baudrillard, *Symbolic Exchange*, 167.

infinitude of capital with the infinitude of time that it receives from the theology of sempiternal survival.

Pre-Capitalist Death

Only in modern capitalist societies is the irreversibility of death established, assuming the objectivity of a biological fact; "every other society says that death begins before death, that life goes on after life, and that it is impossible to distinguish life from death".[55] This indistinguishability, or rather inseparability, is the work of ritual. Ritual 'conjures away,' re-unites, or resists the splitting of life and death and thereby fends off the corollary inescapable fatality that befalls the already declining body.[56] This is possible because in the 'primitive' or symbolic order the body is not understood merely as a machine, valued solely on the basis of its function. Rather, "death articulates life, is exchanged in life and is the apogee of life".[57] There is no definition of death, since death is not the de-finition of life, but a process in which parts of the self (body, language) "fall from life to death";[58] a process that in the 'primitive' order remains symbolically reversible. Accordingly, the significance of death as a finality, a finitude, and a de-finition applies as little here as for the self-dividing protozoa.[59]

So it is that the most abject modes of death must be reappraised. It is not that symbolic death is not cruel; the contrary. Yet, it does not constitute vengeful violence or an eruption of the repressed. There is no guilt or anxiety in the ritual killing of the king, since the latter is not simply a body blocking the way to power, nor is he a disease of the social body that must be sanctioned and removed. Rather, the taking of the life of the king is the taking of the life that the king gives willingly, entering a festive exchange which obliterates division and re-entrenches the solidarity of the collective. Just like the madman, the fool and the bandit in later societies will offer themselves as objects of 'ritual derision' or ritual hate, the king offers his death in a process of symbolic exchange. The body of the king assembles the collective.[60]

In a similar vein, cannibalism proceeds neither from some necessity of a state of nature, nor from a radical disregard for the dead. Cannibalism pays homage to the dead by preventing their decomposition in accordance with the natural order, thereby preventing them from escaping into that order, an inaccessible domain

55 Baudrillard, *Symbolic Exchange*, 179.
56 Baudrillard, *Symbolic Exchange*, 153.
57 Baudrillard, *Symbolic Exchange*, 179.
58 Baudrillard, *Symbolic Exchange*, 180.
59 The question of the death of protozoa is unfortunately glossed over in the way of a convenient example; the tacit assumption that the individual and the species coincide cannot decide this question.
60 Baudrillard, *Symbolic Exchange*, 159–60; 189.

whence the dead can persecute the living. In sum, cannibalism weaves a total nexus of life and death as the symbolic socius, the radically social integration of the enemy. For Baudrillard, it is modern societies that despise what they eat – the animal or vegetable condemned to death and biological assimilation – and, by extension, their own human bodies. Moreover, and this is a statement as challenging as it is significant, "primitive devouring is ignorant of the abstract separation of the eater and the eaten into the active and passive."[61]

For Baudrillard, one must *first* separate life and death in order to effect the division of active and passive, the direct analogue of the subject-object distinction. The individual subconscious and the psychic sphere thus organise themselves within the perimeter established by the threefold 'killing-possessing-devouring' and its ensuing network of prohibition and guilt. In contrast, primitive experience is arranged around the threefold 'giving-returning-exchanging', woven by and through myth and enabling an indefinite symbolic reversibility.[62]

In geometric terms, capitalism counterposes the line to the cycle. More importantly, perhaps, capitalism discretises an interminable plurality of lines, whereas the cycle remains a collective singularity. Autonomous consciousness, and with it the subconscious, emerge as countering responses against the irreversibly fragmented subject-object by placing the object in the conscious, or subconscious, subject.[63] Law and necessity are concretised in a break with nature, an "irreversible castration" that gives rise to history ("the operational violence of man against nature") and of the subconscious ("the redemption of the symbolic debt owed for this operational violence").[64] Capitalism thus replaces a system of reciprocity in which clan measures up against clan, death against death, and gift against gift with a system of equivalences wherein one thing, anything, including death, can be had in the place of another; 'death *contra* death' therefore becomes 'death *for* death'. The subsumption of the totality of equivalence under the sign of universality – a universal value or principle – supports and seals off the system.[65]

The Death Drive: Freud & Bataille

Baudrillard seeks an alternative to the parallel economisation of death by political economy and psychoanalysis. Freud's postulation of a death drive introduced a psychic force of dissolution which strives to unbind the organic constitution of

---

61 Baudrillard, *Symbolic Exchange*, 158–9.

62 Baudrillard, *Symbolic Exchange*, 160.

63 Baudrillard, *Symbolic Exchange*, 164.

64 Baudrillard, *The System of Objects*, 71.

65 Baudrillard, *Symbolic Exchange*, 191.

the living being and return it to the inorganic, countering the constructive work of eros: "entropy of death, negentropy of Eros", writes Baudrillard,[66] underlining the influence of thermodynamics in this development of Freud's thought. In this picture, arranged first in 1920 in *Beyond the Pleasure Principle*,[67] and elaborated upon ten years later in *Civilisation and its Discontents*,[68] "Eros is nothing, but an immense detour taken by culture towards death."[69] This detour delays and defers, through a negentropic 'federation' of energies into ever larger unities,[70] the return of the organic to the inorganic, assuming the guise of (cultural) sublimation.

The structure of the death drive is complicated by its discontinuous character. Because of the resistance of eros, but also because "the organism wishes to die only in its own fashion",[71] the death drive paces death by punctuating life and the linearity of the works of eros with countless micro-deaths. Through the compulsion to repeat (*Wiederholungszwang*) "the non-event of a prior inorganic state of things, that is to say, death",[72] the death drive establishes a recursive process, giving rise to a metaphysics of 'pulsation' that Freud, according to Baudrillard, sets against the tradition of a "metaphysics of anguish", which recognises death only as a singular finality.[73]

For Freud, the death drive's energetic animation of processes of the subconscious order, bestows upon the latter an *objective*, or at least a pre- and extra-subjective status.[74] Baudrillard, however, considers the reality of the drive "indefensible". For him, the intuition of the concept is only meaningful as a "deconstructive hypothesis", which must itself be deconstructed.[75] Not only because the death drive is worthy of all mistrust, fostering the repressive violence of the individual and the collective super-ego, but also because it is peculiar and limited to "*our*" culture – it is only in modern capitalist societies that "death [as psychic drive] undertakes to abolish death [as biological fact] and, for this very purpose, erects death above death and is haunted by it as its own end."[76] For Baudrillard, the concept of the death drive is, in a Nietzschean sense, the residue of the mythic metaphor, axiomatising the

66 Baudrillard, *Symbolic Exchange*, 170.

67 Sigmund Freud, "Beyond the Pleasure Principle," in *The Complete Works*, vol. 18, edited by James Strachey (London: Vintage, 2001).

68 Sigmund Freud, "Civilization and its Discontents," in *The Complete Works*, vol. 21, edited by James Strachey (London: Vintage, 2001).

69 Baudrillard, *Symbolic Exchange*, 170.

70 Baudrillard, *Symbolic Exchange*, 177.

71 Freud, "Beyond the Pleasure Principle," 39.

72 Baudrillard, *Symbolic Exchange*, 170.

73 Baudrillard, *Symbolic Exchange*, 168.

74 Baudrillard, *Symbolic Exchange*, 168.

75 Baudrillard, *Symbolic Exchange*, 170.

76 Baudrillard, *Symbolic Exchange*, 172.

fundamental exchangeability of life and death in the symbolic order, in the form of a recursive, and ultimately regressive, psychic economy.

This economy gains its autonomy only late in the history of the Occident, redoubling at a higher plateau the autonomy that the biological sphere has wrested from the inorganic. The 'pulsation' of the death drive is meant to harmonise the autonomous spheres of the psychic and the somatic, yet it ends up contributing to their arbitrariness and radical autonomisation.[77] It is clear that death cannot be tamed, cannot be controlled. As a "radical, functional principle" the death drive not only has no need of a libidinal economy, whether more or less repressive, but it ineluctably ends up subverting every such economy as it "meanders through successive topologies and energetic calculi".[78] This is why, "as a principle of counter-finality, a radical speculative hypothesis, meta-economic, metapsychical, meta-energetic, metapsychoanalytical, the death (drive) is beyond the subconscious: it must be wrested from psychoanalysis and turned against it."[79] To do so, Baudrillard turns to Bataille.

Death in Bataille functions no longer as a regulator, but rather as the force of excess that drives an incessant exchange with life. This exchange is cyclical, it constitutes a *revolution* of life, rather than its antagonistic opposition. *Contra* Freud, death is accordingly not the 'price' of sexuality, nor is sexuality a detour towards death. Life and death "exchange their energies and excite each other", yet they eschew a single economy in which they would function in separation: in their interweaving, life and death set themselves "beyond economics altogether".[80] Accordingly, whereas the Freudian cycle of involution (as regressive pulsation) facilitates a linear economy of duration premised on scarcity or 'penury', the latter's cycle of revolution breaks with it.[81] In a structure where utility is the supreme value and life is reduced to survival at any cost, "death becomes a useless luxury, and the only alternative".[82]

This death, which opens the possibility of *continuity* – of an indefinite continuum of existence, a continuum of excess – is what Baudrillard discovers in Bataille and what he wishes to counterpose, under the name of the symbolic, to the discretising capitalist apparatus. The excess of the symbolic, localised in the plenitude and luxury of erotic expenditure is, however, both 'anti-productive' and 'anti-reproductive' and is aimed against all order.[83] Bataille, according to Baudrillard, sought ultimately to functionalise sacrificial destruction, play, and expenditure by inscribing it into the

77 Baudrillard, *Symbolic Exchange*, 173.
78 Baudrillard, *Symbolic Exchange*, 174.
79 Baudrillard, *Symbolic Exchange*, 174.
80 Baudrillard, *Symbolic Exchange*, 176.
81 Baudrillard, *Symbolic Exchange*, 176.
82 Baudrillard, *Symbolic Exchange*, 176.
83 Baudrillard, *Symbolic Exchange*, 178.

underlying law of the species, thus resolving into biology the impasses of the psycho-cultural economy.[84]

Discrete Death: Serres' Quasi-Object

It is becoming clear that the spatiotemporal localisation of death at a specific hour and in a specific body is the effect of a capitalist psycho-cultural economy, which employs such localisations to produce discrete subjects: to subjectivise, but also to subject.

Although Baudrillard nowhere discusses this, Michel Serres' theory of the quasi-object affords one of the clearest perspectives on the process. In the eponymous *The Parasite*, Serres queries the ontology of the parasite, a figure that, according to him, balances between relation and substance, between the ontology of "an operator" and that of "a monad".[85] Among the different examples of the parasitical figure that Serres provides is the ferret, or *furet*, which in the French signifies the animal that humans have domesticated and parasitise, using it like the kestrel, but also the game in which the one marked by the sign of the *furet* tries to find an object that is passed around.[86] When the *furet* finds the one who possesses the object, that person, marked now by the object, becomes the *furet*.

At play, the *furet* emerges as both subject and object while being neither completely. What one finds, when one arrests the passing object, is the next *furet*; one discovers the *furet* as an imminent object, an object which incorporates in its constitution the *furet*. In a sense, one chases the *furet* as a quasi-object, an object that upon discovery will produce a new subject, for the object found is integral to the constitution of the subject as *furet*. The *furet* is thus at once a quasi-object – being an object while sought – and a quasi-subject – becoming a subject once found. Those who pass it do not possess it, but in doing so they weave the collective. When they arrest its movement, when they possess it, the collective dissolves, an individual is marked and formed – the new *furet*.

In fact, every ball game utilises this structure. A ball must be held by a subject, but it must also be passed around. It is what it is only as long as it circulates; "over there, on the ground, it is nothing; it is stupid; it has no meaning, no function, and no value."[87] A ball accordingly forces a change in perspective, a revolution "in a Copernican world where objects are slaves", for the ball is not the object for the body, the

---

84 Baudrillard, *Symbolic Exchange*, 178.

85 Michel Serres, *The Parasite*, translated by L. R. Schehr (Baltimore: The John Hopkins University Press, 1982), 224.

86 Serres, *The Parasite*, 225.

87 Serres, *The Parasite*, 225.

body is the object of the ball, the sun around which the subject moves.[88] The ball, like the *furet*, undoes the individual and weaves the collective. The 'I' is undone, the subject is sub-mitted to the ball, which continues to be passed in a collective motion, exchanging 'I's like tokens. This passage is precisely, symbolic, showing our capacity for *ec-stasy* and *ec-centricity*.[89] For Serres, this is a dangerous moment, as one's individuality is abandoned and being is 'transubstantiated' into relation.[90]

Baudrillard opens up the possibility of conceiving this moment, as precisely the instant in which life is symbolically exchanged with death. Death is, accordingly, a quasi-object and a quasi-subject, passed around in the collective, only occasionally marking discrete individuals. It thus takes the "infinitesimal space of the individual conscious subject" to establish death as an irreversible finality and ultimate source of meaning,[91] but it also takes the arrest of death in discrete parcels, or quanta, of mortality in order to produce an individual consciousness. The dissolution of the collective is only the ineluctable corollary.

Discreet Death: On the Natural and the Safe

Parallel to the operation of power, by means of which the master removes the slave's death from the circle of symbolic exchange, death becomes symbolically unavailable though its naturalisation. 'Natural' death is "banal because it is bound to the policed and commonplace [*banalisé*] individual subject, to the policed and commonplace nuclear family, and because it is no longer a collective mourning and joy."[92] Constituted by 'natural' death, the modern subject glorifies and dreads its prospect; it glorifies and dreads the finality of death *because* it is natural, because nature colludes with capital to establish and ensure death's finality.

One dreams, thus, according to Baudrillard, of escaping the "indifferent negativity" of the 'natural' order of capital, which corresponds to an individual yet "impersonal expiry of the body"; a body delivered over to the crushing death of instrumentalization.[93] One dreams of giving and receiving death, of sharing death with other subjects and other objects, of reverting to the symbolic, "primitive order". This impossible dream takes the form of the fatal technical accident, the artificiality of which is invoked as the counterpoint to natural finitude. A fallacious twist of logic

88 Serres, *The Parasite*, 226.

89 A literal figure of this eccentricity was the revolutionary Fosbury flop, performed for the first time in Mexico City in 1968; from then on, placing one's centre of gravity outside oneself would be the only way to reach higher.

90 Serres, *The Parasite*, 228.

91 Baudrillard, *Symbolic Exchange*, 189.

92 Baudrillard, *Symbolic Exchange*, 185.

93 Baudrillard, *Symbolic Exchange*, 186.

that leaves the collective subconscious untroubled equates in the technical accident the non-natural with the *willed*, reclaiming death as a meaningful sign by re-inscribing it in the social and aesthetic orders, thereby setting in motion stifled imagination and its corresponding *jouissance*.[94]

In a system where death is understood as an evil because of and insofar as it escapes the law of value,[95] the fatal accident emerges as an atavistic act of resistance. It is to be expected, then, that such resistance should be pre-empted at all costs. The apparatus of control transitions from 'you shall not kill' to 'you shall not die'. Birth and death are controlled so that they are not only removed from one's will but also from biological chance, ensuring that rational programmability can calculate and certify which deaths qualify as natural.[96]

In order to ensure the economisation of death, life must be secured: "*Security is the industrial prolongation of death*, just as ecology is the industrial prolongation of pollution."[97] A whole complex of "security forces" from social security and life insurance to the seatbelt set up radical, insidious forms of repression that dispossesses the subject from its own death, the death one dreams of beyond the instinct of conservation: "It is necessary to rob everyone of the last possibility of *giving* themselves their own death as the last 'great escape' from a life laid down by the system."[98] It is from this perspective that an object such as the car, as cause and effect of numerous processes, needs to be understood. Assembled as a thing to meet a wide range of computable criteria of efficiency and of professional or private productivity, the car aims not least to anticipate death, not so much by preventing it, as by voiding it:

> mummified in his helmet, his seatbelt, all the paraphernalia of security, wrapped up in the security myth, the driver is nothing but a corpse, closed up in another, non-mythic, death, as neutral and objective as technology, noiseless and expertly crafted. Riveted to this machine, glued to the spot in it, he no longer runs the risk of dying, since he is *already* dead. This is the secret of security, like a steak under cellophane: *to surround you with a sarcophagus in order to protect you from dying*.[99]

Replacing one kind of death for another, equivalence for exchange, the economic for the symbolic, the apparatus is able to anticipate and classify everything. There are henceforth two kinds of things: 'good objects' (and with them 'good subjects'), created "by exuding danger, pollution, usury, deception and haunting" and placed

94 Baudrillard, *Symbolic Exchange*, 185.
95 Baudrillard, *Symbolic Exchange*, 192.
96 Baudrillard, *Symbolic Exchange*, 194–5.
97 Baudrillard, *Symbolic Exchange*, 198.
98 Baudrillard, *Symbolic Exchange*, 197.
99 Baudrillard, *Symbolic Exchange*, 198.

within the circulation of goods as what transacts or what is transacted. 'Bad objects', in contrast – objects beset by disease and frailty such as the human body and 'bad subjects', primitive subjects, or subjects beset by madness, criminality and art – such subjects are obliterated or at best silenced and marginalised, left to long after a machinic-algorithmic efficiency that they cannot achieve.[100]

In this *Gestell* by any other name, programmability, which principally involves predictability and accuracy, presents a finality for both material objects and desiring subjects. This finality is the generalised law of value according to which "everything is arrested as a coded difference in a universal nexus of relations".[101] Death is the critical test that the apparatus must pass to achieve uninterrupted equivalence and thus, for Baudrillard, the sole nodal point lending itself to subversion. For as soon as the apparatus incorporates death, thereby shifting its register and order, all is made interminably available as standing reserve in a network of equivalences. Not even knowledge escapes the fate of a 'cryogenic freezing', which will preserve it at the ready to be resurrected and utilised.[102] Thus, it is that "our societies' true necropolises are the computer banks or the foyers, blank spaces from which all human noise has been expunged, glass coffins where the world's sterilised memories are frozen".[103]

Salute to Life: Reversibility and Artistic Practice

The above exploration has made manifest the function of the symbolic exchange of death as a prime expression of the form of reversibility. Although Baudrillard veers into other figures of reversibility in *Symbolic Exchange and Death*, such as the gift and the anagram, death constitutes the form's exemplary expression, being itself, as shown, subject, object, and process *at once*. Symbolic exchange sets motion thus into motion.

Baudrillard's aim is to explore the limits of "the linearity of time, language, economic exchange, accumulation and power".[104] He offers accordingly a rich diagnosis of the modern obliteration of symbolic death, yet with it comes only a thin cure: the *pharmakon* of death is out of balance. It is clear that Baudrillard stakes his hopes on death itself; "perhaps death and death alone, the reversibility of death, belongs to a higher order than the code. Only symbolic disorder can bring about interruption in

100 Baudrillard, *Symbolic Exchange*, 198.
101 Baudrillard, *Symbolic Exchange*, 205.
102 Baudrillard, *Symbolic Exchange*, 205.
103 Baudrillard, *Symbolic Exchange*, 205.
104 Baudrillard, *Symbolic Exchange*, 23.

the code."[105] His 'solution' is to unhinge or unbind all systemically-bound energies, which like all energies are directed to their own death: "This is why the only strategy is catastrophic, and not dialectical at all. Things must be pushed to the limit, where quite naturally they collapse and are inverted."[106] To achieve this,

> simulation must go further than the system. Death must be played against death: a radical tautology that makes the system's own logic the ultimate weapon. The only strategy against the hyperrealist system is some form of pataphysics, "a science of imaginary solutions;" that is, a science-fiction of the system's reversal against itself at the extreme limit of simulation, a reversible simulation in a hyperlogic of death and destruction.[107]

It seems that in this pataphysical science-fiction, the emphasis is on fiction rather than on science. Yet, Baudrillard does not seem to show the path to new forms of fabulation, a new *aesthesis* and *praxis*. Indeed, he insists on the death of art, a non-exchangeable death, insofar as collectives remain beholden to production made spectacle, to the aesthetisation of politics which for Walter Benjamin constituted the vertigo of fascism, now made into the 'general system' itself. This spectacle becomes twice indispensable, both because it constitutes the source of all aesthetic enjoyment, but also because it preserves the hope of a real catastrophe – a possibility for Baudrillard immanent in every spectacle.[108] This hope seems to be the second gift of Prometheus: along with fire, not ignorance of the time of the arrival of death, but hope for this arrival.

One senses the tensions in Baudrillard's effort. This effort, which is itself, as discussed, a theoretical symbolic exchange, relies on a fictionalisation of anthropology in order to fashion the thanatopoietic form. Baudrillard's form establishes itself immanently out of its own practice. What is being established is the potentiality of death's reversal in conditions which preclude it. According to Baudrillard, the loss of symbolic death constitutes – just like the fragmentation of subject and object – an "irreversible evolution from savage societies to our own".[109] In sum, Baudrillard's theoretical poetics belabours the impossibility of introducing reversibility into an irreversible system of irreversibility. This Sisyphean, or rather perhaps, pataphysical, effort seems to be vindicated one last time out of despair or out of humour: reversibility is proclaimed 'imperishable'.[110]

---

105 Baudrillard, *Symbolic Exchange*, 27.
106 Baudrillard, *Symbolic Exchange*, 26.
107 Baudrillard, *Symbolic Exchange*, 26.
108 Baudrillard, *Symbolic Exchange*, 206.
109 Baudrillard, *Symbolic Exchange*, 147.
110 Boyne and Lash, "Symbolic Exchange," 89.

Perhaps the key to this tension is afforded in the confessional mode. When, in 1995, Baudrillard reflected on *Symbolic Exchange and Death* and his relation to Heidegger, he admited that his erstwhile 'metaphysical nostalgia' couched in his admission of technology as the end and realisation of metaphysics has given way to 'irony'.[111] If irony is understood as dis-semblance – as a second order resemblance, a second order simulation – Baudrillard's effort not to reinstate value, but rather to introduce the old, 'imperishable' form of reversibility into symbolic death can be understood as an attempt to avoid proliferating difference, to play instead with the absolute indifference of simulation. Late Baudrillard wishes to transform simulation, advancing a logic indifferent to the true and the false, as rule of play.[112]

Yet the tension between the immanent play of indifference and the imperishable form of reversibility remains. Irony alone cannot prevent reversibility from becoming a transcendental law. Nothing pata-*physical* remains of Baudrillard's gesture if at the ultimate physical level quantum gravity's reversibility is set against thermodynamic irreversibility; nothing except law against law, theory against theory. Perhaps, however, this is the last theoretical symbolic exchange left to be played out and Baudrillard partakes in it. His thanatopoietics fashions and stakes a form of death through which another life is imaginable. More, unexpected poetics are called for to explore strange objects and the reversible form.

111 Boyne and Lash, "Symbolic Exchange," 85.

112 Boyne and Lash, "Symbolic Exchange," 91.

Co-Production: Towards a Relational Ontology of Aesthetic Objects

Olga Moskatova

When addressing the role of materials in aesthetic poietic processes, the explanatory framework can quickly lead to a hylomorphic paradigm. From this perspective, 'making' is conceived as an imposition of human immaterial forms (*morphē*) upon a passive matter (*hyle*). Thereby, artefacts appear as a mere unification of form and matter. Whereas form is expected to substantiate and determine the nature of a being, matter is defined as an underlying, indeterminate, and receptive substratum (*hypokeímenon*).[1] According to British anthropologist, Tim Ingold, this conception, which goes back to Aristotle's *Physics* and *Metaphysics*, is still common in many studies of material culture today and reduces the process of making to a simple "project."[2] In philosophical aesthetics, too, hylomorphism has a long pedigree. From antiquity to modernity, the Aristotelian-inspired art and image theory, reinforced by Platonic ideas, Christian doctrines, and German idealism, revolves around the dichotomy between form and matter.[3] In the metaphysical art theories of the Middle Ages, in the Renaissance, and in the 19th century, form and content have traditionally taken priority over matter, the alleged inferiority of which makes it destined to be spiritualized, sublimated, and eradicated in the creative process.[4] Moreover, it is not only the artistic practice and process of making which can be modelled on hylomorphism, but also the structure of the aesthetic object itself. If the object is made by unifying form and matter, it inevitably results in a reified compound structure.

---

1 Aristotle: *Metaphysics* Z, 7, 1032a, 16–1033a, 10; Met. H, 1, 1042a, 25–30; Aristotle: *Physics* I, 7, 190a, 13–21; Phys. I, 7, 190b, 1–17; Phys. I, 9, 192a, 2–35.

2 Tim Ingold, *Making: Anthropology, Archaeology, Art and Architecture* (London/New York: Routledge 2013), 20.

3 Dieter Mersch, "Materialität und Formalität. Zur duplizierten Ordnung des Bildlichen," in *Materialität und Bildlichkeit: Visuelle Artefakte zwischen Aisthesis und Semiosis*, ed. Marcel Finke and Mark A. Halawa (Berlin: Kadmos 2012), 21–49, here, p. 27.

4 Dieter Mersch, "Materialität und Formalität," 24–29. Monika Wagner, "Materialvernichtung als künstlerische Schöpfung," in *Material im Prozess: Strategien ästhetischer Produktivität*, ed. Andreas Haus, Franck Hofmann, and Anne Söll (Berlin: Dietrich Reimer 2000), 109–121.

Differentiated in image carrier and image object, figure and ground, *disegno* and *colore*, transparent representation and opaque medium, or medium and form, images and other artistic media are often based on the opposition of material and immaterial, which more or less explicitly inherits the Aristotelian distinction between form and matter.[5]

The French philosopher Gilbert Simondon has famously scrutinized the a-processuality and binarism in the Aristotelian approach and has developed an alternative relational and pluralistic theory of individuation. According to Simondon, hylomorphism is a technological, epistemological, and social paradigm of extreme endpoints, which gives an abstract and all too summarily account of becoming and poiesis.[6] Instead of focusing on operations and processes of individuation, it presupposes two principles—form and matter—that precede the being.[7] With view to poiesis, the hylomorphic concept is quite problematic for its notion of passive and inert matter; it reveals an influential and habitual reduction which conceives matter preferably as raw matter, i.e. as something which has no value in and of itself, which is destined to become something ontologically, epistemologically, and aesthetically different and presumably 'higher.' The hierarchy between activity and passivity which supports hylomorphism also implies a subject-object relationship at the heart of making. It subordinates materials to human ideas and intentions. This understanding envisions a human maker as an autonomous, centered, powerful subject who is not only in control of his intentions, actions, and other entities around him, but who is himself conceptualized as disembodied and immaterial. Neither human nor non-human matter have history or processuality. The process of production is regarded as insignificant. There is no tension between the initial idea and the embodied skills, or between non-human materials and intentions which are actually produced and productive within this very process. For Simondon, the Aristotelian notions form and matter or the material and immaterial only retain the borderline cases of a reality that is organized by degrees, therefore obscuring the crucial moment of operativity.[8] Expressed in the terms of Bruno Latour, all processes and preconditions of construction and becoming are 'black boxed,'[9] turning hylomorphism and its equivalents into metaphysical shortcuts, which only recognize already accomplished results.

5 For a detailed account on Aristotelian heritage see Olga Moskatova, *Male am Zelluloid: Zum relationalen Materialismus im kameralosen Film* (Bielefeld: transcript 2019), 57–79 and 164–167.

6 Gilbert Simondon, *L'individu et sa genèse physico-biologique* (1964) (Grenoble: Millon 1995), 37–43.

7 Gilbert Simondon, *L'individu et sa genèse physico-biologique*, 21–22.

8 Gilbert Simondon, *L'individuation psychique et collective: À la lumière des notions de forme, information, potentiel et métastabilité* (Paris: Aubier 1989), 208.

9 Bruno Latour, *Science in Action: How to Follow Scientists and Engineers Through Society* (Cambridge, Mass.: Harvard University Press 1987), 1–17.

In contrast, Simondon's philosophy of individuation focuses exactly on this operative middle between abstract endpoints and offers an adequate framework for describing it. As in the study of cultural techniques, operations have conceptual priority over entities and finished artefacts.[10] By meticulously analyzing the processes of making, Simondon demonstrates that a mere unification of an abstract, immaterial, non-becoming form and arbitrary matter can never result in a real, existing object because they are simply too incompatible.[11] In order for these two heterogeneous realities to encounter, they first have to be mediated by establishing two different chains of operations and reconciling disparate orders of magnitude.[12] Form and matter are reformulated as "transformational half-chains" (*demi-chaînes de transformations*) of a single technical operation that forges a relationship on the same "level of existence" (*niveau d'existence*).[13] Instead of *basing* the individual on the foundational thought—i.e. on the principles of individuation—Simondon thinks the being *by way of* individuation, i.e. *co*llaborative and *trans*formative operations.[14] In doing so, form and matter become processual, and so their vertical (hierarchical) relationship is horizontalized.

Simondon's critique of hylomorphism and his philosophy became an influential starting point for the processual and agential concepts of matter within the current non-anthropocentric discourses. In particular, new materialists such as Tim Ingold, Manuel DeLanda, and Jane Bennett explicitly draw on his philosophy, while Karen Barad's agential realism displays many similarities to it without directly referring to the French philosopher.[15] They all conceive matter not as a passive receptacle for which immaterial forms are imposed from the outside, but rather as an active and immanent factor in the ongoing processes of becoming and world-making. From this perspective on material agency, non-human actors come to the fore as active

---

10 Erhard Schüttpelz, "Die medienanthropologische Kehre der Kulturtechniken," in *Archiv für Mediengeschichte* 6 (2006):87–110, here p.91.

11 Simondon: *L'individu et sa genèse*, 38.

12 Simondon: *L'individu et sa genèse*, 38.

13 Simondon: *L'individu et sa genèse*, 39 – 41. All translations in the text are mine.

14 Lexically, this shift is expressed through the distinctive use of *à partir* (foundations) and *à travers* (processes) in Simondon's writing. See Muriel Combes, *Gilbert Simondon and the Philosophy of the Transindividual* (Cambridge, Mass./London: MIT Press 2013), 109. Temporally, it can be expressed through the juxtaposition of *before* and *after* with *during*, *trans** and *co** which highlight the operative middle and processuality of individuation.

15 Karen Barad, *Meeting the Universe Halfway: Quantum Physics and the Entanglement of Matter and Meaning* (Durham/London: Duke University Press 2007). Jane Bennett, *Vibrant Matter: A Political Ecology of Things* (Durham/London: Duke Univ. Press 2010). Manuel De Landa, *Intensive Science and Virtual Philosophy* (London/New York: Continuum 2002). Ingold, *Making*, 24–26. Tim: Ingold, "The Textility of Making," in *Cambridge Journal of Economics* 34 (2010): 91–102.

participants in the creative process and as co-producers of aesthetic objects. Simondon's philosophy, however, goes beyond the redistribution of agency and the mere activation and processualization of matter. Instead, Simondon reworks hylomorphism into the philosophy of relations and into a pluralistic ontology that multiplies differences instead of reducing them, as is often the case in the monistic world view of new materialism. Simondon's relational pluralism shows great potential not only for the theory of aesthetic practices—a view that is able to take human and non-human contributions into account—but also for a non-dualistic and non-monistic conception of the aesthetic object. I will unpack this potential using the example of Len Lye's camera-less avant-garde film, *Free Radicals* (1958/79), which is produced by scratching directly onto the filmstrip. While film is generally regarded as a mechanical, auto-poietic medium whose image creation profits from the absence of the human hand, *Free Radicals* imports a manual dimension of drawing, *disegno*, into the film making, thus raising questions about the relationship between non-human matter and human artistic agency. Instead of describing the production process as an asymmetrical subject-object relation, I will elaborate on it as the process of relational co-production of human and non-human in which the aesthetic object originates *from* and evolves *into* a multiplicity.

Beyond Hylomorphism: The Relationality of Becoming Plural

In order to delineate the process of making as a co-production, it is helpful to briefly introduce Simondon's philosophy of relations and plural becoming, as his critique of hylomorphism is first and foremost a critique of a particular metaphysical notion of relationality. For Simondon, Aristotelian hylomorphism and its historical variations exemplify relational thinking of extremes and mutually-external endpoints.[16] Relations are reduced to a simple unification of already-given principles and, thus, to independently-preexisting relata. Simondon names this kind of relationality "rapport" and distinguishes it from relations sensu stricto.[17] Like in Barad's agential realism, the prefix "inter-" denotes this reduced relationality.[18] Barad pleas for the immanence of the prefix "intra-", though Simondon expresses the distinction in terms

16 Simondon, *L'individuation psychique*, 207–210.

17 Simondon, *L'individu et sa genèse*, 30.

18 Karen Barad makes the distinction with reference to the notions of interaction and intra-action. While interactions presuppose the givenness of independent relata, intra-actions signify primitive relations without preexisting relata, i.e. processes from which semantic and ontological differences and relata result in the first place. See Barad, *Meeting the Universe Halfway*, 139–141.

of prefixes "trans-" or "co-."[19] Whereas *rapport* reduces relations to a merely logical and conceptual category, genuine *relations* are elevated to the rank of being within different regimes of individuation and stand for a real, ontogenetically significant activity.[20] Relata and relations do not precede each other, but rather co-emerge. Co-production alludes to this activity of the co-emergent becoming of the human and the aesthetic. Relations, thus, do not connect, but are brought into being during the process of individuation, which turns out to be a process of both differentiation and heterogenesis.

For this purpose, Simondon introduces the concept of the pre-individual in which all principles of individuation are abandoned. Being "more than unity and more than identity" (*plus qu'unité et plus qu'identité*),[21] the pre-individual is an ontically unspecified plurality. It is constituted by orders of magnitude and is full of real potentials, tensions, and different intensities.[22] Simondon further specifies this intensive plurality with the notions metastability (dynamic equilibrium),[23] disparity[24] and the problematic,[25] which he regards as crucial preconditions for becoming. If they are absent and everything is balanced and in stable equilibrium, there is no longer any potential for transformations and, thus, relations.

Simondon uses thermodynamic notions of metastability and also of "dephasing" (*déphasage*) in order to turn them into philosophical notions of plural becoming. The operations of individuation initiate a "dephasing" of the metastable pre-individual, which has no phases prior to it.[26] It is a process of differentiation which resolves the initial incompatibilities between the pre-individual orders of magnitude, turns them into new structures, and results in a simultaneous co-differentiation of the individual and its associated milieu.[27] For the individual, dephasing also implies a differentiation into a "poly-phased being" (*l'être polyphasé*).[28] Simondon calls for the replacement of ontological monism by the "pluralism of phases" (*pluralisme de phases*).[29] A pluri-phasic being, thus, counters the idea of stable, 'mono-phasic' substance which is given at once. This way, individuation indicates a differentiation of the pre-individual in two ways: a doubling of individual and associated milieu, as

19 On "inter-" and "trans-" in Simondon see: *L'individuation psychique*, 179. See also my footnote 14.
20 Simondon, *L'individu et sa genèse*, 26–27, and, 30.
21 Simondon, *L'individu et sa genèse*, 24.
22 Simondon, *L'individu et sa genèse*, 23–25, and, 30.
23 Simondon, *L'individu et sa genèse*.
24 Simondon, *L'individu et sa genèse*, 203–206.
25 Simondon, *L'individu et sa genèse*, 27, 29.
26 Simondon, *L'individu et sa genèse*, 23, 32.
27 Simondon, *L'individu et sa genèse*, 23–25.
28 Simondon, *L'individu et sa genèse*, 230.
29 Simondon, *L'individu et sa genèse*.

well as an unfolding of the structural complexity of a being. Analogous to the pre-individual, the becoming individual is not self-identical. Contrary to the etymology of the individual, its discontinuous plurality makes it divisible. An individual is actually a 'plurividual', so to speak.

Due to relationality and dephasing, the individual is excessive. It always points beyond itself. A being is neither given prior to the relations (as a principle, a predetermining telos of individuation, or a substantial form[30]) nor is it complete after the establishment of the first ontogenetic relations. Rather, the individual unfolds as a pluri-phasic passage *by way of* relations and *as* a relation. Individuations can traverse different domains of existence, such as the psychological, biological, physical, collective, etc. Collective individuation especially makes the excessiveness of individuals apparent. By way of their unresolved tensions and still-contained metastability, individuals can form relations of collectivity and, thus, co-individuate psycho-socially. Simondon refers to this collective individuation as "trans-individuality," wherein "trans-" highlights the horizontal traversing between individuals and is set apart from inter-individuality, which only establishes relationships between already-individualized beings.[31] Trans-individuality and inter-individuality, or rather "trans-" and "inter-," thus correspond to the distinction between relation and rapport. In other words, trans-individual relations can only take place where potentials for becoming still exist.

This relational pluralism is of interest both for the analysis of the processes of making as well as the aesthetic objects resulting from them. With regard to aesthetic poiesis, the pre-individual can be considered a scaled production arrangement of human and non-human entities. This multiplicity acts as a pre-individual relative to the particular emerging aesthetic object. The process of making does not take place between asymmetrical active and passive, immaterial and material parts, but rather constitutes a trans-individual co-individuation or co-production which entails relational becoming for both aesthetic objects and human beings alike. Instead of being a hylomorphic compound, the aesthetic object dephases into a pluriphasic individual and, thus, becomes a multiplicity.

Inscriptions: Co-Production and the Dephasing of the Filmic Art Object

In accordance with the primacy of operativity in Simondon's philosophy, it is necessary to start with an operation in order to examine the co-production of Lye's handmade film, *Free Radicals*. The film was produced by scratching into a 16 mm black film

30 On the substantiality of form see Aristotle: *Metaphysics* Z, 7, 1032b, 1f.; Met. Z, 8, 1033b, 16.

31 Simondon: *L'individuation psychique*, 154, and 191–197. Gilbert Simondon, *Du mode d'existence des objets techniques* (1958) (Paris: Aubier 1989), 248.

strip and, thus, mainly by the operation of inscription that directly refers back to the problems of hylomorphic conceptualizations of matter. For the notion of matter as a site of inscriptions is one of the discursive variations of the antique substratum: here, matter can easily be regarded as a passive and blank state, as natural place, an indeterminate support, ground and foundation waiting for external, allegedly immaterial inscriptions in order to become meaningful and determinate.[32] Moreover, matter as an "inscription surface" not only contains many attributes of metaphysical matter, but also represents a concrete material factor in many pictorial practices—in terms of paper, canvas, or film strips. Numerous avant-garde filmmakers, who produced films without the use of a recording camera—with *Free Radicals* being one of the best-known among them—, have treated the film strip as a surface for drawing, painting, scratching, or writing. With it, the film strip seems to perfectly correspond to the idea of passive matter as a blank sheet ready for the inscriptions of a traditionally male avant-garde artist, since the image support and image carrier are closely intertwined with discourses of substrate, subject, and underlying matter (*hypokeímenon*).[33]

Furthermore, a film strip is a product with a long and rich history. As a result of many time-consuming negotiations of technical, chemical, and opto-chemical properties, and industrial as well as aesthetic necessities, a film strip is never simply a homogeneous entity or a blank surface. As a technical object, it is a "multitude of functionally different zones" (*pluralité de zones fonctionnellement différentes*)[34], which can support certain technical operations and impede others. Although film strips are prepared for recording, among other activities, they are not automatically used as inscription surfaces. Instead, very specific operations have to turn them into surfaces. For example, Józef Robakowski's film experiment, *Test I* (1971), treats a 35 mm film strip as a three-dimensional object by manually perforating it. In projection, too, the film strip operates as a corporeal object for filtering light. Flatness, as Sybille Krämer insists, is not a naturally-given fact of media carriers, but rather an aesthetically and epistemically productive outcome of inscriptions.[35] The drawing of an elementary line already establishes very specific differences.[36] Among others,

---

32 See Judith Butler, *Bodies that Matter: On the Discursive Limits of "Sex."* (New York/London: Routledge 1993), 4–5, and, 38 as well as Barad, *Meeting the Universe Halfway*, 150–151.

33 Jacques Derrida, "Das Papier oder ich, wissen Sie... (*Neue Spekulationen über einen Luxus der Armen*)," in *Maschinen Papier: Das Schreibmaschinenband und andere Antworten*, ed. Peter Engelmann (Wien: Passagen 2006), 221–249, here p. 223, p. 235.

34 Simondon: *Du mode d'existence*, 72.

35 Sybille Krämer, "Übertragen als Transfiguration oder: Wie ist die Kreativität von Medien erklärbar?" in *ZMK* 2 (2010): 77–93, here pp. 81–83.

36 Krämer, "Übertragen als Transfiguration oder: Wie ist die Kreativität von Medien erklärbar?", 83.

the inscription produces a plane, transforming a three-dimensional body into a two-dimensional "surface without depth" (*Fläche ohne Tiefe*) in the first place.[37]

Figure 1: Len Lye, Free Radicals (1958/79), film strips displayed at the exhibition "Zelluloid—Film ohne Kamera," Schirn Kunsthalle Frankfurt, 2010. Courtesy of the Len Lye Foundation from material made and preserved by The New Zealand Archive of Film, Television and Sound Nga Taonga Whitiahua Me Nga Taonga Korero.

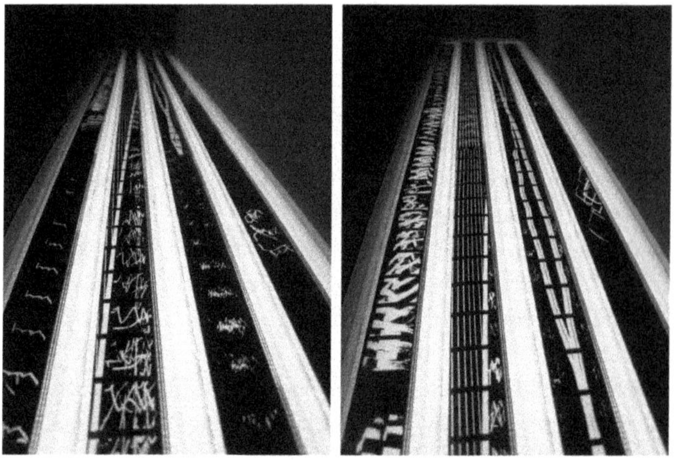

The film strips of *Free Radicals*, which were displayed at the Schirn Kunsthalle in 2010, show the laborious gestural processes of inscriptions (Fig. 1). It took Len Lye several months and thousands of meters of black leader to scratch it. The white lines and figurative constellations were created by means of pointed objects such as dentist's tools, needles, nails, wire brushes, and sections of saw blades.[38] Here, the operation of scratching initially establishes the difference between the marks and the surface of inscription, which figures as a spatial, material, and optical difference at the same time. This internal differentiation constitutes a dephasing of the aesthetic object. Optically, the differentiation between marks and inscription is visible as a contrast of light and dark. Materially, it is a difference in depth between the base and emulsion of the film strip. Simultaneously, the operation of scratching functions as an operation of showing, making visible, and positioning. With it, spatial

37 Krämer, "Übertragen als Transfiguration oder: Wie ist die Kreativität von Medien erklärbar?", 82.

38 Roger Horrocks, *Art That Moves: The Work of Len Lye* (Auckland: Auckland University Press 2009), 168.

orientations and gradations such as left and right, top, bottom, or center, central and peripheral, inside and outside are co-created.[39] In this way, the inscription surface does not remain a "surface without depth" for a long time. The successive scratching produces a visual space—a field (cf. infra)—which conditions further inscriptions and concomitant differentiations. Each new inscription shifts the field and its operative agency.

Also, the white lines are of course traces of hand movements to which they owe their existence. These movements must not only develop an image within a single frame, but also in progression from frame to frame—in more or less constant shifts or in erratic variations of a scratched ensemble. Lye describes this process as a physical activity that involves the coordination of hands and eyes. Furthermore, according to him, a precise execution demands the whole body:

> So, I wriggled my whole body to get a compressed feeling into my shoulders—trying to get a pent-up feeling of inexorable precision into the fingers of both hands which grasped the needle and, with sudden jump, pulled the needle through the celluloid and completed my design.[40]

When drawing directly on a film strip, precision poses a challenge. Compared to a sheet of paper or a canvas, the frames are too small. At the same time, the film strip will be projected at some point. For a continuous impression of movement, the figurative constellations have to be scratched on the diminutive area several times by elaborating the smallest differences frame by frame. A high level of detail and precision is not only a question of the size of the surface, but also of embodied skills. In *Free Radicals*, Lye does not seem to strive for straight, geometrical, or cleanly executed lines—unlike McLaren and Lambart in their handmade films, *Lines Vertical* (1960) and *Lines Horizontal* (1962), in which they used a ruler, scratching across several frames at once[41]—Lye's zigzagging lines seem more spontaneous, less geometric. However, rather than reduce, it increases the difficulties because the zigzagging has to be repeated many times with slight variations and without cutting the film strip.

McLaren's notes on the *Lines*-films reveal what is necessary for a successful co-production. McLaren and Lambart tested different 35 mm emulsions, steel plates, knives sharpened to different thicknesses, and various handlings of the knives in order get straight and uniform lines. Whereas a hard, smooth, steel base made it easier to draw lines, old black leader films were too dry and, thus, got hard

39 On this see also Krämer, "Übertragen als Transfiguration," 83.

40 Len Lye quoted in Sitney, P. Adams: *Visionary Film: The American Avant-Garde 1943–1978* (New York: Oxford University Press 1974), 232.

41 Norman McLaren interviewed by Guy Cotte (Montréal, 1967), in: *Cinema de notre temps* (André S. Labarthe, CND/F 2001).

and brittle. Although the different knives could be used to vary the thicknesses of the lines, even the most careful handling did not guarantee clean lines and could not prevent roughness, jaggedness, or patches.[42] The relational activity slowly arises by harmonizing different processual factors and actors. The singularities of involved materials, their conditions and properties, serve as "implicit forms" (*forms implicites*)[43] which guide the gestures of the filmmakers, as well as the selection of tools, and orient the operation in an informative way. Their implicit character does not contradict the relationality of becoming. Material features are affordances that become significant depending on the particular pre-individual problem; a disparity to resolve. Coordinating different elements of the arrangement helps to do so. Problems and solutions develop and shift in the making. The pre-individual production arrangement is, thus, less of a preexisting infrastructure, but rather a process of mutual arranging, enlisting actors and associating collaborators, to put it in terms of actor-network theory (ANT).[44]

In *Free Radicals*, the challenges result from the differential and sequential character of the frames on the film strip which constitutes one of its 'functional zones,' regulating continuity of the projected movement. Ignoring this functional zone leads to discontinuous aesthetics that isolate and strengthen the individual frame in a painterly or graphic manner. In Lye's artworks, however, "figures of motion"—a notion addressing issues such as processual unfolding, kinetic aesthetics, and embodied kinetic sensation—pose the central problem.[45] Discontinuity is not an option. Accordingly, *Free Radicals* bears witness to a controlled metamorphosis of lines and their constellations, presupposing an intimate collaboration with non-human materials, especially with that of the film strip. The film strip, far from being a passive surface, conditions the operations of inscription and human gestures: the individual frames and their differential functionality set conditions for spatial and temporal aesthetic possibilities. The film strip not only proves to be already structured, but is also structuring and redirecting the operative development. The filmmakers have to "*follow the materials*" and their functional zones, as Tim Ingold counters hylomorphism, seemingly echoing ANT's motto "following the actors."[46]

For a continuous scratching, not only is the size of the inscriptive area important, but also the positioning of the marks on it. The marks have to minimally differ

42 Norman McLaren, *On the Creative Process* (Montreal: National Film Board of Canada 1991), 74–76.

43 On the role implicit forms play for individuation see Simondon, *L'individu et sa genèse*, 53–55.

44 Bruno Latour, "On Technical Mediation: Philosophy, Sociology, Genealogy," in *Common Knowledge* 3(2) (1994): 29–64, here p. 32, p. 37.

45 On a detailed account of Len Lye's notion "figures of motion" see Horrocks, *Art That Moves*, 88–107 as well as Curnow Wystan and Horrocks Roger, ed., *Figures of Motion: Len Lye Selected Writings* (Auckland: Auckland University Press 1984).

46 Ingold, "Textility of Making," 93–94, original emphasis.

from one another while progressing from frame to frame both in their shape and position. Therefore, McLaren recommends either using a grid system as a base or directly drawing it on the blank film.[47] Yet, this solution is out of the question for *Free Radicals* since it utilizes a non-transparent black leader. Additionally, a black film strip is not visibly divided into frames, so the perforation has to serve as a reference. The fact that *Free Radicals* achieves nuanced and elaborate movements despite of this is the result of a process that gradually develops the "figures of motions" and which is open to chances. Looking back at the work on the film in an interview from 1963, Lye describes it as not a simple materialization of an already formed idea, but rather as a lengthy process of trying, searching, discarding, controlled refining, selecting, and arranging:

> You can carry a pictographic design in your head and make a little design. You can't see what you're doing because your hand is in the way. That's why those things have that kind of spastic look ... First of all, I worked for about three or four months with thousands of feet of film, scratching away before I went to see what I had. I wouldn't know what was there. When you see what you've got, you begin to get the control of what you want. You edit the best out of that. Once you've got the stuff and you're really working and you're not sure how it's going, then you look at it. If you're sure how you're going after two or three months, you're pretty sure of your results, so you just work away. Usually when you look at it you're disappointed. You draw a bit, then go to sleep, then draw a little bit more. It took about eight months.[48]

While it is apparent that artistic ideas and imagination can also serve as a prelude to poiesis, they are intensified, redirected, condensed, and dismissed in the course of making. Human ideas represent less of a fixed, predetermining starting point or forms encountering passive materials, but rather a relational, unfolding co-result in a collaborative process of human and non-human bodies. Ideas develop in concrete practices and have a temporal character which also includes previous production arrangements and experiences. While non-human matter is actively involved in the process, human imagination is also materialized. Making is an embodied process, which cannot be reduced to a simple asymmetry or unification of "immaterial" ideas and meaningless materials. Humans and non-human do not oppose each other as

---

47 Norman McLaren, "How to make Animated Movies without a Camera." in *Cameraless Animation: A Technique Developed at the National Film Board of Canada by Norman McLaren*. Information & Promotion Division, National Board of Canada 1958, 2–10, here, p. 5.

48 Len Lye, "Talking About Film," in *Experimental Animation: An Illustrated Anthology*, ed., Robert Russett and Cecile Starr (New York: Van Nostrand Reinhold Company 1976), 66–69, here pp. 68–69.

agents and patients, rather they "intra-act", as Barad calls the relational activity of becoming, which goes beyond simple rapports and interactions.[49]

For Lye, individual moments and figures of motion, which have rich potential for variations and selectivity, typically function as initial impulses.[50] During the scratching process, they give way to new already-accomplished patterns, stimulating further experiments and figurative development. Simondon describes comparable issues as "transduction"—as a step-by-step, directional process of structuring in which each stage can act as a significant threshold and even origin for the next stage.[51] In the transductive process, the difference between the marks and the surface of inscriptions, established operationally, acts as such a threshold for further becoming and dephasing. With it, the aesthetic object differentiates itself into a new phase. Its structures can be described as an aesthetic field. In art and image theory, a field conceptually replaces the figure-ground distinction[52] and denotes a dynamic pictorial constellation in which the "differences of placement and value are correlated" (*Korrelation von Platzierungsdifferenzen und Wertdifferenzen*).[53] Similarly, in Simondon's philosophy, the elements of an individuating field, which conceptually rework the distinction between material and form, have a double function: the elements are located in a field full of differences and gradients and are subject to its forces; but at the same time they constitute the field and, thus, also affect its virtue as a whole.[54] The field is open; further elements can be inserted into it and thereby reorganize the balance of forces and tensions, both on the level of the whole (field) and its parts (elements). Therefore, the field is a metastable constellation in which elements and the whole are co-constituted in a relational way.[55] Unlike the figure-ground distinction, an aesthetic metastable field has to be addressed not as a *rapport* of binary pre-existing relata, but rather as a relational process of pluralization, pervaded by multiple differences.

In *Free Radicals*, the aesthetic field transforms the difference between inscription surface and marks into the relational reciprocity of positional and value differences. Each new inscription—i.e. the introduction of new elements into the field—changes the dynamic constellation and with it its constituting elements. The scratches on the black leader produce differential field zones: contrasts of light and dark, depth and vastness, lateral directions, horizontal and vertical dimensions, imbalances and harmonies, falling and rising gradients, focal points and asymmetries, left and right,

---

49 Barad, *Meeting the Universe Halfway*, 139–140.

50 Horrocks, *The Art of Motion*, 95–99.

51 Simondon : *L'individu et sa genèse*, 30–31.

52 Wolfram Pichler, "Zur Kunstgeschichte des Bildfeldes," in *Der Grund: Das Feld des Sichtbaren*, ed. Gottfried Boehm and Mateo Burioni (München: Fink 2012), 441–472, here pp. 448–449.

53 Pichler, "Zur Kunstgeschichte des Bildfeldes," 443.

54 Simondon, *L'individuation psychique*, 44.

55 Simondon, *L'individuation psychique*, 47.

and also boundaries and delimitations. The shifts in compositional tensions, balances, and densities—i.e. the reconfiguration of the field—are particularly apparent in film sections which aim for the continuity of movement and smooth metamorphosis of the markings, while harsh discontinuities will more likely set new series of fields in motion.

The differentiations in the aesthetic field simultaneously direct and affect human gestures in a transductive way. In such a way, Lye produced material for ten minutes of film, from which he selected passages that best-matched an added soundtrack. He used the music of a Bagirmi tribe which had "the same attack as the visual attack in the tone of the drum and the way that the guy hand-drummed."[56] The rhythmic resonance between the visuals and the music helped to co-create a lively impression and continuity of motion. The selected scratching and the music recorded as an optical soundtrack initially made up a film of five minutes in length (1958). In 1979, Lye rearranged and condensed the film to four minutes.

Résumé: Artistic Practice as Trans-Individual Becoming

Trials, corrections, careful selection, and arrangement, of course, do not suffice for the emergence of *Free Radicals*. Considering the difficulties in precision, positioning, and continuity of movement, embodied know-how is also required: dexterity, habitualized routines, skilled perception, and handling. They are not only productive in the poietic arrangement, but are also co-produced by it and within former processes; thus, making is an operational process in which both an aesthetic individual and a human being are co-produced. Co-production does not only mean that human and non-human entities are jointly involved in the making and performance of an operation collaboratively, as concepts of distributed or material agency suggest. Rather, in Simondon's "operational ontology of relations,"[57] co-production also implies co-genesis or co-individuation. While human beings participate in poietic individuation of an aesthetic object, they also individuate themselves—physically, psychically, mentally, socially, perceptually, etc.

It is one of the distinctive features of living beings that they are capable of perpetual individuation. A physical individual will eventually use up its metastable potential and successively transform it into stable structures; however, the living does not exhaust its pre-individual potentials and maintains metastability from the start, which allows for ongoing becoming.[58] Furthermore, the relational excess of the liv-

56 Lye, "Talking About Film," 69.

57 Alberto Toscano, *The Theatre of Production. Philosophy and Individuation between Kant and Deleuze* (Houndmills: Palgrave Macmillan 2006), 141.

58 Simondon, *L'individuation psychique*, 80.

ing individual, its openness towards his associated milieu and other beings, permanently calls his individuated structures into question. In this way, they can again become problematic, i.e. metastable, and require new solutions in the form of new structures.[59] The living individual, thus, undergoes processes of de- and re-structuring, dis- and re-organization. For the living individual, a problem becomes a necessity not only to change his relation to the milieu, but also to change himself, to create new structures and, with it, to modify the structures of the milieu and his own relation to them.[60] The progression of de- and re-structuring fulfills enabling and restricting functions at the same time insofar as the thresholds in this transductive process, by means of conditioning solutions, continuously limit the scope of future problems and individuations.[61] These processes can take place on perceptive, logical, sensomotoric, social, psychic, etc. levels, since there is no privileged domain of individuation.[62] Perception, learning, emotions, and others are ways for the individual to relate to himself and his milieu. Thus, they continually raise specific problems and require specific solutions. Simondon leaves no doubt that creating artefacts also involves a process of individuation for the living being:

> L'individu s'individue dans la mesure où il perçoit des êtres, constitue une individuation par l'action ou la construction fabricatrice, et fait partie du système comprenant sa réalité individuelle et les objets qu'il perçoit ou constitue.[63]

On the one hand, the production arrangement, including the artist or the filmmaker, constitutes the milieu of the becoming aesthetic object. On the other hand, the production arrangement also forms the milieu for the human individual. In this sense, making can be understood as an individuating, problem-solving activity which involves the questioning of already-established structures. While for the human producer this co-individuation means a prolongation of an initial individuation by dis- and re-organizing his mental, physical, and imaginative structures, the structures of the aesthetic object just emerge in this process. The aesthetic object, resulting from this problem-solving co-genesis, does not pre-exist neither on the human nor the non-human part of the production arrangement and cannot be reduced to a union of form and matter. Starting from a problematic, metastable assemblage, the aesthetic object becomes by way of operations which result in dephasing and differentiation of its aesthetic dimensions. In *Free Radicals*, it is the operation of inscriptions which sets in motion this dephasing. With it, four phases are formed: *Pre-in-*

59 Simondon, *L'individu et sa genèse*, 20; Simondon, *L'individuation psychique*, 57–59.

60 Simondon, *L'individu et sa genèse*, 26.

61 Simondon, *L'individuation psychique*, 81.

62 Simondon, *L'individuation psychique*, 127.

63 Simondon, *L'individuation psychique*, 98.

dividual, on which there is no phase prior to dephasing,[64] constitutes the very first phase of the aesthetic object and remains associated with it as a milieu in the guise of the production arrangement. The second is an operative difference between inscription surface and marks, which, following Donna Haraway, can be named "*material-semiotic*."[65] The third is the *field* phase, which stands for a dynamic plurality that is prone to relational transformations and differentiations of aesthetic structures such as space, orientation, compositional tensions, and balances. Rather than being a hylomorphic compound, the aesthetic object appears to be a "network of differential relations" (*un faisceau de relations différentielles*),[66] which turn it into a coherent and non-arbitrary plurality (*pluralité unifiée et d'unité pluralisée*).[67] The aesthetic object is a plurality not only by being a pluri-phasic individual, but also by way of an intrinsically pluralized field as its third phase. Finally, being a co-individuation, producing an art object establishes a *trans-individual* relation between the artist and the art object as its fourth phase. Artistic poiesis is, thus, a trans-individual becoming plural of the human and the aesthetic.

64 Combes, *Gilbert Simondon*, 4.

65 Donna Haraway, "The Promises of Monsters: A Regenerative Politics for Inappropriate/d Others." in *Cultural Studies*, ed. Lawrence Grosberg, Cary Nelson, and Paula Treichler (New York/London: Routledge 1992), 295–337, here p. 298. Emphasis added.

66 Simondon, *L'individuation psychique*, 83.

67 Simondon, *L'individuation psychique*, 84.

Correspondences: Exploring the Echoes of Jack Spicer's Poetics in the Paintings of Matt Connors

Job Boot

> Poems should echo and re-echo against each other. They should create resonances. They cannot live alone any more than we can.[1]

In her *New York Times* review of Matt Connors's 2010 show, *You Don't Know*, Roberta Smith writes that although his works are "appealing" and display a "wonderful way with paint and canvas," they "seem to need one another, as if they form a single installation." Ultimately, she notes that "despite its intermittent pleasures" the work seems to be in a "transitional phase" which "will seem more interesting once it has led elsewhere."[2] Four years later, Connors's show, *Machines*, was also reviewed in the *Times*. Readers might have wondered whether the "elsewhere" has been reached, but the review, this time written by Karen Rosenberg, had to disappoint, concluding that "[Connors] doesn't seem to trust that a single, fully realized painting, on its own, can set off a conversation."[3] Both reviewers desire independent, fully realised paintings and both are disappointed by what Connors offers them. Ultimately, the interdependent nature of his works is seen as a flaw by both reviewers, but if Rosenberg suggests that a fully realised painting can *set off* a conversation, she misses out on another conversation: not the conversation the viewing public might engage in amongst themselves *about* a painting, but the conversation that takes place *amongst* these works. Connors's paintings, I suggest, invite a different relation to art than one conditioned on the distinction between subject and object where the painting-

1 Jack Spicer, *My Vocabulary Did This To Me: The Collected Poetry of Jack Spicer*, ed. Peter Gizzi (Middletown: Wesleyan University Press, 2008), 163.

2 Roberta Smith, "Matt Connors: 'You Don't Know,'" *New York Times* (New York, NY), Dec. 9, 2010. https://www.nytimes.com/2010/12/10/arts/design/10galleries-MATTCONNORS_RVW.html

3 Karen Rosenberg, "Matt Connors: 'Machines,'" *New York Times* (New York, NY), May 15, 2014. https://www.nytimes.com/2014/05/16/arts/design/matt-connors-machines.html

object is reduced to a topic of conversation for the pleasure of the viewing public. Indeed, far from being an object that is made, finished, and displayed to be gazed upon, the work extends the artistic practice from the studio into the gallery. Each painting becomes an active participant in this practice which unfolds itself as a kind of conversation—or *correspondence*—that involves the paintings, their sources, and even those who come to view them. It is not a matter of *setting off* the conversation, then, but of being open to the conversation that is already ongoing.

In order to explore this aspect of Connors's work, I will turn to one of the painter's literary inspirations: the American poet Jack Spicer (1925–1965). Spicer is a poet who, in recent years, has been increasingly recognised as an important voice within the avant-garde poetics of the San Francisco Renaissance as well as an influence to the poets of the Language school. In a 2012 lecture given at Portland State University, Connors cites a letter that Spicer wrote to his friend, fellow poet Robin Blaser. The letter speaks of a break in the way that Spicer regards the possibility of finishing (or, indeed, *not* finishing) a poem. In the letter Spicer disavows his early poems on the basis of them being "beautiful but dumb." "They are one night stands filled (the best of them) with their own emotions," he writes, "but pointing nowhere, as meaningless as sex in a Turkish bath."[4] The problem with these early works, Spicer explains, is that they were attempts to perfectly capture a singular and "unique" emotion and, insofar as they succeeded, were self-sufficient or, indeed, *fully realised* and therefore closed-off. By the mid 1950s when the letter was written, however, Spicer has discovered a new approach to writing. The "trick," he tells us, is "not to search for the perfect poem but to let your way of writing of the moment go along its own paths, explore and retreat but never be fully realized (confined) within the boundaries of one poem." "There really is no single poem," Spicer adds, because "[p]oems should echo and re-echo against each other. They should create resonances. They cannot live alone any more than we can."[5] Neither poems, nor indeed paintings, can live alone: they need one another in order to resonate and it is in these resonances that their meaning lies, not in the degree to which they are realised. A poem or painting, as I will explore, *needs* its trough edges and open ends precisely because it is not an end in itself but part of a larger conversation, an ongoing correspondence that cannot be limited to a single work, to a single exhibition or volume of poetry, nor even to a single artist. That paintings and poems need one another is not a flaw, but constitutive of their, to Spicer and Connors, inherently *social* existence.

"Things fit together," Spicer concludes his letter. "Two inconsequential things can combine together to become a consequence. This is true of poems too."[6] And, we will

4 Spicer, *My Vocabulary Did This To Me*, 163.

5 Spicer, *My Vocabulary Did This To Me*, 163.

6 Spicer, *My Vocabulary Did This To Me*, 164.

add, of paintings. But if we accept this we must ask ourselves: how *do* artworks combine? If it is clear, almost self-evident, that things "fit together," this is not automatically true for works of art. With Martin Heidegger we can say that insofar the "thing things," its "thinging gathers."[7] That is, the very nature of a thing is to gather around itself other things through which it discloses its being: the pen, for instance, gathers around itself ink and paper and the hammer nails and wood. As Heidegger's use of the workshop as a paradigm for relationality attests to, these relationships are utilitarian: things are tools that are used *for* certain ends and used *with* certain other things and this is why they are relational. But what is a painting or a poem used for? Should we think of the artwork as a tool? And if we should, to what end can the artwork be utilised? What the work of Connors and Spicer requires, and what I will try to formulate in this paper, is a form of relationality without teleology: how can we insist that the artwork's being is a being-with (*Mitsein*) without thereby limiting its uses to any predetermined ends?

"The work is [not] finished until it ends up installed," Connors notes, indicating the challenge of painting without a clearly defined goal, but "then that's also complicated because then it is never going to be installed in that way again."[8] As such, in contrast to the Heideggerian tool, it becomes impossible to determine what a painting is *for* and, as such, the practice of painting never comes to an end: "I think that if you make work like this, there is a really scary fine line because you could stop anywhere. There is a suspension of judgment, it just becomes really fragile."[9] The nature of such a practice is not to work toward something, but to stay with the process as it moves along, creating its own resonances and correspondences. Indeed, if the value of one painting or poem only becomes clear in the way that it not only echoes older work, but also will re-echo in work to come, it becomes quite impossible to tell where a single work begins or ends. In this way, knowledge and mastery proper to the workshop are replaced with the attention that is paid to the constantly evolving relationships between things—between brush and canvas, between one canvas and another, between one colour and another, and so forth—and what is required of the artist is not to limit these possibilities but to go along with them, to suspend one's personal judgement and make space for the fragility inherent to the process.

In the remainder of this chapter I will begin with a brief summation of Heidegger's relational philosophy and indicate how it can serve as a jumping-off point toward a broader notion of relationality. As we will see, Heidegger's emphasis on relationality is crucial but his insistence on relationality *as utility* marks its limitations.

---

7 Martin Heidegger. "The Thing" in *Poetry, Language, Thought*, trans. Albert Hofstadter (New York: HarperPerennial, 2001), 172.

8 Matt Connors, "Matt Connors Lecture at Portland State University," Feb. 1, 2012, PSU School of Art, Portland, OR. video, 47:55–48:05, https://vimeo.com/37696043.

9 Connors, 10:18–10:30.

In order to go one step further, I will turn to the post-Heideggerian philosophies of relationality of Emmanuel Levinas and Maurice Blanchot who, like Spicer, refuse to limit the relational to the useful. From this perspective, I will explore what Spicer calls "correspondence" as a form of relationality that is non-coherent and non-unified but not, therefore, devoid of meaning. Finally, I will return to Connors's PSU lecture as well as to a conversation between the painter and writer Wayne Koestenbaum in which they gesture toward the unrealised not as a flaw but as a condition for future possibilities.

Heidegger's philosophy is born from a critique of representationalist philosophy. In "The Age of the World Picture" (1938), Heidegger explains that modernity is defined by the distinction between subject and object which brings with it the fact that we view the world and its objects through the lens of the imagination: as translated into a mental picture. This picture, Heidegger contends, is not a "copy" or rendering of the world, but constitutive "the world itself, the world as such, what is, in its entirety, just as it is normative and binding for us."[10] In our relation to the world, then, we are less concerned with the things that inhabit it than with the way we represent them to ourselves. Heidegger writes:

> Here to represent [*vor-stellen*] means to bring what is present at hand *[das Vorhandende*] before oneself as something standing over against, to relate it to oneself, to the one representing it, and to force it back into this relationship to oneself as the normative realm.[11]

The German *Vorstellung*, literally means "that which has been put before." And what is put before oneself is the object or, in German, *Gegenstand*, stemming from *das Entgegenstehende* meaning "that which stands over against." Heidegger takes these meanings literally when he interprets representation as the enactment of the subject-object division in the sense that the thinking subject turns a thing into an object by, exactly, putting it in front of himself as something to study and form a mental picture of. Objectivity, as the paradigm of science, then, is nothing other than the way in which man represents reality to himself, thereby reducing each thing to an object that has a meaning only in relation to himself as normative subject. Certainly, the mental picture that arises from this process can tell us all kinds of things about an object—we can discover the materials it contains, its dimensions, colour, or weight—but, Heidegger contends, through none of these aspects does the thing announce itself. What is missing, then, is precisely the way in which it is situated in the world. After all, as when we considered the pen or hammer, these objects are nothing without the things that accompany them. To look at an object in isolation, then,

10 Martin Heidegger, "The Age of the World Picture," in *The Question Concerning Technology and Other Essays*, trans. William Lovit (New York: Garland Publishing Inc., 1977), 129.

11 Heidegger, "The Age of the World Picture", 131

misses out on the very thing that matters most. Heidegger's philosophy shifts the focus from what is present-*at*-hand, from what is placed before us, to what present-*to*-hand, to what is ready to handle. What we should be concerned with, Heidegger contends, is not the way in which the object appears when we gaze at it from a contemplative distance but how it is used. The problem, however, is that when an object is in use, it does not announce itself either. When we pick up a tool, that is, we do not become aware of the object's being, but are simply contend to make use of it without reflecting on its ontological status. As long as the object serves us well, we do not notice it. How, then, can we become aware of its relational being?

Heidegger famously answers this question in §16 of *Being and Time* when he argues that we should focus on the very moment that a tool ceases to be ready to hand. That is, when the tool breaks, goes missing, or is just out of reach, the tool is extracted from its natural environment and comes to stand out in its absence. "Our circumspection comes up against emptiness," Heidegger writes about such moments, and it is in this emptiness that one "sees for the first time what the missing article was ready-to-hand *with*, and what it was ready-to-hand *for*."[12] When we intend to use an object and it does not work, we become aware of the object's *with* and *for*. When we study, say, a hammer, we can form a more or less exact picture of it, but only when we intend to use it and the hammer refuses, do we realise in what relationships the hammer is engaged: we do not only experience the loss of the hammer, but also of the possibility of completing the project we are working on. Alongside the hammer, then, the hammer's context announces itself in the form of the things (nails, wood) that we use it *with* and the project (I am making a table) that it is used *for*. In short, we become aware of the work that the hammer is involved in and from which it derives its meaning and alongside the work "everything connected with the work—the whole 'workshop'—as that wherein concern always dwells." "With this totality," Heidegger concludes, "the world announces itself."[13]

No longer a representation contemplated from afar, the idea of the world resurfaces as the interconnectedness of things, as they way they work together and so constitute a world. The world, then, is not what man puts in front of himself but something he is surrounded by and engaged in: the hammer is connected to the nails and the wood, together they make a table, this table is used as a desk and, together with pen and paper, allows one to write. Taking all of these things together, we come to an idea of the world as the sum of things working together toward what Heidegger calls man's dwelling, his way of being at home in the world. This new totally that takes the workshop as its paradigm is structured, as Heidegger contends, by concern which

12 Martin Heidegger, *Being and Time*, trans. John Mcquarrie and Edward Robinson (New York: HarperPerennial, 2008), 105.

13 Heidegger, *Being and Time*, 105.

we can understand as the natural care we take of our tools so that we may keep using them. Concern, Heidegger writes, "is the "primordial structural totality" which "lies 'before' every factical [i.e. representational or contemplative] 'attitude' and 'situation.'"[14] Before any thematic *analysis* of reality, we are already intimately, if implicitly, familiar with the world around us through the care we take of it. This matter of concern, however, is also where Heidegger's philosophy falls short: concern, and through concern the world, extends only to those things that are useful to us, to those things that serve us and which may cease to do so when we neglect them. Indeed, Heidegger's world is a world of *tools* and has no space for things deemed unworthy or useless. In Heidegger's workshop, we should therefore say, man is still normative.

In his 1947 book *Existence and Existents*, Emmanuel Levinas extends this critique, writing that the "practical structure of activity" (*Zuhandenheit*), like the "theoretical structure of forms" (*Vorhandenheit*), treats the world as what is "given" (46), as that which is *available to us.*[15] Much like the philosophical normativity that Heidegger criticises, Heidegger's own tool-analysis is based on the *a priori* recognition of an object as *this* or *that* specific object or tool. Whether we study it or use it, from the very moment that we recognise an object, this recognition already "delivers that object over to us."[16] If, as we saw, Heidegger places use before contemplation, Levinas believes that contemplation, as the recognition of "an object as something given ... is already a factor in an action."[17] As such, the Heideggerian notion of concern "comprises an illumination"—that is, a recognition of *form* in the Platonic sense—"which makes of it comprehension and thought."[18] Heidegger's concern is still limited to the world as it makes itself available to thought.

Insofar as works of art work toward no clear goals and are, as the modernist invention of the collage shows, perfectly able to incorporate elements that from any other perspective would be deemed waste, we need to think of a form of relationality that, like Heidegger's, is inherently relational but, unlike Heidegger's, is not bound by servitude or availability. In order to approach this other form of relationality, we should return to the moment where circumspection comes up against emptiness. In this transitional moment in which the object is extracted from its environment, we come upon what Heidegger presents as a binary choice: we can either contemplate the isolated thing in order to form a mental image of it, or we can reconstruct the environment it belongs to. A third option arises, however, when we refuse to choose: what if the missing or broken thing leads us neither to construct a representation

---

14 Heidegger, *Being and Time*, 238.

15 Emmanuel Levinas, *Existence and Existents*, trans. Alphonso Lingis (Dordrecht: Kluwer Academic Publishers, 1988), 46.

16 Levinas, *Existence and Existents*, 46.

17 Levinas, *Existence and Existents*, 46.

18 Levinas, *Existence and Existents*, 47.

nor to reconstruct its use value? What if the broken thing is simply there without fitting into any world? What if the thing has no use and refuses to serve us? Such is, according to Blanchot, the nature of the image as well as the artwork.

Normally, an object does not show itself, Blanchot contends echoing Heidegger, because it "never announces that it is, but how it serves." For an object to appear,

> a break in the circuit of usage, a gap, an anomaly has to make it leave the world, leave its senses. And it seems then that, no longer there, it becomes its appearance, its image—what it was before being a useful thing or a significant value. This is also when it becomes . . . a veritable work of art.[19]

To Blanchot, the thing's image is not distinct from the thing's material existence. In fact, it is the material residue of an object that has lost its use value or meaning. The image, that is, concomitant with a thing's becoming-waste. At the sight of waste, as Rudi Visker writes, we may experience these objects as they are randomly placed together when they were discarded, as though they are attempting to free themselves from the world in which they were forced to function.[20] Such an experience may be unsettling but it may also be fascinating. Indeed, that what become waste can also become art becomes clear in the displays of ancient tools and objects of use in our museums: these things have become things to look at because their use value has dissipated. Of course, these objects often urge us to reconstruct the world that they departed from and for Heidegger this is, unsurprisingly, what the artwork does. Like the unavailable tool, Heidegger believes the artwork opens onto the world it has left behind. As such, van Gogh's painted peasant's shoes are not wearable, but as they are extracted from their natural environment they are also the opening of this world:

> From out of the dark opening of the well-worn insides of the shoes the toil of the worker's tread stares forth. In the crudely solid heaviness of the shoes accumulates the tenacity of the slow trudge through the far-stretching and ever-uniform furrows of the field swept by a raw wind. On the leather lies the dampness and richness of the soil. Under the soles slides the loneliness of the field-path as evening falls.[21]

According to Levinas, however, one should not treat an artwork as if it is some kind of "microscope or telescope of artistic vision exposed for the curiosity of an investi-

---

19 Maurice Blanchot, *The Space of Literature*, trans. Ann Smock (Lincoln, NE: University of Nebraska Press, 1982), 222.

20 Rudi Visker, "Kunst en Grofvuil: Heidegger, Levinas en de Overgang," *Tijdschrift voor Filosofie* 68, no. 3 (2006): 604.

21 Martin Heidegger. "The Origin of the Work of Art," in *Poetry, Language, Thought*, trans. Albert Hofstadter (New York: HarperPerennial, 2001), 14.

gator."[22] (1989; 130). This, he insists, betrays the obscurity essential to any artwork. To Levinas, the artwork is not a window onto the world, but the extraction of an object from world and nothing more. "Art makes makes [things] stand out from the world and thus extracts them from this belongingness to a subject," he writes, because it places an image between "us and the thing" (52).[23] Whether we are dealing with Magritte's meticulously painted pipe or Duchamp's ready-mades, in either case we are dealing with an object *extracted* from the world that serves us *neither* as a representation nor as equipment. Neither pipe nor urinal gives us a true picture of itself or the world from which it came. All it gives us is a thing relegated to some stubborn remainder that is simply *there*, freed from the duty to serve. What it shows, if it shows anything, is what an object would be if it weren't there *for us*.

The artwork, then, does not take part in the course of the world. This lack of "world" does not mean, however, that the things in art are devoid of relationships. Levinas draws our attention to modern painting and specifically to cubist collage which, he contends, is engaged in a "struggle against sight" insofar as sight "seeks to draw out of the light beings integrated into a whole." In contemporary painting, however, things shown are *together in a different way*, one that amounts to no "whole." This is exemplified by its fascination "with the pure and simple play of colors and lines" as well as by its

> preoccupation with the correspondence between objects, between the facets and surfaces, inasmuch as it is foreign to the coherence of the world, and the care taken to merge the different planes of reality by introducing a real object in the midst of painted objects or debris of objects.[24]

Where things form no coherent whole that can be limited to a common goal or universal meaning, they still *correspond* with one another, however obscurely. Indeed, Charles Baudelaire's poem "Correspondances" anticipates Levinas's use of the term: "Comme de longs échos qui de loin se confondent," it reads, "Les parfums, les couleurs et les sons se répondent."[25] Baudelaire's correspondences are synaesthetic and, like Levinas' collage, therefore cross the boundaries between different planes of reality: as sounds correspond with colours, painted shapes correspond with the debris of "real" objects. There is no overarching logic, no distinction between imaginary or physical, useful or wasteful, but only the hubbub of material elements engaging with each other somewhere beyond the dominion of our gaze.

---

22 Emmanuel Levinas, "Reality and Its Shadow," in *The Levinas Reader* (Oxford: Basil Blackwell, 1989), 130.

23 Levinas, *Existence and Existents*, 52.

24 Levinas, *Existence and Existents*, 56.

25 Charles Baudelaire. "Correspondances," in *Les Fleurs du Mal* (Paris: Les Éditions G. Crès, 1925), 17.

Spicer's poetry in which poems are thought to "echo and re-echo," too, activates this notion of correspondence. Most specifically in 1957's *After Lorca* in which Spicer plays with the double meaning of the term. On the one hand, the volume contains translations of Federico García Lorca's poetry that correspond *to* their original counterparts and on the other, it contains a series of letters that make up a correspondence *with* the Spanish poet. Throughout the volume, however, the two meanings commingle like the echoes in Baudelaire's poem: the translations do not correspond to the original poems as a proper translation should. "Even the most faithful student of my work," the ghostly voice of "Lorca" writes in the introduction, "will be hard put to decide what is and what is not García Lorca as, indeed, he would if he were to look into my present resting place." "In even the most literal of them," he adds, "Mr. Spicer seems to derive pleasure in inserting or substituting one or two words which completely change the mood and often the meaning of the poem as I had written it."[26] Indeed, the translations are not faithful reflections of Lorca's originals, but original and translation echo and re-echo one another in ways that are difficult to disentangle. What is at stake is not the ossified relationship between author and translator, but the relationship between these authors that escapes all such frameworks: "The fact that I didn't know Spanish really well enough to translate Lorca, was the reason I could get in contact with Lorca."[27] Spicer's poems correspond with Lorca's but not because they are faithful renderings of them.

Indeed, if things fit together, as Spicer argued, things fit obscurely, as if only on their own terms: "Things do not connect; they correspond."[28] Words, Spicer contends, are "what sticks to the real," the immediate object or emotion that one wants to transfer to a poem "always has hundreds of its own words clinging to it, short-lived and tenacious as barnacles."[29] These "words around the immediate shrivel and decay like flesh around the body," Spicer continues, but this decay is not a flaw. Instead, it is the very condition that makes poetry possible: it is because the immediate and fully realized meaning of Lorca's poems has decayed, that they are able to resonate with Spicer. Poetic correspondence works this way not only from poem to poem, but also from poem to real thing. As things decay, the "garbage of the real," Spicer writes, "reaches out into the current world making its objects, in turn visible—lemon calls to lemon, newspaper to newspaper, boy to boy. As things decay they bring their equivalents into being."[30] Correspondences, then, come about through decay, rather than through intellectual sublimation or use. If things bring their equivalents into

26 Spicer, *My Vocabulary*, 107.

27 Jack Spicer, *The House that Jack Built: The Collected Lectures of Jack Spicer*, ed. Peter Gizzi (Middletown, CT: Wesleyan University Press, 1998), 138.

28 Spicer, *My Vocabulary*, 133.

29 Spicer, *My Vocabulary*, 122.

30 Spicer, *My Vocabulary*, 133.

being, then, this does not mean that their equivalency adheres to any recognisable law. Spicer writes, addressing Lorca:

> That tree you saw in Spain is a tree I could never have seen in California, that lemon has a different smell and a different taste, BUT the answer is this—every place and every time has a real object to correspond with your real object—that lemon may become this lemon, or it may even become this piece of seaweed, or this particular color of gray in this ocean. One does not need to imagine that lemon; one needs to discover it.[31]

As in Baudelaire's poem, the correspondence between objects remains obscure and crosses through the different senses: a lemon may correspond with seaweed, or even to a certain colour that is not yellow. Precisely because things can depart from themselves, from their determined position in the world, they can bring about something else, whatever it may be. "Even these letters," Spicer continues. "They *correspond* with something (I don't know what) that you have written (perhaps as unapparently as that lemon corresponds to this piece of seaweed), and, in turn, some future poet will write something which corresponds to them."[32] Through decay and their becoming-image things are extracted from the world and enter into the non-coherency of the poetic collage which allows them to be placed together in new and unexpected ways that create resonances that may not yet be recognisable but are, therefore, no less real. The poem, therefore, is "a collage of the real."[33]

Connors's paintings, too, are collage-like in their fragmented nature. It is not that glue and scissors are involved in their production, but their logic of correspondences is the same. Indeed, it is striking how his current body of work is born from very similar circumstances as Spicer's later poetry. Like Spicer, Connors feels dissatisfied with his early works which, in the Portland lecture, he describes as "quirky abstractions … geometric small scale abstract paintings that were fairly resolved."[34] Having grown tired of their limited scope, Connors cites the desire to "take apart that quirky abstraction thing" as the subject of his later work. "Rather than to draw a picture or to make a symmetry," he says, "my idea of painting was kind of falling apart in a productive way."[35] Similar to Spicer, the idea of 'things *not* working' becomes the guiding principle for Connors. An early example of this new approach is titled *This Will Break*. In the conversation with Koestenbaum, Connors reflects that it was titled this way "because I just thought that I made this system that just wasn't gonna work, like a machine part that was gonna swing wide of its receptor." For Connors,

---

31 Spicer, *My Vocabulary*, 133–4.

32 Spicer, *My Vocabulary*, 133.

33 Spicer, *My Vocabulary*, 133.

34 Connors, 00:45–01:00.

35 Connors, 05:00–05:30.

this swinging wide, the matter of something "not fitting or not working," is an exploration of the theme of "adjacency."[36] Speaking of the same painting in the PSU lecture, Connors explains that adjacency is not (only) a theme internal to a painting, but also involves the adjacency between paintings.

"I started to become less interested in the actual, particular paintings," he relates, "and more interested in what the painting was going to show me about what I was going to do on the next painting and how they would look together."[37] But such interest requires giving up the hope that a single painting can fulfil one's desires and insists on allowing the painting *not* to be self-sufficient. Indeed, contrary to the workshop with its machine-like efficacy, the alignments of Connors are constructed on misalignment, on things that resonate because they swing wide.

Indeed, the show *Machines* (which the *Times* reviewed), explores these suggestions of functionality that lead nowhere. The paintings in the show become like cogs in a machine or tools in the workplace. But their production is never geared toward a set goal. "I have been doing a lot of brushless technique," the PSU lecture reflects, "where I'm using one painting to make another painting." This involves not only "following . . . mistakes and leads from other paintings" but actually using "wet paintings as the paint brush." In this way, "the work started to really represent the actual physical studio or the work that went on in the previous painting" rather than something that is "pictured." Koestenbaum remembers visiting Connors one day and being presented with a "frottage lesson" where "one painting, whether it was done or not, would just get pressed against another one."[38] Paintings, then, become physical tools that, "done or not," still have an active role to fulfill in the studio. As if they are brushes, they are pressed against each other, altering the new painting being worked on, but, of course, altering the old one too, thereby questioning the very notion of "new" and "old": insofar as they are all actively involved in the ongoing process of painterly production, nothing is old or finished. As we have already seen, this process of making and remaking continues in the exhibition space as well. One example of this is a painting that is missing the top section of its frame and which was, therefore, at one point installed in a way to emphasise this. This will change, of course, when the painting is relocated. But rather than to see this as a loss, Connors reflects: "since I work in bodies of work, I get really excited about combining and uncombining, and redestributing, and creating logics, and then creating problems of logic."[39] Or, as Koestenbaum notes: "the issues of contiguity and adjacency

36 Wayne Koestenbaum and Matt Connors, "Wayne Koestenbaum and Matt Connors, a conversation at 356," Apr. 27, 2016, 356 S. Mission Road, Los Angeles, CA., video, 10:53–11:18. https://youtu.be/qhXu9_qVXgo

37 Koestenbaum and Connors, 07:20–08:20.

38 Koestenbaum and Connors, 11:35–11:53.

39 Connors, 12:30–13:40.

were not about objects in one painting but were about the process of making which involves somewhat promiscuous or unintended collisions."[40] "The drama where the worth of the paintings is" he adds, addressing Connors, is that "maybe something unattended happens through something like an accident. But then there's the space of you looking at it, taking time, accepting it, interpreting it, leaving it, or altering it."[41] The image of the painting thus becomes the "image of an act of attentiveness, and, to some extend, self-acceptance . . . a genuine curiosity about the accident, a space of detachment, looking and leaving."[42]

When an "accident" happens, Connors allows the accident to subsist in a suspension of judgment, accepts it (perhaps as part of himself, but at least as part of the work), and works *with* it. Insisting on patience rather than the pursuit of any specified goal, Connors is able to sidestep the demands of the good or fully realised painting and is able, instead, to admit the "useless" as something that is allowed to play a role in his artistic process. "My, I guess, doubt and misunderstanding [have] almost like physically translated into formal issues of misalignment" Connors says, "the idea of anything being good" has made place for the desire for "things to be open which I think is maybe contrary to good or, 'good' the way someone would imagine good: 'finished.'"[43] We can see that, for Spicer as for Connors, such an approach is creative because it allows one to remain open to new possibilities. But, as Koestenbaum emphasises, it is also an ethical imperative: "the unfinished or failed things give lots of very concrete lessons in how to approach the acts of seeing and shaping that make us want to go on."[44] Rather than to limit what, and *who,* is worthy of our care, as Heidegger ultimately does, the practice of correspondences insists that we extend care also to the misaligned, the unfit, and the accidental. What we may take from Connors's paintings, then, is not the satisfaction of a good ending, but a reflection on what it means to go on even if there is no end in sight. Here, meaning is immanent to the process of production and not contingent on the realisation of any predetermined idea.

40 Koestenbaum and Connors, 11:55–12:01.
41 Koestenbaum and Connors, 14:06–14:25.
42 Koestenbaum and Connors, 14:36–15:02.
43 Koestenbaum and Connors, 13:05–13:43.
44 Koestenbaum and Connors, 37:09–37:20.

The Object of Non-Aesthetics

Jonathan Fardy

The work of François Laruelle has in recent years grown in both stature and controversy. His project of "non-standard philosophy" has generated a wealth of critical and creative scholarship. This essay aims to make an intervention in the explication of a central concept in Laruelle's project to rethink the formulation and uses of standard philosophical aesthetics. Here, I attempt to clarify the concept of "non-standard aesthetics" or simply "non-aesthetics" in the context that concerns us in this volume, namely, in the context of questions concerning process, object, and materiality. If non-aesthetics is a doing – a kind of fictional writing, as I argue – then the question remains: what is the object (and I mean this in both senses of the term, as aim, and material object) of non-aesthetics that underlies this doing, these practices or processes? The purpose of this essay, therefore, is to clarify the object (in the two senses) of non-aesthetics in order to lend some measure of clarity to a dense and fascinating corpus of thought that offers a new approach to the practice of aesthetics and philosophy in general.

Non-Standard Philosophy in Brief

It will be useful to lay the groundwork for what follows through a schematic review of the basic axioms of Laruelle's approach. Firstly, Laruelle axiomatically identifies "standard philosophy" with the decisions it makes concering the Real. These various decisions he denotes by the single term "Philosophical Decision." It should be noted here that while there are affinities between Laruelle's work and standard anti-foundationalist philosophies of the later twentieth century, non-philosophy is radically different than most of those approaches in its axiomatic orientation. Laruelle's approach is *axiomatic* in the last instance inasmuch as he never defends the claim that standard philosophy is fundamentally defined by the implicit or explicit decisions it makes regarding reality (or what is of ultimate concern); what Laruelle, again, simply terms the "Real."

Philosophical Decision can take any number of implicit and explicit forms, from the essence of reality to the ontology of art. This decision is underwritten by a presuppositional invariant that Laruelle names "Principle of Sufficient Philosophy." Non-philosophy works by suspending this principle and voiding philosophy of its decisionist pretensions. This might be likened to Husserl's method of bracketing the question of the truth of phenomena in order to focus on the problem of their description. This displacement of the question of truth in Husserlian phenomenology is radicalized and generalized in non-philosophy as the bracketing of philosophy's presupposed power to decide the question of the Real. This bracketing of *philosophy's decisionism* – and its presupposition regarding its ability to decisively settle the question of the Real – transforms standard philosophy into "raw materials." By this he means philosophy should be treated as a collection of conceptual, rhetorical, scientific, and poetic materials – words, phrases, logics, and so on – that offer critical and creative resources for fashioning new objects of thought that lie beyond the scope of traditional philosophical decisions.

The freedom opened up by the non-philosophical reduction of philosophy to "raw materials" is the freedom afforded thought when the irreconcilable nature of diverse philosophies – irreconcilables that are determined by their differing decisions on the Real – are voided and reconstituted in a mode of formal equality that Laruelle terms "democracy-in-thought," but which I think is better formulated as *democracy-in-theory*. This democracy is premised on the formal equality of theoretical approaches (or philosophical schools). This formal equality is founded upon the axiom that no theory has full epistemic access to the Real. This is not relativism as some of Laruelle's critics claim. Rather, for Laruelle, all theories fail the test of the Real and in this respect only are they are formally equal. But how and why and to what extent they fail are not the same. Here then is a theory of theoretical equality that is not founded on the concept of sameness. Democracy-in-theory is both a conceptual object and a conceptual aim to combine hitherto seemingly incompatible philosophical materials and to democratize the uses of philosophical materials by repurposing them and putting them to work in new ways unbounded by the strictures of standard philosophical decisionism.

My interest here is principally in what happens to the philosophy of aesthetics in this non-standard frame. Aesthetics in this light is voided of its standard pretension to grasp the Real of art. Aesthetic philosophy, after Laruelle, can now be taken as materials, as "raw materials," with their own aesthetic dimensions, investments, and strategies. Non-standard aesthetics works at a meta-critical level by exposing and exploiting what I identified in *Laruelle and Art* as the *aesthetics of aesthetics*.[1]

The practice of aesthetic philosophy is necessarily an aesthetic practice inasmuch as any practice of theory (or philosophy) is more or less concerned with the materiality of writing. The idea that standard aesthetic philosophy – and indeed all

1 See Jonathan Fardy, *Laruelle and Art: The Aesthetics of Non-Philosophy* (London: Bloomsbury Academic, 2020).

standard philosophy – is a matter of the materiality of words and the problem of composition, and by extension a problem of the aesthetics of presentation, has important precedents in the work of numerous modern philosophers. But I would like here to note three precedents that have considerably impacted and shaped my thinking and whom I believe serve as crucial and clarifying intertexts for the work of Laruelle. The three precedents I want to focus on are Theodor Adorno, Walter Benjamin, and Jacques Derrida.

Precedents

Martin Jay argues that Adorno's prose sought to achieve an "atonal philosophy" that would achieve in philosophical writing what composers such as Arnold Schoenberg, Anton Webern, and Alban Berg had achieved in music.[2] Adorno's aim, however, was "to 'aestheticize' neither philosophy nor politics," writes Susan Buck-Morss, "but instead to reconstitute the dialectical relationship between subject and object."[3] Schoenberg's so-called "twelve-tone" method of composition demands that all twelve tones of the Western scale be sounded once before any tone is sounded twice. This rule or parameter on composition enabled atonal composers (Schoenberg and his followers) to compose according to a transpersonal rule that as such mitigated against the allure of the romance of subjective freedom that characterized music of the Romantic school against which the twelve-tone school rebelled.

Adorno sought to transpose something of Schoenberg's system of composition into his style of philosophical composition. Above all, he sought to remodel philosophical prose by prizing the dissonance of non-closure or what he called "negative dialectics." As he notes, somewhat cryptically, in *Negative Dialectics*,

> Philosophy serves to bear out an experience which Schoenberg noted in traditional musicology: one really learns from it only how a movement begins and ends, nothing about the movement itself and its course. Analogously, instead of reducing philosophy to categories, one would in a sense have to compose it first. Its course must be ceaseless self-renewal, by its own strength as well as in friction with whatever standard it may have. The crux is what happens in it, not a thesis or a position – the texture, not the deductive or inductive course of one-track minds.[4]

The materiality of Adorno's prose is dense, textured, and marked by an unrelenting staccato-like, paratactic rhythm. Adorno's very style inverted and disrupted the

---

2 Martin Jay, *Adorno*, (Cambridge: Harvard University Press), esp. chapter 2.

3 Susan Buck-Morss, *The Origins of Negative Dialectics: Theodor W. Adorno, Walter Benjamin, and the Frankfurt Institute* (New York: The Free Press, 1977), 123.

4 Theodor W. Adorno, *Negative Dialectics*, trans. E.B. Ashton (New York: Continuum, 1973), 33.

standard relation of philosophy (*qua* subject) to art (*qua* object). Adorno took art not only as an object of philosophical analysis, but as a model and spur for philosophical composition and philosophical thought itself. A music of philosophy then and not only a philosophy of music. Adorno's aim was to combine or matrix together a set of inputs – art and aesthetic philosophy – in order to systematically produce something other than a definition, an ontology, or even a simple critique of music. Adorno composed philosophy, as Schoenberg composed music; against the grain of standard dialectics which prizes synthesis, reconciliation, sublation, and all forms of Hegelianized harmonies. Philosophizing after Schoenberg, for Adorno, meant resisting the tropes of resolution and closure in fidelity to the aesthetics and the philosophy of the fragmentary and the dissonant.

Benjamin too drew on art as a model for philosophical composition, but his model was taken from the visual arts, specially surrealism. As Richard Wolin notes, Benjamin's style reflects his "desire to render philosophy surrealistic."[5] In texts such as *One-Way Street*, his massive yet unfinished *Arcades*, "On the Concept of History," and other texts, Benjamin sought to illuminate the present by means of surrealist-inspired strategies of juxtaposition and montage. Surrealism and Marxism were, for Benjamin, intellectual cousins. Both expose the strange, otherworldly dimension immanent to a world governed by the abstract logic of exchange. Marxism aims not only to dispel the metaphysics of the market, but also to show how this very metaphysical character is actually immanent to its seemingly materialist base. This is precisely what Marx did when he drew attention to the "theological niceties" of the commodity.[6] Marx not only pierced the veil of the commodity's theological shell, but he also showed how that shell was part of reality itself. Surrealism – which historically separated itself off from Dadaism in fidelity to communism – likewise developed aesthetic strategies to illuminate the otherworldly and strange nature of everyday reality under capital. Benjamin matrixed Marxism and surrealism in order to expose, as he put it, "the true surrealist face of existence."[7]

Compacted in Benjamin's phrase is a matrixial movement that spans in six words art (surrealism) and reality (existence). Here in six words, Benjamin also covertly cancels the base/superstructure relation of vulgar Marxism. Art's fiction speaks to the truth of the otherworldly nature of the material world screened from view by the normalization of life under exchange. It is in the "superstructure" of art

5 Richard Wolin, *Walter Benjamin: An Aesthetic of Redemption* (New York: Columbia University Press, 1982), 124.

6 Karl Marx, *Capital: A Critique of Political Economy, Vol. 1* trans. Samuel and Edward Aveling, ed. Frederick Engels (Moscow: Progress Publishers, 1887), 47. Available at https://www.marxists.org/archive/marx/works/1867-c1/

7 Walter Benjamin, "The Image of Proust," in *Illuminations*, trans. Harry Zohn, intro. Hannah Arendt (Boston: Mariner Books, 2019), 153.

that we see what sanitized and normalized processes of exchange and exploitation disavow: the entirely magical thinking that determines and reproduces capitalist domination. But what is key for my purposes is that this surreal-real revelation illuminated for us by Benjamin is precisely made visible by the surrealistic aesthetics of juxtaposition and shock that structure his own style of writing.

Finally, we can turn to our third precedent – Derrida. My interest here is in the fact that not only does Derrida's writing, especially his more experimental texts, prove a useful model for doing philosophy in the manner of an aesthetic practice, but also that his work targets the authoritarian impulse of philosophy in ways that are close to Laruelle's critique of standard philosophy. Derrida's commitment to the displacing (or decentering) of the authority of philosophy provides a set of ethical coordinates for continuing and developing the project of non-aesthetics. The Derrida to which I will appeal is the writer of "Tympan" from *Margins of Philosophy*.

"Tympan" examines and critiques the authority *of* philosophy, especially its authority to determine what *its margins are*. The question of the margins of philosophy is pertinent here since the arts have traditionally been forced to the margins of philosophy. Plato famously exiled the arts from the city of thought, but the philosophy of art or standard aesthetics also makes art into an objects *of* philosophy. "Tympan" is useful for getting traction on the object of non-aesthetics. But here we should sound a note of caution in the very attempt to "get traction on the object of non-aesthetics." What is it that would get traction on it if not a discourse at least marginally determined by philosophy? The problematic that is hereby confronted (if not overcome) is that of the indebtedness of non-philosophy to philosophy and therefore of non-aesthetics to standard aesthetics. First, however, we must consult Derrida. He writes in "Tympan,"

> If philosophy has always intended, from its point of view, to maintain its relation with the nonphilosophical, that is the antiphilosophical, with the practices and knowledge, empirical or not, that constitute its other, if it has constituted itself according to this purposive *entente* with its outside, if it has always intended to hear itself speak, in the same language, of itself and of something else, can one, strictly speaking, determine a nonphilosophical place, a place of exteriority or alterity from which one might still treat *of philosophy*? Is there any ruse not belonging to reason to prevent philosophy from still speaking of itself, from borrowing from its categories from the logos of the other ...?[8]

Is it possible to "treat of philosophy" from a place exterior to philosophy that would not itself be philosophical? As Jason Demers has astutely argued, Derrida identi-

8 Jacques Derrida, "Tympan," in *Margins of Philosophy*, trans. Alan Bass (Chicago: The University of Chicago Press, 1982), xii.

fies philosophy's dangerous impulse to absolutize itself and thereby its "others."[9] "The movement of philosophy towards the absolute," writes Demers, "is premised on the idea that philosophy's other exists in order to be sublated."[10] The "imperialist and fascistic" movement by philosophy to absolutize its authority, to assign its own margins, and to determine those margins as "*its* others," ethically demands a counterforce of resistance to philosophy proper.[11] But what would this resistant other be if not already *philosophy's resistant other*? And where might it be located if not already in philosophy's self-delineated margins? Is there any way to think of the "nonphilosophical" outside without thinking it as the outside *of* philosophy? Derrida doesn't really answer his question. Instead, he reframes the question as an aporetic figure and shows how the question is seemingly as inescapable as it is unanswerable.

The work of Adorno, Benjamin, and Derrida proves important for us by indicating some models for how standard aesthetic philosophy might be reconceived as an aesthetic practice itself. However, I think that Laruelle's work importantly goes beyond simply inverting the expected relation of philosophy to art by rethinking the relationship between the two in terms drawn not from either art or philosophy, but from science. It is to this that I now turn.

Invariance

Laruelle's argument that all philosophies share the single invariant character of an implicit or explicit decision on the Real discloses the structuralist dimension of his thought. Structuralism offers Laruelle a readymade model of thought *about* philosophy that is itself, properly speaking, not a form of philosophy. As Vincent Descombes notes:

> Properly speaking, there is no definable structuralist philosophy such as might be opposed, for example, to the phenomenological school. "Structuralism" is, after all, only the name of a scientific method. The *effect* of structuralism upon philosophical discourse is nonetheless incontestable.[12]

Descombes counters the caricatured image of structuralism that has been one of the unfortunate effects of poststructuralism's academic institutionalization. Structuralism, on Descombes's reading, never meant anything like thinking in wholes or

9 See Jason Demers, *The American Politics of French Theory: Derrida, Deleuze, Guattari, and Foucault in Translation* (Toronto: University of Toronto Press, 2019).

10 Demers, *The American Politics of French Theory*, 23.

11 Demers, *The American Politics of French Theory*, 23.

12 Vincent Descombes, *Modern French Philosophy*, trans. L. Scott-Fox and J.M. Harding (Cambridge: Cambridge University Press, 1980), 77.

totalities. It was always concerned with the invariance of discrete elements that span a set of phenomena. To analyze is not to think in wholes, but precisely to think in discrete parts. It is this sense of structuralism that Ian James astutely detects in Laruelle's work. Laruelle's "characterizations of the structural invariant of philosophy," writes James, "suggests that philosophy will always repeat its deep structure as philosophy whatever form it may take."[13] The invariance of the gesture of decision on the Real, be it the Real of metaphysics, art, politics, etc., "is a kind of stance or posture that the philosopher automatically adopts by dint of philosophizing."[14] Laruelle's structuralist orientation is also resonant with his frequent invocations of the language of science, especially physics and mathematics. His work calls for a "science of philosophy" in which the identity of philosophy is structurally defined and creatively negated and transcended via "fictional" modes of conceptual production.

Non-aesthetics, then, names firstly a structuralist judgment that may be formulated axiomatically as: *standard aesthetics is a set of decisions that subjugate art to philosophy.* This judgement can only be axiomatic. If it was not then Laruelle would be compelled to logically argue in support of his judgment and this would formally commit him to the grammar of philosophical decisionism. Laruelle therefore limits the extent of his judgment to the identification of philosophy's self-constituting gesture. Laruelle makes virtually no other claims in regards to the identity of philosophy since such claims would amount to philosophical claims. Rather, like a structural anthropologist, he identifies a structurally invariant pattern of decisions that operationalize philosophy and its self-legitimating machinery. Beyond this, Laruelle's project of a general "non-philosophy" has no other fixed content. The work of the "non" of non-philosophy lies – beyond the axiomatic identification of philosophy – in the elaboration of ways of thinking and making that resist the philosophical imperative to incorporate the alterity of phenomena within the empire of philosophy.

Non-aesthetics likewise names an axiomatically rendered and structuralist-like judgment on philosophy's imperialistic domination of art. But beyond that axiomatic point, its identity as a multiplicity of processes and practices, is determined experimentally by working with art in non-philosophical ways. This is clear in the opening lines of Laruelle's *Photo-Fiction, a Non-Standard Aesthetics*:

> Aesthetics, particularly since Hegel, is the claimed domination of philosophy over art by which philosophy claims to unpack its meaning, truth ... In its least aggressive, least legislative form, philosophy describes art's figures, eras, its styles, the formal systems according to philosophy's own norms. Art, for its part, resists this

13 Ian James, *The Technique of Thought: Nancy, Laruelle, Malabou, and Stiegler after Naturalism* (Minneapolis: University of Minnesota Press, 2019), 30.

14 James, *The Technique of Thought*, 31.

> enterprise and rebels. We propose another solution that, without excluding aesthetics, no longer grants it this domination of philosophical categories over works of art, but limits it in order to focus on its transformation. It's about substituting for the conflict of art and philosophy the conjugation of their means regulated on the basis of a scientific model.[15]

Every bit of this statement (along with the title of the book itself) deserves careful attention. *Photo-Fiction* is a collection of experimental attempts to think of philosophy from the perspective of photography (rather than the reverse) without getting ensnared in a *philosophy of photography*, which would repeat the domination of philosophy over art that Laruelle resists. Moreover, the essays "fictionalize" aesthetic philosophy via the discursive resources of photography, mathematics, and physics in order to divert and stymie the decisionist machinery that would otherwise reaffirm standard philosophical aesthetics in its standard practice. Laruelle *takes many shots* at doing a non-standard aesthetics. These shots, in their very diversity and plurality, militate against any claim to a singularly sovereign, non-standard approach.

The passage quoted above also articulates the two-sided operation of any non-standard aesthetic practice. First there is the stated axiomatic determination of standard philosophical aesthetics as "the claimed domination of philosophy over art." Note that Laruelle's axiomatic judgment is that the domination of philosophy over art (or anything else) is merely "claimed" axiomatically by philosophy. Laruelle counters philosophy's axiomatic presupposition with his own. Since there is no way to logically decide between two opposed and undefended axioms, one is "free," and this the second move, to choose based on grounds other than those of logic, argument, or philosophy proper. Laruelle, for his part, chooses on the grounds of aesthetics as opposed to philosophy proper. He treats philosophical materials as aesthetic forms as a painter might treat the relation between colors. This freedom to compose and recompose philosophical materials no longer grants philosophical aesthetics its presupposed right to dominate over and legistalte the meaning of art.

Matrix

Non-aesthetics neutralizes the decisionist dimensions of philosophical aesthetics – but to what end? Non-aesthetics provisionally "limits" the "conflict of art and philosophy." Philosophy induces the conflict in its effort to subordinate the alterity of art to its margins. This subordination produces conflicts that are invariably conflicts *for*

15 François Laruelle, *Photo-Fiction, a Non-Standard Aesthetics*, trans. Drew S. Burk (Minneapolis: Univocal Publishing, 2012), 1.

philosophy. Art for its part always "rebels" in the sense that its own materiality resists easy and total assimilation by the logical materiality of philosophy. Art's own materiality resists the materiality of philosophy.

There is no analogy (or other form of translation) whereby the materiality of art can be rendered in philosophy without destroying its material alterity by translating it into verbal-conceptual forms. Non-aesthetics "limits" the standard conflict by experimenting with possibilities for the "transformation" of standard philosophical aesthetics via a "conjugation" of the "means" of art and philosophy on "the basis of a scientific model." The "scientific model" is the matrix, which is both an object and a "structuralist" process, that combines and produces new conceptual objects though operations of conjugating or combining standard philosophical materials that works (and reworks) the relation of philosophy and art without reducing either to the other. Laruelle writes:

> [O]ne must construct non-aesthetic scenarios or duals, scenes, characters, or postures that are both conceptual and artistic and based on the formal model of a matrix ... A matrix is a mathematical mode of organization and a presentation of the data of a problem, when there are at least two heterogenous, conceptual, and artistic data that are linked in what we will call a matrixial manner.[16]

The matrix is a philosophical form used in mathematics to relate at least two data and subordinate them to a relation governed by logic. The "matrix is ordinarily directed by philosophy and its objects," notes Laruelle, "but it can also be directed differently toward generic uses ... rather than philosophy."[17] The matrix is a conceptual-material space for relating the means of art and philosophy, but the matrix itself is also transformed in the process into a "new or third function" that can reformulate the means of art and philosophy into a form that Laruelle names "veritable theoretical 'installations'"[18] What would a "veritable theoretical installation" be? Let us take the phrase in parts.

The term "installation" can be understood in the sense of "installation art." I make this interpretation in light of Laruelle's repeated invocation of the concept of "art-fiction" in *Photo-Fiction* and elsewhere. Installation art is, to reach for a simple definition, a form of art in which the entire environment of the exhibition space is included or matrixed into the phenomenal totality of the work of art. Installation art solicits the viewer to enter a world fashioned in the image of the work of art itself. This is akin to the condition of a "fictional" or invented world that one encounters in the pages of a novel or, for that matter, in the pages of a philosophical system. The novel and the

16 Laruelle, *Photo-Fiction*, 4.

17 Laruelle, *Photo-Fiction*, 4.

18 Laruelle, *Photo-Fiction*, 4.

philosophical system alike – at least in their classical forms – function as environments or worldviews. Novel or systematic environments are neither simply "true" or "false," nor "real" or "unreal." They are of another order of reality for which these dichotomies prove clumsy and inadequate. Laruelle's "installations" are creative exercises in "theoretical" formulations, but here "theoretical" means "speculative" with a determinedly anti-decisionist gaze. In terms of non-aesthetics, this means that the invention of creative and speculative installations, or "art-fictions," is a means of remaking the standard practice of philosophical aesthetics such that "aesthetics becomes a second power of art itself."[19] The matrix-object of non-aesthetics then can serve as way of modeling other "creative and inventive" modes of speculation; a form that Laruelle describes as a "philosophical artistic genre that strives to make a work with pure and abstract thought."[20] Installation artists look at objects, images, acts, and processes as possible raw materials for the matrixing of a form of art capable of physically and conceptually reshaping the environment of the exhibition in the image of art. Likewise, the non-aesthetician turns to the raw materials of philosophy – and especially the philosophy of art or aesthetics – in order to transform them into "an art of thought rather than a thought about art."[21] Yet, these installations are "veritable installations." How are we to take this?

I suggest that we read this phrase as being itself a "veritable theoretical installation" in which the veritableness of its conceptual environment is affirmed by criteria engrained into that world. It is true in its own terms as a fictive installation, but true in a fashion that cannot be reduced to questions concerning its "ultimate" truth-content status. Just as one does not get far in asking whether or not a given work of installation art is "true'" likewise it seems to be a false start to ask of non-aesthetics if it is a true theory of art. It is not a theory of art, but an art of theory. Theory as installation is true in the sense that it is true to its referent which is fictional – which is, again, neither simply true nor false.

We now come closer to answering our question: what is the object of non-aesthetics? It is, considering this previous discussion, an "installation" made of abstract-philosophical thought, but not of a sort that decides the nature of art nor renders aesthetic judgment. "It would be a bit like an artisan, to use a Socratic example," writes Laruelle, "who instead of making a bed following the ideal model of a bed he already had in his mind, got it into his head to make an Idea of the bed that would somewhat resemble the bed but which would also not be its copy, but rather a 'generic' extension of the bed."[22] The non-aesthetician does not turn to the world of ideas in order to conceptualize art. That would affirm the old Platonic or "Socratic"

19 Laruelle, *Photo-Fiction*, 5.

20 Laruelle, *Photo-Fiction*, 6.

21 Laruelle, *Photo-Fiction*, 5.

22 Laruelle, *Photo-Fiction*, 12.

ideology that presumes art to be a material under the conceptual dictatorship of philosophy. Rather, the non-aesthetician treats philosophical work like an artisanal craft that makes concepts; not in an effort to conceptualize or judge the work of art, but to take it as a model for the creation and extension of theory itself.

No work of art, however, can simply be taken as a model without in some measure conceptualizing its materiality. The work of art that non-aesthetics takes as a model cannot be "other than philosophical since all theory would, in any case, include a philosophical aspect."[23] Hence, non-aesthetics always and invariably conceptualizes works of art in some way, even if only as simply a set of materials. We might then reformulate our working definition slightly: non-aesthetics is any process that takes the materiality of philosophical aesthetics as "raw materials" for the making of non-aesthetic art-fiction. The conceptual space in which such processes can be determined is that of the matrix. The matrix of non-aesthetics is that space wherein the "two moments of the structure" (art and philosophy) are "distributed" through a "dual transcendence" in which the two moments are preserved in a "holistic" but "non-totalizing way."[24] Neither is art reduced to thought nor thought to art. The hyphen in "art-fiction," if you like, is the metaphorical image of this matrixial space. It produces a new object entirely irreducible to its constituents.[25] The object of non-aesthetics – because it cannot be determined or decided in advance without defaulting into the metaphysics of the Principle of Sufficient Philosophy – can only be determined as the matrixial space into which the standard relation of art and philosophical aesthetics is reformulated and materially redeployed. "The matrix is," writes Laruelle, "the third term or the term-index that assures the aleatory but necessary conjugation of the two instances, without imposing on them an absolutely necessary analytic or dogmatic link."[26]

In its most general, its most "generic" form, the object of non-aesthetics is the matrix of non-aesthetics itself. Laruelle frequently appeals to the rhetoric of quantum physics in his most recent writings as a means to shore up his concept of matrix. "Finally, art-fiction demands to be understood precisely in its complexity," writes Laruelle, it "is irreducible to the fiction contained in all art and irreducible to an art of the first degree. It is not the identity but the superposition of an art and aesthetics."[27] The matrix may be constructed in an infinite number of ways, but it will be an artisanal creation that "generalizes and confirms as necessary the possibility of the con-

23 Laruelle, *Photo-Fiction*, 5.

24 Laruelle, *Photo-Fiction*, 6.

25 There is a distinct parallel here I believe with the concept of Third Space developed by Homi K. Bhabha. See Homi K. Bhabha, *The Location of Culture* (New York: Routledge, 1994).

26 Laruelle, *Photo-Fiction*, 9.

27 Laruelle, *Photo-Fiction*, 10.

jugations of art and thought instead of practicing them according to chance."[28] The matrix is a non-arbitrary (quasi-scientific) combinatory system that allows art and standard philosophical thought to be "generalized and to be confronted as properties, variables, or parameters of a system X."[29] The "system X" is precisely a given system of non-aesthetics produced out of the matrixial constraints that set the parameters for the extension of art and philosophical thought into a fictive "art-thought."

What then, finally, is the object of non-aesthetics? I have argued here that it is not the fiction produced, but a set of systematic, non-arbitrary limits and parameters that define the matrix for the combinatory superposition of art and philosophical aesthetics. The object of non-aesthetics is the general conditions for the setting of these matrixial parameters. It would therefore appear that the discipline of non-aesthetics will require a familiarity with a certain mathematical form. However, we should note Laruelle's warning here: "Non-standard aesthetics is not founded upon the substitution of the Principle of Sufficient Philosophy with the Principle of Sufficient Mathematics ... but with a mathematics that is itself decontextualized."[30] What then is decontextualized mathematics? I leave this question aside for it demands another interrogation of a very different sort. Let us say that somewhere between art-fiction and decontextualized mathematics lies an even more general and complete theory of non-aesthetics. However, speaking non-philosophically, I will say that it is enough to have rendered a general theory of non-aesthetics without rendering that theory as a totality. What I have done here is itself another fictional installation comprised of raw materials for still other matrixial combinations and non-standard projections.

28 Laruelle, *Photo-Fiction*, 7.

29 Laruelle, *Photo-Fiction*, 7.

30 Laruelle, *Photo-Fiction*, 6–7.

Solid Gifts

Seven Lessons from the Fossil

Luca Trevisani

Figure 1: Luca Trevisani, Notes for dried and living bodies, 2015, UV cured print on dried leave, framed, courtesy the artist, Galerie Mehdi Chouakri, Berlin, Pinksummer Contemporary Art, Genova

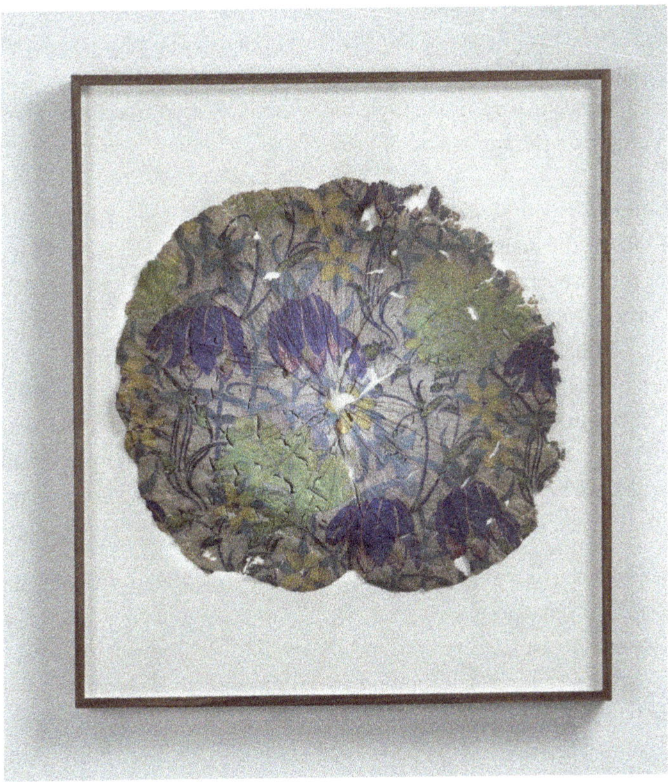

Sometimes projects and ideas show up as they wish, unpredictable like bubbles in a pond. Our burden is to equip them with a method, help them to grow strong and – above all – to let time pass by to tell us what they really are, beyond our own sincere intentions. It is then up to us, when time comes, to try and close the circle; retroactively understand the sense of our actions, and to learn from our vague intents.

In 2015, I started to print nature-based patterns on dried leaves, designed by artists, architects, and authors that were addressing the green world as a deposit of original knowledge and pure value. *Notes for dried and living bodies* (2015-ongoing) is a series of vegetal tattooed skins, flora reified in effigy, in an imaginative political herbarium. The idealization of nature in William Morris' wallpaper, like the ones drawn by Koloman Moser, Ettore Sottsass Jr., and Ernesto Basile, just to name a few of these designers, overknown or outer-known, is put into test here, once and forever, inscribed where it should be. The following year I flew to Kenya to do an *Interview with the unicorn*[1], to screen the last North African white rhino into the future, before its extinction. Sudan was the last living male of his subspecies; all of the instant photos and the short film I made based on his body are fragments of a low–fi monument, dedicated to nature, the ghost we pretend to be a part of. Afterwards, I choose to investigate *The Nature of Nature of Nature* (2019) by printing Paul Klee's geometrical speculation onto dried apple slices using UV rays, thereby imprinting the Bauhaus utopia on the surface of the fruit of Eve and Adam, a juicy emblem of our curiosity.

Our knowledge of the world comes through the senses and the direct manipulation of things: the ones mentioned are just a few examples of a cult of metamorphosis, of the incessant becoming of identities. In a world obsessed with the pure and the certain, we need to nurture highly energetic processes and find the strength to be curious. Curiosity is not a light or innocent behaviour; curiosity is a constant, tiring, and not necessarily peaceful attitude. Being curious is not a party, a playful, childish, or colourful act; being curious means being open to the world, questioning one's own beliefs and balances, looking around for solutions to problems that we do not recognize we have. It's like making artworks while pretending not to have done them, but to have found them, like a fossil discovered in the heart of a mountain.

> "Whenever we attempt to interpret a ~~work of art~~ [fossil], we are at once confronted with problems that are as perplexing as they are contradictory. A ~~work of art~~ [fossil] is an attempt to express something that is unique, it is an affirmation of something that is whole, complete; absolute. But it is likewise an integral part of a system of highly complex relationships. A ~~work of art~~ [fossil] results from an altogether independent activity; it is the translation of a free and exalted dream. But flowing

1 Luca Trevisani, *Interview with the unicorn* (2016) is Fujifilm Instax Wide, passe-partout, frame, 50 x 39 cm; Luca Trevisani, *Sudan. Interview to a body*, 2016, HD film, 16:9, stereo sound, 15'02". Photography: Edoardo Bolli, Editing: Luca Trevisani, Music: Michael Kresna.

> together within it the energies of many civilizations may be plainly discerned. And a ~~work of art~~ [fossil] is (to hold for the moment to an obvious contradiction) both matter and mind, both form and content"[2].

Almost one hundred years ago Henri Focillon began his *Life of forms* with these exact words.

By hacking these wise confabulations, with polite presumption, we may discover a buried, but very precious latent content of this milestone of art writing. Here you go with a crystalline theory of the fossil, intended to be a supreme work of art, an emblem and instrument of the century to come. If, as Focillon taught us, the forms are autonomous entities equipped with an internal principle that makes them dynamic and aim at continuous transformation, then these forms turn out to be precisely fossils, deposits of life suspended as crystals, blind agitation buried in matter. These words are a theory of the fossil as art, and of art as a fossil, understood as any fragment that interrupts space-time continuity, so convenient for us to believe. Here, you will not find organic remains that belong to the purest Palaeontology, but rather a collection of temporal accidents, of bodies suspended in history, such as those surprised by Vesuvius in Pompeii two thousand years ago, or like the remains of the soldiers of the First World War, which the climate change frees from the glaciers with increasing insistence.

If we continue to cripple Focillon's prose to understand the nature of fossils, here's where we find out: "space is its realm – not the space of everyday life involving, say, a soldier or a tourist – but space treated by a technique that may be defined as matter and as movement."[3] The fossil is a challenge to time; life that gives itself a shape without becoming form or sign. The fossil is a message without a code, an enigma so explicit as to avoid any explanation. The fossil is a stinging surprise, a not-invited thing that happens – like space debris, satellites, and probes that surround the earth and often crash into it.

The fossil is a fantastic occurrence, metaphysical and political unforeseen. For example, consider the rusty remains of a car bomb like the one that exploded in Baghdad, the remains of which were exhibited in a paradoxical parade by Jeremy Deller in 2009, entitled *It Is What It Is*. This parade was an American road tour that opposed modern dematerialized war and instead provided a turbulent and cumbersome corpse.

2 Henri Focillon, *The Life of Forms in Art* (New York: Zone Books, 1992), 31.

3 Focillon, *The Life of Forms in Art*, 33.

Figure 2: Jeremy Deller, It Is What It Is (2009). The car in front of a mural depicting the fall of Baghdad near 29 Palms, California. Courtesy of the artist and The Modern Institute/ Toby Webster Ltd., Glasgow

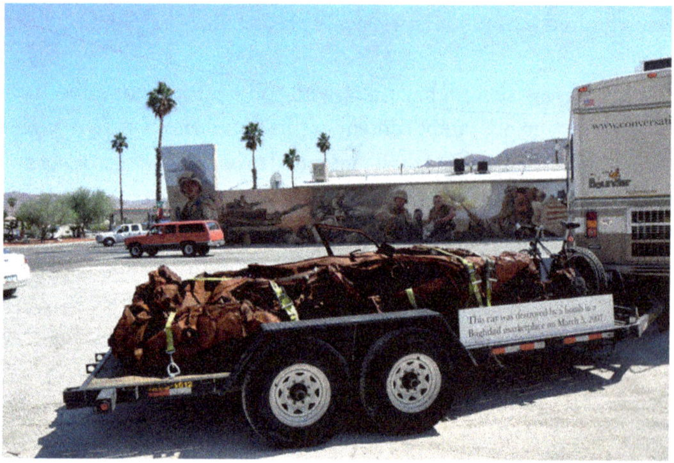

The fossil can be defined as a lump of badly digested, non-assimilated matter spewed out into the world. It's an irreverent analogical message, reminding us that there is no such thing as a neutral body, a fragment of a Theory of Everything, that forces us to redefine our ideas of rhythm and obsolescence. The fossil is not a true evasion of the passage of time, but rather a hiccup, a jolt, made of matter. The memory of a body and an incorporated memory twists in a perpetual feedback, in a real time madness, like that of someone who is lost at sea and can no longer tell where he is.

The fossil about which I am talking here is not a metaphor, but rather a figural image, a way of seeing artistic practice and ignoring current conventions. This is a speculative tale, whose protagonists are objects and processes that withdraw from possession and consumption. It's a deliberately irregular attempt to investigate the material base of our production of knowledge, beyond any technological determinism. Our fossil is related to the hyperobject, described by Timothy Morton[4] as a nonlocal, viscous entity that come and go in multilinear spacetime. Its sense and metabolism go far beyond human understanding; shiny, anonymous mysteries, magnetic and indifferent, they behave like the sphinx in front of which Napoleon stood, dumbfounded, during his Egyptian campaign in 1798. And here is Bonaparte, the modern Emperor par excellence, mounted and speechless before the ancient

4 Timothy Morton, *Hyperobjects, Philosophy and Ecology after the End of the World* (Minnesota: Minnesota University Press, 2013).

Sphinx, facing an unanswerable question, because this, and only this, is the real meaning of a true work of art.

Figure 3: Jean-Leon Gerome, Bonaparte Before the Sphinx (1886). Public Domain

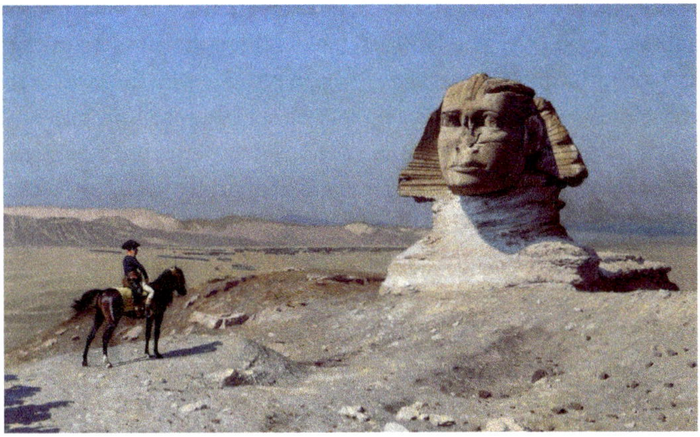

The fossil, in short, trips our will to control and challenges power through the supreme communicative gesture, the one composed of silence. The fossil knows how to disrupt the public with mystery and tragic carelessness. It is, therefore, no coincidence – but is a curious note of colour – that Gérôme's painting of Bonaparte was bought in 1898 by the first true modern media emperor, William Randolph Hearst at the center of Orson Welles's Citizen Kane, but that is another story. Our story, however, is also a story of gifts, because these unexpected encounters which we call fossils break the routine, and refresh our capacity for wonder, proving once more the strength of those who remain curious, open, and ready to be amazed are happy to be surprised and revitalized by a different dimension.

To speak the truth, a fossil is never made by somebody, and you don't even find it, because at most, to be honest, you are found by it, like a message in a bottle that appears from oblivion helped by a severe storm, when and where it wants to. It therefore sounds like a paradox, to ride such a figure of thought to describe the creative process and artistic practice, but that's only an apparent eccentricity. Notions such as that of subject and object, beings and things, and nature and culture need to be constantly renegotiated. The fossil provides us a lens through which we can perceive a different understanding of authorship. Fossils avoids any authority, just as they undermine any idea of a creator. In their world, there are no inventions, only discoveries, hybridization, and syncretism. Their writing proceeds by pollination, a result of a collective metabolism. There is no undo; our cosmos is a system with no way back, no delete, only additions, modifications, and wanderings, so that "all that is needed is to wander and let wander, be this slow boundless whirlwind and every particle of its dust."[5]

Our molecular universe is a combinatorial lottery, a pulsating jungle, a cacophonical state of continuous definition, something that cannot be frozen into a map; the only possible art production happens in a perpetual script, in an endless initiation ritual. The fossil is then a necessary model through which we can re-discuss the modern privatisation of experience, in open polemic with the myth of the omniscient and solitary maker and with the Promethean fable of anthropocentrism. But who's speaking this inhuman semiotic? What is it that sends us these signs? Where do these countless mysterious messages come from?

The fossil is a *sui generis* automatic composer, as concrete as it is non-existent, a message without origin because it lacks a root. It's a signal that speaks loudly, but that does not care about its audience. If language is an affective field made up of emotions, then this is not limited to the human world, as our senses deceive us. If every narrative act is based on exchange, abstraction, and trust, then it is necessary to learn how to engage with any and all 'vibrant matter'.

Contrary to common belief, the medium of the fossil is not time, but psyche. Its fragments belong to a geology of the mind, like the bodies surprised by Vesuvius in Pompeii two thousand years ago, or like the remains of the soldiers of the First World War, which climate change releases from glaciers with increasing impatience. Le Corbusier was aware of this school of thought, which is why he used to put shells in his concrete formwork, so that the pillars would have fossil remains inside of them, like the one you can spot in the lobby of the *Unité d'Habitation* in Marseille. Modernism would therefore not belong to the present, but would be part of an ancient future, reinforced by an imaginative pedigree.

5 Samuel Beckett, *The Unnamable* (New York: Grove Press, 1978), 91.

Figure 4: The shells impressions in the cement of the Unite d'habitation by Le Corbusier, in Marseille, 1947–1952, foto by Luca Trevisani, Courtesy of the artist

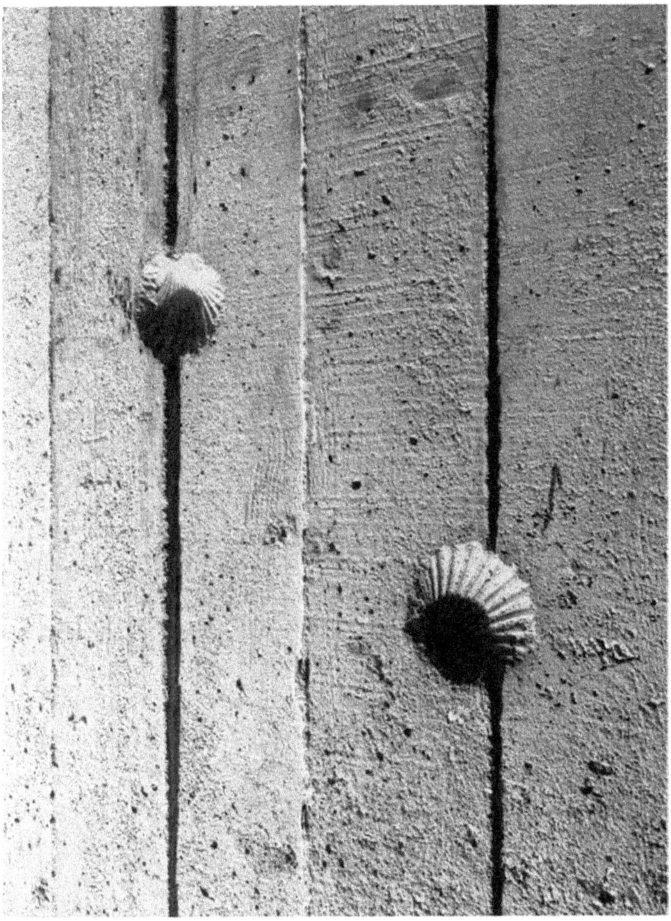

The fossil claims that everything is made of matter, it refutes the narrative of a society that believes in being dematerialized by a technological takeover. As a matter of fact, the explosion of the electronic realm didn't change didn't change anything in the rules of matter: the internet is made up of a metropolis of servers buried in the desert and by ocean cables, the control of which is a strategic and military garrison. All that is solid melted into the air of modernity, as Marx showed us so well[6], but

6 "All fixed, fast-frozen relations, with their train of ancient and venerable prejudices and opinions, are swept away, all new-formed ones become antiquated before they can ossify.

the fossil expresses the wisdom of a timeless corporeality, with a profound animism that gives unlimited credence to the prophecies of matter; a belief that is as simple as it is revolutionary.

Historical land art has very little to do with the syntax of the fossil, which is indeed a wreck, an object of reverie and meditation, but never a muscular and heroic gesture, as – for instance – Michael Heizer's *Double Negative*, or a romantic ruin like Robert Smithson's reading of the mythological Hotel Palenque. Smithson, as we know, was the first and true prophet of entropy, of space-time bewilderment, and he is certainly an honorary member of the fossil club. No doubt that his process-based landscapes, such as the legendary *Asphalt Rundown* and *Partially Buried Woodshed*, are masterpieces of weight accumulation and inverted archaeology, and thus are authentic praises of the fossil. What Smithson did between 1969 and 1970 was pour semi-solid hydrocarbons into a landfill in the Roman suburbs as well as bury a woodlot at Kent State University, staging two reverse re-enactments of the Laocoon group's famous discovery; because if the one – witnessed by a thirty-year-old Michelangelo Buonarroti in 1506 – was the miraculous liberation of classical harmony out of the soil of a Roman vineyard, then Smithson's shrines where sabbaths dedicated to collapse, raw matter serving cosmic energies. The poet from Passaic was well aware of sculptures being born under the sign of that inertial force we call gravity, sometimes equipped with a skeleton, to resist it, or they surrender by rolling downwards. Each fossil, then, is simultaneously a denial of gravity and also its ultimate confirmation, since fossils emerge from the bowels of the soil with movement equal and opposite to Newton's apple. If gravity is the primal component of sculpture, then the fossil is an extreme expression of the sculptural, potent blossoming of pressure, as the ultimate multiplication of gravity enhanced by underground concentration.

The fossil is an aesthetic category of its own, time abeyant but also an active physical engagement, never a melancholic suspension craving for the sublime. No misunderstandings allowed with any rubbles or moribund carcasses: fossils are neither a residue nor leftovers, but a bullet, a rocket with a counterintuitive trajectory, a work of human ingenuity that embraces matter and its laws to pierce the notion of time. Being both here and somewhere else at the same time, in several spacetimes

---

All that is solid melts into air, all that is holy is profaned, and man is at last compelled to face with sober senses his real conditions of life, and his relations with his kind."

In this overquoted passage of their manifesto, Marx and Engels were commenting on the surface on which different modes of production and social systems are sustained, but before everything else, they were celebrating the blasts of revolutionary thinking that casted the 19th century and its myths of progress. Here, on the other hand, it is provoked by trying to contrast a Darwinism of forms and knowledge with a knowledge. If the place of Homo Sapiens has never been so unmoored as today, we need other strategies and effective dramaturgies.

at once, in a concrete way: that of the fossil is clearly a different measure of time. An outdated prophet, in a nutshell, someone unconcerned by current affairs, somebody who radically rethinks the role of art by disobeying the spectator's dictatorship, ignoring the expectations of the audience, and who speaks to his own present by pretending to belong to another temporality, trying to ignore the fixations and tics of his own time.

Figure 5: Han Solo frozen in Carbonite, in Star Wars, Episode VI Return of the Jedi (Screenshot)

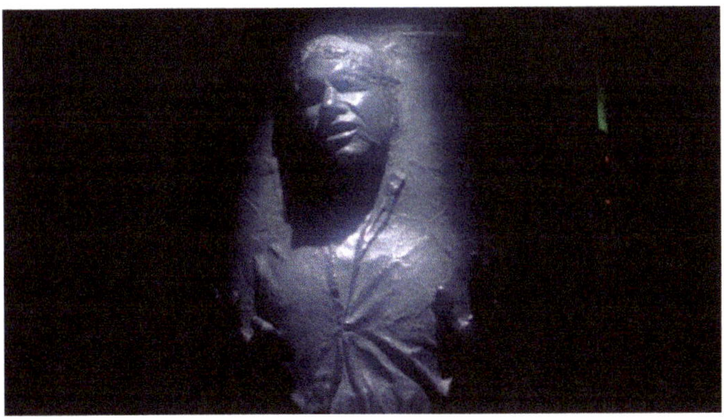

The wisdom of fossils is a matter of bodies, like the fabled one of Han Solo being frozen in carbonite in the original *Star Wars* trilogy, or as the mythological *Wunderkammer* of minerals assembled by Roger Caillois and elaborated upon by the surrealist master in his *The writing of Stones*, which is, for all intents and purposes, an interview with mute minerals. "~~Stones~~ [Fossils] possess a kind of gravitas, something ultimate and unchanging, something that will never perish or else has already done so."[7] One could, here and with great success, fully replicate the hacking to which we have previously submitted Henri Focillon's text, to extract once again the 'essence' of the fossil. And so, in Caillois's words, we understand how the fossil, "consist of subtle and ambiguous signals reminding us, through all sorts of filters and obstacles, that there must be a pre-existing general beauty vaster than that perceived by human intuition- a beauty in which man delights and which in his turn he is proud to create. Stones- and not only they but also roots, shells, wings, and every other cipher and construction in nature – help to give us an idea of the proportions and laws of that general beauty about which we can only conjecture and in comparison with

7 Roger Callois, *The Writing of Stones* (Charlottesville: University Press of Virginia, 1985),

which human beauty must be merely one recipe among others, just as Euclid's theorems are but one set out of the many possible in a total geometry."[8] Caillois' book is a seminal essay of Speculative Mineralogy and is really useful for understanding the dramaturgy of the fossil, of the work of art as an arbitrary sublimation of life into solid, hard, but also very sweet forms.

In his Mediterranean Breviary, Predrag Matvejević taught us how to make a broth from sea stones, giving us a recipe to cook them, and obtain a sauce of the Mediterranean, as if to revive our dormant kinships with Athena and Zeus and Poseidon. Well, Caillois does not stop at the Parthenon, he takes us to the Protozoic, to the third day of genesis, when dry land appeared. What you are reading is a meditation on the power of human imagination, but do not think about the usual story of those who see familiar shapes in the clouds, or of the adepts of pareidolia who perceive faces or grimaces wherever they look. If you look at the photos of the stones Caillois has collected, you will find eyes that peer at us like those of an owl or like the concentric ones of an avid opium smoker, or a section of a red cabbage that is like a drunk face, or a vegetable Rorschach test, but you will also find also the automatic writing of a smartphone screen broken after hitting ... a stone. We will meet the landscape of a spaghetti-western that not even Sergio Leone could have ever made, but then move on to the section of a cooked ham that has clearly gone to hell with its sulphates and nitrites turned into a pistachio green gem. Please keep in mind that with the polished sections of his onyx, Caillois is not playing the part of the cheap decorator, but rather the wrecker, the incendiary, the brawler. This lysergic army of rainbow stones tells us that the writing of the stones is a school of philosophy for which registration is always open.

The school I'm evoking may then look like the cement castles and eerie towers that Paul Virilio started to photograph at the age of twenty-five, between the sands of Normandy and the waters of the English Channel. For seven long years, the furious prophet of dromology, the science of speed, studied the remains of the Third Reich's Atlantic Wall like an entomologist, interviewing the remains with deadpan curiosity. What has sometimes been misinterpreted as an appropriation of a wartime aesthetic is in fact a case study of fossil writing, wherein invisible spaces and inapprehensible boundaries are depicted as an emotional matrix. One could interpret the Nazi water wall, suggests Virilio, as the latest update in the history of frontiers that – from the Roman lime trees to the Great Wall of China – is a matter of borders, separation, and order. If the history of culture is all about how we deal with the dirty, and that of the military one is about predatory control, the bunkers paleology plastically displays the limits of human jurisdiction.

Objects from the past have always been the material support for our historical writings. The construction of meaning develops, as we know, through order, se-

8 Callois, *The Writing of Stones*, 2.

quence, hierarchies, structures, and patterns, but "the history of forms cannot be indicated by a single ascending line."[9] In place of history as an ordered sequence, fossils, these automatic bodies of art, respond with a disordered, fuzzy parade, with an erratic and explosive rhythm. The archive of time becomes messy, dishevelled by anarchic disturbances. Our perception of the world is crumbled into fragments, into parts of a continually-kneaded amalgam. That of fossils is not a diaspora of bodies to be declined to the past; it is a dance that forces us to admit to the existence of a permanent present, unreal but very concrete. So, how do we build our identity, in the shape of a piece of art, following the lessons of fossils?

Decelerate!

The first lesson is in fact a ruthless overhaul of our notions of progress, velocity, and coincidence. Fossils show up in superb delay, out of place like a mismatched sock, never caring about punctuality, and deliberately ignoring any synchronicity with the present; it is precisely this indifference that gives them power. If it's true that a broken analogue clock is right twice a day, then the fossil rivals the generous and smoky oracle of Delphi. Why, then, does art as a practice of political awareness not start from here? Isn't this the supreme example of critical awakening?

The second lesson: if we want to think about a form as a form of life, we must never consider it to be something fixed or unchanged because form, just like a face, has a physiognomy that changes over the years, acquiring new wrinkles and new meanings. Every good work of art listens to its own principle of energetic efficiency, which avoids any superfluous forms, in a synthesis achieved by condensation, compression, and erosion. Fossils remind us that every art form tends to coalesce with the (geological) forms and forces that have moulded it. Art is choosing to say yes to reality, as Henri Cartier-Bresson once said, defining a good shoot; it is a way of becoming part of the material building to which we belong.

Third: A good artist knows how to listen rather than talk. Art is an act of recognitization of the unknown, a question of "proceeding from the I to the other, as a face to face"[10], ethics disguised as aesthetics. You need a good nose, and a lot of practice, because, to counter the current belief, fossils are interspersed in your living environment, simple as cosmic dust, but precious as truffles.

Consequently, fossils are the inspirational alien that is always among us, not as an extra-terrestrial exotic body, but as micro-meteorites that break our perceptual continuity. Yet, the fossil is a multi-scale intruder from another time, another place, and often another culture: it embodies the supreme distance with open innocence, and therefore that can never be fully revealed.

9 Focillon, *The Life of Forms in Art*, 52.

10 Emmanuel Levinas, *Totality and Infinity: An Essay on Exteriority* (Pittsburgh: Duquesne University Press, 1961), 39.

One of the most traditional problems of sculpture is the relationship between body and mind. But what happens to the flesh when it separates from the notion of the individual? The fourth lesson deals with the somatic and with anatomic, and it speaks about a body imprisoned in itself. Vitality now becomes a strange concept, we no longer know who is alive and who is dead, what is biological and what is inorganic. The fossil is an allegory and model for an infinite materiality, which has always been devalued in favour of the soul, the spiritual, and the profound. There is no transcendence except in the flesh. The only possible mysticism is based on matter and achieved by a self-crafted figure, as if the body could write, even lacking hands and pencils. Fossils are solid as a rock because any soft tissue has been absorbed by time, and does not allow any dissection or penetration by the eye; they show up with a skinless and unfiltered flesh, peeled and obscene, like an already unwrapped gift. Nature loves to hide, said Heraclitus, but the mystery of the world is the apparent, not the invisible: this is the traumatic nature of the fossil, of something peeking through the skin of the world This theatre is a virtual striptease of, galling nakedness, flat bodies striking an uncanny pose. The Medusa is the ultimate patroness of sculptors, her gaze is the true mother of fossils, her sons emotionally moving mirages.

Are we a pen or a piece of paper? Are we something that writes or that is, instead, written? The pressure that generates fossils is the same as that which shapes our identities, it is magnetic and irresistible like a black hole, but instead of devouring matter it builds it up. Ask yourself for a moment how a body can be born by itself. The only possible answer is called 'metamorphosis'. My hypothesis consists of affirming that the solidification of things into forms occurs by direct mutations, unseats the myth of the author, and is linked to the transformation of our idea of humankind, its music is meta-human, its score is that of the whole biosphere.

"With painting everything was simple, the original was unique, and each copy was a copy, a forgery" (Wenders 1989). So, was Wim Wenders warning us, with Neoplatonic confidence, in his wonderful documentary dedicated to Yoji Yamamoto, and then reminding us how "with photography and then filming it began to get complicated, the original was a negative, without a print it did not exist, just the opposite. But if it was true that "with photography and then filming each copy was the original." In the epistemology of the fossil, we have copies without an original, which are therefore not copies of anything, but solid ghosts, neither negative nor positive. A mould, such as those in plaster made by Canova's workshop, is a reproduction obtained by continuity so that a point of the original corresponds to a point of the newly generated body. It's an index, as semioticians would say; something that is connected to its referent by physical contact, a copy generated directly from its matrix through pressure. A digital scan, on the other hand, is not a copy of reality but rather an approximation of it, obtained by means of a sum of discrete pixels, collected at a more or less defined density, connected to each other in order to reconstruct an image. Similar to an ultrasound, or sonar, or a depth sounder, eyes that touch from afar, generating a silhouette through a cloud of data. Footprints and signs, you might think of them as useful traces for historical reconstruction or clues for a forensic investigation, but they are firecrackers, they lead to nothing but an explosion. Fossils are not casts; they are spirals, erotic traps, organic beings collapsed in a cryptic encoding. Familiar faces are deformed and reveal the monstrous within the mundane, display the limits of the digital world, and the primitive forces of analogue knowledge.

Sculptures understood as fossils are radical solutions to the problem of storing memories, which are transformed into crazy splinters or still frames, devices for capturing knowledge in the form of a condensed mind. Defeating amnesia through the solid state, giving a memento to a body, this is what the fossil does through fibrous and wild writings. In any fossil library, this must be said, there are never two identical books, as in the mythological library of Babel described by Borges whose bookshelves store everything: "the minutely detailed history of the future, the archangels' autobiographies, the faithful catalogue of the Library, thousands and thousands of false catalogues, the demonstration of the fallacy of those catalogues, the demonstration of the fallacy of the true catalogue, the Gnostic gospel of Basilides, the commentary on that gospel, the commentary on the commentary on that gospel, the true story of your death, the translation of every book in all languages, the interpolations of every book in all books."[11]

The last lesson of the fossil is dedicated to the quick and the dead: a complete biography of the living. The time has come to call a spade a spade, without delay. We are talking about life because this is the realm of art and art deals with life, and nothing else. We are talking about life, and that is why we are dealing with death. The fossil is not the defeat of death, but rather its betrayal, of the corpse it possesses only the rigidity, and of the ghost it completely ignores volatility and sense of escape: no hiding is planned, no burial is possible, but only pure ostension. Nothing is therefore sentenced to dust, but to reincarnation in a hallucinated aberration of the eternal return. Do you remember Duane Hanson's hyperrealistic sculptures or their celebrity pop version by Madame Tussaud? Those, as well as George Segal's chalky cocoons, continue the tradition of royal burials, providing a durable substitute for the dead body, reassuring the public eye, vanquishing any threat to the continuity of power. When compared to those creative sarcophagi, the project of the fossil reveals all its corrosive values, as it disobeys the integrity of the body, doesn't care about cosmetics, is disturbingly dismembered and happily incomplete. This is a manifesto for a necropolitical art, applied political theology: the productive interweaving of death and vitality is insensitive to contradictions. A fossil is solidified life, evaporated but

11 Jorge Luis Borges, *Collected Fictions* (New York: Viking Press, 1989), 115.

backed up; the revenge of biology that defeats death by returning as a simulacrum of itself. The end that does not end, but rebounds in an indigestible form.

Still life, Vanitas, Natura morta – the painters of organic fragility have always chased the accord between the images we create and the world as it is, but our fossil is a profanation of the passage of time, the reincarnation of soft tissues into impetuous bodies. The mission: give a physical dimension to what is constantly fading away, always threatening to vanish. The recipe: a radical metempsychosis and transfiguration, because the link between the mineral and animal worlds is central for our pressing planetary crisis. In order to overcome it we need to mobilise new formats and new interpretations. Humankind is unimaginable without its relationship to the history of the earth and living things, its structure and development links it to the subterranean, to the chthonian, to the general organisation of its environment.

We need a counterpart to the idealized body of modernism, and perhaps the only useful well in which to find it is the surrealist mythological machine. "It is by their failure to harmonize with reality, and owing also to the arbitrary element in their presence, that images so easily assume the forms of reality and that the latter in turn adapts itself so readily to the violence of images, which materialist thought idiotically confuses with the violences of reality."[12] If nature is what is found and culture is what has been made, all we can say is that fossils are a surprising centaur, eternally in between, captious multiple figures, dormant or sibylline deities, composite beasts such as mermaids or erotic chimeras, subversive fetishes. Dali was right when he wrote about his Stinking Ass and noted that their foul putrefaction is other than the hard and blinding flash of new gems.

The ultimate meaning of nature is difference and indifference, a deaf threat to our ego, our sense of possession and completeness. The elusive nature that we feel we could possess by sublimating it in its fetishisation, always slips through our fingers, like a ray of light. Here the fossil shows itself as an eco-monster in the etymological and pure sense of the term: the monster with an echo. Eco, here, does not stand for ecology, but rather for reverberation, for the infinite diffusion of the message of the prodigy, the warning of the white whale, the riddle of the phoenix. Friend of the savage, relative of the freak, the fossil is a potent metaphor for disorientation, but also an operative procedure, a new pair of glasses through which to read the reality we live in.

12 Dali quoted after Lippard, in Lucy R. Lippard, *Surrealists on Art* (New Jersey: Prentice Hall 1969), 97.

Massimo Bartolini's *Untitled Untitled* (2001)
The Strategy for Visualizing the Hyperspace

German A. Duarte

(Praeludium) Massimo Bartolini's Untitled Untitled

In 2001, the Italian artist Massimo Bartolini realized his sculpture *Untitled Untitled,* exhibited for the first time at the SI (Swiss Institute – Contemporary Art) in New York during the winter of 2004. The artwork consists of a solid golden pill, which refers to one of the many Taoist names given to the 'Absolute'. In Bartolini's oeuvre, the pill of solid gold, which is supposed to be one centimeter in diameter and a half-centimeter in length, must be held in the right hand of an old man – never in his pocket or elsewhere. Once the old man grabs the pill in the exhibition place he can start to walk; he can also sit, talk, or do whatever he must do, but always with the pill in his closed fist, always hiding the pill, which can never be shown to the audience. Indeed until now the old man has never shown the pill. Therefore one cannot be sure of the existence of the golden pill, neither of its real material quality nor of its precise size. It is just the information of the caption through which the audience can ascertain itself of the existence of Bartolini's piece. Nobody has ever seen the pill. Regardless of the (non)existence of the pill, what the audience has experienced by the presence of this object is the creation of an space. Bartolini's *Untitled Untitled* can be seen as an instance of the culmination of a millenarian process that, by modifying the traditional understanding of space, radically changed the nature of the object and in so doing deeply transformed our understanding of the body.

A New Nature of Space

Bartolini's *Untitled Untitled* brings me back to the first readings of Euclid's *Elements,* from which emerges a concrete doubt on the veracity of the fifth postulate: the famous *Parallel Postulate*. This postulate states that,

> If a line segment intersects two straight lines forming two interior angles on the same side that the sum to less than two right angles, then the two lines, if ex-

tended indefinitely, meet on that side on which the angles sum to less than two right angles.

Some severe criticism of Euclid's fundamental axiom dates back to the twelfth and thirteenth centuries in some Arabic translations.[1] Some commentators, like Ptolemy, Proclus, or Posidonius, doubted the demonstrability of the postulate. Certainly, this famous postulate, by its axiomatic nature, does not need to be demonstrated. However, once its demonstrability was questioned, it generated an irreversible process the result of which could only be the reformulation and displacement of Euclidean geometry and, by extension, the unsettling change of our comprehension of the space.

This millenarian dispute, accompanied by infinite passionate readings, scientific debates, and philosophical discussions, could be compared to the Pythagorean tragedy of discovering irrational numbers. In turn, the refusal of Euclid's axioms represented not a minor tragedy for humankind. This axiomatic, on which our relationship with the external world was built over the course of millennia, embodied a fundamental tool for analysis that not only allowed us to develop a clear notion of space, but also, above all, to develop the existence of humankind within and through this notion. Thus, to doubt Euclidean geometry meant doubting the foundations of science, philosophy, and culture, and, by extension, it meant doubting any form of human expression. In other words, to express any sort of doubt regarding the Euclidean *ordino* was considered heresy, even up until the nineteenth century. That is the reason why the first studies that developed alternative spaces – or that called into question Euclid's *Elements* – were studies that aimed to demonstrate Euclid's axioms and not to contradict it. An exemplary example of this approach is the case of the mathematician and Jesuit, Gerolamo Saccheri, who devoted one of his works exclusively to demonstrate Euclid's fifth postulate. In Saccheri's *Euclides ab omni naevo vindicatus: sive conatus geometricus quo stabiliuntur prima ipsa universae Geometriae principia* from 1733, one can identify the emergence of a series of alternative spaces that contradict those constructed through the strict rational order dictated by the Euclidean laws.[2] In fact, through a *reductio ab absurdum* Saccheri intended to demonstrate that the fifth postulate was correct; however, this failed and he instead left the basis and unwittingly encouraged the development of alternatives postulates.[3]

By examining Saccheri, the genealogy of the destruction of Euclid's space becomes clear. It is from Saccheri's conclusion that Johann Heinrich Lambert derived

---

1 David Reed, *Figures of Thought: Mathematics and Mathematical Texts* (London: Rutledge, 2013).

2 Roberto Bonola, *Non-Euclidean Geometry: A critical and Historical Study of its Development* (New York: Dover Publications, 1955), Chapter II. The Foreruners of Non-Euclidean Geometry. Gerolamo Saccheri.

3 Jeremy Gray, *Ideas of Space: Euclidean, Non-Euclidean, and Relativistic* (Oxford: Clarendon Press, 1989).

his own geometric theorems developed in non-Euclidean parallel systems. Following the same genealogical line through to the first half of the nineteenth century, the work of both Johan Carl Friedrich Gauss and Georg Friedrich Bernhard Riemann revealed a concrete will to develop a series of alternatives geometrical systems that, presenting a different axiomatic, radically differ from Euclidean geometry. Yet, being a controversial topic, Gauss' works remained unpublished and that is the reason why one identifies the work presented by Nikolai I. Lobachevsky and Janos Bolyai as the first publication which theorizes a non-Euclidean geometry[4]. Still, both authors concluded that there is not a 'universal geometry', but rather that each field requires a special geometry. Lobachevsky and Bolyai assumed that Euclidean geometry is better adapted to the human senses – to our perceptions of the world – whereas other perspectives, i.e. atomic or planetary ones, require a different kind of geometry altogether. What Lobachevsky and Bolyai meant was that in a planetary perspective – meaning planetary spheres and their orbits' circumferences or ellipses – the plane must, under these conditions, manifest some spherical surfaces, as is the case in the ecliptic geometry theorized by Riemann. Following this new hypothesis, from a planetary perspective a straight line must be understood as a circle of maximum radius'.[5]

Despite the fact that Euclidean geometry is materialized by means of a series of geometrical figures that do not exist in nature[6] – a straight line, a square, and a triangle – Euclid's *Elements* guided during centuries the way humankind established a relationship with the object. Above all, after the Renaissance and the introduction of the mathematical perspective, this geometry became a sort of *lingua franca* that guided the processes of pictorial representation and, consequently, it drastically influenced human comprehension of space[7]. It is not by pure coincidence that Kant's notion of space corresponds to Euclidean space in that it also accepted only three dimensions. From this postulation, Kant also derived his assertion that space is understood as a pure form of sensitivity. Thus, following this reasoning, space is a three-dimensional entity that 'contains' objects, but is also, and above all, an essential characteristic of the object 'contained' *in* the three-dimensional space, as per the conclusion one assumes from the Euclidean principle of invariability. Yet, implicit in the development of non-Euclidean geometries was a deep transformation of that very conception of the object: a transformation based on the dissolution of the prin-

---

4 See, Linda Dalrymple Henderson, *The Fourth Dimension and Non-Euclidean Geometry in Modern Art.* Revised edition, (Cambridge MA: MIT Press, 2013).

5 See, Stefano Leonesi and Carlo Toffalori, *Matematica, miracoli e paradossi. Storia di cardinali da Cantor a Gödel* (Milano: Bruno Mondadori, 2007).

6 Benoît Mandelbrot, *The Fractal Geometry of Nature* (New York: Times Books, 1982).

7 Erwin Panofsky, *Perspective as Symbolic Form* (New Jersey: Princeton University Press, 1997).

ciple of invariability.[8] Contrary to the general understanding that regards the emergence of the new nature of the object as the result of a new conception of space, it is instead from the acknowledgement of the object's flexibility and its dynamic form that a new conception of space emerged, one developed within different disciplines during the end of the nineteenth century and the beginning of the twentieth.

It is during the last century that the notion of space decisively lost its pure definition of 'three-dimensional container' of both objects and subjects, and started to be comprehended as a complex set of relationships between flexible, changeable, and dynamic entities. Suddenly space became a *complexus,*[9] a set of relationships. This new comprehension of space was spread through different disciplines and it was 'installed' into the collective imaginary. The new understanding of space represented an important 'conquest' since it not only became a change in the paradigm of the scientific field, but this notion also acquired a central position within the discussions around the avant-garde movements.[10] Furthermore, this new comprehension of space also became pivotal to the development of a critical understanding of the social space; a notion of space that displays a multidimensional nature and that is even able to embrace temporal dimensions and complex technological *agencements*[11]. The impact of this new, complex feature of space is represented by Foucault in the following passage:

> L'espace dans lequel nous vivons, par lequel nous sommes attirés hors de nous-mêmes, dans lequel se déroule précisément l'érosion de notre vie, de notre temps et de notre histoire. Cet espace qui nous ronge et nous ravine est en lui-même aussi un espace! Hétérogène. Autrement dit, nous ne vivons pas dans une sorte de vide, à l'intérieur duquel on pourrait situer des individus et des choses. Nous ne vivons pas à l'intérieur d'une vide qui se colorerait de différents chatoiements, nous vivons à l'intérieur d'un ensemble de relations qui définissent des emplacements irréductibles les un aux autres et absolument non superposables.[12]

As Foucault observes, life develops itself within a set (*ensemble*) of relationships and this *complexus* – in continuous transformation and recombination through processes of abstraction – is what is generally understood as space. In this view, space

---

8 Jean Dieudonné, *A history of Algebraic and Differential Topology 1900–1960* (Basel: Birkhäuser, 1989), 18.

9 About the notion of *complexus*, see Edgar Morin, *Introduction à la pensée complexe* (Paris: Points, 2014), 114.

10 See Henderson, *The Fourth Dimension and Non-Euclidean Geometry in Modern Art.* And Mario De Michelli, *Le avanguardie artistiche del Novecento* (Milano: Feltrinelli, 2014).

11 On this the notion of social space and its complexity see Henri Lefebvre, *La production de l'espace* (Paris: Economica, 1999).

12 Michel Foucault, "Des spaces autres," *Architecture, Mouvement Continuité* 5, (October 1984), 47.

does not represent a container, like under the Euclidean axioms, and it is essentially a set of relationships between flexible entities. Through this lens, as exemplified in Bartolini's oeuvre, space involves both forms of movements and forms of relationships. In fact, Bartolini's sculpture generates a continuum by establishing a series of relationships through which the artist manifests the mechanism that generates the space. In Bartolini's *Untitled Untitled,* space is the product of relationships between entities, between objects and subjects: relationships exclusively deriving from the presence of the invisible pill. The golden pill, if it exists, makes *presenza*[13], sets in motion the *agencement* of forms of movements and forms of processes that would embrace the subject. The latter, once reached by the process instilled by the pill's presence, immediately starts to dwell and, consequently, to experience the space of the sculpture.

The Method of postulation - The object of the system

During the second half of the nineteenth century – and from that point onwards – different disciplines, theories, and practices reached the same conclusion: space is a pure set of relationships and entities which generate space cannot be considered to be isolated entities *in* the space. A fundamental step towards arriving at that conclusion is, without a doubt, Bergson's hypothesis on the non-existence of isolated systems, which also represents the theoretical basis of his concepts of *devenir* and *durée*. According to Bergson, movement not only concerns the subject and its psychological experience, but it also involves the extension, which, under this logic, represents an incessant progression.[14] For Bergson, therefore, movement concerns everything and consequently it traverses all entities in the universe. Nevertheless, according to Bergson, through a process of *fabrication* the human mind (*l'intelligence humaine*) isolates and substitutes the *continuum* of reality with fixed images (*coupes immobiles*)[15]; a continuum emanated by a flexible object under continuous transformation. This is

13 The word '*presenza*' is used in accordance with what Ernesto de Martino attributed to the term, which is close to the heideggerian *dasein*. See, De Martino, *La fine del mondo. Contributo all'analisi delle apocalissi culturali* (Torino: Einaudi, 2019).

14 Herbert Wildon Carr, *Henri Bergson; The Philosophy of Change* (Lodon: T. Nelson & Sons, 1919), 14.

15 This phenomenon can be considered the phenomenon that directed Bergson's attention to the film camera and the way that technology produced the illusion of a fluid movement. In fact, this technology not only allowed him to better comprehend the processes of *devenir*, but also it figured the notion of duration as a sequence of past-present-future. On this subject, see, Gilles Deleuze, *Le bergsonisme* (Paris: PUF, 1966) and German A. Duarte, "Between logos and doxa: The Intelligence of a Machine," *Human and Social Sciences – De Gruyter*, vol. V, no. 1 (2016), 113–134.

to say, for Bergson the apparently static presence of the object contained *in* the space is the product of a mechanical view that *'fabricates'* a perception based on assembling parts of matter that have been isolated and that subsequently were inserted into an action (*autour de l'action*)[16]. The paradigm of *fabrication* generates a preordained system from which derives a series of preordained effects already contained in the cause. According to Bergson, this predetermined universe – which sees the object not as a force of progression but as a static presence – limits the possibility of conceiving what he calls *'organization'*, which, separate from *fabrication*, represents a way of conceiving both spaces and objects outside the mechanical and Euclidean views.[17] This conclusion represents a *'leitmotiv'* for diverse philosophical theories and artistic movements from the second half of the nineteenth century.

Delineated under different words and supported through different solid theoretical apparatuses, a series of contemporaneous concepts displays very close analogies with Bergson's ideas on the non-existence of isolated entities; a theory that, as noted above, is fundamentally based on the assumption that every single entity in the universe is traversed by a *continuum*. A convergent hypothesis could be considered Whitehead's conclusion on the phenomenon of *bifurcation*, which he identifies as the human tendency to divide thought from extension[18]. Different from Bergson's ideas of *fabrication*, Whitehead describes *bifurcation* as a human mistake through which the human mind 'divides' the object from a perceiving subject and, in so doing, ignores the *continuum*. Whitehead proposes a liberation of the human mind from *bifurcation* via *concrescence*, through which humankind could identify the associative character of the extension and could, therefore, identify the complexity of the association of entities.[19] Both theories display clear analogies and above all both represent a departure from the analysis of the subject as the center of the experience.[20] When Bergson asked himself "Qu'existe-t-il de la durée, en dehors de nous?"[21] he was not only concretizing the acknowledgment of the extension as a set of incessant processes, but was also, as in Whitehead's previously-mentioned instance, erecting an apparatus that would allow for conceiving the subject without using the traditional egological understanding of it. In other words, the figure of a

16 Henri Bergson, *L'evolution créatrice* (Paris: PUF, 1907), 93. This nature of the object and it role in the generation of the space can be also identified through Baudrillard's analysis. See, Jean Baudrillard, *Le système des objets*, (Paris: Gallimard, 1978), 38.

17 David Kreps, *Bergson, Complexity and Creative Emergence* (New York: Palgrave Macmillan, 2015), 56.

18 Alfred North Whitehead, *The Concept of Nature* (Cambridge, Cambridge University Press, 1964): 21.

19 Alfred North Whitehead, *Science and the Modern World* (New York: Pelican, 1948): 50–57.

20 Xavier Verley, "Whitehead et la subjetivité," *Les Études Philosophiques*, no. 4, Whitehead (Octobre-Décember 2002): 511–525.

21 Henri Bergson, *Essai sur les données de la conscience* (Paris: PUF, 1889): 170.

subject as an interconnected entity defined by momentary relations of togetherness with other open sets and open processes emerges. Furthermore, this apparatus also suggests that every entity pervades the *continuum*; the sets of mutations established by forces of relations that figure what we call 'space'.

However, the Euclidean understanding of the space at that point represented a limit to conceive such subject. In fact, the general understanding of space is derived from the Euclidean axiomatic: 'container of invariable objects'. Further, this understanding represents the very instrument through which humankind exerts an involuntary act of isolating elements, systems, and phenomena, and, by extension, conceives of the object through series of fixed states distributed in a duration (*durée*). Thus, the notion of space that derives from Euclid's axiomatic embodies a limit to understand forms of *concrescence* and forms of *organization*, and consequently the response to that limit could only come from the field of geometry. In the hands of Henri Poincaré, – who was a contemporary of both Bergson and Whitehead – Leibniz's theorization of *Analysis Situs* acquired an additional and decisive development. In fact, in the nineteenth century, the accomplishment of Leibniz's theory of a different space became, as remarked by Poincaré, an urgent human need[22]. Poincaré's analysis of situation, which characterizes the conceptual basis of modern topology[23], represented not only a fundamental tool for scientists to explain phenomena through abstractions enabled only by highly transformative spatial structures, but it also epitomized the instrument through which humankind could finally discover what is called 'hyperspace'; an instrument, as described by Poincaré, able to 'replace' human senses. In his words:

> Il faut qu'on arrive à le construire [l'Analysis Situs] complètement dans des espaces supérieurs; on aura alors un instrument qui permettre réellement de voir dans l'hyperespace et de suppléer à nos sens.[24]

By re-elaborating some major Leibnizian concepts regarding space, Poincaré's analysis of situation marks a violent rupture from the version of space established by the Greeks. In fact, Poincaré's theories decisively awarded space an amorphous nature shaped by infinite relationships between processes of objects.[25] Certainly, his

---

22 Henri Poincaré, *Science et méthode* (Paris: Flammarion, 1908): 40.

23 Note that Poincaré's work *Analysis Situs* is a research work of multiple volumes, the first of which was edited in 1892 in *Comptes-Rendus* and the last was completed by a paper from 1895 entitled "Analysis Situs." Then, the notion of Analysis Situs was definitively completed in a series of papers edited between 1899 and 1905, entitled *Compléments à L'Analysis Situs*.

24 Poincaré, *Science et méthode*, 40.

25 As described by Günzel, "Für die topologische Raumbeschreibung hilfreich sind dabei Relativierungen, welche von Seiten der Mathematik und Physik nach Newton hinsichtlich der Raumauffassung vorgenommen wurden: Raum wird im Zuge dessen nicht mehr als eine dreifach dimensionierte Entität oder formale Einheit gefasst, sondern anhand von Elemen-

theory signified the loss of space's imperative three dimensions, since the number of dimensions should respond to the necessity of a complex thought able to conceive space as the result of movements and changing forms. Like in Bergson's case – who found a human limitation in the concept of *fabrication* – or in Whitehead's notion of *bifurcation* – which also represented a human limitation – Poincaré found the materialization of this human weakness in the notion of *dimension*; an instinctive concept that, according to him, was somehow inherited from Greek knowledge and was subsequently 'implanted' in our childhoods.[26] Furthermore, instead of theorizing an invariable object, Poincaré proposed a series of concepts that hypothesized an object determined by processes – by relationships and variability. In fact, by replacing Euclid's *notiones communes* with Leibniz's theorization of the analysis situs, one can find notions such as 'nearness', 'congruence', 'homogeneity', 'variability', 'resemblance', and 'similarity' through which emerges the idea that space is just a *situs* determined by a series of relationships between points, which are in continuous transformation.[27] Following these Leibniz theorizations, Poincaré proposed a principle of transformation of elements, as well as the disappearance of both coordinates in space and the principle of the invariability of the object.[28]

The space theorized by Poincarré is basically developed around the flexible nature of the object, whose continuous transformation shapes a series of relationships. Converging with Hermann Grassmann's method of postulation – a method that derives from Grassmann's understanding of geometry as a system that assigns meaning to objects – Poincaré theorized a space constructed through a series of relationships between objects that are in continuous transformation, but whose transformation does not change the object's nature. In other words, within this theory, regardless of both the shape and the series of transformations that the object under-

---

ten beschreiben, die relational zueinander bestimmt werden. – Mit anderen Worten: An die Stelle des Ausdehnungsaprioris tritt eine Strukturdarstellung von Raum." Stephan Günzel, "Raum – Topographie – Topologie" in *Topologie. Zur Raumbeschreibung in der Kultur- und Medienwissenschaften*, ed. Stephan Günzel (Bielefeld: transcript, 2007), 17.

26 Poincaré, *Science et méthode*, 121.

27 In this regard, it would be possible to see Riemann's theories as the *consecutio* of Leibniz thought. By theorizing surfaces that vary their curvature, by hypothesizing irregular shapes, and by challenging Euclid's principle of invariability, Riemann hypothesized that movement implies change in objects' shapes and properties. In Riemann's will to develop a new geometrical space one can identify the necessity to conceive a new nature of the object, a flexible object, which is subjected to the processes of postulation. On the idea of movement as a generator of spaces in the topologic dimension, see Jean Dieudonné, "Une brève histoire de la topologie" in *Development of Mathematics 1900–1950*, ed. Jean-Paul Pier (Basel: Birkhäuser, 1994), 37.

28 Marie-Luise Heuser, "Die Anfänge der Topologie n Mathematik und Naturphilosophie," in Topologie. *Zur Raumbeschriebung in der Kultur – und Medienwissenschaften*, ed. Stephan Günzel (Bielefeld: transcript, 2007), 118.

goes, the object's proprieties remain unchanged. Being that geometry is a purely semantic force, within the field of topology objects can be deformed through motion or inner processes and they can still be considered equivalent: let's say the object 'means' or 'represents' the very same 'signification' even after having undergone radical changes in form and matter.[29]

As remarked by Graßmann in his *Die Ausdehungslehre von 1844*, within the field of geometry the object itself is completely irrelevant; instead, what is important is the meaning granted to it.[30] Yet, in his view, the force that grants meaning to the object is not determined by a kind of formalist structure that satisfies the generation of meaning within the relationship of two different objects *in* space. In Graßmann's theory, the object is determined by its positioning (*Setzen*) in the *complexus*, by its bonding (*Verknüpfen*) with other flexible entities generating the space, and, above all, the object is determined by a force of generation (*Erzeugen*) of processes which grants the object features of the *continuum*. In the multidimensional continuous form theorized by Graßmann, objects do not represent fixed entities that determine a state and that can enter into a univocal relation; rather, their existence is in fact determined by their bonding, position, and continuous generation. This new conception of the object allows for theorizing forms of *concresence* instead of univocal relationships between objects present *in* the space. To follow a Merleau-Ponty's formula through which he described the presence of the subject in the world, the same could be said of the object conceived by Graßmann and by the modern topology: L'objet est au monde, et non pas seulement dans le monde.[31]

To conceive the object *in* space (as the subject *dans le monde*) is indeed to construct isolated systems to and through them to build serialized states. Consequently, this approach would bring our analysis to miss not only the object's nature – its flexible nature as determined by series of processes in becoming – but also the way its nature produces the space by creating it through forces of *concrescence*. It is important to note that by reformulating Euclid's *notions communes* one was indeed establishing a new form of postulation, one that reveals that the object is subjected to diverse changes and that it does not represent a state, but a process. This is to say, the status of the object was no longer a status defined by the relationship between form-matter, but by a temporal modulation that implies continuous variations of both matter

29 This object's nature within topology was certainly popularized through the phenomenon of homeomorphism.

30 Hermann Graßmann, *Die Ausdehnungslehre von 1844: oder Die Lineale Ausdehnungslehre, ein neur Zweig der Mathematick* (Leipzig: Wigand, 1878).

31 Merleau-Ponty's original sentences is refering to the subject, and he posits that as subjects "(...) nous sommes au monde, et non pas seulement dans le monde." ("(...) we belong to the world, we are not just in the world". My translation) Maurice Merleau-Ponty, *Phénoménologie de la perception* (Paris: Gallimard, 1945), 281.

and form.[32] At the same time, this new form of postulation reveals a different nature of the subject which becomes, as defined by Deleuze, *a point of view on a site*.[33] This is to say, the subject is no more than a point of view on a set of variations.[34] Nevertheless, it does not mean that the point of view varies with the subject; instead, it is that a possible subject grasps a variation, a passage from form to form (metamorphosis), or a subject that grants form to the amorphous (anamorphism).[35]

Figuring the topologic condition

The subject experiencing Bartolini's sculpture dwells in the space; it is embraced by the set of relationships established by means of the pill's *presenza*, the latter, invisible, but developing its existence through the use of an old man's body. Yet, in Bartolini's oeuvre, the object generating the *complexus* could be seen as the static and immutable object *par excellence*: a solid golden pill, one centimeter in diameter and a half-centimeter in length. In Bartolini's artwork, this solid object, which in its form personifies the invariability, unveils the semiotic forces that traverse and form the object, from which derives the space. *Untitled Untitled* is basically a sculpture that lays bare the *in becoming* essence of the object and the way the object's *devenir* pervades the continuum and grants spatial features to it. Bartolini highlights it through a remarkable strategy of unveiling the postulation process that generates the notion of the invariability of the object; i.e. that constructs from a *continuum* a static and immobile entity *in* space. The pill, in fact, after being subtracted from the physical place, becomes a purely semiotic construction via archetypical forces triggered by the supposed material of the object (gold) as well as by its hypothetical shape (pill). As already noted, the apparent material and the shape of the object allude to the Taoist name of the absolute, which adds an ulterior semiotic dimension to the oeuvre. If analyzed from the point of view of western philosophy, the notion of the absolute triggered by the pill in Bartolini's work would open the notion of 'complete independence' of the pill. This notion, in my opinion, would be reinforced by the hypothesis of the extraterrestrial origin of the gold. Further, the notion of the absolute, which on the one hand describes a completely independent entity, alien to all synergies of the imperfect systems, on the other hand implies the existence of a series of dependent entities – the dependence of which is directly linked to the presence of the pill. As one can note in

32 This was described by Deleuze as the essence of the object of the Baroque, but above all, Deleuze describes in that way the status of the object in our digital technological context. See Gilles Deleuze, *Le Pli. Leibniz et le Baroque* (Paris: Minuit, 1988), 26.

33 On this subject, see Gilles Deleuze, *Différence et repetition* (Paris: PUF, 1968), 96. And Deleuze, *Le Pli*, 27.

34 *Ibidem*.

35 Deleuze, *Le Pli*, 50.

Bartolini's work, the space is fully dependent on the pill's presence, but its presence is at the same time completely independent, so independent that it is even invisible. The result of this semiotic force is that the subject perceives the pill as a clear presence *in* the space, but it is a purely generative force that produces relationships.

Considering the work of Rosalind Krauss, a first analysis would suggest that the pill's invisibility responds to a tendency of sculpture to pursue a kind of ontological absence.[36] Through this phenomenon, Krauss intended to identify some subtracting forces of opposition between *no-landscape* and *no-architecture* in order to better comprehend the field of intervention in which the sculpture develops during the second half of the last century. However, Krauss' examples tend to transfer the object's absence to other media, thus making the object present via its media representation. There might be a need to document the ungraspable object, but the fact is that the absence identified by Krauss opened an obliged detour to the use of representative media; a detour that coerces the object's absence to deal with the realm of representation. By noticing this phenomenon, Krauss identified a new relationship between the sculpture and the media universe. Just to mention one example, in her essay she dealt with Robert Smithson's *Spiral Jetty* (1970), the construction of which was documented in a 32-minute color film.[37]

This media detour was already seen as a need, but was pushed further to be a need that brought any expression of the artistic practice to face an intermedia approach. It was in the same decade that Dick Higgins published his groundbreaking work, *Statement on Intermedia* (1966). In this text, Higgins claims that there is an urgent need to place artistic expression within a "dialectic between the media" and that "A composer is a dead man unless he composes for all the media and for his world."[38] The intermedia behavior presented by Higgins could be seen as the need to grasp the ungraspable objet; the illusion to grasp its perpetual process. In fact, the need to regain an object already dissolved in its process generated an artistic approach aware of the media universe and its whole gamut of mechanisms of representation. Thus, this need also encouraged to establish relationships between media. In other words, it seems that the need to document the object through any media at our disposal responded to the cognitive necessity of 'catching' the object and constructing it

36 Rosalind Krauss, "Sculpture in the Expanded Field," October, Vol. 8, (Spring 1979), 36.

37 Also consider *Partialy Burried Woodshed* (1970), another of Robert Smithson's artwork mentioned in Krauss' essay. Nevertheless, in this case, the artist turns his attention to the entropy, a word able to describe the new nature of the object analyzed in this short essay since its etymology brings us to the semantic sphere of 'forces of transformation' or 'transformational contents'. It would also be imperative to recall Joseph Kosuth's *One and Three Chairs* (1965), former piece that offers some insights into the complexity granted to the object and its relationship with realm of representation.

38 Dick Higgins, "Statement on Intermedia," *Dé-coll/age* (Décollage), n.6, Frankfurt, Typors Verlag – New York, Something Else Press, July 1967.

via *coupes immobiles*: states determined by a well-defined relationship between matter and form. As follows, the intermedia approach, as well as the need to document the ontological absence of the object, might respond to the human need to *bifurcate* or *fabricate* the object; a human need to construct an isolated and invariable object *in* a well precise *dimension*. Nevertheless, a sort of paradox emerges since the intermedia approach was a direct product of a precise technological context, which was mainly shaped by the introduction and popularization of video technology. It is important to remember that video-electronic technology is basically a technology that 'dissolves' the object into an electrical *continuum*. In fact, this technology represents a non-representative medium since it does not establish the traditional relationship with the existing object, as was imposed by the photochemical process of photographic technology.[39] In fact, the very same nature of the video-electronic medium transformed the optical input, produced by the object, into an electrical signal – into a variation, a frequency, a process. As remarked by Lorenz Engells, video is just time that becomes image; it is a *continuum*. Thus, he posited that this technology presents objects that 'just-cannot-continue-to-exist' (*nicht-einfach-vorhanden-bleiben-können*), they are processes in becoming.[40]

Bartolini's *Untitled Untitled* does not belong to the development identified by Krauss with the ontological absence of the object. As remarked above, this phenomenon was mainly accompanied by a new regard towards the use of media through which the artist could supplant the object's absence in the exhibition space. It is at that point that the main difference between Krauss' identification and Bartolini's piece appears. In fact, the golden pill was never (at least for the moment) documented, represented, or visualized in any medium currently at our disposal. Nobody –except, of course, for the artist and the old man carrying the pill in his fist- has ever seen the object. Nobody has seen a representation of it, neither a pictorial representation nor a photographic image. Curiously, by fully subtracting the pill from any form of presence, from any document or any mechanism of representation, its complete absence transforms the pill into an absolute presence from which it derives the set of relationships (the space) that the subject experiences in the exhibition. Illustrating the way through which a purely semiotic process becomes an isolated an invariable state (an object), Bartolini's artwork allows the subject in the exhibition space to experience an invisible *presenza* as a concrete object, a well-defined *ob-iectum*, a *Gegenstand* perceived by the subject as different from himself.

---

39 See, Edmond Couchot, *Des images, du temps et des machines dans les arts et la communication*, (Paris: Actes Sud, 2007).

40 Lorenz Engell, "Fernsehen mit Gilles Deleuze," in *Der Film bei Deleuze / Le cinéma selon Deleuze*, eds. Oliver Fahle and Lorenz Engell, (Weimar: Verlag der Bauhaus-Universität Weimar and Presses de la Sorbonne Nouvelle, 1999), 470.

In *Untitled Untitled*, the pill is an entity that becomes an object through its absence. By means of archetypical figures and semiotic mechanisms, the pill *fabricates* and brings the object into existence. Furthermore, as one can see, the existence of the pill is fully dependent on the rupture it generates with the subject, i.e. on the *bifurcation* between the object and the perceiving-subject. Once the rupture is accomplished, the object appears. Yet, the rupture is founded on the generation of a static and invariable object, a presence *in* a three-dimensional space. In other words, the rupture is this precise moment – the *movimentum* – which characterizes the continuum of the whole, becomes *momentum*, becomes instant, a *coupe immobile* that gives shape to the present moment and that shapes a duration. At that point, the object, by becoming invariable form-matter, differentiates itself (bifurcates itself) form the perceiving-subject. Nevertheless, the sculpture manifests this complex process that determines our perception of reality in a purely geometric construction. It is the construction of a three-dimensional space, a container in which the subject deploys its cognition. That is the reason why Poincaré posited that the development of topology would also represent the development of an instrument able to replace human senses.[41]

Untitled Untitled by Bartolini is an artwork that encapsulates the way in which our comprehension of space has changed during the last century. By sculpting a solid criticism on Kant's understanding of space as a pure form of sensitivity, Bartolini's *Untitled Untitled* generates some important insights on the flexible nature of the object and, above all, supports the hypothesis that the topological space – the space seen as a set of relationships – is no more than the product of the object's dynamics. This is to say, space is the direct product of the object's flexibility and its procedural character.

Object + Subject = Body. An Equation for a non-Euclidean dimension (*peractio*)

The question of the subject carrying the pill in his close fist still remains. Eclipsed by the pill's *presenza*, as well as by the creation of the space experienced by the audience, this old man passes into the background. Yet, as one can see, he represents a crucial element of the sculpture. I would like to propose a last remark on the figure of the old man as a way to conclude this short essay, since I also considered his figure as conclusive. I personally ignore the reason why the artist always and exclusively requires an old man to exert this task. As mentioned above in the *praeludium*, it must always be an old man and he can never take the pill in his pocket, always in his closed fist. As one can imagine, for the audience this old man is nothing more than an element

41 Poincaré, *Science et méthode*, 40.

witnessing the pill's presence. This is to say, the old man is the initiator element that sets the object's process in motion; the initiator element for the semiotic forces that produce the object and subsequently the space, the latter of which is experienced by the audience. As one can see, the old man is not a subject experiencing the space generated by the pill nor is he an object part of the series of relationships of the *complexus*. I would suggest that the old man is just a body.

By involving the figure of the old man, Bartolini brought into play a conclusive corporeal dimension. In fact, once the artwork unveils the mechanism through which the rupture of object-subject occurs, and unveils the way our cognition generates a static and invariable object, Bartolini creates the place in which all of these complex semantic forces happen: the body. By doing so, Bartolini not only provided a figure for the topologic condition, but also, by encapsulating the phenomenological lesson, created a sculpture that is a clear statement about the body as a sensitive space wherein both object and subject meet[42]. Following this framework, Bartolini's *Untitled Untitled* would be a statement on the topologic character of the phenomenological approach. Furthermore, this sculpture would offer some solid insights on sensitivity, a fundamental part of human intelligence. In my opinion, this would be the undertone that places Bartolini's sculpture in the current social debate around the illusory exclusion of the body as the center of the sensitive experience. This is to say, if placed in the middle of the social debate around the illusory and hypothetical migration of the being into another body, dispositive or hardware, this sculpture would offer a clear figure that generates some doubts about that transhuman hypothesis. In fact, by encapsulating the millenarian process that brought about the development of the non-Euclidean geometries – and by giving a clear figure on the role played by the object in the development of a topological space that extends the phenomenological conception which proclaims the body as the exclusive place wherein the sensitive encounter between object and subject occurs – this sculpture would create a fundamental argument that the transhuman hypothesis ignores.

This might also be the reason why the object in the sculpture does not cover its absence by entering into the realm of representation. To open the possibility of re-presenting – or, presenting the object again via a technologically-mediated process – would generate the false and illusory idea of being in the condition of relating such complex experiences through a technological process. To place the object into another mechanism of creation of meaning, into another method of postulations, and above all, to eliminate the body from the unique equation that allows a sensitive encounter between object and subject would reinforce the transhuman hypothesis. Instead, by radically avoiding the media detour, this art piece can fully accomplish its hypothesis, which is grounded on the topological approach towards the

42 On this understanding of the body, see, Roberto Esposito, *Le persone e le cose* (Torino: Einaudi, 2014).

phenomenological lesson, which states that the body is the space in which object and subject meet. Further, this lesson also allows us to see the body as a space traversed by the immanent *continuum,* and thus as a space subjected to forces of concrescence, which one describes as experience.

Figure 1: Massimo Bartolini, Untitled (1993). Courtesy of the Artist.

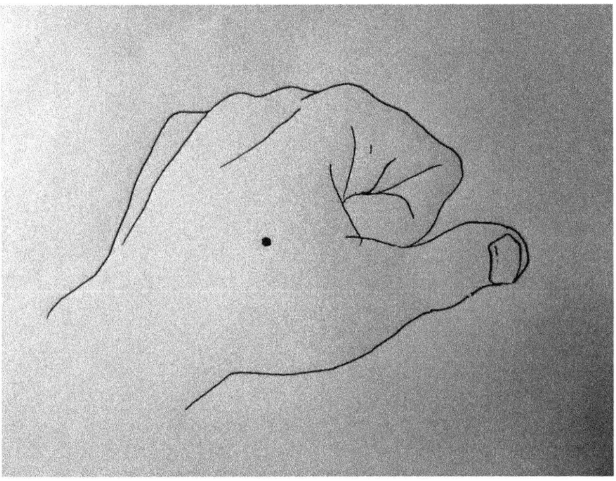

The Lure of Absence: Can there be Process without Artists?

Heidi C. Gearhart

Artistic process is an elusive thing. Most often when viewers engage with artworks they do so in the galleries of museums, wherein objects are presented as cultural artefacts, made in the recent or distant past. The labels that accompany them usually indicate the artist, if known, a title, and a date; they also might indicate the materials that comprise the work, or, in cases when the artist is unknown, perhaps a region or country of origin. They rarely, however, describe the process by which raw matter was transformed into the object the viewer encounters. The changing of materials from one state to another is often assumed to be something of the past, of a time before the object was "finished", before it reached the state in which, one imagines, it was intended to be seen. In the following pages, I wish to suggest that this idea of process coming to an end does not always apply, and that in the Middle Ages in particular the object was understood as a site of continuous potential.

In the last fifty years, artists have sought to put process on display, in part by exposing the making of art in the gallery through actions, performance, mutability, or even decay. The ephemerality of these works brings problems of temporality to the fore. A performance, for example, might only occur in a brief moment, to be known after the fact solely through memory, photographs, or documentation. In contrast, the work itself might be in flux, decaying or changing over time. The former reveals the gaps between a present *now* and a past *then*, and the variability of interpretation; the latter reveals the instability of the object itself. The 2010 retrospective exhibition, *Marina Abramović: The Artist is Present*, displayed in the Museum of Modern Art, New York, addressed this transitory nature of performance, as it sought to review the career of the artist, Marina Abramović, by presenting digitally re-mastered films of her past performances and displaying the objects used in those works. Yet the highlight of the exhibition was Abramović herself: for the duration of the exhibition, Abramović sat in a chair in the gallery, across from an empty chair in which viewers could sit. As Abramović explained, the piece was about bodily presence and bodily encounters, but also involved viewers in an ongoing creation of art.[1] It made process present.

Figure 1: Marina Abramović, The Artist is Present, 2010, Museum of Modern Art, New York, 9 March – 31 May 2010. Photo: Andrew Russeth. Creative Commons.

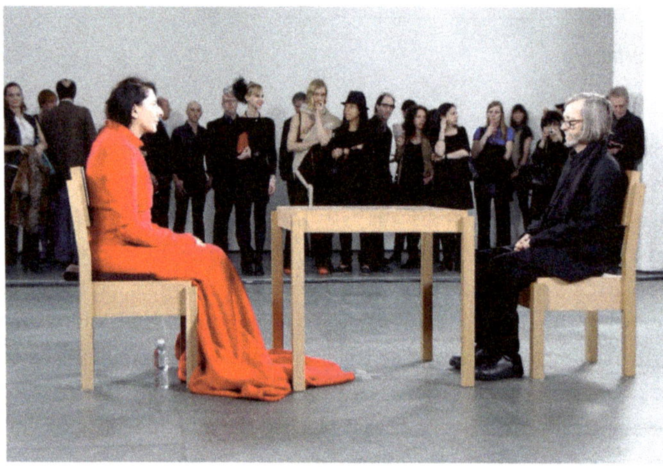

Interestingly, in its attempts to retrospectively display Abramović's body of work, the exhibition revealed the problems of displaying an art form which is durational and dependent on presence. As Amelia Jones pointed out, through the photographs, films, and object remnants of Abramović's performances, the MoMA exhibition "reveals the dependence of any concept of presence on … documentation."[2] Such documentation even extended to the current moment, creating a spectacle of Abramović's presence, as Jones noted, because photographs of visitors sitting across from the artist were posted on the museum's website; "the event, the performance, by combining materiality and durationality (its enacting of the body as always already escaping into the past) points to the fact that there is no 'presence' as such."[3]

1 "Marina Abramović: The Artist Speaks," *Inside/Out: a MoMA/PS1 Blog*, June 3, 2010, https://www.moma.org/explore/inside_out/2010/06/03/marina-abramovic-the-artist-speaks/ Accessed 30 March, 2020.

2 Amelia Jones, "'The Artist Is Present': Artistic Re-enactments and the Impossibility of Presence," *TDR: The Drama Review* 55 / 1 (2011): 16–45, at 18. See also Jones, "'Presence' in Absentia: Experiencing Performance as Documentation," *Art Journal* 56, no. 4 (1997): 11–18.

3 Jones, "'The Artist Is Present'," 16–45, at 18.

Abramović's retrospective highlights the challenges of thinking about process as a quality of a work of art. Like 'presence', the term 'process' is also ambiguous. Even if the production of a work of art is put into practice in front of the viewer – as a piece of performance seeks to do – it is nevertheless always reaching into the past. As Derrida explains, "we see very quickly then that the presence of the perceived present is able to appear as such only insofar as it is in *continuous composition* with a non-presence and a non-perception, namely, primary memory and primary anticipation (retention and protention)."[4] Records, photographs, descriptions, or narratives of process may present themselves as evidence, but they also belong to their own systems of signification, and bear the mark of yet another process of gathering, curating, and editing.[5] Language-based records, for example, must transpose a bodily experience into the abstraction of words, and are then arranged to suit a linguistic organizational system – an alphabetical file, perhaps – that may distort the topic at hand. As Michael Baxandall put it, "Any language... is a conspiracy against experience in the sense of being a collective attempt to simplify and arrange experience into manageable parcels."[6] Thus we often think of process, like performance, as something grasped retrospectively; a visual or linguistic account of an event that occurred in the past. Physical traces, like a thumbprint or toolmark, for example, serve these narratives, but is there a way to consider process as a part of the work itself? In the following pages I take a historical approach to the problem of process, and consider how, in the medieval era, process was never finished. Objects were continually amended, changed, or adjusted; therefore, their materiality can be regarded as continually in flux.

Before we begin, we must consider the parameters at work in contemporary accounts of process. Often, descriptions of procedure put the artist first – the artist is assumed to be the agent who transforms the material. For example, in the first weeks of Abramović's "Present" piece, a table sat between her and the other chair. Partway through the exhibition, it was removed in order to better facilitate connections between the two persons. As she recalled this experience in an interview with MoMA, Abramović said, "I decided to remove the table and when I removed the table

---

4 Jacques Derrida, "The Sign and the Blink of an Eye," *Voice and Phenomenon: Introduction to the Problem of the Sign in Husserl's Phenomenology*, trans. Leonard Lawlor (Evanston: Northwestern University Press, 2011), 55. See also Jones, "'The Artist is Present'," 17 and note 4.

5 For the traces of events as representations see Jones, "'The Artist is Present'," 21 and Jacques Derrida, *Speech and Phenomena and Other Essays on Husserl's Theory of Signs*, trans. David B. Allison (Evanston: Northwestern University Press, 1973), 64–65; and Robin Kelsey, *Archive Style: Photographs & Illustrations for U.S. Surveys, 1850–1890* (Berkeley: University of California Press, 2007).

6 Michael Baxandall, *Giotto and the Orators: Humanist Observers of Painting in Italy and the Discovery of Pictorial Composition* (Oxford: Oxford University Press, 1971), 44.

then the piece started having sense to me. I know now that I'm really interested more and more in immaterial art, that removing the table is just this direct connection."[7] The table, then, was thought to hinder the performance of the work – by adding too much distance – but the agent of change in the narrative is Abramović herself. The table was the passive prop. If we look more closely, however, we begin to see that the table too had agency – it was large, hard, and formed a barrier between people. It was like a being itself and thus was able to hinder the connection between two persons. Though it might appear to be static, non-descript furniture, the table, in fact, played a significant role in the piece, hindering or enabling the connections between persons. To consider this as the proper force of the table is to take up the challenge set by Fernando Domínguez Rubio to pursue "an approach that takes seriously the seemingly banal fact that things are constantly falling out of place... that takes temporality, fragility, and change as the starting points of our enquiry."[8] In other words, the table in Abramović's performance throws into question the assumption that it was only the people – Abramović and her visitors – who had agency in the work.

In order to decenter the role of the artist with regards to process, we might look to current thinking about materiality. Tim Ingold, for instance, argues that we shift focus from human acting upon material to consider how materials operate in the world:

> Like all other creatures, human beings do not exist on the 'other side' of materiality but swim in an ocean of materials. Once we acknowledge our immersion, what this ocean reveals to us is not the bland homogeneity of different shades of matter but a flux in which materials of the most diverse kinds – through processes of admixture and distillation, of coagulation and dispersal, and of evaporation and precipitation – undergo continual generation and transformation. The forms of things, far from having been imposed from without upon inert substrate, arise and are borne along – as indeed we are too – within this current of materials.[9]

Ingold suggests we consider how materials and humans are in the same "ocean", continually changing and transforming each other through various processes. By examining how process might be ongoing regardless of the artist or other human agent, I hope to show how objects might be understood as the composite of a series of ongoing interactions and resistances between materials, tools, and human agents. Like the performance, which laid bare the forces of artist, visitor, table, and space, so too the object might be understood as if an exuberant amalgam of the

7 Marina Abramović: The Artist Speaks," *Inside/Out*; and Jones, "'The Artist is Present'," 17.

8 Fernando Domíguez Rubio, "On the Discrepancy Between Objects and Things: An Ecological Approach," *Journal of Material Culture* 21 / 1 (2016), 59–86, at 60.

9 Tim Ingold, "Materials against Materiality," *Archaeological Dialogues* 14 / 1, (2007): 1–16, at 7.

traces of its experiences. A group of medieval manuscripts, which bear evidence of multiple interactions, demonstrate this point.

The medieval era left few traces of its artists. It was long assumed that this absence of named artists was regrettable and signaled some lack of confidence in art-making; thus scholars sought to identify artists from the Middle Ages, collecting inscriptions and delving deep into archival sources. In 1857, for example, Jacques-Remy-Antoine Téxier (1813–1859), published the *Dictionnaire d'orfévrerie, de gravure et de ciselure chrétiennes*, which gathered names of artists, alongside definitions of objects and techniques for goldsmiths' work.[10] Since then, artists have remained a topic of interest: in 2009 Anton Legner, a great force in the study of German medieval art, published a large tome which collected images of artists from the Carolingian era to the age of Dürer, arranged according to such themes as "Donation und Devotion," and "Personal Presence."[11] Yet I suggest that we see this absence of artists not as a lacuna to be filled, or as a handicap to be overcome or, at best, ignored; instead, let us consider it as an opening towards different ways of thinking about art-making. In the high Middle Ages the artist's labor was but one part of a much larger spectrum of activities that led to the production of an object.[12] So too, for medieval audiences, the mutability of an object – the tendency of its materials to decay or change over time, or the ways in which materials might resist an agent's intervention or invite later interventions – was accepted as an essential aspect of the object itself. Making – and viewing and reading – made space for material's changeability; it was often visible, sometimes even celebrated. As long as the object lived in the world, process didn't come to an end. Understanding process and material from this point of view, we might reconsider how we read objects that are otherwise seen as passive props, like Ambramović's table.

10 Jacques-Remy-Antoine Téxier, *Dictionnaire d'orfévrerie, de gravure et de ciselure chrétiennes* (Paris: J.-P. Migne, 1857); for a short biography of Téxier himself and his concern for archaeology and music, see most recently Jane Alden, *Songs, Scribes, and Society: the History and Reception of the Loire Valley Chansonniers* (Oxford: Oxford University Press, 2010), 23–26.

11 Anton Legner, *Der Artife: Künstler im Mittelalter und ihre Selbstdarstellung: eine illustrierte Anthologie* (Cologne: Greven, 2009).

12 See especially Therese Martin, "Exceptions and assumptions: women in medieval art history," *Reassessing the Roles of Women as 'Makers' of Medieval Art and Architecture*, ed. Therese Martin, (Leiden: Brill, 2012), 1–33; and Therese Martin, "The margin to act: a framework of investigation for women's (and men's) medieval art-making," *Journal of Medieval History* 42 / 1 (2016) 1–25. For more technical studies of workshop practice see Jonathan J. G. Alexander, *Medieval Illuminators and their Methods of Work* (New Haven: Yale University Press, 1992).

Persistent Materials

A manuscript containing a collection of liturgical works, now bound together and preserved at Saint Gall, contains a drawing of a man peering into a tube, which leads to a large hole in the middle of the manuscript (Figure 2).[13]

Figure 2: Composite manuscript with liturgical works. Abbey of St. Gall, c. 1000, 245 x 175 mm. Saint Gall, Stiftsbibliothek Cod. Sang. 18, p. 43. Creative Commons.

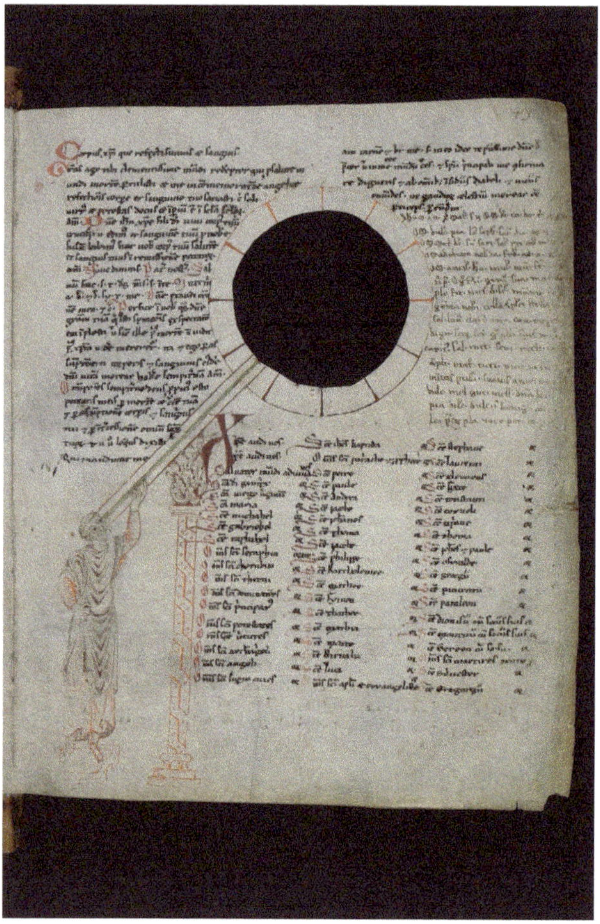

13 St. Gall, Stiftsbibliothek Cod. Sang. 18, p. 43.

The drawing dates back to around the turn of the millennium, and the circular hole, divided into twelve parts, may once have contained an image of an astronomical clock.[14] Sometime in the 15th century, the text that once surrounded the image was scraped off in order to make room for a new text: litanies and prayers for local saints. The large black hole, meanwhile, must have been cut, or at least enlarged, at yet a later date, for on the reverse side of the page the cutting has eliminated lines of the 15th-century text.

The page reveals the natural qualities of parchment and the traces of its many interactions with human hands. The large black hole, with its jagged edges and imperfect proportions, attests to the awkward task of cutting a circle out from a bound page, and to the resistance of the parchment itself. Made from animal skin, often of sheep or cow, parchment would be soaked in a lime solution, stretched, scraped, and polished before being cut to form bifolia. The two sides of the page thus correspond to the two sides of the skin, usually referred to as the skin side and the hair side. The former is often of a lighter colour, with a smoother appearance, while the latter might retain the slightly spotted appearance left by hair follicles. In our manuscript, the drawing has been placed on the skin side, and the page has evidently been well-thumbed, for dirt has accumulated on the edge of the textured surface of the verso, revealing the hair follicles more clearly. For example, on the lower left side of the page, faint white lines appear across the drawing of the figure, which lead to pin pricks along the right side of the margin, testimony to the malleability and thickness of the folio when it was inscribed with lines to rule the page. Also, ghostly images of letters emerge at the bottom of the page, a clue to us, as later readers, that another text once filled the space, as if a witness to the words that were there before, and to the ink that cannot be scraped from the skin.

The page, then, reveals several instances in which the makers of the manuscript, or its later readers, interacted with the parchment of the page itself. These actions happened over time, as evidenced by the change in script, and were likely done by different agents. The page becomes an aggregate of the traces of interactions between parchment, agent(s), and knife or pen, and it is a testimonial to later readers' continued acceptance of the vestiges of those occurrences and willingness to work with them. It is a palimpsest – carrying and consisting of the cumulative, continuing, effects of multiple events. The page is not solely the recipient of interactions but is also agent of them. In what Bernard Cerquiglini has termed a "joyful excess," medieval works "copied by hand, manipulated, always open and as good as unfinished,

14 Anton von Euw, *Die St. Galler Buchkunst vom 8. bis zum Ende des 11. Jahrhunderts*, Band I: Textband, St. Gallen 2008 (Monasterium Sancti Galli, Bd. 3), S. 502–503, Nr. 144. Joachim Wiesenbach, "Der Mönch mit dem Sehrohr. Die Bedeutung der Miniatur Codex Sangallensis 18" *Schweizerische Zeitschrift für Geschichte* 44 (1994): 367–388.

invited intervention, annotation, and commentary."[15] Cerquiglini's concept focused largely on variation in written texts, but I argue that the cut, scraped, and dirtied parchment of the page suggests that this excess extends to the material aspect of the object as well.[16]

Readers would have likely seen holes in manuscripts many times before. Holes – albeit smaller ones – often appear in manuscripts, and indeed, are the traces of the processes of its production. The process of stretching, scraping, and polishing animal skin in order to transform it into a thin, smooth surface for writing was laborious, and parchment thickness and quality can vary greatly. Some manuscripts contain very fine delicate pages that feel almost like modern paper, while others have thick pages that become stiff with age. During this stretching and scraping process, holes can appear in the skin. The holes might emerge from uneven scraping or they might be a flaw in the original skin. As the skin is strained, a small hole might become larger, just as a hole might emerge in a pizza dough as it is rolled out. Such holes are not uncommon in manuscripts, and more importantly, as demonstrated with the hole cut into in St. Gall, Cod. Sang. 18, they were not considered problematic. Sometimes they were ignored: a manuscript copied in Aquitaine in the first half of the 12th century, for example, containing the psalter along with other litanies, hymns, and a translation of the Gospel of St. John into Occitan, has a page with a hole in the text, but the scribe seems to have thought nothing of it, for he continued writing around the gap. The rubricator however, then circled the hole in red, as if to call attention to it, or perhaps to allay confusion about which words belonged where (Figure 3).[17]

15 Bernard Cerquiglini, *In Praise of the Variant: A Critical History of Philology* (Baltimore: Johns Hopkins University Press, 1999), 34.

16 This might also be considered what Gilles Deleuze and Félix Gutarri term an "agencement," often translated as "assemblage." Deleuze and Gutarri, *A Thousand Plateaus*, trans. Brian Massumi (Minneapolis: University of Minnesota Press, 1987); for the problems of translating agencement, see also John Phillips, "Agencement/Assemblage," *Theory, Culture & Society* 23 / 2–3 (May 2006): 108–109.

17 London, British Library Harley MS 2928, fol. 193r.

Figure 3: Psalter, Southern France (Aquitaine), first half of the twelfth century, 160 x 90 mm. London, British Library Harley MS 2928, fol. 193r.

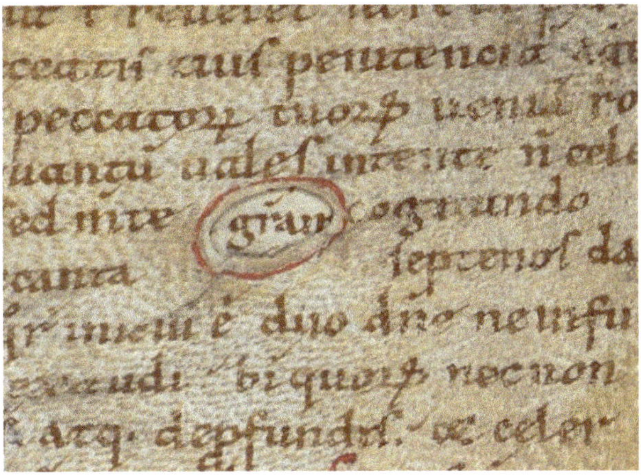

In other cases they were decorated or lovingly repaired or incorporated into the text itself. A manuscript of Isidore of Seville's *De natura rerum*, for example, copied in the early ninth century for the emperor, Otto III, and later given by Henry II to the monastery at Bamberg, contains a folio with quite a large hole in it; yet the scribe has written the text around the hole and he may well have also arranged the image on the prior folio so that it would peep through the hole and fill the space (Figure 4).[18]

18 Bamberg, Staatsbibliothek Msc. Nat.1, fol. 26v. It is likely that the scribe would have copied the folia before the gathering was assembled, thus we cannot say for certain that the placement of the animal on the preceding folio was planned. It also follows the pattern set by other initials in the manuscript. Nonetheless, faint ink lines on the folio 25v marking the space by the hole may suggest that the drawing was planned around the hole. See Erik Kwakkel, "The Skinny on Bad Parchment," *Medieval Books blog*, October 24, 2014: https://medievalbooks.nl/2014/10/24/feeling-good-about-bad-skin/ accessed 6 March, 2020; and https://erikkwakkel.tumblr.com/post/101115772496/parchment-face-heres-something-special-last, accessed 6 March 2020.

Figure 4: The shells impressions in the cement of the Unite d'habitation by Le Corbusier, in Marseille, 1947–1952, foto by Luca Trevisani, Courtesy of the artist.

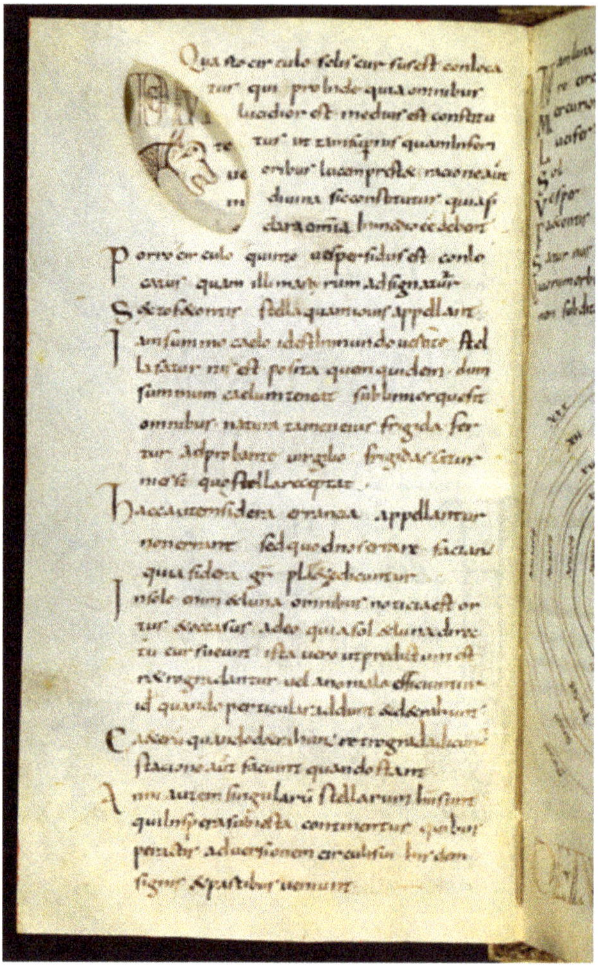

Another example is provided by a manuscript copied in Winchester, England, in the late ninth or early tenth century, which contains a hole that the scribe transformed into an animal, using the hole as the body and adding a head (Figure 5a, 5b).[19]

19 London, British Library Add. MS 47967, fol. 62v. See https://blogs.bl.uk/digitised-manuscripts/2018/03/if-youve-got-it-flaw-nt-it.html

Figure 5a: Orosius, Historia adversus paganos, Winchester, late 9th or early 10th century, 295 x 205 mm. London, British Library Add. MS 47967, fol. 62v.

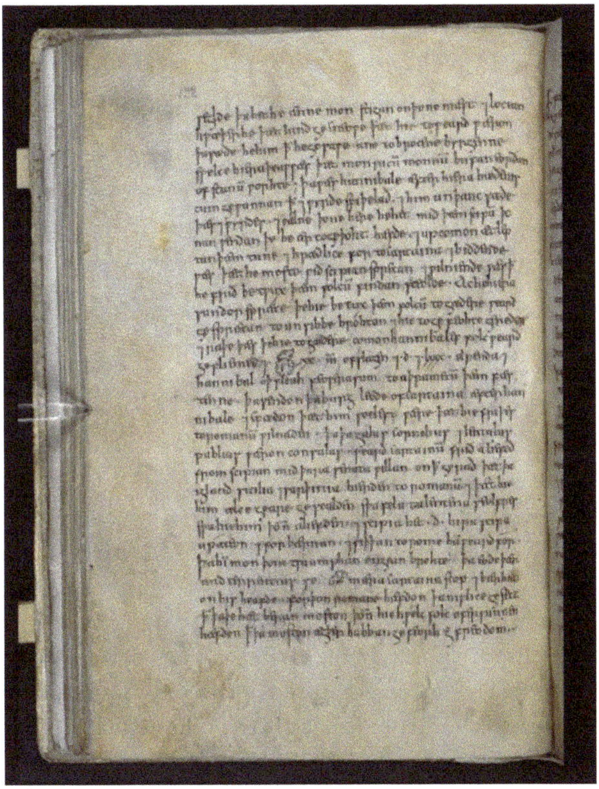

Figure 5b: Orosius, Historia adversus paganos, Winchester, late 9th or early 10th century, 295 x 205 mm. London, British Library Add. MS 47967, fol. 62v. Detail.

These parchment flaws are often cited by manuscript historians as examples in descriptions of the process of parchment making, and they are usually cited with praise for the cleverness and resourcefulness of medieval scribes.[20] They also, however, demonstrate an acceptance of the parchment's quality as parchment. In each of these cases, the scribe or rubricator has worked with the flaw rather than against it, so that from the natural elasticity of the parchment something new emerges: in the Winchester manuscript, the scribe has turned the hole into the body of an animal; in the Aquitaine manuscript, a scribe has encircled the hole with red, as if to highlight it, perhaps in deference to the word which emerges on the page beneath: *gratiam*, or grace. Decorated, written around, or drawn upon, the holes function as if agents themselves, as if a witness to a dialogic relationship between multiple persons and their tools – scribes, rubricators, and readers – and parchment.

The writing of books was certainly considered a physical process, and thus such deep engagement with materials such as parchment is not surprising. The spacing of a page's ruling were marked with pricks in the margins and the lines indented with a fine metal point, which made no mark, but rather changed the surface of the parchment. Mistakes, meanwhile, could only be corrected by scraping off parchment, and scribes are often shown holding a pen in one hand and a knife in the other expressly for this purpose. There is also evidence of the pain caused by long hours of writing:

20 See for example Alison Hudson, "If you've got it, flaw-nt it," *British Library Medieval Manuscripts Blog*, 27 March, 2018; and Erik Kwakkel, "The Skinny on Bad Parchment," *medievalbooks.nl*, 24 October, 2014; for parchment making, see Christopher De Hamel, *Making Medieval Manuscripts* (Oxford: Bodleian Library, University of Oxford, 2018).

the 10th-century scribe Florentinus of Valerancia, who copied several manuscripts, composed a lengthy colophon for a volume of the book of Job (Figure 6).[21]

Figure 6: Gregory the Great, Moralia in Job, Valerencia?, c. 945, 490 x 340 mm. Madrid, Biblioteca Nacional de España, Cod. 80, fol. 500v-501r.

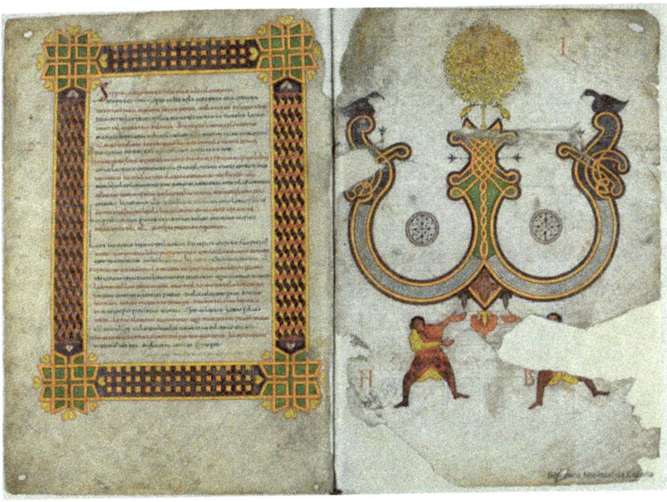

In an elegant script, carefully inscribed within a decorated frame, Florentinus extensively describes the physical suffering related to writing, saying, for example, how it makes one's eyes fog over and bends the back, perhaps comparing his own suffering to that of Job himself.[22]

The idea that art making might be a process of wrestling with materials, rather than mastery over materials with a definite end point, is evident in other texts from the period as well. *On Diverse Arts*, or *De diversis artibus* in its original Latin, is the only complete treatise on art that survived from the period. Written in early 12th century Germany by a monk using the pseudonym Theophilus, the tract presents the reader with instructions for the practices of painting, staining glass, and metalwork. Yet within this treatise, the author says precious little about how art-objects should

21 See John Williams, "A Contribution to the History of the Castillan Monastery of Valeranica and the Scribe Florentinus," *Madrider Mitteilungen* 11 (1970); 231–248.

22 Madrid, Biblioteca Nacional de España Cod. 80, fol. 500v; see also *The Art of the Medieval Spain, A. D. 500 -1200*, (New York: Metropolitan Museum of Art, 1993), 161–162, n. 84; and John Williams, "A Contribution to the History," 231–248; and André Grabar and Carl Nordenfalk, *Early medieval painting from the fourth to the eleventh century : Mosaics and mural painting*, trans. Stuart Gilbert (New York: Skira, 1957), 168.

look. In the prologue, for example, Theophilus writes of the effects of stained glass, but makes no mention of images. Instead, his concern is focused on the material of glass and the craft required to produce the window, writing: "if [the human eye] regards the profusion of light from the windows, it marvels at the inestimable beauty of the glass and the infinitely rich and varied workmanship…"[23] Indeed, throughout the text Theophilus focuses on how things are to be constructed: one creates a censer, for example, by cutting out a series of tiers: four segments are removed from the first tier, in order to shape a cross; eight sides are removed to create the next two levels, with four rounded and with one rotated over the other; finally, the top tier is "formed with eight walls of the same size and without roofs."[24] The finished product is a four level censer, the first level in the shape of a cross, the second a square with rounded corners and protruding flat sides, the third the same, but rotated forty-five degrees, and the fourth an octagon.[25] This manner of description puts process in the forefront: as readers, we are not told of the overall shape, or how to imagine it; instead we are told how each level is made and our own mind is left to determine what the finished product might look like. There are several reasons for this emphasis. One is certainly technical, for it seems certain that Theophilus' tract was used at least some of the time, as a reference for artists. But it has also been suggested that such modes of description were intended to invite the reader to meditate and visualize, as he or she slowly puts together the pieces in his or her head, carefully shaping each level.

Theophilus' reticence about what a finished object looks like reveals a concern for the nature of matter and its mutability. Materials, for example, are treated according to their origins, and Theophilus carefully describes their respective character. He writes:

> Copper is formed in the earth. When a vein of it is found, it is obtained with the utmost labour of digging and breaking. It is an ore of a very green colour, very hard and in its natural state mixed with lead. Dug up from the earth in large quantities, this ore is placed in a heap and burned like lime. It does not change colour, but it does lose its hardness so it can be broken up…[26]

So, too, he describes colours by the process by which they were made:

23 Theophilus, Prologue III, trans. and ed. C.R. Dodwell, *De diversis artibus* (London: Thomas Nelson and Sons, 1961), 63.

24 Theophilus, Book III, ch. LXI, "The Cast Censer," Dodwell, *De diversis artibus*, 113–114.

25 For a diagram of the levels see Theophilus, *On Divers Arts, the Foremost Medieval Treatise on Painting, Glassmaking and Metalwork*, trans. and ed. John G. Hawthorne and Cyril Stanley Smith (New York: Dover, 1963), 134.

26 Theophilus, *On Diverse Arts*, Book III, ch. lxiii, "Copper," Dodwell, *De diversis artibus*, 120–121.

> The colour, which is called the flesh tone, with which the face and nude bodies are painted is composed as follows. Take flake-white, which is white made from lead – and, without grinding it, put it just as it is, dry, in a copper or iron pot, place it over a fire and heat it until it has changed to a yellow colour. Then grind it and mix with some ordinary flake-white and vermilion until it becomes the colour of flesh.[27]

The idea that materials were valued for their potential and transformative properties, rather than any kind of fixed existence, emerges in other writings too. The historian, Flodoard of Reims, for example, composed his *Gesta* of the bishopric at Reims sometime after 948. Flodoard's history presented a line of bishops that established Reims as the inheritor of Roman establishment, and asserted the high status of the office and its personae.[28] Within this history, the gift of fine objects plays a primary role: the seventh century bishop, Sonnatius, for example, is said to have given to the church a plate of gilded silver, twelve spoons, and a salt cellar of silver. Sonnatius' generosity extended beyond his own church as well, for he gave to the basilica of St.Martin at Tours the gold for a chalice and silver for the tomb of Theodulf. Yet for our purposes, the most interesting gift he gave is one to the church of Saint-Vite, for there he gave a vase of silver which could be transformed into a chalice and fifteen sous of gold.[29] Most of these gifts are not to be taken as is, for, as the source specifies, the gold is given in order that it be made into a chalice, the silver intended for the tomb. The amount given is not specified, nor is the maker. The vase, then, is valued not for the name of its artist nor for its material worth, but rather for its transformative possibility – for its potential to be transformed into a chalice. Indeed, while values of materials occur often in treasury inventories, they do not occur in monastic chronicles or *gestae*. It is as if in both cases the value of the object is in its potential, not in its current form. As a gift is noted in a chronicle, it is valued for the object it will become; as a treasury item, it is valued as the raw material to which it could be converted.[30] Flodoard's text was written in the 10th century, and his agenda was clearly to establish the high standing and achievements of the bishops of Reims and,

27 Theophilus, *On Diverse Arts*, Book I, ch. I, "The Mixing of Clours for Nude Bodies," Dodwell, *De diversis artibus*, 5.

28 See Michael Sot, *Un Historien Et Son Église Au Xe Siècle: Flodoard De Reims* (France: Fayard, 1993); and Peter Christian Jacobsen, *Flodoard von Reims. Sein Leben und seine Dichtung 'De Triumphis Christi'*, Mittellateinische Studien und Texte 10 (Leiden: Brill, 1978), 60 ff.

29 Flodoard of Reims, Historia Remensis ecclesiae, ed. J.-P. Migne, *Patrologia Latina* 135 (Paris: Migne, 1853), cols. 23–408, at col. 105.

30 On treasuries see Joseph Salvatore Ackley, "Re-approaching the Western medieval church treasury inventory, c. 800–1250," *Journal of Art Historiography* 11 (2014): 1–37; and Joseph Salvatore Ackley, *Offer him gold; that is true love': Ottonian Gold Repoussé and the Western Medieval Church Treasury*, Ph.D. Diss. (New York: Institute of Fine Arts / New York University, 2014).

by extension, that of the city.[31] Thus it becomes clear that the patronage of objects is amongst the deeds recorded for the bishop, and these deeds constitute his benevolence.[32] Yet it is nonetheless significant that the bishop's benevolence is measured not by materials but by potentials, and the potential maker makes no appearance. It is the nature of the materials for transformation that drives the value of the gift.

In all of these examples, save for that of Florentinus, the name of the artist is unknown. The medieval context, it seems, puts little stock in the identification of the artist. This tendency is clear throughout the 12th century. In most cases, as with Flodoard of Reims and Theophilus, artists' names are not mentioned, and indeed, they seem unimportant. Far more significant, as we have seen, are the transformative qualities of materials.

I have tried to demonstrate how artistic processes, for medieval audiences, were quite broadly construed. Objects were made and re-made by numerous makers and users. By taking into account the qualities of materials and the transformations of objects over time, it becomes clear that process extends far beyond the maker. Objects and materials are used and re-created by generations of users and subject to years of preservation, neglect, renovation, or decay. The relationship between makers, viewers, and materials is dialogic and ongoing. The gifts to the church treasury, the repurposed manuscript, and the decorated holes demonstrate that for medieval audiences the object was never "finished" – it was always in flux, always in process, always changing and changeable. From this point of view, we can see the larger system at work in Abramović's performance. As the table showed us, the artist, the spectators, and the participants operate in relation to the furniture – but they also operate in relation to the gallery itself, as bright lights blaze down, viewers crowd into the edges of the rectangular space, pushed back by a line inscribed on the floor. The entire system is a part of the process of the work. So too are we. Ten years on, as we examine photographs of this piece, read about viewers' experiences, and consider the reflections of the artist, we too are a part of the ongoing making of the work, which remains, and will continue to be, ever evolving.

---

31 See Yitzhak Hen and Matthew Innes, eds., *The Uses of the Past in the Early Middle Ages* (Cambridge: Cambridge University Press, 2000); Rosamond McKitterick, *Perceptions of the Past in the Early Middle Ages* (Notre Dame: Notre Dame University Press, 2006); and Robert F. Berkhofer, *Day of Reckoning: Power and Accountability in Medieval France* (Philadelphia: University of Pennsylvania Press, 2004).

32 For more on the idea of the benevolent abbot see for example Dominique Iogna-Prat, *La Maison Dieu: une histoire monumentale de l'église au Moyen Âge (v. 800–v. 1200)* (Paris: Éditions du Seuil, 2006), 347–53.

A noisy love affair: The Language of Things in the Works of Mark Leckey and *Musa paradisiaca*

Miguel Ferrão

British artist Mark Leckey, 2008 Turner Prize winner, has dedicated a significant part of his practice to popular culture and to particular sound scenes. Both played a formative role in his late teenage years at Ellesmere Port, to which his family moved when he was nineteen. Ellesmere Port — a town and port of Cheshire, a county in England south of Liverpool — was "a strange place that felt constantly toxic"[1], as the artist observes. Surrounded by oil industry facilities, the town connected Leckey to a deep feeling of lostness, but also, in a contradictory sense, to freedom. This in-between sensation has often been described by Leckey as a peculiar mode of being in the "periphery of the action (...), on the edge of the dance floor looking at everyone else having a good time"[2]. His reference to Ellesmere Port as one of the key locations in the Soviet Union's nuclear target list, and his mention of its proximity to Capenhurst's uranium enrichment plant, are major examples of the context Leckey turned into his territory of exploration; a territory characterized by imminent emergency embedded in ordinary life.

Corresponding to the working-class background Leckey left behind while attending university at Newcastle or later entering the art world, this territory of exploration has been mapped by his involvement with *underground* activities of young people including the *casuals*[3], the *rave* movement, and, specifically, *hardcore* — a genre associated with electronic dance music characterized by a fast tempo, an intensity of kicks, and an extensive use of repetition. In 1999, Leckey would define

1 Mark Leckey and Paul Farley, "In Conversation: Under the Bridge," *Tate Etc.*, September 20, 2019, https://www.tate.org.uk/tate-etc/issue-47-autumn-2019/mark-leckey-paul-farley-conversation-under-the-bridge.

2 Mark Leckey, "TateShots: Mark Leckey – 'I Wallow in the Mire of Nostalgia'," October 28, 2016, https://www.youtube.com/watch?time_continue=80&v=CATey5LcEF4&feature=emb_title.

3 Defined by the casual wearing of expensive designer clothing, the *casuals* sub-culture is majorly associated with the peripheral effects of the hooliganism movements operating within the European and, particularly, British football context, which emerged during the late 1970s and the early 1980s.

this frame with his breakthrough work, a 15-minute short video entitled *Fiorucci*[4] *Made Me Hardcore* (fig.1).

Figure 1: Mark Leckey, "Fiorucci Made Me Hardcore," video, 14:44, https://www.youtube.com/watch?v=-dS2McPYzEE.

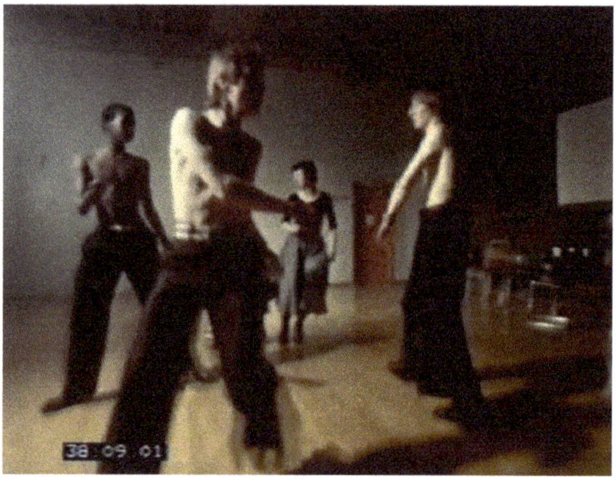

Using VHS footage that covers a rough "overview of 30 years of British nightclub culture"[5], the video portrays a sense of collective youth thrill focused on solo performances and, in particular, on expressive dance moves. It proposes a complex and fluid sound-people construct achieved through an exploration of transition/repetition dynamics which cause a strong sensation of slipping between images, sounds, characters, and places. This feeling of hypnotic movement conducted by unexpected dialogues would resonate through Leckey's following body of work. Accordingly, the communication between both immaterial and material elements that spreads across time and space has been one of its major forces since. Leckey's practice — a survey developed through the relation between technology, nostalgia, and freedom — is permanently challenging the constraints of body and action limits. As Catherine Wood recently affirmed, at the heart of it "there is a desire to dis-

4 *Fiorucci*, an Italian iconic fashion label founded in 1967, played a crucial role in the relationship between fashion and street culture, being associated with popular denim outfits, angels' t-shirts, and vinyl trousers.

5 Bryony Stone, "Anxiety, Speed and Rave Flyers: Artist Mark lackey on His Iconic Video 'Fiorucci Made Me Hardcore'," *It's Nice That*, February 27, 2017, https://www.itsnicethat.com/features/artist-mark-leckey-270217.

appear into time"[6] and, with this, the development of a trust in an undetermined interaction among things that are apparently disengaged from each other.

Figure 2: Mark Leckey, "BigBoxStatueAction," 2003–11, Sound Systems 'in conversation' with Henry Moore's "Upright Motive No.9," Installation view, SEE, WE ASSEMBLE, Serpentine Gallery, London, 19 May – 26 June 2011, Photograph by Mark Blower, Image courtesy the artist and the Cabinet, London.

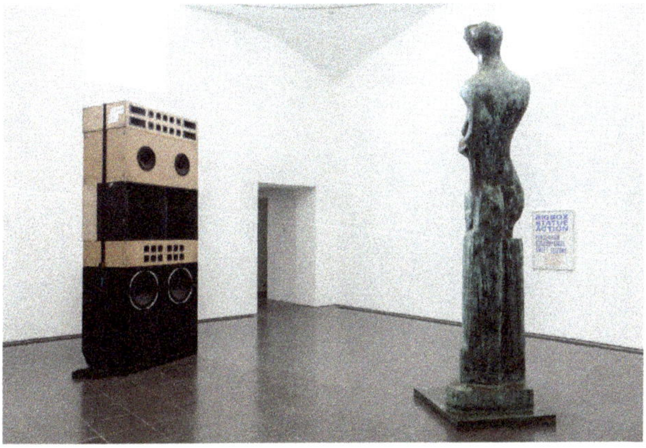

In 2011, the art critic Jonathan Jones visited *See, We Assemble*, a solo exhibition by Leckey in London's Serpentine Gallery. In what seems to have been a terribly deceptive walkthrough, Jones chose a specific work — *BigBoxStatueAction*[7] (fig.2) — to exemplify what he declared as "the arrogance (…) in which [Leckey] has the insolence to juxtapose one of his own speaker-stack sculptures with a bronze abstract statue by Henry Moore"[8]. This *arrogance*, as Jones puts it, lies precisely on Leckey's staging of unrelated subjects as available to communicate with each other. As so, *BigBoxStatueAction* works as a provocation directed to the stability of things — something that Jones was apparently not willing to give up, at least relatively to an art giant like

6 Catherine Wood, "Under the Bridge," in *Mark Leckey: O' Magic Power of Bleakness*, ed. Clarrie Wallis and Elsa Coustou (London: Tate Publishing, 2019), 41.

7 The documentation of the performance *BigBoxStatueAction* at Tate Britain, in 2003, was made available online by Mark Leckey, on his YouTube channel, at https://www.youtube.com/watch?v=XjTDmirVoaE&t=1s.

8 Jonathan Jones, "Mark Leckey's Art Creates Noise Without Meaning," *The Guardian Blog*, May 23, 2011, https://www.theguardian.com/artanddesign/jonathanjonesblog/2011/may/23/mark-leckey-exhibition-serpentine-gallery.

Henry Moore. More than a temporary *insolence*, this process by Leckey constitutes a creative proposition that began years before, in 2003, when the first version of *BigBoxStatueAction* was debuted at Tate Britain. There, as at The Serpentine Gallery, this *action*, as Leckey addresses it, was a performance shaped as a "pummelling sonic sermon via monumental sound systems"[9], directed to similarly monumental sculptures, objects, or structures. At Tate Britain, the chosen partner was *Jacob and the Angel* (1940–1) (fig.3), a Jacob Epstein (1880–1959) sculpture[10] which had a similarly hard journey across the sensitivities of the critics of its time.

Figure 3: Jacob Epstein, "Jacob and the Angel," 1940–41, alabaster, 214 × 110 × 92 mm. © Tate, London.

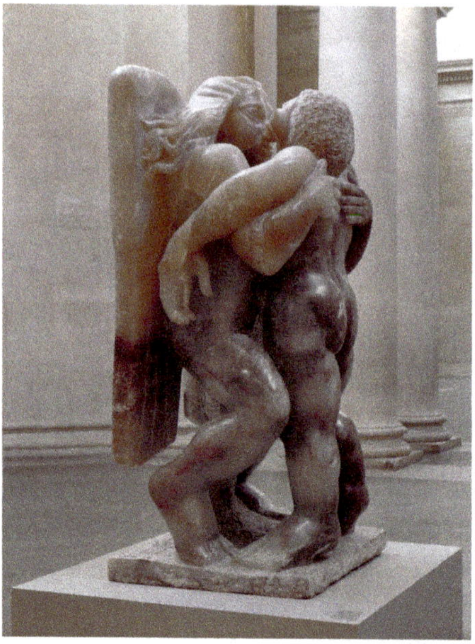

This choice is not only relevant for the definition of the specific spatial, material and immaterial qualities Leckey was looking for with the *BigBoxStatueAction* series,

9 Ed Atkins, "Possession/Commotion," in *Mark Leckey: O' Magic Power of Bleakness*, ed. Clarrie Wallis and Elsa Coustou (London: Tate Publishing, 2019), 78.

10 Carved from alabaster, the voluminous figures depict a scene from the book of Genesis wherein, attacked by an unknown aggressor during the night, Jacob wrestles until losing his strength at daybreak, only to understand that this unbeatable opponent was, in fact, the presence of God himself (Gen 32:22 [NRSV]).

but it also matters as a sign for his awareness for unexpected links. His defiance of time[11] is, therefore, within his will to communicate with others — all the Others — and within the desire to provide them a stage for their their own languages. Thus, from the point of view of Epstein's language of Modernism — which Leckey openly didn't relate to[12] — *BigBoxStatueAction* looked for an entrance to a dialogue only possible because of this fundamental linguistic discord. *Jacob and the Angel* paired *BigBoxStatueAction*, while Leckey paired Epstein, exactly because of their differences.

Stuart Tulloch, in an historical approach to the career of Jacob Epstein[13] — a British sculptor mainly devoted to portraits and monuments — highlights the long-lasting love for *Jacob and the Angel* as a solitary example in the public appreciation of Epstein, although the first reactions to it were between surprise and shock, something that Leckey also found with his own work. As Epstein acknowledges, the most common charge against his work was that it had no "formal relations"[14] and that it lacked connection with the recognition, historicity or contingent rules of sculptural representation.

Debuted in 1942 at the Leicester Galleries in London, *Jacob and the Angel* was originally purchased by the London-based entrepreneur Charles Stafford, who supported its travel to Blackpool where it was shown as an experience for 'Adults Only.' Placed "on sand against a painted backdrop of dunes and palm trees (...), it was illuminated by coloured spotlights and accompanied by an American juke-box playing soft music, and a loudspeaker giving an explanation of the work".[15] Earlier on, Epstein had declared his indifference to the use of "special lighting (...) and colouring of sculpture," characterising it as "trivial and not worth [of] serious consideration"[16]. Thus, surprisingly enough, the staging of *Jacob and the Angel* on Blackpool's central promenade seems to directly contradict Epstein's principles — a kind of defiant attitude or a long-lasting anecdote. In the same way we also have to judge the use of sound, both in the 1942 installation and in the 2003 reappearance of the sculpture in *BigBoxStatueAction* at Tate Britain. The similarities between both contexts transform this encounter into an exemplary long-term relationship without any time constraints, something that Leckey was clearly aware of.

11 Wood, *op. cit.*, 41.

12 Mark Leckey, "Mark Leckey: transformed by the digital realm," *The Double Negative*, April 12, 2013, http://www.thedoublenegative.co.uk/2013/04/mark-leckey-transformed-by-the-digital-realm/.

13 Stuart Tulloch, "Miracle or Monstrosity? Story of an anwork.," *Tate Etc.*, May 1, 2011, https://www.tate.org.uk/tate-etc/issue-22-summer-2011/miracle-or-monstrosity.

14 Jacob Epstein, *Let There Be Sculpture* (United States of America: G. P. Putnam's Sons, 1940), 212.

15 Tulloch, *op. cit.*, 4.

16 Epstein, *op. cit.*, 212.

Leckey would eventually address this time-travel possibility when recently describing *BigBoxStatueAction* during a lecture at Liverpool's John Moores University:

> The idea here was trying to wake and move the sculpture, in order for it to communicate what it was or what it is (…). Trying to get it to speak to me. In order to do that, I thought it needs something equivalent in scale, in volume, to itself. It is not going to listen to me asking questions, it needs something with the same kind of mass. And so, I had this sound system made (…). And the idea was to play music, play sounds, to play just noise at this thing until it starts to speak. Or starting to potentially, hypothetically, sympathetically vibrate, through resonance. So, it was divided in a three parts performance: *Persuasion*, that's where I'm trying to seduce it with a kind of music (…); *Borborygmus*, that was just (…) playing this very low base frequencies at it; and *Sweet Seizure*, (…) kind of a celestial, celebration of the thing (…). It is like trying to understand something through feelings.[17]

It is clear that a dialogic equivalence process is being settled here. Imaginably, in some distant future, it may even be included in a history of sonic weapons, given its ability to make people faint, like what happened during the second presentation of *BigBoxStatueAction* at the Serpentine Gallery[18]. In fact, we find it reasonable to assume that this transmission effect played between the sound system, Epstein's sculpture, and the audience — which Leckey describes as a sympathetical vibration — forms not only an actual response from *Jacob and the Angel*, but also an answer from the *action* itself as a whole. Even if this answer comes indirectly, through the effects of Leckey's intervention in the audience and the space surrounding the sculpture he is trying to *wake up*, an answer is nevertheless provided.

This quest for a physical response through the use of sound, which Leckey's performance attempts, is also reminiscent of another biblical episode — *Jericho Taken and Destroyed.*[19] Here, Joshua is encouraged to conquer the city of Jericho using sound to break its walls and he does so alongside a group of priests playing horns, joined by the people in a collective shout. Perhaps, in an unexpected way, the main difference between this episode and Leckey's *BigBoxStatueAction* is only based on volume control; i.e., between breaking and vibrating, desire and transcendence,[20] Leckey's *actions* require, after all, a direct participation of several interveners in different, although equally vital, degrees. Audience, sculptures, space, and sound are not only elements apart from each other, they are members of a collective conjuring — an

---

17 Mark Leckey, "Mark Leckey – Masters Lecture," April 5, 2017, https://www.youtube.com/watch?v=MJHyg4g8MzQ&feature=youtu.be.

18 Ibidem.

19 Josh 6:20 (NRSV).

20 Atkins *op. cit.*, 79.

entity born of a conversation in real-time. This conversation is the actual *object* arising from the *action*.

In a performance script titled *The Stone Tape Theory – 1979*, Leckey articulates this transformative *action* with the notion of aura; he 'concretizes' it, in a double sense of the word:

> The Stone Tape theory speculates that certain building material, such as stone, wood, or concrete, have properties similar to that of magnetic tape. These materials can store the energy created by an emotional disturbance or traumatic event (...). These 'stone tapes' can be recorded over and over and over and over again (...), growing fainter through successive generation loss while never completely dying away. By identifying the signal, these earlier perturbations can be regenerated and retransmitted.[21]

The gibberish performed by Leckey's DIY sound system installed in front of the monumental sculpture seems to be an challenge to the silence of matter. At the same time, it offers the opportunity to learn new languages and it urges a translation method between them. To meet the urgency implicit in an event recorded by non-standard mediums and materials, *BigBoxStatueAction* functions, therefore, as a formal introduction to a broader relational system. This coincides with what Leckey acknowledges in the term *disturbance* — to act, to record, to translate, to retransmit, and to relive, join into one continuous process of becoming. Ultimately, to create a disturbance means, in this case, to actually become reachable. In this context, *BigBoxStatueAction* can not only be considered as an instrument with which matter can *speak*, but also as an effort to establish a two-way communication channel between the different players involved in this dialogue; namely the audience, the sculptures, the sound work and the space where the *action* is performed.

This particular *disturbance*, based on an ontological displacement between subjects, objects, and *voices*, is also present in two recent solo exhibitions by *Musa paradisiaca*[22], a duo formed by the Portuguese artists Eduardo Guerra and Miguel Ferrão. Although built as a closed system without a live component — apart from its activation by the presence of a visitor — the two installation projects explore the same

21 Mark Leckey, "The Stone Tape Theory – 1979." in *Mark Leckey: O' Magic Power of Bleakness*, ed. Clarrie Wallis and Elsa Coustou (London: Tate Publishing, 2019), 106.

22 *Musa paradisiaca* is an artistic project started in 2010 concerning the transmutation of temporally-restricted private events (sound recorded encounters) into publicly broadcasted durational sound objects (edited sound recordings). Firstly, through virtual and individualized channels of distribution (online) and, later, within more open and collectively-attended formats (gatherings, talks, exhibitions), *Musa paradisiaca* has been transversally characterised by a performative and continuous exploration of the different modes of interaction between orality and object making.

promise of an open relationship with diverse criteria that *BigBoxStatueAction* considered, namely the formal equivalence between subjects as a way to make them speak to each other.

Cavazaque Piu Piu[23], presented at the Galeria Quadrado Azul in Porto (Portugal), and *The I of the Beeholder*[24], shown at Fundação Carmona e Costa in Lisbon (Portugal), were both based on choreographies that synchronized sound, light, and objects. Each of these components was operated by a program that governed the space of the exhibition and turned it into a single organism. The system seemed to have a life of its own and it could give the visitor the deceptive feeling of a loss of freedom, as if the experience of the exhibition could be performed without him or her. But the system waited to be joined in. When the lights would finally initiate its cycle of in, out, fade in, and fade out, the illuminated objects — painted fiberglass reliefs with a sometimes-recognisable identity such as a car door [fig.4], a cactus [fig.5] or fins [fig.6], for example — would be accompanied by a voice coming from speakers.

Figure 4: Musa paradisiaca, "Car's door," 2018, painted fiberglass, 115 × 130 × 50 cm. Installation view, Curveball Memory, Galeria Municipal do Porto, Porto, October 6 – November 18, 2018, Image courtesy the artist and Galeria Municipal do Porto, Porto.

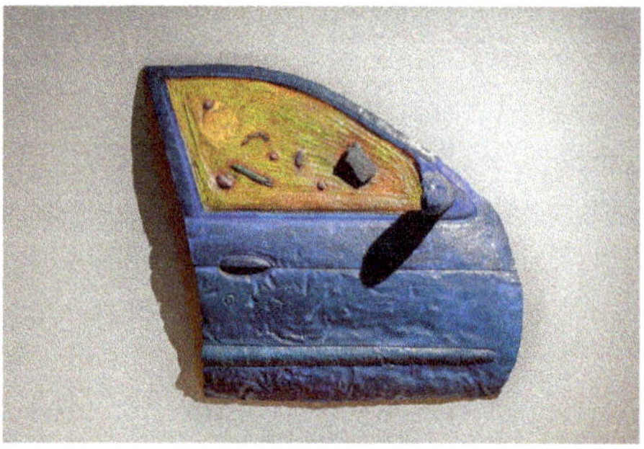

23 The video documentation of the exhibition *Cavazaque Piu Piu*, by *Musa paradisiaca* at Galeria Quadrado Azul, is available at https://vimeo.com/340688457/3268cf3d76.

24 The video documentation of the exhibition *The I of the Beeholder*, by *Musa paradisiaca* at Carmona e Costa Foundation, is available at https://vimeo.com/392018099/692b9b69e5.

Figure 5: Musa paradisiaca, "Cactus," 2019, painted fiberglass, 56 x 60 x 2 cm. Image courtesy the artist and Galeria Galeria Quadrado Azul, Porto.

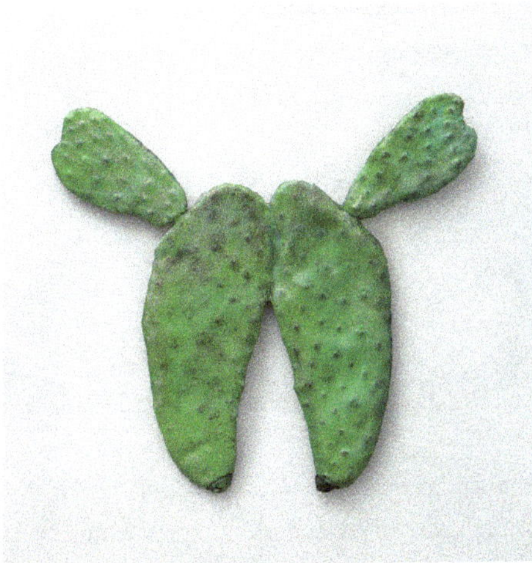

Figure 6: Musa paradisiaca, "Fins and Eggs," 2020, painted fiberglass, 180 × 170 × 15 cm. Installation view, The I of the Beeholder, Carmona e Costa Foundation, Lisbon. Courtesy the artist and Galeria Quadrado Azul, Porto.

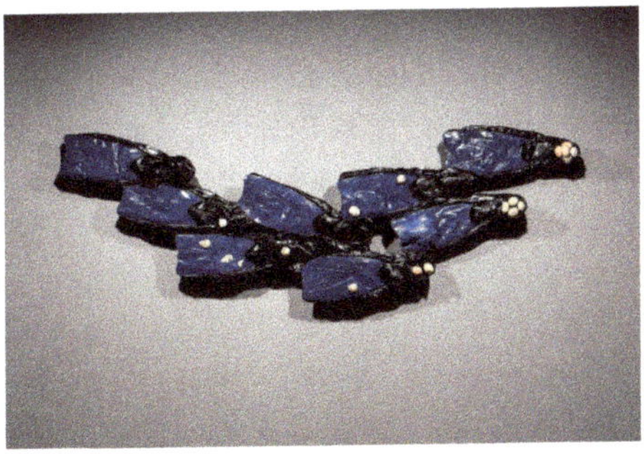

Figure 7: Musa paradisiaca, "Mat, TV and Potatoes," 2020, painted fiberglass, 155 × 310 × 20 cm. Installation view, The I of the Beeholder, Carmona e Costa Foundation, Lisbon. Courtesy the artist and Galeria Quadrado Azul, Porto.

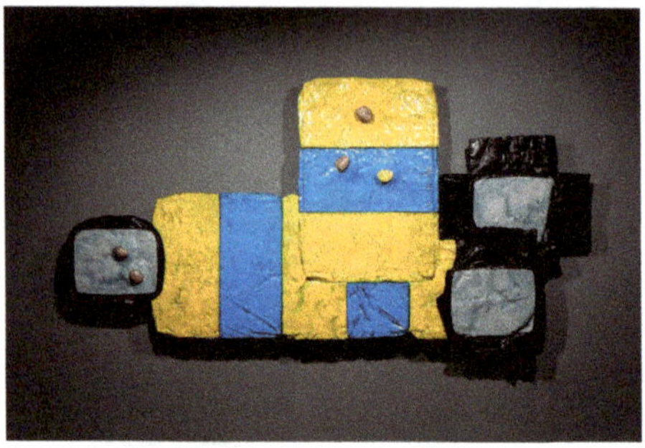

The sound—verbal and reflexive in *Cavazaque Piu Piu*, mostly non-verbal and descriptive in *The I of the Beeholder*—was a dialogue performed by a single voice, though its multiple tones and intonations placed doubt on its existence as being of a single origin. Adding up to the *conversation* between lights and objects, all operated by the central nervous system of a computer, the presence of technical equipment—cables, speakers, and plugs — not hidden from sight, also played a role as a reminder of the physical attachment between space and objects. Eventually, the discreet but stable reverberation of the installation rooms, caused by the electric circuits which allowed the space to be reactive and sensitive to movement, personified the whole space as a kind of half-sleeping mind "running through a permanent state of alertness".[25]

Both exhibitions combined a spoken voice with objects in order to continuously question the speaker's position. Violently addressing the pieces in *Cavazaque Piu Piu* or smoothly outlining them in *The I of the Beeholder*, these were the voices of an unknown. Of course the objects did not move, but the sound and the light/dark rhythm turned the objects into temporary *talk-makers.*[26] Provided with an acoustic ability to manifest themselves, all of the objects that were displayed — sculptures, drawings, and speakers — inverted the conventional link between speaker and spoken-about. This provocation is in line with Mark Leckey's attempt to "understand things through feelings"[27], but also corresponds to a desire to experience "subjectivity in

25 David Revés, "Musa paradisiaca: The I of the Beeholder," *Contemporânea*, February 2020, https://contemporanea.pt/edicoes/01-02-03-2020/musa-paradisiaca-i-beeholder.

26 Bruno Latour, "Fetish–factish," *Material Religion: The Journal of Objects, Art and Belief* 7, no. 1 (2011), 44.

27 Mark Leckey, "Mark Leckey – Masters Lecture." April 5, 2017, https://www.youtube.com/watch?v=MJHyg4g8MzQ&feature=youtu.be.

multiplicity and in continuous fragmentation".[28] Although the physical limitations of the object are not altered, here the object appears to exist only in communication — its existence is grounded in duration and transitivity.

Conversation, a word that "derives from being together in conversion"[29], has always been a central methodology of *Musa paradisiaca*'s artistic practice. It builds up a space "in which each person, or each thing, merges in a distinct albeit related manner, perceptible through oral, textual, sound, film, sculptural, and performance-based objects".[30] The objects *in action* in *Cavazaque Piu Piu* and *The I of the Beeholder* exemplify a specific use of conversation — the ability to create hybrid entities. Embedded in a discourse that leans towards a fluency among signs, these objects are simultaneously receptive to voice and a contribution to it with sensorial depictions of uncommon, yet somehow identifiable, features. This open dialogue marks, as in *BigBoxStatueAction*, a chance for language to develop, to be experimented, to be redistributed. At the same time, it is an effort to disconnect it from petrifying conventions.

"When I speak to you in your language, what happens to mine? Does my language continue to speak, but in silence?"[31], asks Sofia Lemos quoting Vincent Rafael[32], who, on his part, cited the Moroccan critic, Abdelkebir Khatibi. Would this mean that the relational qualities of the objects in *Cavazaque Piu Piu* and *The I of the Beeholder*, of Epstein's *Jacob and the Angel*, or of Leckey's sound system in *BigBoxStatueAction*, disappear when soundless? Certainly not, we would reply. Their soundless existence does not steal the voice of their single, autonomous presence. This is particularly evident in the sculptures of *Musa paradisiaca*. Their ordinary appearance suggests a familiarity with a world shared by many and thus in their individuality they are already of a plural nature.[33] Their connection is not theoretical, it is founded in the *collective grammar*[34] wherein no memory ever disappears.

In Carl Einstein's writings, we can find an impulse to deconstruct the *concept* through an opposition between *gestalt* and *form*. Amid a view of the *concept* as a ratio-

---

28 Sofia Lemos, "Moving Syllogisms." in *Musa paradisiaca: Views on Misunderstanding*, ed. Sofia Lemos, Claudia Pestana, Miguel Ferrão, and Eduardo Guerra (Porto: Galeria Municipal do Porto and Bom Dia Books, 2018), 28.

29 Lemos, "Moving Syllogisms", 29.

30 Ibidem.

31 Ibidem, 27.

32 Vincent L. Rafael, *Motherless Tongues: The Insurgency of Language Amid Wars of Translation*. (Durham: Duke University Press, 2016), 7.

33 Filipa Oliveira, "The Text as an Experiment." in *The I of the Beeholder* (Lisbon: Fundação Carmona e Costa and Documenta, 2020), 114.

34 José Bragança de Miranda, "Carl Einstein e a Força da Arte," *Caleidoscópio: Revista de Comunicação e Cultura*, no. 11/12 (September 2012), 9.

nal, constructed fixpoint and a view on *gestalt* as a defamiliarization of the world and its qualities, Einstein promotes a criticism of the mechanism that "deadens powers that were once dominant or, at least, equal to [man]"[35]. Einstein is thereby recognising a negative response which, through the act of generalisation, devalues any "spirits, gods, and cosmic powers (...) into mere ideas or elements, mythic processes dimmed into rational metaphysical operations"[36]. He is proposing a dissolution of the pleura that divides an *internal* from an *external* space — a division he considers to have been ruled by fear and insecurity, and amplified by disbelief in a repeatable and predictable continuum. In this framework, the artistic activity arises, for the German writer, "as a counter-impulse, a refusal to accept the world as given"[37].

The result of this refusal is an expansion of art itself through a movement that thrives on the valorisation of conflicts between forms[38] as their *anima*. It is actually through the investigation of the contrast among elements that, accordingly to Einstein, this expansion occurs. To expand means, in this context, to manifest features which were unavailable or silenced before. It requires, consequently, the affirmation of a hypothetical language of things operated by an exaggeration of their existing qualities, while not losing the ability to preserve a relation with the same things before being exaggerated.

Here, *language* corresponds to the right of things to speak. If, accordingly, objects are taken as a mobile set of disconnected signals, a horizon of equity for the language to be spoken has to be established. This does not only mean that one must dismantle conventional connections — artist/spectator; artist/mediator; viewer/participant; producer/consumer, to name a few — but rather the new *language* of things also has to question the authority attributed to human subjectivity, as the Italian sociologist Maurizio Lazzarato proposes.[39] Einstein would envision, in this perspective, a need for a collectivized art, one that would allow for social reconstruction.[40] Lazzarato, on his part, refers to Félix Guattari, who claimed that there is "no reason at all to deny living and material assemblages the equivalent of a-subjectivity"[41].

This new status of objects may, ultimately, be linked with the "trans-individual, polyvocal, animist and multi-referential operation (...) also found in madness, child-

---

35 Carl Einstein, "Gestalt and Concept (Excerpts)," *October* 107 (Winter 2004), 171.

36 Ibidem.

37 Ibidem.

38 Miranda, *op. cit.*, 14.

39 Maurizio Lazzarato, "'Exiting Language', Semiotic Systems and the Production of Subjectivity in Félix Guattari." In *Cognitive Architecture: From Biopolitics to Noopolitics: Architecture & Mind in the Age of Communication and Information*, ed. Deborah Hauptmann and Warren Neidich (Rotterdam: 010 Publishers, 2010), 506.

40 Carl Einstein, "On Primitive Art," *October* 105 (Summer 2003), 124.

41 Lazzarato, *op. cit.*, 506.

hood [and] artistic creation"[42]. While referring to *archaic societies*, but also to poetic and artistic projects, Lazzarato acknowledges this process of continuous reconfiguration, negotiation, and fine-tuning as a "*bringing-into-existence* (...) relation between 'words and things' (...), [wherein] language does not only describe, denote or name reality"[43] but effectively bridges the divisions between subject and object. The language of things that merges object and subject could, therefore, be positioned as a kind of *lingua franca*, depending solely on a disturbance of the relationships taken as granted, as we have outlined in the artistic and dialogical practices of Leckey and *Musa paradisiaca*. The right to speak may, after all, be pulverised into a condition of absolute orality, not only in which everything is urged to speak but, specially, in which everything is always speaking to something else. As a form of relational overture, the recognition of a possible language between things may allow for a performative understanding of a temporary community or, simply, the praise of a noisy love affair[44] among apparent strangers.

42 Lazzarato, *op. cit.*, 507.

43 Ibidem.

44 Mark Lewis, "Mark Leckey: Formal Love," *Afterall: A Journal of Art, Context and Enquiry*, no. 33 (Summer 2013), 52.

The photographic multiples of Joseph Beuys as an extension of himself

Pierre-Emmanuel Perrier de la Bâthie

> We don't need more museums that try to construct the historical narratives of a society, community, team, nation, state, tribe, company, or species. We all know that the ordinary, everyday stories of individuals are richer, more humane, and much more joyful.
> *Orhan Pamuk, A Modest Manifesto for Museums*, 2012.

How does a photograph become an object? Theorists have often asked this question more or less explicitly. The canonical texts of Walter Benjamin and Roland Barthes, for instance, approach it from a rather sociological angle. Many scientific disciplines, which use photographs as instrument of study, have spent time questioning their objecthood. Nevertheless, as other images, one primarily sees in a photograph what it refers to rather than the substrate presenting it. Whether it is a historical painting, a cartoon or a photographic portrait, one relates more easily to its content than to its medium. Indeed, the supposed two dimensions of the image deny its materiality, and, by extension, a large part of its objecthood. The medium must have a clearly visible materiality – the impasto of the painting, the grain of the paper – to be considered. Here lays the trap of photography: its lack of texture and the absence of an individualising feature make it easy to overlook the object and concentrate instead on the image[1]. Paradoxically, the physical imprinting that took place at the origin of the recording process – the presence in the same place of the photographer and what was photographed – is easily forgotten because of the transparency of the support combined with the supposed neutrality of the gesture that produced it.

1 Geoffrey Batchen, *Burning with Desire: The Conception of Photography* (Cambridge: MIT Press, 1997), 2.

Moreover, far from pointing out its obvious material reality, photography's great capacity for remediation – its ability to move from one substrate to another without changing its content, at least not completely – ends up convincing viewers that it is valid only for what it represents and not for its physical presence in a place and time. Digital media, permitting anyone to appropriate and transform a photograph unlimitedly, have just exacerbated this impression. In art exhibitions, for example, it is often necessary to give photographs an imposing dimension – a frame, a monumental reproduction, vertically displayed on a cyma, and the like. It is a way to assert their artistic value instead of a simply illustrative value that is so easily ascribed to them.

However, this first observation may be nuanced. Admittedly, in the absolute, the multiplication of an image seems to make it immaterial. But taken individually, each of these reproductions may be physically accessible and thus singularised, like a postcard on the fridge, a family photograph in the living room or a picture autographed by a celebrity in an album. The book *Photographs Objects Histories: On the Materiality of Images*, edited by Elizabeth Edwards and Janice Hart and released in 2004, explore the genealogy of the photographic object by discussing its materiality. In their own way, each chapter underlines the idea of materiality being linked to the value that an individual or a community attributes to the image and its medium: "photographs are both images and physical objects that exist in time and space and thus in social and cultural experience. They [...] are thus enmeshed with subjective, embodied and sensuous interactions[2]". Photography's objecthood depends above all on the use made of it, and thus on their attributed value: economic, scientific, social, religious, symbolic, heritage, sentimental, etc.

In the 1960s and 1970s, precisely by opposition to traditional art forms and to the concepts of uniqueness and authenticity, performers or conceptual artists, amongst others, suggest a new approach to photography. Using it as a tool or a material for their creations, or even as a conceptual reference, they give it a new place in the artistic process. The exhibition, *Photography into Sculpture,* held at the Museum of Modern Art in New York in 1970 is an example of such a landmark in this change of status; just as the Golden Lion obtained by Bernd and Hilla Becher in 1990 is a full validation. Among the many artistic achievements of that period, the photographic multiples by Joseph Beuys (b.1921, Krefeld; d.1986, Düsseldorf) are in this respect particularly significant. Obsessed by materiality – like a sculptor – and fascinated by immaterial forces – like the shaman he intends to be – Beuys has a great interest in the principle of the multiple, artistic object industrially produced in a large number of copies and

2 Elizabeth Edwards and Janice Hart, "Introduction. Photographs as objects," in *Photographs, Objects, Histories: On the Materiality of Images*, ed. Elizabeth Edwards and Janice Hart (New York: Routledge, 2004), 1.

affordable by a large number of collectors. He sees them as "object-vehicles[3]" that allow the dissemination of his artistic ideas. In the creating process of multiples, Beuys gives to photographs of himself, which he appropriates from others, a great importance as a symbolic material that embodies the concepts he works on. Indeed technically, thanks to its ability for remediation, photography combines easily with properties of multiples. Beuys' photographic multiples question the values attached to photographs, then singularised as objects, and allow him to consider their permanence in time and space as an extension of himself. He manages to establish a clear relationship between the photographic image and its material substrate, giving weight to the objecthood of the photograph as much as his artistic persona, both at the service of the exposure of his work.

Beuys and his own image

As an artist, Beuys first of all acknowledges the damaged German identity after World War II. He then extends this observation to the general malaise of Western civilisation, which has lost itself in an excess of rationalism, of which the cold and triumphant capitalism of the 1960s is a symptom. Conceiving an expanded concept of art, he decides to heal the wounds of the occidental society by returning to the primordial myth of a freely creative humanity. In this process, he asserts himself as a mediator, a stimulus: "I do not want to take care of my own person, but on the contrary use it to track down forces that, in my opinion, belong to the buried consciousness[4]". His material achievements are only the physical part of a profoundly metaphysical work, in which the figure of the artist is a catalyst: "both [the artist and the materials] are sculptural elements. That is a very important concept for me. If I produce something, I transmit a message to someone else... Here is the borderline between physics and metaphysics: this is it what interests me about theory of sculpture[5]". Establishing himself as the cornerstone of his work, he brings any interpretation or analysis back to his artistic persona. He embodies the myth of the shaman, whose action is entirely dedicated to the proper functioning of the social group. This myth is not hidden, but rather is fully assumed as a model to be followed in the chaos of the modern world.

---

3 Bernd Klüser and Jörg Schellmann, "Questions to Joseph Beuys," in *Joseph Beuys: the Multiples. Catalogue Raisonné of Multiples and Prints*, ed. Bernd Klüser and Jörg Schellmann (Munich/New York: Schellmann, 1997), 9.

4 Marianne Eigenheer and Martin Kunz, *Joseph Beuys: Spuren in Italien* (Lucerne: Kunstmuseum Luzern, 1977), 9.

5 Willoughby Sharp, "An Interview with Joseph Beuys," *Artforum* 8, no. 4 (December 1969): 49.

The shaman is an evocative figure of a social order based on belief more than rationality. Embodying it, Beuys embraces the associated mysticism. He expresses it through the ritualisation of his acts, opening up an 'extraordinary setting' in the 'ordinary space' or, in other words, a sacred moment in a profane continuum. The theatricality of his interventions physically breaks with a normalised social attitude and contributes to founding the rite: his ceremonial dress – hat, fisherman's jacket, fur coat –; the use of an indistinct primordial language; the realisation of codified gestures; the reference to a metaphorical sculptural vocabulary; his bestiary of psychopompous animals; and his favourite materials, fat, felt, honey, gold, etc. All of these gives his persona a "symbolic efficacy", "a language in which unformulated and otherwise unformulable states can be expressed immediately[6]". Constantly nourished by the present and the near past, this "symbolic efficacy" finds a perfect space to express itself in contemporary media. Beuys masters media-tools at his disposal – photography, television, video, press, etc. – and knows perfectly how to fully exploit the potentialities of his image as a support and extension of the verbal narrative he is progressively building. The many films[7] and television reports[8] dedicated to him during his lifetime testify to this, as does the publication of numerous books that try to maintain a fair balance between text and photographic reproductions. For instance, he even clearly influences the writing and editing of his biography by Adriani, Konnertz, and Thomas in 1973 and of the catalogue of its personal retrospective at the Guggenheim Museum in New York in 1979[9].

Beuys does not want his artistic vision to be seen by a limited audience of experts and enlightened amateurs. To overcome the spatial and temporal restrictions imposed by the performative act, he knows that his work required a circulation medium whose impact has to be stronger than that of a scientific publication. Paradoxically, Beuys always denies – or at least avoids admitting – the importance of photography in the transmission of his artistic message, which thereby invokes the loss of aura like Benjamin: "[photography] cannot show [...] life, facial expression, body language, the way of speaking, the very particular mark of time on his face[10]". The photographic process fragments a continuous temporal and spatial reality into several instantaneous prints, abusively reducing the whole interpretation of a work or of an action, and at the same time deprives him of his words, his immaterial

6 Claude Lévi-Strauss, *Anthropologie structurale* (Paris: Plon, 1958), 218.

7 Samuel Bianchini and Julie Heintz, "Filmographie," in *Joseph Beuys: films et vidéos*, ed. Fabrice Hergott and Harald Szeemann (Paris: Centre Pompidou, 1994), 73–79.

8 Maïté Vissault, *Der Beuys Komplex : l'identité allemande à travers la réception de l'œuvre de Joseph Beuys (1945–1986)* (Dijon: Les Presses du Réél, 2010), 268.

9 *Ibid.*, 12–13.

10 Eugen Blume, "L'expression la plus forte de l'art chez Beuys est dans son visage," in *Joseph Beuys: films et vidéos*, ed. Fabrice Hergott and Harald Szeemann (Paris: Centre Pompidou, 1994), 31.

tool for sculpting thought. Moreover, because he does not practice photography, he has to rely on the vision of someone else. Nevertheless, even if he minimises its possibilities, Beuys knows that there is an extra potential of meaning, more or less exploitable, provided that he has some control over its mechanisms. His striking entry into the media space comes through a photograph of his action on July 20, 1964 in Aachen. Heinrich Riebesehl took a picture of the artist after being struck by a spectator during his performance *Kukei, akopee-Nein!, Braunkreuz, Fettecken, Modellfettecken* at the Fluxus Festival for New Art. The significance of his performance is ideally condensed in a single shot, in which clash the symbols, the Hitler salute and the crucifix. For its synthetic composition, as well as for its provocative part, this photograph is widely disseminated in the following weeks[11]. It is also symptomatic of his future relationship with the camera. Never really posing, he obliges all photographers to work with a series of shots of which only a few are selected. Beuys' photographs are characterised by this aesthetic of the snapshot – captured on the spot, in a burst, often badly framed, sometimes blurred –, an expression of his creative personality always in movement. Then, in the very large number of photographs at his disposal, he makes specific choices by appropriating and readapting this new material to his discourse[12].

His installation, *Arena – Where Would I Have Got If I Had Been Intelligent*, is largely based on his photographic image. In 1972, Beuys exhibits in Naples, then in Rome, 100 panels on which he displays, among a few drawings, 264 photographs showing the artist's work through some performances, but also private photos; notably one of his mother. There is no logical organisation, no chronological or informational references as in archives, but rather the exhibit is an accumulation of conceptual layers, which insists on the inextricable entanglement of work and life. This work could be described as a sculptural autobiography for posterity[13]. Photographs gain materiality as artistic material, in the same way as fat and felt, which are also present on the panels. Even though they are confined to the specific space of the installation, they retain the symbolic load of the artistic act that selected it, and thus singularised it from the mass of anonymous archive reproductions: "Beuys' selection of materials, limited tonal palette, and the photographs' erratic arrangement on the mattes collectively strip the images of any 'evidence of their historicity by endowing them with

11 Ingrid Burgbacher-Krupka, *Prophete Rechts, Prophete Links* (Nuremberg: Institut für moderne Kunst, 1977), 65–69.

12 Eugen Blume, "Joseph Beuys and the Photography," in *Joseph Beuys: Make the Secrets Productive: Scultpure and Objects*, ed. Ute Klophaus (New York: PaceWiledenstein, 2010), 45.

13 Gabriele Guercio, *Art as Existence: The Artist's Monograph and Its Project* (Cambrige/London: MIT Press, 2006), 274–76.

a kind of objecthood that has clear affinity with his sculpture".[14] More than having a performance documented by a photographer and released on specific document-oriented publications, Beuys creates an additional permanent expression to what was only ephemeral by integrating these photographs into his own sculptural work. The rite is not experienced directly, but is rendered by the complex structure in which symbolic materiality substitutes for the performative experience.

"I'm a sender, I transmit"

Beuys might have been nourishing *Arena* all his life as a work constantly in progress. But the static condition of the installation clearly limited the scope of his discourse. Taken as a coherent whole, the multiples of Beuys could be seen as an extension of *Arena*, freed from the constraints of the exhibition space, to become part of everyday life and to act more effectively and democratically. It is no coincidence that he conceives his first multiples in the same period – the late 1960s – as 'antennae' that broadcast his artistic discourse[15]. "I am a sender, I transmit!" – the phrase, which he chanted throughout his *Vitex Agnus Castus* action in Naples in 1972[16], became the ideal formula for summarising his conception of the multiple; a formula which is also widely used in publications and exhibitions on the subject. It is no longer a matter of multiplying for the sake of multiplication, but of considering the principle of multiplication in art and all that it implies: circulation, democratisation, audience enlargement, and development of different relations between the artist, the public, and the work, the status of which is then profoundly transformed.

The principle of a mechanically reproduced work of art in multiple copies has existed for a very long time. It is always a technological innovation that brings us to consider a new type of work; in previous centuries this included, etching, mezzotint, or lithography. The origin of the multiple is the same, stemming from the industrial development of the 20th century, and is therefore as varied in its expressions as were the technological innovations during this period. It follows in the footsteps of the Duchampian ready-made, even if their intentions are opposed; the latter aims at the authenticity of the unique, while the former assumes its multiplicity right down

14 David Green and Joanna Lowry, "Splitting the Index: Time, Object and Photography in the work of Joseph Beuys and Yves Klein," in *Sculpture and photography: envisioning the third dimension*, ed. Geraldine A. Johnson (New Haven: Cambridge University Press, 1998), 151.

15 Klüser and Schellmann, "Questions to Joseph Beuys," 9.

16 Uwe Schneede, *Joseph Beuys – Die Aktionen. Kommentiertes Werkverzeichnis mit fotografischen Dokumentationen* (Stuttgart: Hatje, 1994), 318–23.

to its name[17]. Ideologically, the multiple emerges in the 1960s, the era of mass consumption. It is quickly imbued with a democratic vocation, emancipatory vis-à-vis an overly elitist art market: "by the end of the 1960s, young gallerists specialising in editioned works, along with dedicated art fairs, large-scale public exhibitions, and displays in popular venues like department stores had helped place multiples in the hands of a new and larger audience for art[18]".

Beuys quickly understands the full potential of this art form, which is ideally suited to his expanded concept of art. As an echo to his work, using the same references, the same materials, he sees the multiple as a 'physical vehicle', whose strength lies more in its communicative capacities than in its ability to convey complex ideas[19]. Beuys already uses the term 'vehicle' in 1964 to refer to his performances[20], insisting on his ability to intervene at a distance and, over time, on the consciousness of the anonymous spectator, as well as that of the community. In the case of the multiple, it is more precisely the consciousness of the one who owns it – because it must be owned: "I can talk to just about anybody who owns such things, such vehicles. There are also cross-connections between people, or deviations[21]". The artistic concept can only take shape because it is founded on the ownership of an object as a way for the owner to make it his own, to singularise this specific exemplar among the many copies. It creates a personal and material link that constantly connects it to its transmitter and that connects the owners to each other. This link is also spiritual, like the symbolic load imposed by the shaman, which takes the appearance of a signature, a stamp, a dedication, or any other mark specific to the figure of Beuys, derived from his very personal and recognisable visual vocabulary.

La Rivoluzione siamo Noi (Cat. 49)[22] is a good illustration. For the poster of a forthcoming exhibition in Naples in 1971, Beuys poses in his well-known ceremonial dress. The idealistic vision of the man who walks against difficulties, is driven by a desire to unite, who anchors his artistic persona in a collective imagination, and who becomes exemplary in its synthetic simplicity. On site, he signs and stamps

17 Dieter Daniels, *Duchamp und die anderen. Der Modellfall einer künstlerischen Wirkungsgeschichte in der Moderne* (Cologne: DuMont, 1992), 227.

18 Julia Robinson, "Multiple Manifestations. Nouveau Réalisme and Fluxus," in *The Small Utopia. Ars Multiplicata*, ed. Germano Celant (Milan: Fondazione Prada, 2012), 137.

19 Klüser and Schellmann, "Questions to Joseph Beuys," 9–10.

20 Vissault, *Der Beuys Komplex*, 168.

21 Klüser and Schellmann, "Questions to Joseph Beuys," 10.

22 The multiples are numbered according to the catalogue raisonné published in 1997 by Bernd Klüser and Jörg Schellmann. See Bernd Klüser and Jörg Schellmann, ed, Joseph Beuys: the Multiples. Catalogue Raisonné of Multiples and Prints (Munich/New York: Schellmann, 1997).

200 copies of the poster[23] – physical imprints that make these photographic reproductions stand out as objects. Then, in 1972, he has 180 copies of the poster printed and signed with the eponymous dedication. The words themselves are included, reflecting Beuys' desire to inscribe the formula normally pronounced orally: the artist's handwriting should be seen as a preserved form of his words. Imposing his symbolic load, he transforms the image into a solid object, no longer only visual. He also produces a postcard which has been published more or less continuously since the 1970s and which can be ordered today on the internet from Edition Staeck. Beuys' image circulates easily and more democratically under this form and with great fluidity. He is particularly fascinated by postcards that could be distributed on a very large scale for a very low price, imitating the banality of souvenir objects that can be easily owned and singularised by anyone[24].

Beuys also develops several photographic scenarios in order to play with the materiality of the photographic image. The multiple, *Bonn Kunstverein 8.11.1977*, becomes a poster in 1981 for the exhibition *Multiples 1968–80* in Regensburg (Cat. 224) and illustrates the confusion of visual fields. Seen from behind, recognisable only by his iconic hat, Beuys pretends to sign the white background of the photograph. Signing it afterwards, he thus gives the impression that he has just stepped out of the field of the image and appropriated the object onto which he is presented. Using trompe-l'oeil, Beuys puts the notion of object and image into abyss and projects his artistic character directly onto the object. Another remarkable example is one of the photographs of the multiple *3 Ton Edition B* of 1975 (Cat. 74). Standing in front of white background, face in profile, mouth open, Beuys seems to be shouting his name for all eternity, inscribed on the surface like a phylactery in medieval manuscripts.

The aura of Beuys transmitted through appropriation

As artistic media, photography and multiples equally question the concepts of technical reproducibility and democratisation. Their interaction in Beuys' work is therefore not casual, each one breaking with a more traditional vision that links artistic value with uniqueness. As a vehicle, the multiples become artistic extensions of Beuys' work. Those made from photographs of him therefore occupy a particularly important place, as they help to establish his artistic persona at the centre of his discourse. In fact, the multiples that have been most successful retrospectively are those in which he appears. At the opening of Documenta 6 in 1972, his friend and

23 Vissault, *Der Beuys Komplex*, 343.

24 Benjamin Dodenhoff, "Die Multiples," in *Joseph Beuys: Parallel Prozesse*, ed. Marion Ackermann and Isabelle Malz (Düsselorf/Münich: Kunstsammlung Nordrhein-Westfalen/Schirmer-Mosel, 2010), 170.

colleague, Nam June Paik, explains it in these terms, "the most powerful image of Beuys' art is in his face"[25]. And his ceremonial dress, particularly his felt hat, to be precise. Together these elements create a silhouette that stands out and makes him quickly recognisable to the public, even from behind.

By repeatedly emphasising his expanded concept of art, Beuys has managed to occupy a very special position in the public sphere, astride the artistic and the political. In Germany, where the artistic subject matter is much more politicised, his use of the photographic multiple goes far beyond simple aesthetic production; it was attached to the idea of a public fame which the artist uses to his advantage[26]. He knows that he owes his first media success to the political dimension of his actions and quickly builds his artistic statement on his desire to heal a wounded Germany[27]. His fame goes beyond the more restricted circle of art amateurs, to become part of a much more extended, real, and responsive political sphere[28]. In addition to his already committed work, he makes himself known through political interventions – the concretisation of his artistic will to transform mentalities. This includes his stance in favour of the student unions of the Düsseldorf School of Fine Arts, the creation of various politically oriented organisations (Organisation for direct democracy through plebiscite in 1971, Free International University in 1973, etc.), and his candidacy for the political party *Die Grünen* in 1979. Visually, he takes up many of the codes of the political campaign which he applies to his artistic proposals, such as meetings with his public, posters, slogans, signed objects often bearing his effigy, and stamped logos[29].

Beuys only takes half a step into the political arena, maintaining a certain detachment that his artistic status could allow him. He does not fully engage with all of his responsibility. For that, he receives the sharpest criticisms from many contemporary intellectuals, who consider the dangers of this attempt to aestheticise politics[30]. Beyond these considerations, his freedom to go in an in-between allows Beuys to seize the codes of one field for the benefit of his action in the other. His political fame increases his artistic presence while remaining coherent. Beuys' great strength is being able to give a concrete image of his revolution of consciousness through arts. The multiple, *Demokratie ist lustig* (Cat. 68), is a perfect illustration of

25 Blume, "L'expression la plus forte de l'art chez Beuys est dans son visage," 23.

26 Vissault, *Der Beuys Komplex*, 130–33.

27 Joseph Beuys, "Reden über das eigene Land," in *Par la présente, je n'appartiens plus à l'art*, ed. Max Reithmann (Paris: L'Arche, 1988), 19.

28 Nathalie Heinich, *De la visibilité. Excellence et singularité en régime médiatique* (Paris: Gallimard, 2012), 145–46.

29 Jean-Paul Gourévitch, *L'imagerie politique* (Paris: Flammarion, 1980), 8, 17 and 21; Peter Schmieder, *Unlimitiert: Der VICE-Versand von Wolfgang Feelisch; Unlimitierte Multiples in Deutschland* (Cologne: Walter König, 1998), 191; Vissault, *Der Beuys Komplex*, 181–82.

30 Vissault, *Der Beuys Komplex*, 12–13.

this, as it conveys the dose of reality that the fictional *Rivoluzione Siamo Noi* lacks. It is edited in 1973 as a dedicated poster, then as a postcard. Beuys is shown evicted from his studio in the Fine Arts Academy by a cohort of policemen, because he had defended his students who were opposing the administrative established order[31]. Evoking the iconography of an *Ecce Homo*, the image's composition ideally underlines the character of the prophet he wishes to embody[32]. His political act is revealed here by a press image, which he reinterprets with codes of political communication by adding a slogan – *Democracy is merry* – on political visual media – posters and postcards which consequently become leaflets. By doing so, he gains part of the 'surplus of being' contained in the political imagery. Even if he transforms this rebellious act in an art object, he no longer refers to fictitious actions but to concrete realities. The entire object is thereby impregnated with the aura that emanates from the image, an aura all the stronger as it is catalysed by the renown of his effigy. The appropriated and transformed press-photograph becomes an extension of his artistic persona.

Beyond this particularly well exploited political act, there is also the concept of appropriation that impacts photography because it is about considering the objecthood of what is appropriated. Beuys calls upon a large number of contributors in the realisation of multiples: "I cannot create the multiplications all by myself[33]". But the process of appropriation by Beuys, while reinforcing auctorial erasure, underlines the artistic gesture at the origin and at the completion of the object. There is all the weight of the Duchampian choice, that of valorisation through individualisation, which summarises the creative act as an agreement between the artist and the spectator. But such appropriations are rare in Duchamp's work, which shows the disinterest he makes his own, and which Beuys criticises[34]. On the contrary, Beuys makes excessive use of appropriation, a manifestation of a creativity that he wants to make the main tool for transforming society and that he wants overflowing, without limits.

This practice of appropriation becomes almost systematic with the shamanic-star Beuys, whose signature – or stamps or any other kind of mark – revalues all kinds of objects, in addition to his multiples. As a proof of physical contact with the artist, it may be seen as a symbolic load, whose action depends on the public's acceptance to believe in it in return. Beuys' skilfully constructed fame is at the heart of this

---

31 Burgbacher-Krupka, *Prophete Rechts, Prophete Links*, 87.

32 Pierre-Emmanuel Perrier de La Bâthie, "La photogénie de l'artiste en action : six exemples de l'acte créateur photographié au XXe siècle," *Les Cahiers de l'École du Louvre*, no. 2 (March 2013), http://journals.openedition.org/cel/531.

33 Clara Bodemann-Ritter, *Beuys – Jeder Mensch ein Künstler, Gespräche auf der documenta V / 1972* (Francfort/Berlin/Vienna: Ullstein Verlag, 1988), 18.

34 Fabrice Hergott and Harald Szeemann, ed., *Joseph Beuys* (Paris: Centre Pompidou, 1994), 275–76.

belief in the touched object, which is all the stronger if it can also relate to a recognisable effigy that naturally reinforces it. In 1979, Beuys appropriates the mocking front page of *Spiegel* Magazine (Cat. 321), whose catchphrase denounced a kind of speculation on artistic value that he was the instigator: "Artist Beuys: The greatest world fame for a charlatan?". He signs 100 copies, thus defusing the criticism, turning it into an act of creation. Bringing the focus to the appropriation rather than the content, he proved that creativity prevailed once again, despite the 'bad buzz'. His face and his signature are signs of this fame whose creative power he was only redirecting. The aura of the shamanic artist is thus found as much in the process as in the result, conferring on his photographic multiples – more than on other multiples whose relationship to the artist is less immanent – the value of a relic, precious because it bears the trace of him. Almost fetishist in nature, these photographs became an extension of Beuys himself.

And today?

To answer our initial question, we could say that a photograph becomes an object when the image and the medium justify each other. In his desire to stage himself and extend this staging, Beuys perfectly manages this process of objecthood. The fame of his persona is at the heart of the material value of the photographs which represent him and which he takes the time to singularise. He adds a symbolic load that individualised these photographs and freed them from the immaterial flatness of the image. Using supports suitable for the public daily space, he disseminates his aura through these photographic objects that relate directly to him and his artistic discourse. Beuys has always left a doubt as to the number of multiples he has created, not counting them automatically and often letting others do so. He explains that he never wants to impose a multiple, but rather lets them emerge arbitrarily[35]. This great freedom – or facility, depending on one's point of view – makes it possible to envisage a limitless set in which any article with Beuys' mark could be associated with him, extending more or less in the same proportions the artist's impact on his public.

The democratic project of the Beuys multiples quickly failed, as the price of these reproductions soared[36]. But this is paradoxically a good sign because the failure of the democratisation of the object, through its circulation and its capacity for transmission, confirms its value for the person who possesses it and the strength of its

35 Isabel Siben, ed., *Beuys Posters* (Munich/Berlin/Londres/New York: Prestel, 2004), 13; Bernd Klüser and Jörg Schellmann, ed., *Joseph Beuys: the Multiples*, 10 and 30.

36 Dodenhoff, "Die Multiples," 170.

relationship to its creator. What about the effects of the increased remediation permitted in the digital era, an age that Beuys could not have anticipated? Beuys' photographic multiples, with their hard-won objecthood, find themselves deprived of their material substance. From three dimensions, they move to only one, that of the code providing their digital expression[37]. This loss of substance is also associated with a loss of resistance because the image can be retrieved and manipulated by everyone: 'Beuys the appropriationist' is now appropriated.

Nevertheless, it may be beneficial for his work, because it gives the photographic image a great fluidity while also reinforcing, by contrast, the material value of the multiples that exist in a precise place, giving them singularity. Another conception of the aura is to be considered in the digital period, an aura that cannot be separated from the one already existing in Beuys' many photographs. These "poor images" circulating on the internet are proof of a renewed fame based on their unrestrained multiplication[38]. But wherever they appear, they all remain linked by the recognisable effigy of Beuys. The man with the hat is the common denominator of all his appearances in viewers' minds. All of these photographs – issued from the multiples or not – come to compose a network of images, which reconstitutes piece by piece Beuys' artistic persona as the photographs in *Arena*: "[they] do not cohere into a unified narrative. They instead problematize the nature of the work as a whole and calling attention to the distance between what is visible and what was once there[39]". From *Arena*, through the network of multiples, Beuys has successfully made his transition to digital, giving new importance to copying, not anymore in terms of quality, but in terms of quantity by appropriation, multiplication and finally singularisation.

37 Joanna Sassoon, "Photographic Materiality in the Age of Digital Reproduction," in *Photographs, Objects, Histories: On the Materiality of Images*, ed. Elizabeth Edwards and Janice Hart (New York: Routledge, 2004), 189–90.

38 Hito Steyerl, "In Defense of the Poor Image," e-flux, Journal #10 (November 2009), https://www.e-flux.com/journal/10/61362/in-defense-of-the-poor-image .

39 *Marin R. Sullivan, Sculptural Materiality in the Age of Conceptualism: International Experiments in Italy* (New York: Routledge, 2010), 142.

Obsolescence and reinvention: the case study of João Maria Gusmão and Pedro Paiva[1]

Filippo De Tomasi, Maura Grimaldi

Colors, geometrical shapes, elementary figures, animated forms: an orange resembling an evening; a twilight on a two-tone background; white circles that look like snow; squares inside squares. The orange (is it on a table?) is not just a fruit, it reminds us of Paul Cézanne. The squares address the memory of Josef Albers. These are some suggestive imaginings that come from six different works by the Portuguese artist-duo, João Maria Gusmão and Pedro Paiva, created between 2017 and 2018. *Sunset*, *Camels in Egypt*, *Faucet*, *Jumping White Square on a Green Square*, *Snowfall*, and *Green Orange* together made up an immersive installation in the exhibition *A Dog with a Remarkable Tail* (2018) at Fortes D'Aloia & Gabriel | Galpão in São Paulo. The titles of these works are descriptive and suggest an interpretation of the visual effect presented. Each piece is created by a slide projector that simulates an animation through the alteration of its original technique: the still images morph into a chromatic and kinetic variation. We are confronted with a technical device that is no longer in use and which has undergone changes. These old projectors are extracted from the transience and decadence our societies need to keep the economic system working.

As the North American art critic, Jonathan Crary, affirms, contemporaneity is based on the constant acceleration of technological updates. He also highlights that "novelty production" disables our collective memory: "The conditions of communication and information access on an everyday level ensure the systematic erasure of the past as part of the fantasmatic construction of the present."[2] A kind of acceleration that steers toward the erasure of the past in the present. Following Crary, this essay scrutinises whether artists could inquire the constant "demand for replacement or

1 A former version of this paper was presented at the International Conference Counter-Image (2019), Lisbon, and was published in Portuguese at the *Revista de Comunicação e Linguagens: Counter-Image* nº 52, a peer-reviewed, biannual journal of communication and languages of ICNOVA – NOVA Institute of Communication, of the Nova University of Lisbon.

2 Jonathan Crary, *24/7. Late Capitalism and the Ends of Sleep* (London and New York: Verso, 2013), 47.

enhancement"[3] by bringing overtaken technologies into play again. It is intended to observe how these projects challenge the dimension of obsolescence and the technical lens-based image. Also, it will be considered how the concept of obsolescence and the works of Gusmão and Paiva relate to other relevant notions such as "zombie media" or "Do It Yourself" (DIY). Finally, the text will provide a relationship between the artist-duo and other authors working in a similar way such as Francisco Tropa, and Rosângela Rennó.

Media obsolescence

The word "obsolescence" can be found in the majority of occidental languages which share a common root word, *obsolete*. The Cambridge Dictionary describes the adjective obsolete as something "no longer practiced or used," "a discarded type or fashion," or "effaced through wearing down, atrophy, or degeneration."[4] Etymologically, the Latin word is formed by the prefix *ob* – meaning "counter" – and *solèscere* – derived from *solère*, i.e. "used to". Thus, the term obsolescence concerns an object or concept no longer in use. In our context, the word classifies an apparatus discarded by technological evolution[5].

Apart from an etymological approach, obsolescence also mirrors multiple meanings in Media Archaeology. In his essay, "Media Archaeology as the Poetics of Obsolescence" (2016), the German film historian, Thomas Elsaesser, uses the term to comprise four dimensions. At first, the term had a negative connotation, which concerned "the technicist economic discourse of 'progress through creative destruction'."[6] Then, through a Marxist perspective, one could observe the "planned obsolescence"[7] strategy and the protests against it in the 1950s[8]. The concept later obtained a

3 Crary, *Late Capitalism and the Ends of Sleep*, 44.

4 James A. H. Murray, ed., "Obsolete," in *The Oxford English Dictionary* (Oxford: Clarendon Press, 1978), 34.

5 In English, obsolescence is also applied to biology: the technical term recognizes an organ "very imperfectly developed, hardly perceptible". See Murray, 34.

6 Thomas Elsaesser, "Media Archaeology as the Poetics of Obsolescence," in *Film History as Media Archaeology* (Amsterdam: Amsterdam University Press, 2016), 331–50, at 335.

7 The "planned obsolescence" is a commercial strategy by which a technological product has a predefined life cycle. The real-estate agent Bernard London was the first to write about this concept. Indeed, the planned obsolescence strategy was first utilized by industries in the 1930s. See Garnet Hertz and Jussi Parikka, "Zombie Media: Circuit Bending Media Archaeology into an Art Method," *Leonardo* 45, no. 5 (2012): 424–30, at 425.

8 A similar position appears in current political and public debate when, in defense of customers' rights, the European Parliament Resolution of 4 July 2017 points out some "*Measures on Planned Obsolescence*". See "European Parliament Resolution of 4 July 2017 on a Longer Lifetime for Products: Benefits for Consumers and Companies (2016/2272(INI)),"

positive redrafting as "heroic resistance to relentless acceleration, and in the process has become the badge of honor of the no longer useful."[9] Currently, it is considered as a convergence of the sustainability and recycling spheres; moreover, it works as "an eloquent plea for an object-oriented philosophy and a new materialism of singularity and self-sufficiency of being."[10]

Elsaesser also points out that in the twenty-first century both artistic research and media studies have focused their attention on objects and technologies, which became useless for contemporary production. As well as Elsaesser, in the artistic field, the American art historian, Rosalind Krauss, also analyzes obsolescence, namely in two texts from 1999: *A Voyage on the North Sea: Art in the Age of the Post-Medium Condition* and "Reinventing the Medium". The first one is a critical analysis of artworks by Belgian artist Marcel Broodthaers, while the other concerns the slide projection pieces of the Irish artist James Coleman. Krauss underlines the philosophical dimension of obsolescence, following Walter Benjamin[11]. For Krauss, Broodthaers and Coleman utilized obsolete technologies to reveal the specific potentialities inscribed into the apparatus itself. In other words, both artists developed new practices excluded from the conventional use of the medium; these revelations happen only when the device falls "into obsolescence of its final stages of development."[12]

Krauss argues for these potentialities beyond historical and social configurations; conventional norms are set aside, therefore a universe of new associations and relations can be found in the device. Krauss' concept of media is essential for understanding the technological conventional norms: the term no longer identifies a technical instrument and its specifications, but rather "a set of conventions derived from (but not identical with) the material conditions of a given technical support, conventions out of which to develop a form of expressiveness that can be both projective and mnemonic."[13] In the artistic context, obsolescence involves overcoming

---

European Parliament, accessed July 4, 2017, http://www.europarl.europa.eu/doceo/document/TA-8-2017-0287_EN.html.

9 Elsaesser, "Media Archaeology as the Poetics of Obsolescence," 335.

10 Elsaesser, "Media Archaeology as the Poetics of Obsolescence," 335.

11 In his text, "A Short History of Photography" (1931), Walter Benjamin points to the creative character of the photographic image that can be triggered by the recuperation of obsolete processes, providing the development of a new aesthetic language. See Walter Benjamin, "A Short History of Photography," translated by Stanley Mitchell, *Screen* 13, no. 1 (1972): 5–26, at 24.

12 Rosalind Krauss, *A Voyage on the North Sea. Art in the Age of the Post-Medium Condition* (New York: Thames and Hudson, 1999), 45.

13 Rosalind Krauss, "Reinventing the Medium," *Critical Inquiry* 25, no. 2 (1999): 289–305, at 296.

the physicality of a technology in order to reinvent the medium, thereby developing other practices beyond the routines defined by the historical conditions.

To deepen this critical perspective, we will turn to the work of James Coleman, who, early in the 1970s, adopted media like film, photography, and video – he created his first piece using slide projectors in 1972. Krauss specifically analyzed his works from the 1980s and 1990s, and she identified two retrospective dimensions of the image: on the one hand, the language of the photo novella, and on the other, the example of the advertising panel. In addiction, Krauss writes: "photography functions against the grain of its earlier attempts at self-destruction, becoming, under precisely the guise of its own obsolescence, a means of what has to be called an act of reinventing the medium."[14] Here, obsolescence does not concern the technical apparatus, but rather the photographic image in itself.

Figure 1: Rosângela Rennó, Survival Image, 2015. © Rosângela Rennó. Exhibition view at Cristina Guerra Contemporary Art Gallery. Photographer: Bruno Lopes. Courtesy: Cristina Guerra Contemporary Art, Lisbon.

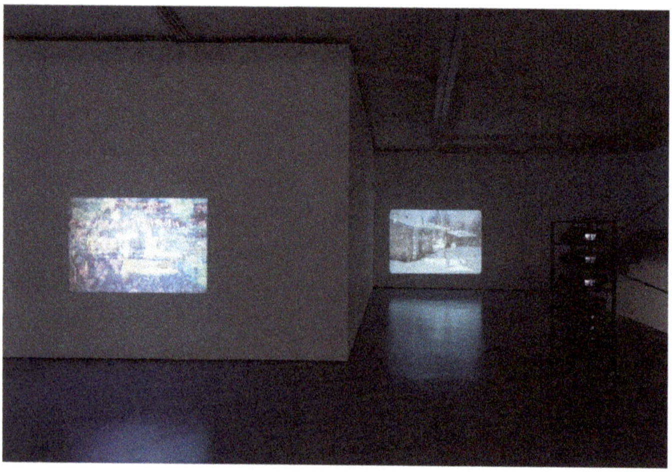

Apart from Krauss' position, there is also another way of referring to the obsolete: image appropriation. i.e., the act of using photographs previously taken by other authors. *Survival Image* (2015) by Brazilian artist Rosângela Rennó (Figure 1) can serve as an example. This artwork is made up of racks holding Kodak projectors, their projections, and some extra trays. The slides used were found in secondhand markets. The device follows a normative use – a projection on a wall –, but the visual

14 Krauss, "Reinventing the Medium," 296.

effect changes because the images are overlapped. They show everyday private life, but places, figures, and objects look faded, seemingly on the edge of disappearance. According to Portuguese curator João Silvério, the installation "creates a residual, almost overexposed, image" evoking "an almost spectral relation to memory."[15] Even though Rennó usually uses photography, she is not a photographer in the narrow sense, as she also works with text, video, and installation. According to the Brazilian curator Moacir dos Anjos, the artist "prefers to draw on the vast inventory of already-existing images", building up, in a Foucaultian perspective, "an *archaeology* and a *genealogy* of photography, situating it as an integral part of a system of knowledge and values that anchors forms of power in society, be they clearly defined or more indistinct."[16] When Rennó works with anachronistic optical devices – in this case slides –, obsolescence focuses on the modes of reception, the way a profusion of photographs was shared throughout the twentieth century. The viewer does not see a subversion of the technological equipment, but rather an interest in the survival of existing images and the mode in which they were handled.

The appropriation of photographic images and of objects refers to the work of the German photographer, Andreas Müller-Pohle, specifically his essay "Information Strategies" (1985) and his concept of "ecology of information", as Rennó herself indicates. In that text, Müller-Pohle proposes a critical attitude through "recycling or revitalizing consumed information" and a "reintegration of 'waste' information into the communications cycle."[17] In this case, the word "waste" can be interpreted as dissipation, disposal, residual, spoilage or even garbage and trash. Moreover, this concept is reminiscent of the verse, "O que é bom para o lixo é bom para a poesia" (what is good for the trash is good for poetry)[18], from a 1974 poem by Brazilian poet, Manoel de Barros. Indeed, Rennó chose this excerpt to refer to her own work. If forgotten and out of use objects can be thought of as a kind of obsolescence, *Survival Image* can be viewed as a reintegration process of obsolete information.

"Zombie media" and material reinvention

Until now this analysis has mainly referred to the normative use of technological equipment, which subverts its visual effects – i.e. artists' work to re-construct/re-

15 João Silvério, "Rosângela Rennó – Insólidos" (Cristina Guerra Contemporary Art, 2015), http://www.cristinaguerra.com/exhibition.past.php?&year=2015.

16 Moacir dos Anjos, *Rosângela Rennó* (Recife: Museu de Arte Moderna Aloisio Magalhães, 2006), 31.

17 Andreas Müller-Pohle, "Information Strategies," Equivalence, accessed July 12, 2019, http://equivalence.com/labor/lab_mp_wri_inf_e.shtml.

18 Manoel de Barros, *Poesia Completa* (São Paulo: Leya, 2010), 147.

present the conventional use of the photographic image. This analysis has also addressed obsolescence in connection with topics like sustainability, material ecology, and the informational domain. Beyond the mere use of obsolete technology, the Canadian artist, Garnet Hertz, and the Finnish researcher, Jussi Parikka, observe in some art pieces a different reconfiguration of media on a technical-material level, which they call "zombie media". In their essay of 2012, the authors use the concept to identify technology which had fallen into desuetude, and their system and functions were altered by artists. According to Hertz and Parikka, the machines are modified through a technique of bending the circuits: a manipulation of 'inner' mechanisms by amateurs, rather than specialists. This technique permits the use of obsolete, broken equipment that is often completely unusable and becomes a "black box."[19] The machines are constituted as closed-circuits that could be used without one needing to understand their components. Their function is no longer known *a priori*, but through the end-result of the operation.

This kind of intervention could result from two approaches: DIY and hacking. The first concept defines a self-made manipulation of any apparatus or object[20], converting original functions into other uses. In addition to this, the second term expresses a desire to overcome normative uses and limits. Although the word 'hacker' usually refers to informatics and the internet, it also names authors with a deeper knowledge of hidden systems whose purpose is to find gaps in said systems. Artists are included in both dimensions. Even without the necessary technical equipment, they redefine the limits of the apparatus. "Hardware hacking and other hacktivist exercises," confirms historian Wanda Strauven, are "contemporary artistic methods to resist the media industry's planned obsolescence."[21]

Additionally, the concept of "zombie media" also concerns "media that is not only out of use, but resurrected to new uses, contexts and adaptations,"[22] similar to Krauss' definition of "media reinvention". Another perspective therefore opens up: reusing obsolete media signals "the importance of operability of the newly repurposed devices, even if they are often totally useless or purposeless."[23] Although the reinvention of media establishes new functions, it does not utterly replace the apparatus. The obsolete device does not disappear, it physically remains as modifications are worked into its existing functions and highlighted when the machine

---

19 Hertz and Parikka, "Zombie Media: Circuit Bending Media Archaeology into an Art Method," 424–30, at 428.

20 Hertz and Parikka, "Zombie Media", 426.

21 Wanda Strauven, "The (Noisy) Praxis of Media Archaeology," in *At the Borders of (Film) History: Temporality, Archaeology, Theories. FilmForum/2014: XXI Convegno Internazionale Di Studi Sul Cinema*, ed. Alberto Beltrame, Giuseppe Fidotta, and Andrea Mariani (Udine: Forum, 2015), 33–41, at 36.

22 Hertz and Parikka, "Zombie Media", 429.

23 Strauven, "The (Noisy) Praxis of Media Archaeology," 36.

is activated. In spite of its alterations, the media continue somehow to keep part of the conventions that defined them during their historical-social life. Even if the device loses its old operations, it retains some of its appearance and it evokes a past time. The "zombie media" concept reveals how past and future meet in the modified, outdated apparatus: new functions coexist with elements from a conventional and normative past. Hacking intervenes with a linear understanding of time; it breaks the idea of progress connected to the machine.

Case study: Portuguese artist-duo, Gusmão and Paiva

João Maria Gusmão and Pedro Paiva have developed art projects together since 2001. For two decades their practice has been characterized by a discourse of "philosophical-poetic fiction,"[24] influenced by, for example, French writer Alfred Jarry and his concept of Pataphysics, as well as French philosopher Henry Bergson and his concept of Intuition[25]. In terms of media, Gusmão and Paiva prioritize analog, lens-based apparatuses, such as photography and 16mm and 35mm film, but also sculpture and installation. In an interview with the Portuguese curator Miguel Amado, they say that analog media was chosen not in opposition to digital technology, "but for the characteristic of verisimilitude that an analog image produces."[26] Thus, photographs and films are regarded with a double interpretation: "on the one hand, as fake construction inside an illusionistic narrative, like a trick, or, on the other, as depiction of a fictional factual event, or better, the true quality of what is shot during a magical performance."[27] Their explanations point to a relevant aspect in their work, the play between reality and fiction of/in the image. For instance, in their film *3 Suns* (2009), the viewer witnesses an unlikely scene: a seascape with three shining stars that destabilizes the spectator's vision and undermines a rational presumption. Another example is *Colombo's Column* (2006): in this film, a man stacks a series of eggs,

---

24 Macba, "João Maria Gusmão + Pedro Paiva," Macba, accessed January 29, 2020, https://www.macba.cat/en/art-artists/artists/a-z/gusmao-joao-maria-paiva-pedro.

25 Several of Gusmão and Paiva catalogs and books present literary and philosophical influences – e.g., *Experiments and Observations on Different Kinds of Air* (2009), that includes essays by Honoré Balzac, Fernando Pessoa, and Paul Valery, among others. See Natxo Checa et al., *Experiments and Observations on Different Kinds of Air de João Maria Gusmão + Pedro Paiva* (Lisbon: Direcção-Geral das Artes – Ministério da Cultura, 2009).

26 "mas pela característica de verosimilhança que a imagem analógica produz". See Miguel Amado, "Condição Do Enigmático," *L+arte*, no. 28 (September 2006): 18–22, at 20.

27 "por um lado, enquanto construção falsa dentro da narrativa ilusionista, isto é, o truque de magia, ou, por outro lado, enquanto representação de um acontecimento ficcional factual, isto é, a qualidade verdadeira do que está a ser filmado num espectáculo de magia". See Amado, 22.

one on top of the other. This action creates a precariously balanced egg structure and a representation of impossible equilibrium. Gusmão and Paiva's pieces work intertwining reality and fiction, which questions the analogue optic system as a generator of knowledge and truth.

As British curator Mark Nash points out, Gusmão and Paiva's works might be characterized by a "surrealist discontinuity;" although there seems to be very little connection between the films, they "recreate something of the originary strangeness and disorientation [that] the early silent films would have created for their first viewers."[28] For Nash, Gusmão and Paiva's choice of analog media resumes issues related to the suggestive power of cinema from the beginning of the twentieth century. The Portuguese curator Pedro Lapa also agrees that these films allude "to another time" and to the advent of the moving image that "implies its selective and critical return in a different historical context."[29]

Although critics have focused primarily on their films, the latest works of Gusmão and Paiva extend the aforementioned aspects. The slide-projections *Sunset, Camels in Egypt, Faucet, Jumping White Square on a Green Square, Snowfall* and *Green Orange* – henceforth referred to as *Sun, C, F, J, Snow,* and *G* – were compounded into a unique installation using outdated projectors (Figure 2)[30]. The works were exposed in three different spaces in 2018: a collective exhibition, *Estudos do Labirinto* (Labyrinth-Studien) at Calouste Gulbenkian Planetarium in Lisbon, as well as two solo shows, one at Sies + Höke Gallery in Düsseldorf entitled *Green Orange* and the other at Fortes D'Aloia & Gabriel | Galpão in São Paulo named *A Dog with a Remarkable Tail*. In each presentation the installation followed a different design.

28 Mark Nash, "Memories_of_celluloid," in *Celluloid – Tacita Dean, João Maria Gusmão and Pedro Paiva, Rosa Barba, Sandra Gibson and Luis Recoder*, ed. Marente Bloemheuvel and Jaap Guldemond (Amsterdam e Rotterdam: Eye Filmmuseum e nai010 publishers, 2016), 17–23, at 20.

29 Pedro Lapa, *Intrusão: The Red Square*, translanted by 100 Folhas (Lisbon: Museu do Chiado – Museu Nacional de Arte Contemporânea, 2005), 17.

30 The first piece of these new works was *Sunset* (2017), presented in the exhibition *Os Animais que ao Longe Parecem Moscas*, at Oliva Creative Factory (São João da Madeira, Portugal).

Figure 2: João Maria Gusmão & Pedro Paiva, A Dog with a Remarkable Tail, 2018 © João Maria Gusmão & Pedro Paiva. Exhibition view at Fortes D'Aloia & Gabriel | Galpão, São Paulo. Photographer: Eduardo Ortega. Courtesy Fortes D'Aloia & Gabriel, São Paulo/Rio de Janeiro.

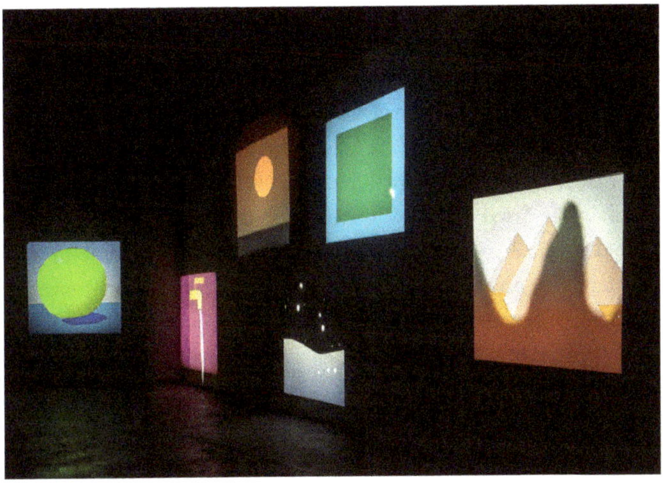

As previously mentioned, the latest works of Gusmão and Paiva are made up of modified slide projectors that produce animated images. The main difference between their older and newer works is that in previous works the projector was used in a normative way following technical conventions. *The Big Game* (2005), for example, used a slide projector to project nineteen enigmatic and parodic images. *Sun, C, F, J, Snow,* and *G*, however, demonstrate a change in how conventional technology is used: the slide projector is redefined by DIY and hacker practices. Various devices such as riddled discs, colored filters, metallic tapes, and so on, intervene in real-time within the appearance of the static images, lending movement. In a conversation on November 18th, 2019, Gusmão mentioned the aim to develop pieces "of continuous light," using *camera obscura* as an example. This optical device is a progenitor of lens-based images. Here, light flows through a tiny pinhole into a completely darkened room. The picture of the world outside appears upside down. This visual transposition keeps the characteristics of the objects and functions without the mediation of photo-filmic supports.

These latest artworks of Gusmão and Paiva also share characteristics with the older magic lantern technology[31]. Both the magic lantern and the altered slide projector achieve a kinetic experience by adding unusual parts to a conventional mech-

31 The magic lantern was a projective instrument mentioned in the book, *Ars Magna Lucis et Umbrae* (1646) by German Jesuit Athanasius Kircher. The device was made up of a lens,

anism. In these works by the Portuguese artists, we deal not only with a material issue, but also with an immersive dimension. Returning to some historical uses of magic lanterns such as entertainment, illusion, and persuasion[32], the two artists highlight the experience of enchantment through the movement effect of their analog machinery.

The altered slide projections of Gusmão and Paiva are similar to the works of the Portuguese artist Francisco Tropa. We will consider the works in the exhibition *Scenario*, in the Portuguese pavilion at the *54th Venice Biennale – ILLUMInations* (2011). Here, Tropa showed objects, sculptures, and seven works using projectors similar to magic lanterns. Their structures included converters, fans, light bulbs, lenses, and other materials like dried leaves, water, sand, insects, and incandescent filament. The projectors produced reversed (left to right) and inverted (upside-down) images: the water droplets of one of the sculptures did not fall, but rather moved upwards. According to the Portuguese curator Sérgio Mah, Tropa creates projections that "are strange and spellbinding, a bewildering experience that causes wavering between the recognizable and the indiscernible."[33] As in the works of Gusmão and Paiva, this astonishment grows when the viewer understands that Tropa's devices no longer "reproduce the movement" or, more so, they are not kinematic projections, but instead that the movement of continuous light occurs in real-time, produced by the mechanism of the projector itself.

---

a light source, and an image on the glass; it reproduced the blown-up images on a wall or screen.

32 To deepen the history of the magic lantern and its forms of entertainment, we suggest reading Jennifer F. Eisenhauer, "Next Slide Please: The Magical, Scientific, and Corporate Discourses of Visual Projection Technologies." *Studies in Arte Education* 47, no. 3 (2006): 198–214 and Friedrich Kittler, *Optical Media: Berlin Lectures 1999*, translated by Antonhy Enns (Cambridge: Polity press, 2010).

33 Sérgio Mah, *Scenario. Francisco Tropa*, translated by Brad Cherry, Paola D'agostino, and Kennis Translations SA (Lisbon: Direcção-Geral das Artes – Ministério da Cultura, 2011), 12.

Figure 3: Francisco Tropa, Pharmacie, 2019 © Francisco Tropa. Courtesy artist and galleries Jocelyn Wolff (Paris), Gregor Podnar (Berlin) and Quadrado Azul (Lisbon).

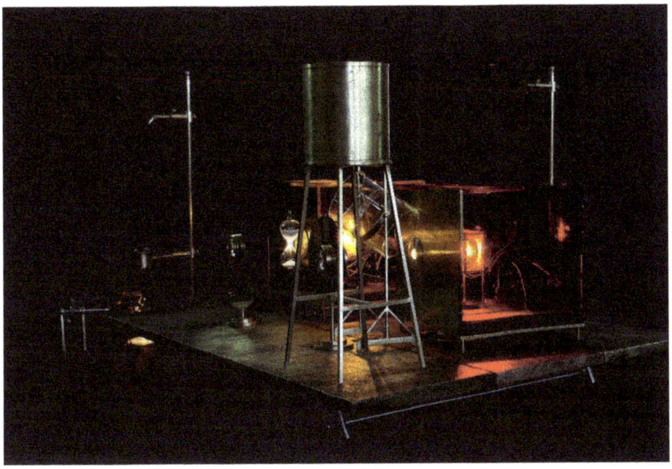

Tropa called his devices "lanterns" (lanternas) because he intended to emphasize "the idea of a moving mechanism that emitted a beam of light with a certain scintillation, with a certain degree of magic, of enchantment."[34] In fact, the movement in these projections destabilizes the chronological conventions of the spectator. The artist comments, "[t]he different mechanisms always presupposed the attempt to show different forms of measuring time."[35] In Tropa's works, time-measures are unsorted; both the standard ones – such as the rolling of sand grains – and the irregular, non-standard ones – such as the climbing of water. This mixing of time reaches its most sophisticated form in *Pharmacie* (Pharmacy) from 2019. It not only has one mechanism to project, as in the previous works, but also is a complete installation composed of four lanterns (Figure 3). They all add up to a singular image in which various movements – a drop, clockwork gears, an hourglass – are co-presented with a static image of agate; the visual result is a play between lights and shadows in a continuous flux of unrepeatable combinations.

34 Francisco Tropa, *Arénaire* (Paris: Galerie Jocelyn Wolff, 2014), 37.

35 Tropa, *Arénaire*, 37.

Figure 4: João Maria Gusmão & Pedro Paiva, A Dog with a Remarkable Tail, 2018 © João Maria Gusmão & Pedro Paiva. Exhibition view at Fortes D'Aloia & Gabriel | Galpão, São Paulo. Photographer: Eduardo Ortega. Courtesy Fortes D'Aloia & Gabriel, São Paulo/Rio de Janeiro.

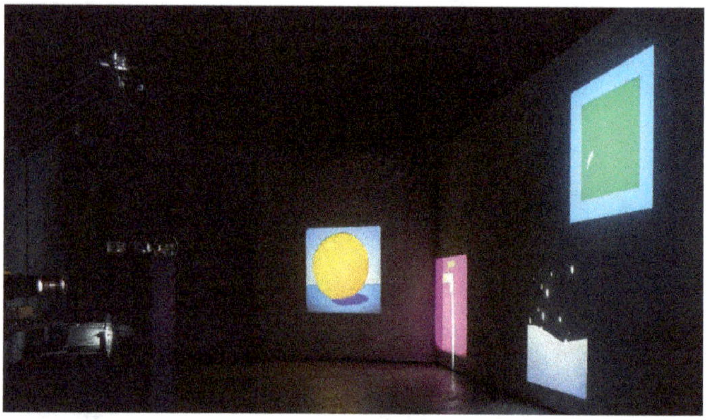

Similar to Tropa's works, one might consider Gusmão and Paiva's *Sun, C, F, J, Snow,* and *G* (Figure 4). Their installation also suggests a transformation of the viewer's experience of time, which is no longer represented chronologically or as a narrative, but rather as a layering of distinct durations and events reverberating in the body of the beholder. Another factor that impacts on the physical experience of the visitor is related to the exhibition environment and architecture, since in each presentation the installation changes: while the spectator in the Calouste Gulbenkian can relax in the reclining chairs of the auditorium of the Lisbon Planetarium, in the "white cube/black box" of Fortes D'Aloia & Gabriel | Galpão in São Paulo, the visitor wanders around the space.

The projectors of Gusmão and Paiva are programmed to randomly change images. The spectator can not see the projections simultaneously or in synchronicity, but rather as a set of appearances and dissipations. In this obscure space, wherein color and shape continuously change, attention seems to be captured not only by the projections, but also by the sound. Even if the projected images remind the viewer of a silent movie, the installation should not be taken as noiseless: the machines themselves rumble. The noise is present, evoking memories. Sound belongs to the technical side of the installation and plays a significant role[36].

36 In the conversation mentioned above, Gusmão claims that the projectors and their sounds are not important for the practice or diegetic construction of their exhibitions. For the artist-duo, the projectors should not be considered as a sculptural element and the sound is just a technical consequence of analog devices.

In all of these works, Gusmão and Paiva have utilized outdated slide projectors inserting recently developed pieces and mechanisms – their devices are a kind of machine collage from different contexts. In this sense, a linear understanding of time is undermined. Gusmão and Paiva's constructions do not provoke a return of the past in the present, and do not constitute a mere reenactment of no longer times. This process triggers a combination of temporalities. Their altered machines suggest something that could have happened in the past: it is not clear if these machines ever existed in history, or if a fictionalization of the past.

The critique of a linear understanding of time, proposed by these artworks, echoes the work of German philosopher Walter Benjamin in "On the Concept of History;" taken up by Media Archaeology in order to not limit itself to identify the old in the new[37]. Following this thought, Wanda Strauven notices that Media Archaeology "can be conceived of as history hacking, as circuit bending the false image of linear history, which is still so dominant today."[38] (2015, 38). Also, Elsaesser's *Media Archaeology as the Poetics of Obsolescence* may be useful in helping to understand the change concerning the concept of time from Benjamin's perspective. Through obsolescence, he writes, "the present rediscovers a certain past to which it then attributes the power to shape aspects of the future that are now our present."[39] He calls this the "loop of belatedness."[40] To design an interrelation of different times, proposing a hypothetical tense, determines "*the need to re-invent history*,"[41] "invoking alternative histories" and "imaginary media."[42] In these forms of different conjunctions of time, one should regard Gusmão and Paiva's machines in *Sun, C, F, J, Snow* and *G*, which use an obsolete and uncommon mechanism and therefore conjoin various real and fictional temporalities.

---

37 Strauven recognizes in Media Archaeology "four different, sometimes opposite approaches adopted by key figures of the field, which consist in seeking: 1) the old in the new; 2) the new in the old; 3) recurring topoi; or 4) ruptures and discontinuities". See Wanda Strauven, "Media Archaeology: Where Film History, Media Art, and New Media (Can) Meet," in *Preserving and Exhibiting Media Art: Challenges and Perspectives*, edited by Julia Noordegraaf, Cosetta G. Saba, Barbara Le Maître, and Vinzenz Hediger (Amsterdam: Amsterdam University Press, 2013) 59–79, at 68.

38 Strauven, "The (Noisy) Praxis of Media Archaeology," 38.

39 Elsaesser, "Media Archaeology as the Poetics of Obsolescence," 331–50, at 348.

40 Elsaesser, "Media Archaeology as the Poetics of Obsolescence," 348–49.

41 Elsaesser, "Media Archaeology as the Poetics of Obsolescence," 336.

42 Jussi Parikka, *What Is Media Archaeology?* (Cambridge: Polity press, 2012), 139.

Final considerations

To conclude this essay, let's consider some reflections of Portuguese artist Miguel Leal in "Obsolescência e Inoperatividade: a Arte como Contrafluxo da Mediação" from 2011 (Obsolescence and Un-operativity: Art as Counter Flux of Mediation). Here the author outlines an apparent contradiction of the discourse around obsolescence in art: on the one hand, it has often become a normative operation, constituting for many artists "a true method" (um verdadeiro método)[43]; on the other, it could be a disruptive "questioning of the function of media and its operability" (um questionamento da função dos *media* e da sua operatividade)[44]. Considering this duality, the most recent works by Gusmão and Paiva unfold to expose two aspects: resistance and a methodology. Moreover, their works are not simple investigations into the machine and its inscribed meaning, but rather they are an attempt to reorganize the relation between the spectator and the mechanism of projection, the spectator and the images.

A shared meaning can be identified in the arguments collected in this essay: a dialectic in the approach to obsolescence in contemporary art. Following Leal, obsolescence has lost its nostalgic character, which lent to it "something reassuring, familiar and nostalgic, sometimes in a fad phenomenon" (algo de tranquilizador, familiar e nostálgico, por vezes mesmo num fenómeno de moda)[45]. Similarly, Elsaesser points out the risk of possible fetishism when treating obsolescence as nostalgic. In this sense, the Portuguese curator João Pinharanda finds that Gusmão and Paiva's works "seem to hover in a 1800s time frame [...] creating a certain nostalgic atmosphere. Yet, this fact does not come across so much as belong to the realm of nostalgia and fetichism [...], but rather as a staging determined by a humorous, parodic expression."[46] In fact, Gusmão and Paiva's works are less related to a nostalgic sphere, as Pinharanda points out, but are more concerned with obsolescence as "re-enactment, recovery, and redemption,"[47] as Elsaesser highlights.

Taking into account that the "acceleration of novelty production is a disabling of collective memory,"[48] then the practice of replacement or enhancement in projecting machines could be a critical reflection on power structures of today. The artworks of Gusmão and Paiva, Tropa, and Rennó propose a discontinuity. They question the

43 Miguel Leal, "Obsolescência e Inoperatividade: A Arte Como Contrafluxo Da Mediação," *Interact Revista Online de Arte, Cultura e Tecnologia* 18 (2011), http://interact.com.pt/18/obsolescencia-e-inoperatividade/.

44 Leal, "Obsolescência e Inoperatividade: A Arte Como Contrafluxo Da Mediação,"

45 Leal, "Obsolescência e Inoperatividade: A Arte Como Contrafluxo Da Mediação,"

46 Anabela Sousa and João Pinharanda, eds., *Fundação EDP: Prémio EDP Novos Artistas, 2000–2004*, translated by José Gabriel Flores (Lisbon: Fundação EDP, 2005), 76.

47 Elsaesser, "Media Archaeology as the Poetics of Obsolescence,", 334.

48 Crary, *24/7. Late Capitalism and the Ends of Sleep*, 47.

disappearance of certain objects and information, highlighting obsolescence as a strategy for rethinking and reformulation. Gusmão and Paiva's works in particular can be understood as a turn in the contemporary modes of production; as an opportunity to develop other histories, once again, a way to "re-enactment, recovery, and redemption."[49]

49 Elsaesser, "Media Archaeology as the Poetics of Obsolescence," 331–50, at 334.

A Two-Way Mirror: Narcissism and Surveillance from the Closed Circuit to the Network[1]

Olivier Asselin

The *technical* object (as a tool) and more specifically the *media* (as a tool of communication) both occupy a central place within the realm of objects. The technical object is not just an object like the others since it is a *mediation* between subject and object, between one subject and another. And this mediation is not passive since it is constitutive of the subject and object that it mediates.

In this essay, I would like to consider a singular technical object: video, which has made it possible to capture, record, and disseminate sounds and images through an electronic signal. This tool developed piecemeal over the course of the 20th century. In the 1950s, it became a form of mass media as television, and later, in the 1960s and 1970s, as a type of household technology with the advent of the Portapak. Artists quickly appropriated the latter, often diverting it from its essentially documentary vocation and transforming it into a closed-circuit system and a means for making self-portraits, like a mirror. The space that subsequently opened up here may help us to better understand what is happening today regarding social media with its video selfies, webcams, and videotelephony.

In her famous text, "Video: The Aesthetics of Narcissism", Rosalind Krauss noted the recurrence of self-portraiture in emerging video art[2]. More specifically, she discovered, with her usual perspicacity, a singular encounter between form and motif, physical and psychological characteristics, a technological apparatus and a psychoanalytic situation. On the one hand, there is "the simultaneous reception and projection of an image," the "recording and transmitting at the same time," "instant feedback"— simultaneous *recording* and *reception*, what we call *live* transmission, but fed back into itself; on the other hand, there is "the human body as its central instrument," "the human psyche as conduit," —that of the artist (in the case of single-channel videos) or the viewer (in the case of installations). Enclosing the body between two machines, the camera and the monitor, the apparatus functions like a

1 The text was translated by Donald McGrath.

2 Rosalind Krauss, "Video: The Aesthetics of Narcissism," *October*, Vol. 1 (Spring 1976): 50–64.

mirror and cultivates a certain degree of narcissism. Indeed, Krauss would even go so far as to claim that narcissism was the very "condition" of the medium[3].

Here, as elsewhere, Krauss pursued her extended critical dialogue with the formalism of Clement Greenberg and his reading of modernism. In her view, video art, like minimalism, broke with the modernism as conceived by Greenberg. As we know, modernism for him was a self-critical tendency that led each art form to abandon what it shared with the other arts so as to manifest its own *essence*, i.e. what was *specific* to *it*—in other words, its medium, physical properties, and specific effects – which led to a progressive separation of the arts. For Greenberg, the essence of painting, for example what modernist painting unceasingly manifested, was "flatness, the delimitation of flatness and the properties of pigment" as well as the illusion of a "purely optical space" (what Michael Fried was to call "opticality"). But video art's narcissism is of another kind.

Modernist Reflexivity and Video Reflection

At a first glance, video art *reflection* may appear to be in perfect continuity with modernist *reflexivity*: in both cases the medium points to itself. But Krauss, for political and other reasons, wanted to set them in opposition to one another, as if there was a historical "rift" between them. In modernist painting, the object doubles back on itself (as in Jasper Johns' *Flag*) while in video art it is excluded; in modernist painting, the artist "locates his own expressiveness through a discovery of the objective conditions of his medium and its history" and in the "recognition of the material and historical independence of an external object," while in video art the feedback loop is the instrument of a "double repression" – the "consciousness of temporality and the separation between subject and object" are "submerged," and the artist and the viewer are abandoned in the "suspended space of narcissism," etc[4].

But a more attentive analysis that draws mainly on the semiotics of Charles Sanders Pierce (whose work Krauss would address a few years later in her "Notes on the Index," 1977[5])— clearly reveals that the distinction between the *reflexivity* of modernist art and the *reflection* of video art is not so sharp after all. Modernist reflexivity could very well have a narcissistic dimension and, conversely, the narcissism of video art could just as well be a form of auto-reflexivity.

In order to display its essential flatness, modernist painting often strove to represent it, bringing figure and ground, motif and form, the represented sur-

3 Krauss, "Video: The Aesthetics of Narcissism," 52.

4 Krauss, "Video: The Aesthetics of Narcissism," 56–57.

5 Rosalind Krauss, "Notes on the Index: Seventies Art in America," part 1, *October*, Vol. 3 (Spring 1977): 68–81; part 2, *October*, Vol. 4 (Autumn 1977): 58–67.

face and the literal surface into dialogue. Krauss calls this process a *doubling*, a *dédoublement* (she uses the French term), but it involves more precisely an icon of an icon, in the sense intended by Pierce. However, modernist painting sometimes has recourse to another process that consists not in representing the literal surface but in presenting it through collage – which shows flatness while simultaneously concealing it – or through a "deductive structure" – which shows the limits of flatness by repeating it, like an index of an index. In the first case (*dédoublement*), representation, the difference between what represents and what is represented, is manifested through infinite repetition, as in a *mise en abyme*; in the second case (collage or deductive structure), the distinction is blurred in dialectic reference, as in *metalepsis*. In its ideal version, the modernist painting no longer alludes to an external referent (since the motif disappears along with all tactile space), but it is not yet a mere object in the world (since it presents a purely pictorial optical space). Nor does the painting allude to the sender (the painter is denied when the brushstrokes are minimized) or the receiver (the viewer is denied when motif, perspective, and depth are abandoned in favour of a pure opticality that offers an exclusively visual experience involving only the sense of sight).

While the separation of subject and object is maintained at this point, it has been considerably weakened: the painting has been reduced to a pure surface—it no longer produces an image of an external object, but is not yet a mere object in the world—and the viewer's experience is reduced to vision alone—he or she is no longer a mind but not yet a body.[6] Painting has become an autonomous surface that refers only to itself, like a double index coiled back upon itself. To simplify this, one could say that modernist painting is itself a sort of primary narcissism yet an objective one, from which the outside world, the artist, and the viewer are excluded. In formalism, painting is constructed like a *psychotic* alterity marked by foreclosure—or better still, like a *maternal* alterity whose gaze is elsewhere and whose desire is incomprehensible. However, it may be that the aesthetic experience here is akin to a regression toward an essentially oral (visual) and pacified pre-Oedipal world that precedes the formation of the self and the separation of subject and object, sexual difference, desire and the law of the father, the fear of castration and repression, etc.

In video art, things are not any simpler. First, we must remember that instant feedback, which Krauss presents as specific to video, was not really something new. It was, rather, a modality of direct, or live, transmission and already a key feature of telephone, radio, and television technology. It would soon become central to the Web as well. Its existence was contingent on the development of electricity and electronics, coding and decoding, and electronic information storage and transmission,

6 The modernist separation of the arts presupposes, in effect, a separation of the senses, a division of the subject and a fragmentation of experience; Greenbergian formalism is a strictly visual (not corporal) phenomenon.

wired or wireless. It must also be understood that, despite all of the received ideas about the rupture from analog to digital, electronic transmission possesses, apart from its pronounced iconic character (its resembles its referent), an essential indexical dimension (it is physically connected to its referent).

The Indexical Beyond the Imprint and the Photograph

Reflections on the indexical in art history and in film studies have undoubtedly been skewed by the hegemony of the photographic model. Hence, Krauss came to identify the indexical in general with the "photographic," as if the two terms were perfectly synonymous, and Georges Didi-Huberman was able to reduce the indexical exclusively to the logic of the imprint while ignoring all of its other dimensions[7].

In his inaugural reflections on the sign, however, Peirce developed a broader concept of the index. As we know, unlike the symbol (whose mode of reference is based on convention) and the icon (which is construed in terms of resemblance or, more generally, analogy), reference in the index is rooted in a physical and real "contiguity" or "connection" with its object in a relationship of causality. Pierce cites many examples of the index: cast objects and photographs, of course, but also thunder, the North Star, moist air, the barometer, a knock on a door, a weather vane, an arrow sign, a shadow, a demonstrative pronoun, etc. From this set, one can undoubtedly single out two fundamental types—the *trace* (imprint, fragment, etc.) and the *pointer* (pointing-finger sign, arrow, smoke, etc.)—which Umberto Eco named differently: *indice* and *indizio* in Italian, or, in the words of his French translator, Jean-Marie Klinkenberg, *indice* and *index*[8]. The trace and the pointer both refer to their object by virtue of their physical connections with it: the first *in absentia* (in the absence of the designated object) and the second *in presentia* (in the presence of the object), as Eco puts it. However, the distinction is deeper than that; it is not so much the presence or absence of the object that matters, but rather the temporality and spatiality of the connective relationship. In the *indice* (trace), the physical connection is broken and the sign refers to something in the past; in other words, it operates through a *delay* (*en différé*). In the case of the *index* (pointer), the physical connection is maintained and the sign refers to something in the present—*live*, so to speak. Whether an *indice* or *index*, the sign can be located or relocated depending on whether it occurs in the very location to which it refers (*in situ*) or elsewhere (*ex situ*). In what follows, I prefer therefore to retain the word *indice* for the general term and use the expressions *live indice* and *deferred indice* to specify their spatial and temporal relationship to the referent.

---

7 Georges Didi-Huberman, *La Ressemblance par contact* (Paris: Minuit, 2008).

8 Umberto Eco, *Le Signe*, trans. Jean-Marie Klinkenberg (Bruxelles: Labor, 1988), 62, note 1.

One therefore sees more clearly what constitutes both the resemblance and the difference between the monument, the relic, and the telephone and (live) television: they all engage in a dialectic of presence or absence, which is why they are all surrounded by an aura[9]. But their spatial and temporal configurations differ: while the arrow pointer presupposes spatial and temporal proximity to its referent (a sort of *this-is-here-now*) and the monument is founded on spatial proximity and temporal distance (a sort of *that-has-been-here*), the relic and the photograph are founded on both spatial and temporal remoteness (*that-has-been-there*)[10], the telephone and live television are founded on temporal proximity and spatial remoteness (*this-is-there-now*).

Between the trace and the pointer, however, all sorts of variations are possible depending on the spatial distance between production and reception (ranging from the few inches in front of a mirror to the kilometres involved in the remote viewing of television) or on the temporal distance (from the few second's delay of live transmission to the thousands of years of relics and ruins). Moreover, these differences fade when a TV show is recorded and broadcasted at some later date, or when a photograph is posted as soon as it is taken on social media. The electronic signal, like light, constitutes an indexicality; in other words, a physical continuity, a contiguity, a causality, and a kind of contact. Both belong, moreover, to the same electromagnetic spectrum.

The Delay and the Recording: The Irruption of the Other's Gaze

The "instant feedback" that interests Krauss is therefore a live electronic transmission that is looped back on itself; in other words, it is no longer a remote transmission from one location to another, more distant one, but rather a sort of auto-transmission from one place to itself. The site of production and the site of reception are folded over one another, making the communication process circular; hence television, in this context, is somewhat akin to a mirror, and the communicational experience to narcissism.

But two elements—two overlooked but crucial elements—alter the mirror. First of all, feedback is often complicated by a delay in transmission that artists do not try to reduce or conceal; on the contrary, they attempt to show it, even to widen it, and play with it incessantly in real time. Secondly, this feedback is often *recorded* and can therefore be presented elsewhere at a later time.

---

9 Cf. Jeffrey Scounce, *Haunted Media: Electronic Presence from Telegraphy to Television* (Durham: Duke University Press, 2000).

10 Roland Barthes, *La Chambre claire* (Paris: Gallimard, Seuil, 1980), 120.

These two elements—the delay and the recording—break the perfect circularity of auto-transmission and narcissism, opening it to time and space and revealing the impossibility of the subject's encounter with itself. These same two elements also introduce an otherness, the Other (the "big Other") into the apparatus on which the subject depends. When the artist considers her image in her studio, she knows that the viewer will look at her later in the gallery; and when, in the gallery, the viewer contemplates his own image, he knows that the artist has already seen him and is looking at him again now because she, the artist, is in control of the apparatus.

By now we can better understand why, in her text, Krauss seems to neglect the difference between the videotape and the video installation, the pre-recorded and the live, the position of the artist and that of the viewer: the electronic apparatus always has a certain degree of indexicality; it works in real time at least and, if it is not live, it can nonetheless seem to be. Moreover, the communication the apparatus establishes and the positions it presents—sender and receiver, artist and viewer—are potentially *reversible*—like psychoanalytical positions and relations: exhibitionist and voyeur, masochist and sadist, etc. (At this point one would do well to reread Freud's text, "A Child Is Being Beaten").

The video apparatus is somewhat reminiscent of the classical situation of the self-portrait in painting: the video artist is placed between the monitor and the camera just as the painter is placed between the canvas and a mirror. The genre of the painted self-portrait occurs in many variations depending on whether or not one sees, inside the frame of the painting, the very painting that the artist is in the process of making and the mirror in which they see their reflection; it also depends on whether the painting's viewpoint is identified with the gaze of the artist in the mirror, on what the mirror shows us of the artist, or on the viewpoint of the third party. Most of the time, the painter seems to look toward the viewer, but is actually looking at their own image in the mirror and, in this narcissistic circularity of the painting, viewers are simultaneously excluded (since they are not "seen") and included (since they see), like a voyeur.

This rupture in circularity—the hollow presence of the Other—is why, above and beyond narcissism, the video apparatus is also a one-way mirror; in other words, a surveillance system.

The Forms of the Electronic Apparatus

This close relationship between narcissism and surveillance is not new (we will come back to it later) but it became explicit when the gaze was remediated by electronic signal and live transmission, which have always been used in a double manner. We must keep in mind that, in the 1970s, the video apparatus found another application, one that was neither domestic nor artistic – like with the Sony Portapak – but corporative, in the form of closed-circuit television (CCTV). Likewise, the webcams that appeared in the 1990s at the same time as reality TV (both phenomena are connected) made it possible for individuals to "film" and exhibit their lives in real time, live, 24 hours a day, and 7 days a week; but they also enabled the police to monitor entire cities. We would undoubtedly also have to examine the integration of video and videotelephony into social media on platforms like Windows' Skype, Google's YouTube and Hangouts or Meet, and Apple's FaceTime from this same angle, as, once again, the live (or almost live) self-portrait links up with surveillance.[11]

Obviously, not all electronic devices are alike. First of all, the telephone uses point-to-point (P2P) and two-way (unicast) transmission. Radio and television, on the other hand, use point-to-multipoint (P2MP) and one-way (broadcast) transmission. CCTV, inversely, involves one-way multipoint-to-point transmission, while video generally proceeds by way of one-way point-to-point transmission. The Internet, for its part, is open to all of these models: unicast, multicast, or broadcast; one-way, two-way, or multidirectional. The scope of this communication network varies just as much from one device to another, ranging from the two points of video and the many points of CCTV to the billions of points of the Web. Some of these apparatuses are rather amateur while others are professional—in other words, artisanal versus industrial. But, they all partake in the same paradigm in that they establish similar, essentially electronic (i.e. indexical) connections. In other words, they presuppose a reversibility—at least potentially—with respect to both transmission and position (because electronic technology, its instruments, and its infrastructure are generally reversible). Hence, their use apart from communication is twofold and encompasses both narcissism and surveillance.

Narcissism and Surveillance, Spectacle and Discipline

In a brief and somewhat unexpected passage in her text, Krauss questions the sociohistorical causes of this interest in the video apparatus and speaks of "the problem of narcissism in the wider context of our culture," "the specific inner workings

---

11 Facebook, for example, is cost-free for individual users but not for companies because the members profile—an individual's network with its activity history—makes it possible to present targeted advertising along the search paths of users who are already interested in the products featured (remarketing). This revolution in advertising was inaugurated by Google (with the AdSense network and the AdWords system) and launched on Facebook in 2008, when Sheryl Sandberg, a sales and operations manager, left one company for the other. The system made Facebook profitable, enabling it to grow by 2000% in a year (between 2004 and 2005) and raising its revenue from $400 000 dollars to $40 billion in the dozen years from 2004 to 2020.

of the present art market," and (in order to explain both) the hegemony of mass media[12]. She says, "[t]he demand for instant replay in the media—the creation of a work that literally does not exist outside that replay (...)—finds its obvious correlate in an aesthetic mode by which the self is created through the electronic device of feedback"[13]. In this passage—and in her praise of the work of Peter Campus that closes her text—we come to understand, in the final analysis and despite the attention she devotes to the phenomenon, that Krauss disapproves of the narcissism of video art.

It is undeniable that these autofilmic uses of electronic media—not only the video apparatus examined by Krauss, but also the webcam, and videotelephony on social media that have developed since—are often the expression of a certain kind of contemporary narcissism. Subjects who film themselves take pleasure in seeing and showing themselves and in being seen by a few or as many people as possible within the public sphere (in whatever form that may take today). They seem to have completely internalized the logic of mass media—television, followed by the Internet—and the celebrity culture that it both produces and feeds on.

At the same time, these same uses of electronic media extend well beyond narcissism. They attest, as well, to an interiorization of the logic of surveillance, which is one of the most powerful tools for ensuring compliance with social norms. As Foucault showed in his analysis of the panopticon and the society of modern disciplinary control, surveillance works not because "prisoners" are monitored at all times but because they know that they can be. Power is exercised not directly by a central authority, but rather indirectly by the detainees themselves—"automatically." Foucault has shown how surveillance moved outside of the carceral institution and spread its rites and effects—particularly interrogation and confession—into other institutions and practices that do not seem, at least at an initial glance, to involve any relationships of domination, not even constraint.

> "Today", he writes, "the obligation to confess is now relayed through so many different points... that we no longer perceive it as the effect of a power that constrains us; on the contrary, it seems to us that truth, lodged in our most secret nature, 'demands' only to surface; that if it fails to do so, this is because a constraint holds it in place, the violence of a power weighs it down, and it can finally be articulated only at the price of a kind of liberation."[14]

Foucault thus shows us the close connection that exists today between the desire for truth, authenticity, and recognition, and surveillance. "Power" is no longer a *centralized* and *repressive* body that operates by means of obligations and prohibitions,

---

12 Krauss, "The Aesthetics of Narcissism," 59.

13 Krauss, "The Aesthetics of Narcissism," 59.

14 Michel Foucault, *History of Sexuality Volume I: An Introduction*, trans. Robert Hurley (New York: Pantheon Books, 1978), 60.

according to the model of the *law*, but is rather a set of *dispersed* and *hortatory* forces that operate through a broad range of corporal techniques and power apparatuses, following the logic of the *norm*. The forms of subjectivation are often also forms of subjection. The practice of filming oneself is one of both self-surveillance and self-normalization.

Big Mother

This desire to be seen or monitored, however, like the desire to see and monitor, may not be so narrowly narcissistic nor guilty. At a minimum, it is paradoxical—indeed doubly so. People enjoy using electronic devices to show and see themselves and to be seen by others, be it a few people at a time or as many as possible. But, strangely enough, the number of viewers, visits, messages, and likes sometimes seems less important than the number of cameras, monitors, and friends, or than the mere presence of a camera or webpage. It is as if the essential point was not actual recognition but potential visibility; not so much the real gaze of others as the possible gaze of the Other. Used in this way, the electronic apparatus may feed into exhibitionism in its pure state—an *object without a gaze*.

Viewers, likewise, enjoy using electronic devices to see and surveille. However, oddly enough, there is generally little to see, indeed nothing exceptional or remarkable: no important events, no real story, but merely the ordinary mundaneness of bland bodies, actions, and words—in short, daily life. Yet, viewers continue to be fascinated by these electronic images. From a certain perspective these images are suspenseful; viewers never know what is going to happen. If they are attentive enough, they may notice slight variations in repetition—micro-events—and they generally do find enough of them to entertain the hope that there will be other, more significant ones—in short, real events. They wait for something but they do not know precisely what, or perhaps they do not want to know; whatever it is remains vague and, consequently, always imminent. Used in this way, the electronic apparatus involves voyeurism in its pure state—a *gaze* without an *object*.

But what trauma is one attempting to replay and thereby ward off? What is the obscure object of desire and fear? Is it the primal scene, separation, sexual difference, castration? In terms of the forms of narcissism and surveillance, exhibitionism and voyeurism that operate in the electronic apparatus (albeit practically to no purpose), it is not so much the subject or object of the gaze that matters, but rather the gaze itself, the connection that it establishes. It is crucial that this audiovisual link be electronic—whether in real time, live, or recorded—and always indexical, for this link, as it is fantasized here, is essentially neither a communication connection nor a power relationship—very little is exchanged or placed under control—but is instead a contact, an almost physical contact, a quasi-umbilical relation.

From a psychoanalytical point of view, narcissism is a neurosis in which the libido makes use of a defence mechanism to turn away from the object and back towards the self. In melancholy, for example, the loss of the love object can produce, through inversion, ambivalence, identification with the lost object, and regression towards narcissism. However, psychoanalysis makes a distinction, which Krauss overlooks, between this form of narcissism – understood as an adult and secondary form – and another more archaic form that is said to be primary: that of the child whose libido is directed toward his or her own body as the love object *before* selecting exterior objects. The mirror stage is a concrete illustration of this. We are familiar with the story: the child, who still lacks motor coordination and experiences their body as fragmented, identifies immediately with the image encountered in the mirror (as if with an other); the child gleefully enjoys the control they have over their image and experiences a first imaginary identification. It is on this basis that they will later construct their ego.

When used in this way, however, the electronic apparatus may very well take the subject beyond both secondary and primary narcissism to an even more primal moment wherein the child experiences separation from the mother and the intrusion of the father on the scene. As we know, children, regardless of their sex, enjoy a privileged relationship with the body of the mother; a proximity that forms the basis of a strong imaginary unity that is broken by the law of the father. The formation of the ego, i.e., the subject's entry into the symbolic order—into language, economy, society—depends on the repression of the body of the mother and the acceptance of the law of the father (Kristeva calls this rejection of the mother's body the "primal repression" and deems it the matrix of all subsequent repressions[15]). From this perspective, of course, the electronic apparatus can provoke regression—not necessarily to narcissism, but to a kind of crisis of narcissism, with the re-enactment of this primal scene: the fundamental experience of contact with and loss of the maternal body, which is acknowledged yet denied, in the perverse and incessant interplay of presence and absence. This also brings the moment in which the cry becomes language back into play, as this is when the child's somatic need becomes a psychological demand and when the always incomplete intervention of the mother, both satisfying and unsatisfying, demonstrates the fundamental lack, the infinite demand for love that constitutes every subject: nothing will ever bring complete satisfaction and desire is inextinguishable. The subject would like for contact to be maintained everywhere and at all times, but is ever fearful that it may be severed and therefore return it (the subject) to its fundamental solitude. The pleasure here is oral and the anxiety centred on separation. It is not surprising that the exemplary video works mentioned by Krauss often involve not only the gaze but also the voice, and not only the body but also speech, an elementary form of speech consisting mainly of those

15 Julia Kristeva, *Les Pouvoirs de l'horreur* (Paris : Seuil, 1980), 18.

singular words known as *shifters*—I, you, here, there, now, today, yesterday—which are, precisely speaking, *indices*, pivotal points between the body and language.

With these, as with many other uses of the electronic apparatus, contact is paradoxically both desired and feared. Virtual contact is preferred over actual contact or, more precisely, strictly audiovisual contact is preferred over physical contact. The electronic apparatus offers proximity without the disadvantages of promiscuity, love without sex, attachment without responsibility, and a quasi-umbilical connection without social relation.

Thus, video—like the electronic apparatus more generally, which makes it possible to transmit recorded or live content via a closed circuit or network—is not an object like the others. In a certain manner, it calls into question the very concepts of object and subject as already perfectly constituted. Beyond the technical object and the media, video is neither an autonomous entity nor an extension of the subject. Rather, it emphasizes the relationships between subject and object, between a subject and its image, between a subject and the other's gaze, between a subject and other subjects, and between different places and times. Above all, video shows the active role that technology plays in the very constitution of the subject and the object. Video is, as it were, a kind of philosophical model—phenomenological and psychoanalytical—like the mirror.

Shape of Things, Shapes of Time

Hans-Jörg Rheinberger

Two things fascinated me above all else when I made, over three decades ago, the acquaintance of George Kubler's *The Shape of Time*;[1] a book that accompanied my way out of the laboratory and into the archives of the history of science. The first were the scansions of temporality in which artistic as well as scientific processes of development take place, or, more appropriately formulated, *through* which these processes take shape and realize themselves. The second was the vehemence with which Kubler defended the role of *things* in these processes. In other words, his focus on the materiality of the aesthetic and epistemic objects around which these processes revolve, and their role as genuine actors in the constitution of the respective shapes of time. Both themes are addressed by the title and the subtitle of the book, respectively.

Kubler does not see the flow of time in the field of the arts as a massive, homogenous stream with rising and ebbing phases, cesurae and cascades, but rather as a structure composed of elementary material trajectories, each carrying with it its own temporality. One could also refer to them as contingency networks: "We can imagine the flow of time as assuming the shapes of fibrous bundles [...] The cultural bundles therefore consist of variegated fibrous lengths of happening, mostly long, and many brief. They are juxtaposed largely by chance, and rarely by conscious forethought or rigorous planning."[2] In the image of the fibrous bundle, structural dimensions and forms of concatenation come together, manifesting themselves in the transverse as well as the longitudinal section of the fibers.

For the characterization of historical times, the general historiography as well as the historiography of the arts and the sciences have had recourse again and again to the *longue durée* of biological evolution or the *courte durée* of individual development, each with their specific scansions. Kubler distances himself decidedly from both of these biological metaphors. What he aims to capture is the movement patterns of genuine cultural-historical processes in their specific materiality and temporality of

1 George Kubler, *The Shape of Time. Remarks on the History of Things* (New Haven and London: Yale University Press, 1962).

2 Kubler, *Shape of Time*, 122.

a middle range; in short, the shapes of time located between ontogenesis and phylogenesis, between biographical trajectories and biological evolution.[3] In doing so, Kubler targets the peculiar characters and properties of the *objects* of culture in particular.[4] Unlike many cultural and art historians before him, Kubler is not interested in defining repeating stages or even laws of cultural development. Rather, he aims to provide a conceptual arsenal that makes it possible to capture temporal patterns or trajectories of sequences of objects. His interest is directed toward identifying *patterns* – figures of temporal condensation of a medium range that he himself calls "shapes."

The aspiration to reflect upon the categories in which the history of works of art can be represented does not simply aim to capture meaningful temporal figurations in their formal and symbolic content, but also to arrive at something like a material semantics of things. Ernst Cassirer has formulated this same aspiration in his late Gothenburgian studies on *The Logic of the Cultural Sciences*, as follows: "What emerges is a 'meaning,' which is not absorbed by what is merely physical, but is embodied upon and within it; it is the factor common to all that content which we designate as 'culture'."[5] Thus the late Cassirer himself was on the verge of overcoming that "partial definition of art as symbolic language"[6] that, according to Kubler, was Cassirer's and that had dominated art studies for a long century.

In his short and dense essay, Kubler sketches a history of art way beyond a history that merely concentrates on the symbolic content of works of art. He pleads for – if only programmatically – a rapprochement of the history of the arts and the sciences under a common denominator: "Although both the history of art and the history of science have the same recent origins in the eighteenth-century learning of the European Enlightenment, our inherited habit of separating art from science goes back to the ancient division between liberal and mechanical arts. The separation has had most regrettable consequences. A principal one is our long reluctance to view the processes common to both art and science in the same historical perspective."[7] With this approximation, Kubler did by no means intend to blur the differences between artistic and scientific things, and certainly not those between works

3 On this point, compare Edgar Zilsel, "Geschichte und Biologie, Überlieferung und Vererbung" (1931) in *Wissenschaft und Weltauffassung. Aufsätze 1929–1933*, ed. Gerald Mozetic (Wien: Böhlau, 1998), 101–144.

4 For Kubler's perspective on things, consider Esther Pasztory, *Thinking with Things. Toward a New Vision of Art* (Austin: University of Texas Press, 2005); see also Sarah Maupeu et al., eds., *Im Maschenwerk der Kunstgeschichte. Eine Revision von George Kublers "The Shape of Time"* (Berlin: Kadmos, 2014).

5 Ernst Cassirer, *The Logic of the Cultural Sciences. Five Studies*, trans. Steve G. Lofts (New Haven: Yale University Press, 2000), 98.

6 Kubler, Shape of Time, vii.

7 Kubler, Shape of Time, 10.

of art and technical things. On the contrary, he kept stressing their distinctness: "Although a common gradient connects use and beauty, the two are irreducibly different: no tool can be fully explained as a work of art, nor vice versa."[8] However, he saw comparability in the processes of the *genesis* of epistemic things, including the technical things emerging from them and of works of art; that is, what he called their "common traits of invention, change, and obsolescence"[9] in the temporal dynamics of their becoming, thus in the structures of their emergence.

This induced Kubler to perform a radical turn. Until today, the history of the arts and the history of the sciences are replete with reports about great men in the mode of what Edgar Zilsel once aptly called the "genius religion."[10] Novelty, here, is not only represented as the result of genial strokes of an extraordinary individual, but also as a brainchild, as the sudden inspiration of an exceptionally gifted, ingenious mind. The historical structuralist Kubler is vehemently opposed to this existentialistic image. In his book, novelty is not presented as a result of the illumination of a genius, but rather, if one can say so, as the unprecedented result of retrojection. He compares the situation of the artist with that of an ore digger who, standing at the end of a shaft, can assess the tunnels that others before him have digged, but has no guarantee that the direction which he is about to take will not lead him astray.[11] Kubler's artists – and scientists – thus traverse a terrain whose materiality and opacity challenges them and motivates them in their decisions. They are not led by their dreams, but by the paths that have been trodden before them and which they wish to escape. This by no means implies a denial of the art works' uniqueness, for "[w]orks of art are as unique and irreplaceable as tools are common and expendable."[12] Kubler stresses this point in a comparison between things created to be used and things that are not predominantly destined for perusal and consumption. But, and this is the decisive point, Kubler sees the arts – like the historian of science, Thomas Kuhn, sees the sciences – as "a process that move[s] steadily *from* primitive beginnings but *toward* no goal."[13] We therefore do not have to do with an "evolution-*toward*-what-we-wish-to-know," what we have to do with is instead an "evolution-*from*-what-we-know";[14] a development whose goings-on are determined by choices in the context of the prevailing conditions of possibility. Consequently, a work of art is likewise the result of the pathways that have already been taken, but from which nevertheless it cannot be

---

8 Kubler, *Shape of Time*, 11.

9 Kubler, *Shape of Time*, 10.

10 Edgar Zilsel, *Die Geniereligion. Ein kritischer Versuch über das moderne Persönlichkeitsideal, mit einer historischen Begründung* (1918) (Frankfurt am Main: Suhrkamp, 1990).

11 Kubler, *Shape of Time*, 125.

12 Kubler, *Shape of Time*, 16.

13 Thomas S. Kuhn, *The Structure of Scientific Revolutions*. Second Edition, Enlarged. (Chicago: The University of Chicago Press, 1970), 172.

14 Kuhn, *Structure of Scientific Revolutions*, 171. (Emphasis added).

derived; whether where – and if – the next bonanza will hit, whether where – and if – one will encounter the next escarpment.

This is the point of departure of Kubler's vision of a rapprochement between the history of the sciences and the history of the arts. It is also here that he brings the concept of "series" or "sequence," alongside its variants, into play. He distinguishes between open and closed sequences, intermittent and arrested classes, and extended, wandering, and simultaneous series of objects of art, each of which is characterized by its peculiar forms of manifestation in time.[15] Such series or sequences of works of art – or formal-material problem solutions for that matter – are to be considered, to stay in Kubler's imagery, as temporally-stretched threads in the fibrous bundle of the arts. Kubler's own attempt at defining the concept of sequence reads as follows: "The closest definition of a formal sequence that we now can venture is to affirm it as a historical network of gradually altered repetitions of the same trait. The sequence might therefore be described as having an armature. In cross section let us say that it shows a network, a mesh, or a cluster of subordinate traits; and in long section that it has a fiber-like structure of temporal stages, all recognizably similar, yet altering in their mesh from beginning to end."[16]

Sequences therefore form ensembles; they can proliferate, they can exhaust themselves, they can ramify and spawn new series, they can become fused, intertwined, and transposed temporally and spatially – there is a whole arsenal of relational forms of movement that is connected to them. Yet their material characteristics continue to underlie the actual movement patterns with their frame of contingencies. We shall see that such temporal forms of movement are also characteristic for experimental systems and their constituents in the sciences.

Epistemic Trajectories

It is now time to put Kubler's views on "series" or "sequences" of things of art in relation to my own reflections on epistemic things, their technical surroundings, and their trajectories in the history of the sciences. Instead of strict equivalences, family resemblances in the temporal structures in both realms are to be expected. I would like to briefly present five kinds of trajectories, or sequences, that can be discerned in the empirical sciences. All of them constitute different shapes of time, carrying their own traits and material characteristics with them.

---

15 Kubler, *Shape of Time*, in particular Chapters 2 and 4.

16 Kubler, *Shape of Time*, 37–38.

Trajectories of Experimental Systems

First of all, there are the experimental systems, the frameworks in which the production of experimental traces and data as well as the articulation of epistemic things take place. As a rule, experimental systems form trajectories that can extend over longer periods of time.[17] Their lifespan often coincides with the productivity cycle of a particular research group. Experimental systems are loose compositions of materials, research technologies, and procedures, whose couplings are sufficiently tight in order to structure a research process – in the framework of a certain stage of development of a research field and around a particular research object – in such a way that there is hope regarding finding out something new about the target object. Experimental systems are temporally limited and spatially localized research environments, but they are endowed with an underlying, material continuity over a limited period of time. Along this axis of continuity, however, they change permanently and in unforeseeable fashions.

Migrations of Epistemic Things

Experimental systems and epistemic targets have to be distinguished from one another. The epistemic objects are the materially and theoretically underdetermined entities on which the scientific interest of those who run experimental systems is directed. The system comprises the research technologies with which one seeks to learn about the things of epistemic interest. In a concrete research environment, the investigated phenomenon and the research technology are specifically correlated; they condition each other. Yet, materially they can be of very different natures, as with, for instance, an enzyme isolated from a cell and an ultracentrifuge. Without an epistemically-productive interface between phenomenon and technology there will be no system effects. An instrument that cannot be adjusted to an epistemic object has no scientific value; and an epistemic object that, in one way or another, cannot be made compliant with the instrument is not a phenomenon that can be investigated under scientific auspices.

The concept of the epistemic – epistemicity – is here doubly connotated. Firstly, it designates the object of knowledge in its essentially underdetermined form, a circumstance that renders it relevant for research at all. For that very reason I speak about epistemic *things*. The notion of a thing carries with it an indeterminacy of

17 Please see, for the trajectory of an *in vitro* system for the investigation of protein biosynthesis, Hans-Jörg Rheinberger, *Toward a History of Epistemic Things. Synthesizing Proteins in the Test Tube* (Stanford: Stanford University Press, 1997); as well as Hans-Jörg Rheinberger, *An Epistemology of the Concrete* (Durham and London: Duke University Press, 2010), Chapters 4 to 7, for other examples.

sorts that lies at the core of research objects. The etymology of the word refers to the circumstance that a thing is something in question and on trial. The concept of a technical object, in contrast, we normally associate with determined and sharply-delineated contours. Its shape is not up for debate; it has a closed character. Secondly, the concept of the epistemic, in contrast to the technical, refers to the idea that epistemic things only exist and take shape in an instrumentally-mediated environment and are therefore, ontologically, of a transitory form and duration. Thus, the epistemic and the technical remain mutually dependent on each other and draw their respective contrasting specificity from said relationship.

As already mentioned in passing, the material continuity of an experimental system does by no means imply the continuity of the epistemic things dealt within it. On the contrary, at certain turning points in the development of an experimental system, abrupt changes in the realm of the epistemic can happen without necessarily having a disruptive effect on the system as a whole. The trajectory of epistemic things is not identical to that of experimental systems, not only because the former can be displaced from an existing system and replaced by a different epistemic thing, but also because epistemic things can jump from one experimental system to another. As a rule, they emerge from a particular experimental system and are developed there to a certain degree. It happens rather infrequently that an epistemic object remains completely in the context of a single experimental system. What I would like to emphasize is that epistemic things can migrate from one experimental context to another. These migrations are not linear and unidirectional; they rather ramify, multipy, and cross over in unexpected ways. On the one hand, epistemic things can promote the stabilization of certain aspects of the system in question – they can themselves eventually assume an instrumental character. For example, in biotechnological production, precision-tailored genes function as molecular replication machines. On the other hand, epistemic things do not come to rest because their uses as tools goes along with the emergence of new blind spots. Through migrations of this kind, the experimental systems involved become interconnected. The resulting experimental webs are traversed by multiple, materially-mediated pathways. In this way and in the context of experimental cultures, experimental systems can communicate with each other even if they are only marginally related in terms of their relevant technical components.

The Pathways of Technical Objects

The technical components of experimental systems – that is, the research technologies and other more-or-less standardized parts of such systems – also exhibit characteristic migratory movements and trajectories. In contrast to the history and migratory movements of experimental systems and of epistemic things, there exists an extended literature on the history and dissemination of research technologies.[18] Of particular interest in our context are the trajectories that research technologies undergo in the space of the epistemic. Since the action radius of experimental systems can be widened and altered by grafting new research technologies onto an existing set-up, migrations of research technologies are frequent. In the phase of their emergence, new research technologies mostly take shape by handling and manipulating the materials, procedures, and energy forms that determine their core structure, as has been shown in the case of microscopy.[19] Here it is often the unthought-of effect of the investigated material that opens prospects for a new technology – such as the use of accelerated electrons for the production of enlarged representations of material structures in the case of electron microscopy. In the development that ensues, instrument and object of investigation enter into a tight reciprocal interaction with each other. Interactions of this kind are particularly evident when one looks at the uses of electron microscopy for the enlarged representation of organic materials. Epistemic object and research technology engage in a process of mutual instruction that can trigger epistemic as well as technical effects. It is not unusual, therefore, that research technologies themselves – electron microscopy is again a good example here – will operate for longer timespans in an experimental, essentially epistemic, mode and even can assume the status of something like a technical experimental system *sui generis*. Sooner or later, however, most research technologies become pocketed into more-or-less closed packages. For their users, this transforms them into *black boxes* that can be used without a detailed knowledge

---

18 For example, almost all of the research technologies of molecular biology have received their own account: Paul Rabinow, *Making PCR: A Story of Biotechnology* (Chicago: The University of Chicago Press, 1996); Nicolas Rasmussen, *Picture Control: The Electron Microscope and the Transformation of Biology in America, 1940–1960* (Stanford: Stanford University Press, 1997) and Bruno Strasser, *La Fabrique d'une nouvelle science. La biologie moléculaire à l'âge atomique* (Florence: Olschki, 2006); Angela N. Creager, *Life Atomic. A History of Radioisotopes in Science and Medicine* (Chicago: The University of Chicago Press, 2013); Miguel García-Sancho, *Biology, Computing, and the History of Molecular Secquencing. From Proteins to DNA, 1945–2000* (London: Palgrave Macmillan, 2012). For research technologies in general, compare Bernward Joerges and Terry Shinn, *Instrumentation between Science, State, and Industry* (Dordrecht: Kluwer, 2001).

19 For light microscopy comparison, as a more recent example, consult Jutta Schickore, *The Microscope and the Eye: A History of Reflections, 1740–1870* (Chicago: The University of Chicago Press, 2007). For scanning tunnel microscopy, consult Jochen Hennig, *Bildpraxis. Visuelle Strategien in der frühen Nanotechnologie* (Bielefeld: Transcript, 2011). For electron microscoppy, consult Eric Lettkemann, *Stabile Interdisziplinarität. Eine Biografie der Elektronenmikroskopie aus historisch-soziologischer Perspektive* (Baden-Baden: Nomos, 2016); as well as Falk Müller, *Jenseits des Lichts. Siemens, AEG und die Anfänge der Elektronenmikroskopie in Deutschland* -Habilitation – (Frankfurt am Main: Goethe Universität Frankfurt, 2018).

of their inner workings.[20] As such, they are withdrawn from being tinkered with in the laboratory; only the intersections with the system in question are still open to experimentation. With that, however, their horizon of application becomes widened. Their migration is facilitated and they can become integrated into a greater number of experimental systems.

Something akin to black-boxing can also happen to experimental systems as a whole. They can be transformed into test systems and become part of other experimental systems as subroutines. All of this makes it evident that all these components and configurations of the experimental process can and must be differentiated from one another. Nevertheless, the different components are not fixed in their actual roles forever. Rather, they can change their places in a dynamic manner. Only concrete historical analysis can convincingly show what function a particular element fulfills in a given experimental context.

On the Movement Patterns of Experimental Cultures

The constituents of the process of experimentation are not inert material entities. On the contrary, they are in constant movement, and their migrations define the contours of epistemic spaces that can be addressed as experimental cultures. As reticulated ensembles, they are held together by the experimental trajectories of the different kinds of components described above. In such compound experimental structures, fusions or hybridizations of experimental systems can happen that originally were developed separately from each other. Other experimental systems, having become too rich in options, can split up. Within an experimental culture, such bifurcations or ramifications can lead to niches in which the exchange between the involved systems is particularly intense. Other experimental systems can be superseded and made obsolete by the introduction of new experimental configurations that simply outperform their predecessors. Existing systems that have their place in an experimental culture at a particular point in time are thus confronted with the permanent challenge to be kept abreast of these potential developments by constantly shifting their own boundaries.

Organismic Migrations

Let me round up this survey of the movement of materials through the space of the epistemic with a particular case. It is neither an experimental system nor an experimental culture, neither an epistemic nor an exclusively technical thing. We could perhaps capture it with the concept of "strategic research material" that we owe to

20 Compare Bruno Latour, *Science in Action. How to Follow Scientists and Engineers Through Society* (Cambridge MA: Harvard University Press, 1987).

Robert Merton.[21] Merton uses the notion to designate materials that for usually contingent reasons have revealed themselves as particularly suitable for the study of the natural phenomenon in question. They exhibit this phenomenon in a particularly pregnant form or they can make it accessible in a particularly ostensive way. Although such materials often have a long preliminary history that was not situated in the space of the epistemic to begin with, they can end up in science on their way through completely different cultural contexts.

In the biological sciences this role is often played by particular organisms. A good example is the sweet-water polyp from the *Hydra* genus so vividly described by Abraham Trembley around the middle of the 18th century.[22] The amazing capacities of the animal for regeneration served as a model for epigenetic thinking throughout the second half of the century. In the early 20th century, expressions such as "material for experimental purposes,"[23] "laboratory object,"[24] "laboratory animal,"[25] and experimental organism were popular; today, the concept of "model organism" has gained the upper hand.[26] In a very special way, model organisms are carriers of shapes of time that are essentially determined by their reproductive cycles. This intrinsic clock of the "research material" itself has a decisive influence on the epistemic time regime of the laboratory and its material flows. In the life sciences of the 20th century, there was a tendency to focus on the economization of time. The transition to ever more quickly reproducing model organisms ensued. At the turn of the 19th century, classical genetics still worked with plants subject to an annual reproduction rhythm. With insects – in particular the fruit fly, *Drosophila melanogaster*[27] – model organisms were introduced into the laboratory which had a procreation cycle in the order of months or even weeks. Early molecular biology finally specialized in unicellular organisms

---

21 Robert K. Merton, "Three fragments from a sociologist's notebooks: Establishing the phenomenon, specified ignorance, and strategic research materials." *Annual Review of Sociology* 13 (1987): 1–28.

22 Abraham Trembley, *Mémoires, pour servir à l'histoire d'un genre de polypes d'eau douce, à bras en forme de cornes* (Leiden: J. & H. Verbeek, 1744).

23 Phineas W. Whiting, "Rearing meal moths and parasitic wasps for experimental purposes." *The Journal of Heredity* 12 (1921): 258.

24 Alfred Kühn and Karl Henke, *Genetische und entwicklungsphysiologische Untersuchungen an der Mehlmotte Ephestia kühniella Zeller, I-VI*. Abhandlungen der Gesellschaft der Wissenschaften zu Göttingen, Mathematisch-Physikalische Klasse. Neue Folge, Vol. 15. (Berlin: Weidmannsche Buchhandlung, 1929), 2.

25 Albrecht Hase, "Insekten." *Methodik der wissenschaftlichen Biologie*, Vol. 2, Tibor Péterfi (ed.) (Berlin: Springer, 1928): 265–289.

26 For an overview, see Jean Gayon, "Les organisms modèles en biologie et en médecine." in *Les Organismes modèles dans la recherche médicale*, ed. Gabriel Gachelin (Paris: Presses Universitaires de France, 2006), 9–43.

27 Compare Robert E. Kohler, *Lords of the Fly. Drosophila Genetics and the Experimental Life* (Chicago: The University of Chicago Press, 1994).

such as lower fungi or bacteria with a reproduction cycle in the range of hours. The impact of these organism-specific time regimes on the rhythmicity of experimental systems in the life sciences cannot not be underestimated.[28]

I have followed the scientific career of one such model organism, the flour moth, *Ephestia kühniella*, elsewhere.[29] Its course through the epistemic space lasted for roughly a century. It formed a chain that had its starting point around the middle of the 19th century and that ended around the middle of the 20th century. As an object of knowledge, it began its career as an unwanted colonial import from the Americas that had made itself known as a food pest, but then advanced to a taxonomic unit in entomology, gained new life as an experimental organism in biological insect control, and finally mutated to a model organism in the epistemic space of emerging physiological genetics. After this trajectory, the moth abruptly disappeared as a model organism from the scene of knowledge. Likewise, the French 19th century physiologist, Claude Bernard, once remarked in his notes on the epistemic chains of physiological research that they would form chains and thus constitute a historical trajectory; the links of the chain, however, could by no means be derived from each other by logical necessity.[30]

A history of science that orients itself toward a history of things will have to follow such migrations and gain color from such chains and nexuses of contingency. Seen from this perspective, the "concepts nomades" of Isabelle Stengers as well as the migratory entities that Peter Howlett and Mary Morgan capture with the traditional category of "facts" could both appear in a new light.[31]

Epistemic Matters, Artistic Matters

The multiplicity of cross-connections that can be observed in experimental cultures over longer periods of time notwithstanding, it remains beyond doubt that the dynamics of the individual systems that interact in such cultures is determined, in the last instance, by their intrinsic times.[32] They also determine the points at which, in a given system, epistemic effects can emerge, without any guarantee that such effects

28 James Griesemer and Grant Yamashita, "Zeitmanagement bei Modellsystemen. Drei Beispiele aus der Evolutionsbiologie," in *Lebendige Zeit*, ed. Henning Schmidgen (Berlin: Kadmos, 2005), 213–241.

29 Hans-Jörg Rheinberger "Die Mehlmotte," in *Zoologicon. Ein kulturhistorisches Wörterbuch der Tiere*, ed. Christian Kassung, Jasmin Mersmann and Olaf B. Rader (München: Fink, 2012), 259–262.

30 Claude Bernard, *Philosophie. Manuscrit inédit* (Paris: Editions Hatier-Boivin, 1954), 14.

31 Isabelle Stengers, ed., *D'une science à l'autre. Des concepts nomades* (Paris: Seuil, 1988); Peter Howlett and Mary Morgan, eds., *How Well Do Facts Travel? The Dissemination of Reliable Knowledge* (Cambridge: Cambridge University Press, 2011).

32 Griesemer and Yamashita, "Zeitmanagement," 2005.

actually materialize. Here, we can turn again to Kubler: "Sequence classing stresses the internal coherence of events, all while it shows the sporadic, unpredictable, and irregular nature of their occurrence."[33] For the arts as well as the sciences this means that, "The field of history contains many circuits which never close. The presence of the conditions for an event does not guarantee the occurrence of that event."[34] Consequently, scientists – as well as artists – have to acquaint themselves with the microscopic givens of a particular system – its materiality as well as its peculiar temporality – in order to put themselves in a position to capture its options from within. The "ingenious ideas" which are so often talked about in hagiographies consist, as a rule, in becoming aware of an option that such a system offers by either displacing one of its elements, inserting a new technique, or pursuing a signal that has surfaced in a hidden corner of the system. This holds also for the dizzy heights of theoretical physics, as Werner Heisenberg stresses: "The modern theories have not resulted from revolutionary ideas that from outside would have been carried into the exact natural sciences; rather, they have been forced upon research in its endeavors to consequently complete the program of classical physics [...] It goes without saying that everywhere experimental research is the necessary precondition for theoretical insights, and that fundamental progress can be achieved only under the pressure of experimental results, not through speculations."[35] Or, as molecular biologist Mahlon Hoagland once put it, "[In] science a new vision of reality arises from mystery by the action of experimentation [...] In science, an idea can become substance only if it fits into a dynamic accumulating body of knowledge."[36]

In order to be able to grasp its options, however, researchers must develop a particular affinity for the system in and with which they work. So too, Kubler asserts, with respect to the artist: "Each sequence affords the opportunities of its particular systematic age to only that group having the temperamental conditions for a good entrance."[37] In a somewhat more colloquial form, in scientific circles one often hears the saying "to be in the right place at the right time." The phrase implicitly refers to two points that coincide with the charactzerization that has been given of the epistemic space: the highly articulated fine structure of an experimental culture, and the specific developmental stage – or the age – of an experimental system. It also refers to the interaction between a scientist and his or her system, an interaction in which, in the last instance, the system will prevail.

33 Kubler, *Shape of Time*, 36.

34 Kubler, *Shape of Time*, 36.

35 Werner Heisenberg, *Wandlungen in den Grundlagen der Naturwissenschaft. Zwei Vorträge* (Leipzig: S. Hirzel, 1935), 7.

36 Mahlon Hoagland, *Toward the Habit of Truth. A Life in Science* (New York and London: W. W. Norton, 1990), p. xx.

37 Kubler, *Shape of Time*, 91.

Of course, we cannot expect a strict parallel in the sense of a one-to-one homology between the exploratory moves and systems in both realms, the epistemic and the artistic. Thus, Kubler's "sequences," presented as attempts at the solution of a form problem, can be directly compared neither with experimental systems nor with experimental cultures devoted to the solution of epistemic problems. Here, more often than not, old problems are not solved, but are rather replaced by newly emerging ones. But both Kubler's sequence perspective on the arts as well as the experimental system perspective on the sciences are carried by the common search for the "shapes of time" of their objects. It is a search for new categorial options to make history in its different materializations visible and tangible. Kubler has given weight to this search with the following words: "A net of another mesh is required, different from any now in use." With respect to the concept of style, all too often invoked in this context, he added: "The notion of style has no more mesh than wrapping paper or storage boxes."[38]

The concrete shapes in which human invention – that is, cultural novelty – is realized in history are lastly to be understood as a history of things and as tightly bound to the respective materials and the options that emanate from these materials. I have been arguing for an approach to the history of science and art that is stamped by a commitment to afford the logic of the materials the place that it deserves. The shapes of time that the materials carry with them and along which they unfold their options will differ more or less significantly according to the different artistic activities that can be envisaged. The same holds, *ceteris paribus*, for the differentiations encountered in the realm of the epistemic. What needs to be done, therefore, is not to level out these differences, neither within nor across these realms, but rather to find a common ground on which they can be made comparable and conceptually recoverable in a productive manner.

38 Kubler, *Shape of Time*, 32.

El Anatsui

"Triumphant Scale": Material Realism and the Logic of Things

Karen van den Berg

In a newspaper article published in January 2020, art theorist Wolfgang Ullrich argued that an increasing number of artists were trying to "add weight to their works by imbuing them with material from the real world".[1] He argues that the fictional moment of art or aesthetic quality standards are no longer in the foreground, instead, that the authenticity of the materials is used as proof of artistic quality. One of his examples of this development is the so-called 'assault troop' "Center for Political Beauty", which supposedly used the real ashes of Holocaust victims in an artistic undertaking; another example is Ai Weiwei, who creates installations from the objects left behind by refugees.[2] With regard to these works, Ullrich observes that contemporary art takes a similar approach to authentic materials as did medieval art; that the material value of gold or ultramarine was rated more highly than the artistic skills, composition or the aesthetic concept of a painting. Accordingly, Ullrich condemns such artistic strategies as clumsy co-options of the "real" and discredits them as "reality art". From this perspective, meaning is supposedly borrowed from real life and is not obtained by specific artistic means. In this respect, these strategies reveal certain regressive tendencies through which art threatens to lose its uniqueness.[3]

1 Wolfgang Ullrich, "Der falsche Zauber der Wirklichkeit. Plädoyer für die Fiktion," *Frankfurter Allgemeine Sonntagszeitung*, January 12, 2020, 37. I thank Amarachi Okafor, Joachim Landkammer, Ursula Pasero, and Stephan Schmidt-Wulffen for their careful reading, numerous helpful suggestions, and critical comments on this contribution. My special thanks go to El Anatsui.

2 Cf. Anna Pritzkau, "Show und Schock. Was ist eigentlich das Problem des Zentrums für politische Schönheit?" *FAZ*, December 22, 2019, 34; Carlotta Wald, "Zentrum Für Politische Schönheit: Die Kunst, keine Kunst zu sein," *Die Zeit*, December 7, 2019, https://www.zeit.de/kultur/2019-12/zentrum-fuer-politische-schoenheit-kunst-aktivismus; Mirna Funk, "Stellt euch nicht so an," *Süddeutsche Zeitung*, December 5, 2019, 11 and Dorian Batycka, "Ai Weiwei Floats a New Project About the Refugee Crisis," *Hyperallergic*, April 17, 2017, https://hyperallergic.com/372831/ai-weiwei-floats-a-new-project-about-the-refugee-crisis/.

3 Cf. Ullrich "Der falsche Zauber."

Weiwei's installations of life jackets and refugees' clothes can be used as evidence that a new material realism can be observed in art at the beginning of the 21st century.[4] However, Ullrich's disparaging term "reality art" defames prematurely an interesting epistemological shift in the use of materials in art which has been taking shape since the 1960s. Since then, not only has the much-described conceptualisation of art taken place, as Lucy Lippard and John Chandler diagnosed in their influential essay, "The Dematerialization of Art," in 1968, but also a fundamentally new artistic approach to the employed materials can be observed as well. Particularly in sculpture, materials began to be selected for neither their aesthetic criteria nor based on whether they can be used to implement certain aesthetic or design concepts alone. Instead, the classic material repertoire was expanded considerably, often turning the material from which a work of art is made into a decisive factor. Think of the mythologically-infused use of beeswax, felt, and fat by Joseph Beuys, or Walter De Maria's "Five Continent Sculpture" of 1989, which brings together marble, quartz, and magnesite stones from five continents. In these examples, historical, ecological, and physical properties – including the contextual origins of materials – all play a decisive role in the production of artistic meaning. The material itself becomes part of what is being said; in the sense of Marshall McLuhan's dictum, "the medium is the message."[5] From this point of view, it makes a difference that the stones of the "Five Continent Sculpture" do actually come from five different continents.

This turn towards a *materialistic realism*, as I would call it, is worth a closer look. Ullrich's interpretation seeing it as a relapse into a pre-modern substantialism falls short. Instead – and this would be my reading – very different epistemological interests in certain substances and types of matter become apparent. Materials are rarely found separate from their usage contexts and the political and social norms in which they are set. For more than half a century now, many artists have been trying to render meaningful the materials with which they operate as entities embedded into different aspects of life.

El Anatsui, who was born in Ghana and has been living in Nigeria for the last four decades, is one of these explicitly material-related artists. I would like to use his work as an example to illustrate how the use of a particular material can not only redirect the view of the very material itself, but also transform the entire understanding of production and labour, right up to the concept of authorship. The main focus of this essay lies on his large-scale installations made from used bottle tops, which have turned the Ghanaian from a well-known 'African artist' into an international star while leading to a radical change in his production method.

4 Cf. Batycka "Ai Weiwei."

5 McLuhan, *Understanding Media: The Extensions of Man.* (New York: Mentor, 1964), 4.

His example also shows the extent to which the historical, social, and geopolitical narratives embedded in trivial everyday things are made visible by an artistic transformation, and how only with the release of things from their everyday use do their substantiality and the symbolic meanings stored in them become apparent.

The Bag in the Bush

El Anatsui, The Beginning and The End (2015) (detail). Aluminium and copper wire. Photo By Karen van den Berg.

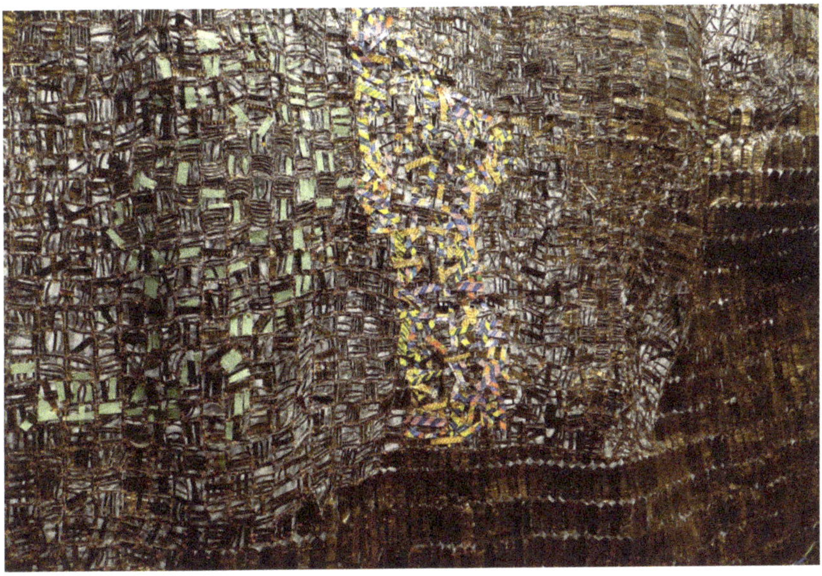

When Anatsui talks about how the creation of monumental tapestries from aluminum caps and metal bottleneck strips from gin, rum, whisky, and brandy bottles came about, he emphasizes the consistency of this development in particular. For him, the use of these materials is the consequence of an artistic attitude developed long before; meanwhile, the work in his studio is no longer like it was in the years before he began working with the screw caps. Not only has his artistic technique changed since then, but also the dimensions in which he works, and the way he now runs his studio. This connection between the work process, the materials, and the studio as a social space is examined in more detail below.

In a series of interviews and reports, the artist tells us that he initially owed the discovery of this material, which then became a trademark of sorts, to a coincidence. In 1998 while walking to a traditional Igbo monument at the gates of the Nigerian university town of Nsukka, where he has lived since 1975, he came across a bag in the bushes full of used aluminum screw caps from liquor bottles, and which he took to his studio to see if he could make anything with these.[6] But the fact that Anatsui attached any importance to this find was not just coincidental, as the artist had begun to experiment with found materials from his immediate living environment many years earlier.[7] For a long time, Anatsui had created reliefs and sculptures from found wood and broken vessels, and had adorned them with patterns that recalled loosely various Ghanaian or Nigerian non-figurative artisanal traditions.[8] In his series of works using broken ceramic vessels, he had already demonstrated his fascination in the traditional usage of things that, having lost their functionality, suddenly take on a different meaning. This approach is deeply embedded in the regional culture. Broken vessels, for example, are used to mark graves, becoming symbols of life itself;[9] this attachment of a deeper meaning to broken or discarded objects foreshadowed the working principles he later used with bottle tops.

The artist, who was born in 1944, often talks about what this specific artistic strategy is rooted in. When he studied at the Kwame Nkrumah University of Technology, Kumasi in Ghana from 1965 to 1969, Anatsui soon noticed – as he tells it – that the materials usually made available to artists, such as plaster, were the materials of former colonizers.[10] This use of materials disagreed with his understanding of art for two reasons: first of all, Anatsui pursued an anthropological concept of art, according to which artists should always use the materials available in their immediate living surroundings; and secondly, he was close to a movement that pursued the indigenization of art and therefore turned away from concepts learned during

---

6 Cf. Laura Leffler James and El Anatsui, "History, Materials, and the Human Hand—an Interview with El Anatsui," *Art Journal* 67, no. 2 (Summer 2008): 38, https://www.jstor.org/stable/40598941;
Susan Mullin Vogel, *El Anatsui. Art and Life* (München, London/New York: Prestel, 2012), 53–54; Raphael Rubinstein, "Full-Metal Fabric," *Art in America* 95 (2006): 162 and Polly Savage, "El Anatsui. Contexts Textiles and Gin," In *El Anatsui, Asi*, New York: David Kurt / October Gallery, 2006.

7 Lisa M. Binder, "El Anatsui: Transformations," *African Arts* 41, no. 2 (Summer, 2008): 24.

8 Cf. on the earlier works John Picton, *El Anatsui. A Sculptured History of Africa*, London: Saffron, 1998.

9 Vogel, *El Anatsui. Art and Life*, 34; also cf. Anatsui in Ayo Adewunmi, "El Anatsui Studio," *art is everywhere Production*, Youtube, Accessed Month Day, 2020, https://www.youtube.com/watch?v=axF_yVzy_Y8 .

10 Cf. for instance Vogel, *El Anatsui. Art and Life*, 100 and James, "Interview with El Anatsui," 38.

his university art studies, which closely followed Parisian art events and the curriculum of Goldsmiths' College in London.[11] In an interview with the filmmaker Susan Mullin Vogel, he describes it like this:

> The materials that we used in school – I knew that they were strange. In art history we learned that in the caves, they painted on the cave wall, or did engravings on the walls. It means that you do art with whatever is around you. They don't make plaster in Ghana! So, using plaster of Paris and things which are imported means that you are not going by the norms of the profession as established by the cavemen.[12]

For Anatsui, the rejection of the European art tradition in the name of the "cavemen" specifically meant working with what belonged to his own cultural environment. When the then-31-year-old artist was appointed to the first independent, and still quite young, university in Nigeria, in Nsukka, in 1975, he passed on this conviction to his students as a professor of sculpture.[13] Anatsui worked at the university until 2011. He still lives and works nearby.[14]

However, the shift to materials from his immediate surroundings did not mean a return to the pre-colonial "traditional art", which anthropologists and art historians long regarded as the only authentic African art.[15] As with a great number of his colleagues at the time, Anatsui was concerned with escaping the aesthetic stipulations of colonial powers as well as what John Picton calls the "tired myth of primitivism", and so he was instead interested in searching for a new identity.[16]

After he came across the bag of aluminum caps, apparently collected for recycling, Anatsui did not immediately find a purpose for the parts. While he had nailed individually cut and flattened metal screw caps onto a wooden relief before (for example in the 1993 work "Harvest Moon") it took him a while to come up with the idea of not only cutting them, pressing them together, and flattening them, but also turn-

11 Cf. ibid.: "The ideology of Africanizing art also called for the use of local materials, implicitly those of indigenous rural life." He received first impulses from his teachers, Gerd von Stokar (a Bavarian ceramic sculptor) and Ghanaian sculptor Azzi Akator, Anatsui explained in an interview on Art Radar, "Renowned African contemporary artist El Anatsui says African art now receiving attention again – Art Interview," December 20, 2008, https://artradarjournal.com/2008/2012/2020/renowned-african-contemporary-artist-el-anatsui-says-african-art-receiving-attention-again-art-interview/.

12 Vogel, *El Anatsui. Art and Life*, 103; also cf. Rubinstein, "Full-Metal Fabric," 200.

13 Cf. Binder, "Transformations," 24.

14 I obtained these details from an email from Amarachi Okafor, a studio assistant of the artist in an email dated 17 June 2020.

15 Picton, *Sculptured History*, 22.

16 Cf. Picton, *Sculptured History*, 19.

ing and folding them and forming them into distinct recurring shapes by linking them to copper wire. He explains:

> I kept the bottle tops in the studio for several months until the idea eventually came to me that by stitching them together, I could get them to articulate some statement. When the process of stitching got underway, I discovered that the result resembled a real fabric cloth. Incidentally too, the color of the caps seemed to replicate those for traditional *kente* cloths [...] I worked on the first set of bottle top pieces from 1998 but showed them publicly almost five years later. It's been a long slow gradual breaking-in, but even with that I had to adjust at two levels: the pace slowed down and process was more labor intensive.[17]

Right after the discovery, the artist reports, he was aware of what interested him about these bottle caps; and this interest was not at all limited to an aesthetic appeal or the connection to traditional fabric patterns. Since the bottle tops were exclusively those from local brands of strong liquor, the artist quickly realized that the history of African colonization was inscribed in this material:

> Several things went through my mind when I found the bag of bottle tops in the bush. I thought of the objects as links between my continent, Africa, and the rest of Europe. Objects such as these were introduced to Africa by Europeans when they came as traders. Alcohol was one of the commodities brought with them to exchange for goods in Africa. Eventually alcohol became one of the items used in the transatlantic slave trade. They made rum in the West Indies, took it to Liverpool, and then it made its way back to Africa. I thought that the bottle caps had a strong reference to the history of Africa.[18]

Even years later, Anatsui makes it clear that he deliberately confines himself to the bottle tops of local distilleries and explains why the caps of Coca-Cola, soda, and soft drinks are out of the question for him:

> Well, Coca-Cola is not liquor, and its cap is also of a different metal from the aluminum of liquor bottles. The bottle caps I use are linked to liquor, which has historical associations, since hard drinks played a prominent role in the earliest contact between Africa and Europe. The caps I use are all from local brands of liquor. The act of stitching them into sheets is to me like melting the different circumstances of these continents together into an indeterminate form. The distillers recycle bottles. The caps are more or less by-products of this process. The distilleries discard them because they have to rebrand the bottles. This yields a

---

17 Vogel, *El Anatsui. Art and Life*, 54; also cf. Gerard Houghton, "El Anatsui," In *El Anatsui, October Gallery*, 27–36, London: October Gallery, 2015.

18 Vogel, *El Anatsui. Art and Life*, 53–54.

fairly wide range of colors of these caps to choose from, with reds and yellows predominating.[19]

It becomes clear from these statements how important the origin of the bottle top is. Not only are they inscribed literally and metaphorically with their former everyday usage, but they also stand in a very wide-reaching historical context: they refer to the history of the African continent, the slave trade, the economies of early colonization, as well as a specific approach to recyclable waste and related economic conditions.[20]

In an interview with the London-based *October Gallery*, Anatsui sums up the ambiguity and rich post-colonial narratives that he sees inscribed in the bottle caps, saying, "The amazing thing about working with these metallic 'fabrics' is that the poverty of the materials used in no way precludes the telling of rich and wonderful stories."[21] Said richness of the 'work materials' is therefore due to symbolic, imaginative, and aesthetic dimensions, and has to do with the fact that they are decorated with countless imaginative signets such as Flying Horse, Castello, Canon Distilleries, Rexton, Chairman, and King Solomon. It is clear, therefore, that "For every magnificent wall hanging, several tanker fillings of alcohol were drunk before."[22]

Royal Coats, Industrialization, and Reappropriation

In addition to the imaginative priming of the functional screw caps, collected for recycling purposes, some of the allure of Anatsui's work lies in the sheer mass of labor-intensive linkage that has transformed these caps into incredibly graceful monumental tapestries. Thrown into elegant folds, they seem meaningful, striking, and at odds with their actual material value. The gold, silver, red, and black shimmering metal fabrics, which often offer hints to traditional Ghanaian weaving patterns

19 James, "Interview with El Anatsui," 48.

20 About this, Anatsui says: "When I saw the bottle tops, what struck me was that they are from bottles that have been used, and therefore human hands have touched them. . . People have really drunk from these bottles, and therefore human hands have left a charge on them. Also, I like to expand my vocabulary, especially of the materials that I use. In terms of media vocabulary, I'm constantly looking for anything that has that connection to human hands in a meaningful way. In the latter part of my wood phase, I developed a predilection for wooden objects that have been put to intense use but are no longer viable – old mortars, for instance. Somehow the media I work with have something to do with food or consumption as well." James, "Interview with El Anatsui," 38.

21 October Gallery, "El Anatsui," accessed February 10, 2021, www.octobergallery.co.uk/artists/anatsui/.

22 Ivo Nagelweihler, "El Anatsui – Triumphant Scale," Kunst und Film, April 1, 2019, https://kunstundfilm.de/2019/2004/el-anatsui/.

in their rhythm and color, are reminiscent of oversized old royal coats or sumptuous wall hangings. The 2001 works, "Man's Cloth" and "Women's Cloth," for example, are Anatsui's first works of this kind.[23] Timeless, handmade, and venerable are the adjectives that come to mind.

The impressive dimensions and simultaneous intricacy of the artwork – the size of the artifacts tower over the individual – inspired the title "El Anatsui Triumphant Scale" for the first major international touring retrospective of Anatsui, which opened in March 2019 at Haus der Kunst. The dimensions of the tapestries, which can span entire facades, are an especially central factor for the artist, as he says, "The individuality of each piece is lost, and it's subjected now to a generality of a bigger form."[24] On seeing these huge works, what is immediately apparent is the immeasurable manual labour involved. It is more important than the recycling aspect. Anatsui therefore repeatedly refuses to regard his works as recycling art or eco-criticism.[25] For him, it is more about a mental and cultural transformation.[26] Although works like "Rising Sea" (2019), the Venice Bienniale work, "Earth Shedding its Skin" (2019), or the installation, "Ozone Layer and Yam Mounds" (2010), created for the Alte Nationalgalerie in Berlin, suggest an eco-critical significance through their titles, Anatsui says that he is not concerning himself with sustainability or the climate crisis. Of much greater importance to him is the reference to certain cultural practices, geopolitical implications, and the element of the works being handmade.[27] The tangibly understood craft of cutting, flattening, folding, and linking with small copper wires, i.e. the recognizable "make" of the work of art, is of great importance to him, without simple "artisanal dominance", as Okwui Enwezor pointed out[28], getting the last word. Rather, Anatsui succeeds at a very specific thematicization of collective processes, evoking a collective-imaginary, in which something intimate and personal remains visible. His works, as the theorist, artist, and curator Chika Okeke-Agulu puts it, combine monumentality with "intimate

23 Time and again it was pointed out that they are reminiscent of traditional Ghanaian Kente and Adinkra fabrics, which Anatsusi's father also weaved in his spare time. "My father wove Ewe kente – as a hobby, though, it wasn't his profession per se," says Anatsui in an interview with Gerhard Hougthin, Binder, "Transformations," 27. See also Rubinstein, "Full-Metal Fabric," 161.

24 Art Basel, "Meet the Artists | El Anatsui," June 7, 2019, https://www.artbasel.com/news/meet-the-artists-el-anatsui

25 Cf. Nagelweihler, "El Anatsui".

26 He also emphasized this in a telephone interview, that I conducted with him on March 17, 2020.

27 "His work can interrogate the history of colonialism and draw connections between consumption, waste, and the environment, but at the core is his unique formal language that distinguishes his practice." https://elanatsui.art/biography.

28 Okwui Enwezor, "A Ceaseless Search for Form," *Parkett* 90 (2012): 34.

fragility"[29] because both the material (that is, the screw caps of Nigerian spirits) and the manufacturing process owe themselves to a specific cultural identity and certain concepts of work, which are clearly different from the ideas that prevail in the Global North. Industrial production and handiwork are intertwined in a completely different way and overlap one another. In Anatsui's tapestry, the industrially-manufactured and machine-printed aluminum caps absorb something surprisingly spiritual, almost sublime, through thousands of embedded hours of manual work. All the while, this elevation – and this is what makes Anatsui's work so special – remains fully anchored in the everyday: it can plainly also be found in the discarded elements of an industry or can, through his intervention, become visible.

In larger exhibition contexts, where huge gallery spaces are filled by wall hangings and semi-transparent curtains, as in his first major survey exhibition at Haus der Kunst in Munich in 2019 or on the facade of Palazzo Fortuny in 2007, it is the moment of collectively contributed creative power that is prominent initially. Installations like this make it immediately clear that an effort of the many is articulated here, which includes each individual's experienced time; always, one specific individual has hand processed each specific bottle top.

But the collective-imaginary is more than that. "I'm constantly looking for anything that has that connection to human hands in a meaningful way,"[30] says Anatsui about the human manipulation that has passed into his works; addressing not just the reflection of the manufacturing process in his own studio, but also the former use of the alcohol bottles, and the cultural practices that arose in the aftermath of colonial history, pithily reflected in countless little pictures and imprints. For the artist – as the statements quoted above demonstrate – it is essentially about the historical and everyday cultural depth, about the imaginative and fanciful that is recognizable in the individual bottle caps – up to the point that alcohol is also associated with spirituality and healing in many African cultures.[31] In addition to the rich aesthetic and compositional possibilities Anatsui's fascination with the material therefore owes something to the conviction that the celebratory, exuberant, or delusory occasions of alcohol enjoyment reverberate in the screw caps with their printed flying horses, crowns, buffalo heads, and the elegant logos of the distilleries, together with some of the life, thoughts and actions of countless people. For him, this reflects

---

29 Tobias Krone, "El Anatsui im Münchner Haus der Kunst – Gardinen-Labyrinth im Nazibau". *Deutschlandfunk*, March 7, 2019, https://www.deutschlandfunkkultur.de/el-anatsui-im-muenchner-haus-der-kunst-gardinen labyrinth.1013.de.html?dram:article_id=443028.

30 James, "Interview with El Anatsui," 38.

31 Cf. Anatsui in an interview with Kate McCrickard, "October 2006, Telephone Interview with El Anatsui in Stockholm," In *El Anatsui 2006, Asi*, New York: David Kurt / October Gallery, 2006.

the stories and images of the deep history of the continent, questions of cultural identity, and the reappropriation of what was taken. The artist is therefore interested in an evocation of the imaginary that can be found in the banal everyday.

Anatsui's great international success therefore probably owes something to the fact that his works align an aesthetic elegance and magnitude with this deep history of work and labor, industrialization, self- and foreign determination. Dealing with prepackaged industrial waste obviously strikes a chord in current discourses – even beyond the field of art. Similar to Ai Weiwei, Dan Peterman, or other well-known contemporary artists, Anatsui is showing an interest in unfolding an epistemic dimension that is locked away in real everyday objects. Working with found objects is therefore not aimed at the certification of a borrowed authenticity and does not follow a clumsy realism, as Ullrich suggests with Ai Weiwei, but unlocks symbolic and allegorical knowledge that shines through in everyday items.

In order to uncover this dimension for the observer, the artist needs, as Anatsui emphasizes, time and experience in dealing with the material in order to develop appropriate work routines. He says,

> When you pick a medium you stay with it for some time. You don't do one or two pieces with it and then flit on to another one, because that way then you wouldn't be able to get into understanding that media and therefore be able to get something intrinsic out of it."[32]

Against this backdrop, it is understandable why Anatsui has remained faithful to his material for almost two decades. What this involvement means in practice, what consequences the manipulation of bottle caps has for his identity as an artist, what specific conception of work and labor his artworks reveal, and how this is embedded in the cultural setting of a university city with about 36,000 students in south-eastern Nigeria is further examined in more detail below.

Contemplation, Intuition and Repetitive Work

The dimensions in which Anatsui has been working for almost 20 years naturally is also directly related to the economies of attention which dominate the global art world. Only since his works have grown to a huge size can they fill the monumental exhibition spaces of major museums, and only since Anatsui has gained a certain level of prominence can he produce works whose production visibly takes thousands of hours of work. But how should we imagine the fabrication? What is the role of the artist? And how does his work relate to the global art market?

---

32 Akron Art Museum, "Gravity and Grace: Monumental Works by El Anatsui," From August 2, 2012, https://www.youtube.com/watch?v=5I7XZL9KjFQ.

For many years, Anatsui's studio was located on a thoroughfare on the northern outskirts of Nsukka, about 20 minutes from the university campus by foot, in a very unpretentious industrial building, surrounded by modest craft businesses, workshops, crude stalls, and small gas stations.[33] In 2018, the artist finally moved to a more spacious but still relatively unpretentious industrial building designed by Lagos-based James Cubitt Architects, built on a 2,300 square meter plot of land on the outskirts of the city.[34] The space in his old studio had long since become too cramped, as, for example, the test hangings of his installations had to take place outside and the 10 to 40 employees sat close together.[35] In his new building, he can finally test-hang larger projects in a light-flooded hall.

During the busiest phases, for instance directly before his retrospective at the *Haus der Kunst* in 2019 in Munich, the number of his employees occasionally rose to more than 100.[36] Since Anatsui stopped using wood and ceramics as a material frequently, his work style has changed considerably. Production has become slower and much more labor-intensive. For the production of a larger wall work from bottle caps, his studio expects several thousand hours of work. "An average piece takes 25 people working on it 60 days. Just imagine if one person would do this work," the artist notes in a film feature by the *Akron Art Museum*.[37] 60 workdays of eight hours multiplied by 25 employees equals 12,000 hours. In this way the studio only produces one wall hanging every two to three months.

This indicates what has changed for Anatsui since he stopped creating wooden sculptures with a chainsaw. One thing is that he can dispense with most machinery: "Initially I found it problematic to work at a snail's pace, but now I'm very much at home with the shift from power tools where I relied on machines that at times could break down,"[38] he says. So, while Anatsui used to need machines but hardly any helping hands to make his wood reliefs or ceramic works, it would be impossible

33 Cf. Art21, "Studio Process", July 20, 2012, https://art21.org/watch/extended-play/el-anatsui-studio-process-short/.

34 Cf. Adewunmi, "El Anatsui Studio" and James Cubitt Architects, "El Anatsui Studio, Nsukka," accessed February 10, 2021, http://www.jamescubittarchitects.com/projects/. It is interesting that all the elements in the design by the architects, which somehow seem rather extravagant, have apparently not been executed.

35 Cf. the film by Susan Vogel, "Fold, Crumble, Crush. The Art of El Anatsui", Price Street Pictures 2011, http://www.susan-vogel.com/Susan-Vogel/Fold_Crumple_Crush.html.

36 Artist Talk: Chika Okeke-Agulu in conversation with El Anatsui about his work and the exhibition at Haus der Kunst. Chika Okeke-Agulu, "Artist Talk: Im Gespräch mit El Anatsui.", 2019, https://museumsfernsehen.de/artist-talk-chika-okeke-agulu-im-gespraech-mit-el-anatsui/; also cf. Ayodeji Rotinwa, "A Major New Survey Celebrates the Creative Reclamation and Nurturing Spirit of Ghanaian Artist El Anatsui," *Wallpaper*, October, 2019, https://www.wallpaper.com/art/el-anatsui-nsukka-studio-doha-mathaf-exhibition.

37 Akron Art Museum, "Gravity and Grace."

38 McCrickard, "El Anatsui in Stockholm."

to get by with only one or two assistants today. The large wall works consist of tens of thousands of elements. The entire work model therefore had to be organized anew. But the exhibitions also became bigger and bigger, and thus the installations as well. While he spoke of a "workshop of up to fifteen hands" in 2006,[39] today there regularly are 30 – 40 assistants working in his studio.

In a telephone interview, Anatsui describes how on an ordinary workday, he gets to the studio at about nine or ten o'clock in the morning.[40] Some of his staff come earlier to open up the studio. Most of the helpers – mostly students who have just finished school and are waiting for a place to study, university students, and young men from the neighborhood who work with him on a daily basis – are more or less constantly busy with creating units comprising of about 200 bottle caps each, folded in different degrees of complexity. These units are called "blocks" in the studio vernacular. Anatsui regularly discusses with the employees which blocks are needed and how they are folded.[41] For the different patterns and links there are code words: Crumpled, Chain, Crushed, Four Corners, Flower, etc.[42]

When there are enough blocks, work begins on the compositions, which often are four to seven meters wide. For this purpose, countless blocks are spread out on the floor to try different arrangements. Anatsui describes this process by saying, "And so, you take these units and start playing around with them ... and you try to see what it can suggest... and take photographs and put them on the computer."[43] Again and again, the employees cast out longer strips or individual blocks, smooth them out, adjust them, and trim them. From either the floor or the upper gallery, Anatsui looks at the composition, discards it, has it rearranged, takes photographs from time to time, and pushes it back and forth until the result seems right to him.[44] This process takes many hours, even days.[45] Anatsui frequently underlines the playful nature of this approach, saying, "Art is about play. You are more honest when you

---

39 Ibid.; also cf. Nkgopoleng Moloi, "A Collaborative Force. Artificial Intelligence and the Art of El Anatsui," *Art Africa*, February 27, 2018, https://artafricamagazine.org/a-collaborative-force-artificial-intelligence-el-anatsui/?v=e4dd286dc7d7 and a documentation by the Metropolitan Museum of 2008, where Anatsui talks about 16–20 assistants: MET, "El Anatsui installing "Between Earth and Heaven"," from August 6, 2008, https://www.youtube.com/watch?v=G7UBvknG8c4

40 The interview was conducted by me on April 17, 2020, 10:30 PM, Nigerian local time.

41 Cf. ibid.

42 Also cf. Vogel, *El Anatsui. Art and Life*, 74–75; "I believe that is the G8. This is the assistants' name for the particular pattern; they have this penchant for devising code names for different patterns, textures and stitches. I believe they were working on this pattern at the time of the Scottish summit. The codes are very useful and handy and make communication faster when work is underway." McCrickard "El Anatsui in Stockholm."

43 Art21, "Studio Process."

44 Cf. Adewunmi, "El Anatsui Studio."

45 Anatsui in Art2, "Studio Process."

are playing."[46] Additionally, it is important to him, when composing, that the end product does not amount to the completion of a fixed structural order, but rather to "floating relationships" and "indeterminant forms."[47] Many of his works are therefore also reminiscent of maps of eroded areas that are either coming into being or in the process of disintegrating.

In this compositional work, Anatsui does not use elaborate design drawings as a template, but rather arranges freely and intuitively in situ, with the material itself. Having to adhere to preliminary drafts would run contrary to his self-image. Even with a drawing, he emphasizes repeatedly, he would feel restricted:

> I will say the process is a very fluid and open one. I do not produce drawings because I want the materials to lead me on, not to follow the dictates of any sketch. I could for instance ask the assistant to pick any color and work with it, or I could impose some restrictions. I could ask for a particular texture or stitch at a point. There are so many variables. Certainly, the alternating freedom and restriction means that there are inputs from the workshop. So, work develops organically and in most cases in unpredictable ways.[48]

The process follows a playful trial-and-error attitude that is guided by the material. Only once the composition seems meaningful to Anatsui are the blocks knotted or sewn together with copper wires by his employees directly on the floor, and individual parts are exchanged for different colored caps where needed.[49] Afterwards, the monumental tapestries are put to the test and, if necessary, refined some more.

His studio has different workshop areas on three levels. The Great Hall is where monumental formats can be developed, viewed from above as they lie on the floor, or test-hung on the walls. The large main room is a workshop wherein exhibition situations can be tested simultaneously.[50]

Most of the helpers sit on stools in the approximately 10-meter-high hall, in pairs or groups of three or four, around smallish tables, and manufacture more "blocks" with small pliers, pricking tools, and copper wires. The working atmosphere is almost contemplative. "I try to impress upon them that a studio is a sacred place," notes Anatsui in a report,[51] "When I come in, they all keep quiet," he says with a

---

46 Anatsui in Art Basel, "Meet the Artists | El Anatsui."

47 MET, "Between Earth and Heaven."

48 McCrickard, "El Anatsui in Stockholm."

49 Adewunmi, "El Anatsui Studio."

50 "A high headroom enables the building to serve effectively as a gallery and workshop", write the architects about the spatial concept. James Cubitt Architects, "El Anatsui Studio, Nsukka."

51 Caroline Goldstein, "'A Studio Is a Sacred Place': Get a Behind-the-Scenes Look at How El Anatsui Builds Glittering Tapestries out of Bottle Caps," *Artnet*, July 25, 2019, https://news.artnet.com/exhibitions/art21-el-anatsui-1609927.

laugh, because when he is in his studio, there has to be as much peace as feasibly possible.[52]

Again and again, Anatsui emphasizes how important it is to him to always stay very close to the manufacturing process: "For each new pattern or texture, I show them how it's done," he says, "if you don't maintain physical contact with handling the material, the work might end up not having a soul."[53] This artisanal ideal of immediate material contact, which Anatsui had initially followed,[54] has now given way to a mediated attitude. He sees himself as more of a "generator and conductor of ideas" who is connected with the material via his employees.[55] About this he says:

> They are more a part of the process; they are not all the time just hands. Working this way, I have got to understand both the material and the different touches or styles of each assistant. It is like conducting an orchestra of musicians each with peculiar performing skill.[56]

Consequently, the work of the employees is not the same thing as the invisible work of third parties, like mixing paint or preparing canvases, because for Anatsui it is indeed important that the helpers have different styles and leave individual traces of themselves on their work. Anatsui's interpretation of authorship is, thus, not based on "the idealism of a self-enclosed subjectivity" – to quote a phrase John Roberts used in his general reflections on authorship – but rather it is "decentred".[57] When the works are shown in museums or galleries, Anatsui often leaves the hanging and the way the tapestries are placed to the local curators. "El regards the making and hanging of the cloths as a collaborative process, and in Nigeria his team of studio assistants is integral to the creation, handling, displaying and photographing of the large pieces," says Elisabeth Lalouschek, Artistic Director of the *October Gallery*.[58] Anatsui himself says,

---

52 Art2, "Studio Process."

53 Ibid.

54 "Initially as an artist I thought that I should be the one doing everything." Art Basel, "Meet the Artists | El Anatsui."

55 Anatsui in an interview with Elizabeth Harney, "El Anatsui – When I Last Wrote to You About Africa," *Michigan Museum of Art (UMMA)*, 2013, https://www.youtube.com/watch?v=PWYCPV1c8YE.

56 McCrickard, "El Anatsui in Stockholm."

57 John Roberts, *The Intangibilities of Form. Skill and Deskilling in Art After the Readymade*, London/New York: Verso, 2007, 103.

58 Bronwyn Law-Viljoen, "Snapshots from the Past – Notes Taken from an Interview with Elisabeth Lalouschek, Artistic Director, October Gallery," In *El Anatsui 2006, Asi*, New York: David Kurt / October Gallery, 2006.

> My work has freedom as its watchword, the idea of freedom being able to shape itself or get shaped in different ways. Each time it is an opportunity to do something new. This has been my principle leading up to the bottle cap series.[59]

It therefore is also important that the works can easily be rolled up, folded, and transported. Many curators were rather astonished that Anatsui did not convey more specifics concerning the hanging of his works, which, the artist admitted with a laugh in a conversation with Chika Okeke-Agulu, did not always go well.[60]

Anatsui's interaction with the assistants plays an important role when composing the overall texture of the works. Unlike in the past, when he was working alone or with a single collaborator, today the mood in the studio is more exciting and this energy is conveyed to the works. Yet despite this, he mainly needs calm and concentration for his work. In a telephone conversation, he emphasized that he spends little time on things other than artistic activities.[61] In his studio, the administrative work is reduced to a minimum. Only a few former students, such as Amara Okafor, support him in this, as he prefers to leave the managerial part of the planning of exhibitions to the galleries and inviting museums, especially since neither he nor his staff are trained for such tasks, as he says.[62]

The artist calls the structure of his studio and the interaction with his employees "very informal." For instance, although many of his freelancers have been working for him regularly for years, there are no fixed contracts.[63] When larger projects come up, the artist engages the larger community, sometimes working with over 200 people. Working with him is "a very good deal" for his employees, Anatsui says. Many finance their studies in this manner, or pursue other professions at the same time, thereby earning qualifications elsewhere, and they are supported by the artist in the long term.[64] Advanced prior knowledge is not necessary to work with Anatsui; one only needs a certain dexterity in order to be able to carry out the routine low-tech manual work.

Unlike many artists who prepare exhibitions on his scale and are in the public eye to a comparable extent, Anatsui has no formal meetings in the studio and no departments that systematically deal with documentation, the tending of Instagram accounts, and the like. While artists such as Olafur Eliasson maintain their own publishing and finance department, Alicja Kwade and her accountant attend to applica-

---

59 Rotinwa, "Creative Reclamation."; elsewhere, Anatsui says about the hanging of his work: "they have to be configured afresh, most of the time by other parties apart from the artist." McCrickard, "El Anatsui in Stockholm."

60 Cf. Okeke-Agulu, "Artist Talk."

61 Telephone interview of April 17, 2020.

62 Ibid.

63 Ibid.

64 Ibid.

tions for reduced working hours during the Coronavirus pandemic, and Ai Weiwei employs his own department of bloggers, Anatsui's studio follows completely different rules.[65] Here, despite the large number of helpers, the studio remains a sheltered place for work that is geared entirely towards the manufacturing of art objects. It remains a contemplative space that is based on an understanding of authorship that is mostly due to a dialogue of the artist subject with the material and the activities and inscriptions of others.

It would however be a disservice to him to simply see the reproduction of the much-criticized, fantastically-imbued artist studio in Anatsui's method; where long-outdated ideas of the lone protean geniuses of the 18th and 19th centuries live on.[66] The artisanal ethos of the numerous helpers plays too central a role for the works and their aesthetic power. If one wants to understand the work process and the work ethic of the artist more clearly, two aspects are important to consider. First, that he does not call his studio a "sacred place" because a tribute must be paid to a great master. The place is 'sacred' only to the extent that he demands respect for the required concentration and silence. From this perspective, it is not so much a workshop as it is a kind of counter-space that is closed off from the restless hustle of the surrounding workaday world. Secondly, working with recycled materials is closely integrated in this very workaday world on the outskirts of Nsukka, as well as in the social fabric of south-eastern Nigeria and its specific economy. Additionally, the product that is manufactured in the studio turns aspects of the worker's world into an issue. In so doing, Anatsui exposes that his skills and intentions are embedded in a specific social environment, in an "ensemble of techniques", and a kind of "collective intellect", as Roberts would call it.[67] As an artist and author he is not "a stand-alone 'expressive' figure, whose agency is external to the employment of [...] particular skills".[68] On the contrary, his works as well as his studio practices are completely embedded in the local economies and modes of production. As a result, the studio is not a foreign body in the setting of the surrounding workshops. This additional aspect is therefore worthy of a concluding examination.

Garbage and a Different Understanding of Things

Some are astonished that Anatsui who is one of the stars of the art world, has received the Golden Lion of the Venice Biennale for his life's work, and has considerable

65 Tobias Timm, "Es bricht eine neue Phase an," *Die Zeit*, April 15, 2020: 49.

66 Isabelle Graw, "Vorwort," *Texte zur Kunst* 49 (2003): 5.

67 Roberts, *Intangibilities of Form*, 103.

68 Ibid.

commercial success[69] still lives and works in the non-metropolitan city of Nsukka, given that the city does not have its own airport and is not counted among the creative hotspots of Nigeria. Unlike Lagos and the much larger provincial capitals of Jos, Ibadan, Enugu, Aba, and Onitsha, where major parts of the film and music industries are based and a start-up scene is booming, Nsukka is – despite its sizeable university – rather provincial.[70]

When asked why he still lives there, Anatsui replies laconically: that his studio is there. Upon closer examination, the idea that he could do his job better anywhere else is rather naïve. His creative work is far too intertwined with the socio-economic and cultural environment on the ground to allow for a simple relocation. Anatsui's local networks in Nsukka are based not only on his decades-long occupation at the university, but rather everything – from material procurement to employee recruitment and work mode – is integrated in the local socio-cultural context. "My studio is in a rural setting and therefore it is possible to get people who would be willing to volunteer to come and help,"[71] is how he explains this aspect of his work arrangements. The informal employment relationships in his studio not only have to do with the fact that in Nigeria about 60% of the population already works in informal employment,[72] but this is also due to a dense local network, both with the rural population as well as with the local tradesmen and his contact with students. This networking is an ultimately indispensable basis for his entire work, and could therefore not easily be relocated to a metropolis.

The connection to recycled materials would also be different in a mega-city like Lagos and even more so in a major city in the Global North. The fact that Anatsui came across the material of the bottle caps has to do with the existence of both small local distilleries, homegrown forms of waste disposal and doing business, and finally with the modest lifestyle of the artist in this setting.

The screw caps, the tin cans, and the used printing plates with which he works do not come from an economy of complete misery, as one might find in the slums of Lagos, nor are they diverted from an industrially- or municipally-managed waste dis-

---

69 His retrospective at the Haus der Kunst was the most successful exhibition of the past ten years at the Munich institution with 118,000 visitors and his works are traded for more than a million dollars. Monopol, "El Anatsui erfolgreichste Schau seit zehn Jahren am Haus der Kunst," August 7, 2019, https://www.monopol-magazin.de/el-anatsui-erfolgreichste-schau-seit-zehn-jahren-am-haus-der-kunst.

70 See Kizito-Ogedi Alakwe, "Defining the Cultural and Creative Industry: An Exploration of the Nigerian Cultural and Creative Ecosystem," *Journal of Creative Industries and Cultural Studies (JOCIS)* 3 (2018): 27.

71 Art Basel, "Meet the Artists | El Anatsui." https://www.artbasel.com/news/meet-the-artists-el-anatsui.

72 See Kate Meagher, "Informal Economies and Urban Governance in Nigeria: Popular Empowerment or Political Exclusion?" *African Studies Review* 54, no. 2 (2011): 68.

posal system. They come from recycling yards, middlemen, or breweries that clean recycled bottles. Due to the poorly equipped state infrastructure for waste management, Nsukka has its own waste economy, with its own markets for materials and countless informally-employed waste pickers who collect bottles, plastic, metal, and compost every day. In Nsukka, the average monthly income is 56 US dollars and so garbage collection is a comparatively profitable activity for unskilled workers. Particularly in scrap-metal collection, some can earn an average income of 110 US dollars per month; which is what Thaddeus Chidi Nzeadibe, geographer and senior lecturer in the Department of Geography at the University of Nsukka, documents in a recent study.[73] Yet, waste disposal and its high proportion of recycling do not rely on the 'self-employed' "waste pickers" alone, but also on a number of intermediaries who clean, sort, and occasionally also remove labels and any fasteners from the bottles in order to return them to local breweries in a clean condition. The aluminum caps are collected separately so that they can be melted down to produce plates, cooking utensils, grates, and coatings in local companies. In addition to intermediaries, separate markets exist for the waste trade – for example, the Orie Orba Market.[74] This is from where Anatsui obtains his material, in addition to middlemen and distilleries. What he buys here is therefore by no means waste; it is regarded a raw material.

As a result, the small industrial work setting of Nsukka is a curiously harmonious fit for his studio. The work behind the impressive weavings does not seem out of place here. Even though garbage collection itself undoubtedly is a hard and dirty activity and miserably paid from the standards of the Global North, the image of the "waste pickers" drawn up in the Nsukka investigations has little to do with the notion that the "children of the poorest" rummage "around in landfills for (toxic, sharp-edged) metal scraps".[75] The idiosyncrasies ruling the precarious economy in Nsukka render the handling of garbage in everyday life very visible. The waste trade is not a shadow economy. Waste is sorted and then traded in public markets.[76] Anatsui is interested in all of these correlations. He does this not in terms of socio-cultural

---

73 "This will tend to suggest that waste picking is a profitable occupation in Nsukka. It would therefore be argued that waste pickers in Nsukka earn more than the statutory minimum wage of about US$56 monthly." Thaddeus Chidi Nzeadibe, "Development Drivers of Waste Recycling in Nsukka Urban Area, Southeastern Nigeria," *Theoretical and Empirical Researches in Urban Management* 4, no. 3 (2009): 144.

74 Ibid.

75 Peter von Becker, "Einer von Afrikas Größten. Das Gedächtnis der Tropen," *Tagesspiegel*, May 19, 2019, https://www.tagesspiegel.de/kultur/einer-von-afrikas-groessten-das-gedaechtnis-der-tropen/24357546.html.

76 On the self-image of the African economy, also see Felwine Sarr, *Afrotopia*, London: University of Minnesota Press, 2019.

analyses, but in the sense of a performative physical realization of ordinary identity-inducing life practices, which usually remain closed to scientific observation.

A series of sculptures made from the printing plates of local newspapers, a material from which Anatsui has made sculptures several times in recent years, also exemplifies this interest by way of the artistic handling of materials. Fragments of obituaries and birth announcements are still visible on the crumpled plates. He notes that he is concerned with how things connect people to each other.[77] 'Whole' and 'useful' objects are not what seem particularly enlightening to Anatsui. Instead, his work highlights that things are things only when in use; yet their thingness and their cultural depth are only recognizable when they are no longer used for their original purpose. Alfred Sohn-Rethel already knew how to describe this in his striking and humorous reflections on the Neapolitan understanding of technology. He claimed that in the mid-1920s in Naples the broken was the actual state of an apparatus and recognized a unique epistemological truth in this. In this vein, it can be said: Only when the screw cap no longer works does it come to light as a thing.[78]

This is why for Anatsui, too, the things that fascinate him are those that fall out of their traditional functional usage contexts but still reveal the characteristics of the former thing. Neither the screw caps nor the printer plates are reduced all the way down to their pure substance, materiality, or shape, as Anatsui never quite strips the work material of its thingness. The screw caps remain recognizable as such, even crushed, and broken as they are. They still carry traces of the former usage contexts, norms, and narratives. But the sediments of accumulated instructions and social scripts now suddenly become moldable and open toward the imaginary.

Anatsui's work, then, is not about revealing that things follow or create rigid social structures, nor is it a powerful conceptualist act of decontextualization, which, like the Readymade, declares everyday objects to be works of art by way of an altered institutional framing or through a changed perspective. The intentional puncturing of traditional aesthetic and art-related hierarchies of perception that energized Marcel Duchamp, for instance, hardly play a significant role for Anatsui. His works do not reflect issues of artistic interpretative sovereignty or for the mechanisms of inclusion and exclusion within the art field, nor does the distinction between conceptual and "retinal art"[79] or between art and non-art seem particularly relevant here. More accurately, Anatsui's work revolves around a performative understanding of materiality and thingness. It is a question of loosening the functions as well as

77 "Things which link people together." Oyiza Adaba, "The El Anatsui Interview," May 21, 2013, https://www.youtube.com/watch?v=WLE_YK2XARw.

78 Alfred Sohn-Rethel, "The Ideal of the Broken Down: On the Neapolitan Approach to Things Technical," (org. 1926 transl. 2018) https://hardcrackers.com/ideal-broken-neapolitan-approach-things-technical/.

79 Calvin Tomkins, *Duchamp: A Biography*, New York: Museum of Modern Art, 1996,158.

the social and political patterns of everyday objects. This becomes even more clear in comparison to Minimal Art wherein "the materials do not represent, signify or allude to anything" but instead "they are what they are and nothing more."[80] Anatsui's materials, by contrast, always remain bound to everyday practices and refer to all kinds of previous non-artistic modes of active use. The artist's epistemic interest in certain materials such as bottle caps follows the objective of demonstrating an understandable imaginable historical depth of everyday things and to show us that they have always belonged in different spheres, times, or contexts.

His usage of certain materials is not concerned with the idea of recycling nor with a clumsy embrace of the "real", as Ullrich has assumed regarding other artists. What Anatsui's work aims at is a linkage between worlds *through* materials. It combines different perceptions of materials, working environments, horizons of meaning and culture. The connection between distilleries, consumers, waste pickers, studio assistants, the global exhibition business, and the Nigerian economy – with its publicly visible garbage that immediately becomes the raw material for something new – is exemplified in Anatsui's work. All of this suddenly acquires its own unique dignity as a nexus of life and the world.

80 Michael Fried, "Art and Objecthood," *Artforum* (Summer 1967): 22.

Authors

Olivier Asselin is a full professor in the Department of Art History and Film Studies at the Université de Montréal, wherein he teaches expanded cinema and media arts. His current research focuses on the use of mobile platforms and locative technologies in contemporary media arts. He co-edited *Espaces de savoir* (Presses de l'Université Laval), *Menlo Park. Trois machines uchroniques* (Presses de l'Université Laval), *The Electric Age* (University of Ottawa Press), and *Precarious Visualities: New Perspectives on Identification in Contemporary Art and Visual Culture* (McGill-Queen's University Press). He has contributed essays to several books and catalogues, such as *Architectures de mémoire* (Presses du Réel), *Pós-fotografia e Pós-cinema* (Ediçoes Sesc), *The Oxford Handbook to Canadian Cinema* (Oxford University Press), *Cartographies of Place: Ways of Representing the Urban* (Mc Gill-Queen's University Press), *3D Cinema and Beyond* (Intellect), *Le réel à l'épreuve des technologies* (Presses de l'Université de Rennes), *Extended Cinema* (Campanotto), *Rafael Lozano-Hemmer* (San Francisco Museum of Modern Art), *Installations* (Musée National des Beaux-arts de Québec), *Edmund Alleyn* (Musée d'art contemporain de Montréal), and *Angela Grauerholz* (Canadian Museum of Contemporary Photography). He has also written and directed several feature films — *La Liberté d'une statue* (Festival des films du monde, Prix Ouimet-Molson), *Maîtres Anciens* (nomination Gemini Awards), *Le Siège de l'âme* (Festival des films du monde, Toronto International Film Festival), *La Fin de la voix* (nomination Gemini Awards), *The Last Days of Paris* (Festival du nouveau cinéma), *Un Capitalisme sentimental* (opening film, Festival du nouveau cinéma), and *Le Cyclotron* (Festival du nouveau cinéma, Shanghai International Film Festival, Whistler International Film Festival, Borsos Awards for Best Screenplay and Best Cinematography, nominations Iris Awards and Canadian Screen Awards) — and he has completed two projects in augmented reality —*Necropolis* (Festival du nouveau cinéma, Gamescom, Augmented World Expo, South-by-South-West) and *MuseumAR* (Musée des beaux-arts de Montréal).

Pierre-Emmanuel Perrier de la Bâthie (b. 1984, Vienne) has been a program director and teacher of Art History and Semiology at the Catholic University of Paris since

2010. He is a former student of *École Normale Supérieure* and *École du Louvre*, and he has just defended his PhD at the University of Poitiers, entitled *Photographic Strategies and Artistic Mythologies: the Construction of an Auto-Photo-Biographical Narrative by Artists in the 20th Century*. He is a specialist in Historiography and the history of photography, he works on visual strategies developed by artists of the 20th century (Pablo Picasso, Marcel Duchamp, Salvador Dalí, Joseph Beuys, Andy Warhol, and Yves Klein) to stage their own artistic mythologies. He is particularly interested in the reception and remediation of "photo-biographical" stories by the public, whether experts or amateurs. His research brings together notions of semiology, mediology and narratology, and highlights the concepts of the creative act and photogenic construction. Since 2012, he has co-directed the annual cycle of conferences, "Jeudis de l'Art," at the Catholic University of Paris. He has also published several articles on the adaptation of literary conceptual tools for the benefit of visual analysis, in particular by working on exhibition catalogues.

Karen van den Berg is Professor of Art Theory and Curating at Zeppelin University, as well as Academic Director of the University's arts program. She studied Art History, Classical Archeology, and Nordic Philology in Saarbrücken and Basel, whereat she received her doctorate. She has worked as a curator since 1988. Between 1993 and 2003, she served as a Research Fellow and Lecturer at the University Witten/Herdecke. She has also undertaken visiting research and teaching opportunities at significant international institutions, including the Chinati Foundation in Marfa (Texas), IKKM Bauhaus University Weimar, the Europäisches Kolleg Jena, and at the Department of Comparative Literature at Stanford University. Her research focusses on art, politics, and activism; artistic working practices and studio research; museum studies; and educational architecture. Along with numerous publications within these fields, she has written monographs and essays on artists and collectives, such as Richard Serra; Joseph Beuys; Forensic Architecture; Korpys/Löffler; Christian Jankowski; Rirkrit Tiravanija; and the Center for Political Beauty. She is currently one of four Directors of Studies within the Innovative Training Network, "The Future of Independent Art Spaces in a Period of socially Engaged Art (FEINART)," supported by the Marie Skłodowska-Curie Actions of Horizon 2020 (www.feinart.org).

Job Boot studied Graphic Design at ArteZ University of the Arts in Arnhem, The Netherlands, before transferring to Comparative Literature, in which he obtained a BA and a research master's degree from Utrecht University and the University of Amsterdam, respectively. He wrote his master's thesis about the poetry of Jack Spicer and its relationship to phenomenology, with a specific focus on Levinas' critique of the utilitarianism implicit in Heidegger's ontology. Job's other research interests include the work of Maurice Blanchot and other French thinkers inspired by the Paris student revolts in May '68, and in particular their continued relevance for contemporary anti-authoritarian social movements. Questioning traditional hierarchies is also a key concern of the visual artists Job writes about, and a central element of his own painting practice. As a critic and painter, Job is interested in contemporary abstract art, the legacy of the Supports/Surfaces movement and Raphael Rubinstein's notion of "provisional painting". In addition to his painting practice, Job currently works as an educator and independent researcher.

German A. Duarte (Ph.D.) is Assistant Professor of Film and Media Studies at the Free University of Bozen-Bolzano. His research interests include history of media, film history, cybernetics, cognitive-cultural economy, and philosophy. He is the author of several publications, including authored books, edited volumes, and essays and papers in international journals. Among them, he recently authored the monograph *Reificación Mediática* (UTADEO – 2nd edition 2020), the book *Fractal Narrative: About the Relationship Between Geometries and Technology and Its Impact on Narrative Spaces* (Transcript, 2014), and co-edited the volumes *Reading "Black Mirror". Insights into Technology and the Post-Media Condition* (Transcript, 2021), *Transmédialité, Bande dessiné & Adaptation* (PUB, 2019), and *We Need to Talk About Heidegger: Essays Situating Martin Heidegger in Contemporary Media Studies* (Peter Lang 2018).

Jonathan Fardy, PhD is Associate Professor of Art History and History at Idaho State University. His research examines the history and structure of theories concerning art and politics since 1960. He has published research on François Laruelle, Louis Althusser, Jean Baudrillard, and Walter Benjamin, among others. He is the author of four books: *Laruelle and Non-Photography*, *Laruelle and Art: The Aesthetics of Non-Philosophy*, *Althusser and Art*, and *The Real Is Radical: Marx after Laruelle*. His current book project is *Ideology After Althusser: Laruelle, Ranciere, Baudrillard.*

Miguel Ferrão (Lisbon, 1986) is a visual artist, a PhD candidate in Artistic Studies – Art and Mediations at NOVA University (Lisbon, Portugal), and a Professor in Fine Arts BA at ESAD.CR (Caldas da Rainha, Portugal). He holds an MA in Philosophy-Aesthetics from NOVA University and a BA in Painting from FBAUL (Lisbon, Portugal). Since 2010, he has been partnered with Eduardo Guerra as Musa paradisiaca; a duo shortlisted for EDP Foundation's New Artists Prize (2013), SONAE Media Art Prize (2015), and FLAD Drawing Prize (2021), and with work presented at Anozero – Biennial of Contemporary Arts of Coimbra (2022); Les Laboratoires d'Aubervilliers (2022); Frac des Pays de la Loire, Nantes (2022); Whitechapel Gallery, London (2019); MAAT – Museum of Art, Architecture and Technology, Lisbon (2018); Galeria Municipal do Porto, Porto (2018); Haus der Kulturen der Welt, Berlin (2017); BoCA – Biennial of Contemporary Arts, Lisbon (2021 and 2017); Vdrome (2017); Calouste Gulbenkian Museum, Lisbon (2017 and 2013); José de Guimarães International Art

Centre, Guimarães (2016); Serralves Museum of Contemporary Art, Porto (2016 and 2015); Videoex Film Festival, Zürich (2015); Malmö Art Academy – Moderna Museet, Malmö (2015); Fondation d'Entreprise Ricard, Paris (2015); Palais de Tokyo, Paris (2013); and Cinemateca Portuguesa, Lisbon (2013). He collaborated with ZDB Gallery (2008–2010) as a curatorial assistant, and coordinated the cultural program "Aguêdê-Alê" in São Tomé and Príncipe (2010–2013).

Heidi C. Gearhart is Assistant Professor of Art History at George Mason University. Her research focuses on artists and art theory of the Middle Ages, and the manuscripts and sacred arts of medieval Europe. She is especially interested in issues of memory, craft, and manufacturing. She has taught at the Humboldt-Universität zu Berlin, Assumption College, and the University of Michigan. Her first book, *Theophilus and the Theory and Practice of Medieval Art* (Penn State University Press, 2017), examines the only complete treatise on art to survive from the high Middle Ages – a text known in English as *On Diverse Arts* – and argues that the tract be read as a cohesive unit that yields precious insights on the values embedded in medieval art-making. *Theophilus and the Theory and Practice of Medieval Art* won an Honorable Mention from the International Center of Medieval Art Book Prize in 2018. She has also published in journals including *Gesta, Studies in Iconography,* and *Word & Image,* and she has received fellowships and awards from the Institute for Advanced Study at Princeton, the Getty Research Institute, the Kress Foundation, and the Busch-Reisinger Museum/Harvard Art Museums. Her current book, *Names to Remember: Medieval Artists in Word and Image, c. 800–1200*, looks at how artists and artistic projects were recorded in Northern Europe in the Middle Ages. By examining images of artists and texts about art-making as deliberately-recorded memories, this book analyzes the functions they serve: as tools for defining social hierarchies, as expressions of morals and power, and as wordplay or memory hooks that open new avenues of meaning. She received her Ph.D. in the History of Art from the University of Michigan.

Maura Grimaldi is an artist and researcher, approaching subjects related to phantasmagoria, obsolete technologies, archeology, and media geology. Based on her experimentation with different optical devices, Maura seeks to reflect on the economy of attention and the forms of subjectivation in contemporary times. Among her main exhibitions and projects are: Utopiana space residency in Geneva (Pro Helvetia / COINCIDENCIA South America / Swiss Art Council 2021); the solo show "The work appearing in your memory is not mine" (Galeria Virgílio, 2018); PIMASP critical monitoring program (MASP, 2016/2017); HANGAR residence (Lisbon, 2017); PIVÔ Research (Sao Paulo, 2017); VI Bolsa Pampulha (Belo Horizonte, 2016); XI Red Bull Station Residence (Sao Paulo, 2015); a residency at Centro de Arte Jardim Canadá – JACA (Belo horizonte, 2014); the exhibition "The avant-garde is in you" (Coimbra,

2014); an artistic residency at the École Supérieure des beaux-arts TALM-Tours (France, 2013); Exhibition of the Photography Program 2012/2013 (CCSP, 2012); and the exhibition "Corners" (MAC USP, 2012). Grimaldi holds both a bachelor and a master's degree from the University of São Paulo in Brazil, and is currently a PhD candidate in Lisbon at the Universidade Nova de Lisboa, Portugal.

Olga Moskatova is an Assistant Professor for Media Studies at Friedrich-Alexander-University Erlangen-Nuremberg. Her main research fields include theory and aesthetics of visual media, materiality of media, new materialism, and networked images. Selected Publications: *Male am Zelluloid. Zum relationalen Materialismus im kameralosen Film* (transcript 2019); *Images on the Move: Materiality-Networks-Formats* (transcript 2021); and *Networked Images in Surveillance Capitalism* (special issue of *Digital Culture & Society* 02/2021, together with Anna Polze and Ramón Reichert).

Hauke Ohls (Ph.D.) is Research Assistant for the Chair of Modern and Contemporary Art History/Art Science at the Institute of Art and Art Science at the University of Duisburg-Essen. His research focuses on theoretical, sociological, and philosophical questions of modern and contemporary art; especially political-ecological aesthetics, discourses on objects, materiality, and image, as well as the relationship between art, economy, and neo-liberalism. Further emphases include the interface between art and music, writings by artists, media art, and transcultural art history. Since 2013, he has worked as an assistant to the artist Mary Bauermeister, and since 2017 he has been compiling her catalog raisonné.

Martina Olivero is a Lecturer in Aesthetics and Philosophy of Art. She holds a Doctorate in Aesthetics from Université Paris 1 Panthéon-Sorbonne, and has obtained both a Bachelor's (*Laurea*) and a Master's (*Laurea Magistrale*) in Philosophy from Università Cattolica del Sacro Cuore (Milan). She focused mainly on Existentialism and Psychoanalysis before specializing in the Critical Theory of the Frankfurt School and its discussed relationship with both of the abovementioned methodological approaches. Her doctoral dissertation accounts for the tragic dimension inherent in Walter Benjamin and Theodor W. Adorno's concerns about aesthetics and the philosophy of history. She is currently preparing a monograph on modern tragedy as an aesthetic and political performative form, exploring its revolutionary potentiality in the Western dialectical scheme at work within the Enlightenment and its creative promise for a stage of immanent emancipation among irreconcilable contradictions and suffering. She has taught courses in philosophy of art, aesthetics, and critical theory across all undergraduate levels and has given seminars in critical theories of culture at the master's level. Besides presenting at international philosophy, aesthetics, and media conferences, she has also published articles on literary theory, film, theatre, and documentary practices. She is currently an Alliance Visiting Scholar in the Department of Philosophy at Columbia University.

Tom Palin was born in Birkenhead in 1974 and studied at Liverpool John Moores University and The University of Manchester (BA Fine Art and MA Art History and Visual Studies respectively). He completed a PhD in Painting at The Royal College of Art in 2018. His doctoral thesis was titled "The Condition of Painting: Reconsidering Medium Specificity". He has exhibited widely and undertaken professional residencies in Munich, Dublin and Prague. Solo exhibitions include: *Pride of Place: A Painter's Perspective* (Yorkshire Sculpture Park, Wakefield, 2002), *A Room with a View* (The Atkinson Gallery, Southport, 2004), *Between Then and Now* (Dean Clough, Halifax, 2005), *A Room with a View 2* (View Two Gallery, Liverpool, 2008), In Two Minds (Ashton Art Gallery, Ashton Under-Lyne, 2010), Small Works (Gallery on the Green, Settle, 2017) and Elegies in Grey, (Leeds Arts University, 2018). Awards include: *The Hunting Young Artist of the Year Award* (RCA, 2000), *The Feiweles Trust Bursary* (YSP, 2002) and *The Gilchrist-Fisher Memorial Award* (Rebecca Hossack, 2004). Publications include: *Pride of Place: A Painter's Perspective* (YSP Press, 2002), *Readings in a Rumour of the End of Art* (Workshop Press, 2012), *Tom Palin: Artist Statements 1993–2012* (Workshop Press, 2013), "The White Paintings of Maurice Utrillo" (Turps Banana, 2019) and "The Context of Medium Specificity: From Riegl to Greenberg" (Journal of Contemporary Painting, 2020). Papers include: "To See or Not to See: Pareidolias and Abstract Painting" (*British Abstract Painting in the Eighties* (Herbert Art Gallery, Coventry, 2018), "Pictures, Truths and Methods: From Function to Form in Abstract Painting" (*Abstract Painting Now*, Royal West of England Academy, Bristol, 2019), "Performing Research: Painting and its Words" (*Is Painting research?* Manchester School of Art, Manchester, 2020, postponed). Currently, Tom teaches Painting at the Royal College of Art.

Hans-Jörg Rheinberger is Director Emeritus of the Max-Planck-Institute for the History of Science in Berlin. He studied philosophy, linguistics, and biology in Tübingen and Berlin. After completing a master's degree in philosophy in 1973, he earned a Ph.D. in biology in 1982 and a Habilitation in molecular biology from the Free University of Berlin. Stations in Berlin, Stanford, Lübeck, and Salzburg followed. From 1997–2014, he was Director at the Max-Planck-Institute for the History of Science. Hans-Jörg is also a member of the Berlin-Brandenburg Academy of Sciences, of the National Academy of Sciences Leopoldina, and of the Académie Internationale de Philosophie des Sciences. His newest book: *Spalt und Fuge. Eine Phänomenologie des Experiments*, Suhrkamp, Berlin 2021 (English version: *Split and Splice. A Phenomenology of Experimentation*, The University of Chicago Press, Chicago, in press).

Stephan Schmidt-Wulffen (Prof. Dr.) is a philosopher, art theorist, curator, and is currently a professor of art theory and curatorial studies at the Freie Universität Bozen. He was a visiting professor at Columbia University in New York, and he was the *Rektor* of Akademie der bildenden Künste Wien (2001–2011). His research focuses on art theory, philosophy, artistic practices, and contemporary art.

Filippo De Tomasi lives and works in Lisbon, Portugal. He is a PhD Candidate in Artistic Studies at the NOVA School of Social Sciences and Humanities, NOVA University of Lisbon – FCSH/UNL (Portugal). His research concerns the relationship between contemporary art and photography. He graduated from Alma Mater Studiorum – University of Bologna (Italy) in Visual Arts in 2014, specializing in contemporary art history and photographic theory and practice. Previously, he collaborated in the production of artistic projects at Galeria Luís Serpa Projectos and he has published some articles in contemporary art magazines. In the last few years, he worked as an assistant professor and he participated in some international conferences. He is a member and co-founder of the research group Estudos Visuais e Arqueologia dos Media – Visual Studies and Media Archaeology (EVAM) at the NOVA Institute of Communication (ICNOVA), FCSH/UNL. Moreover, he collaborates in artistic projects with the curatorial group Da Luz Collective.

Luca Trevisani is a visual artist. His multidisciplinary practice has been exhibited internationally in museums and institutions. Trevisani has published several books including *The Effort Took Its Tools* (Argobooks 2008), *Luca Trevisani* (Silvana Editoriale 2009), *The Art of Folding for Young and Old* (Cura Books 2012), *Water Ikebana* (Humboldt Books, 2014), *Grand Hotel et des Palmes* (Nero, 2015), and *Via Roma 398. Palermo* (Humboldt Books, 2018). Trevisani's research ranges between sculpture and video, and crosses borderline disciplines such as performing arts, graphics, design, experimental cinema, and architecture in a perpetual magnetic and mutant condition. In his works, the historical characteristics of sculpture are questioned or even subverted in an incessant investigation of matter and its narratives

Georgios Tsagdis currently teaches at Leiden University, Erasmus University Rotterdam, and the Architectural Association, and is founder of the theory network, *Minor Torus*. His essays have been published in numerous collections and international journals, including *Parallax*, *Philosophy Today* and *Studia Phaenomenologica*, among others. His editorials include the special issues 'Intersections: at the Technophysics of Space' (*Azimuth*, 2017) and 'Of Times: Arrested, Resigned, Imagined' (*International Journal of Philosophical Studies*, 2020), as well as the collective volume, *Derrida's Politics of Friendship: Amity and Enmity* (Edinburgh University Press, 2022). The collections *Memories for the Future: Thinking with Bernard Stiegler* (Bloomsbury, 2023) and *Re-Imagining Europe* (SUNY, 2023) are in preparation.

Cultural Studies

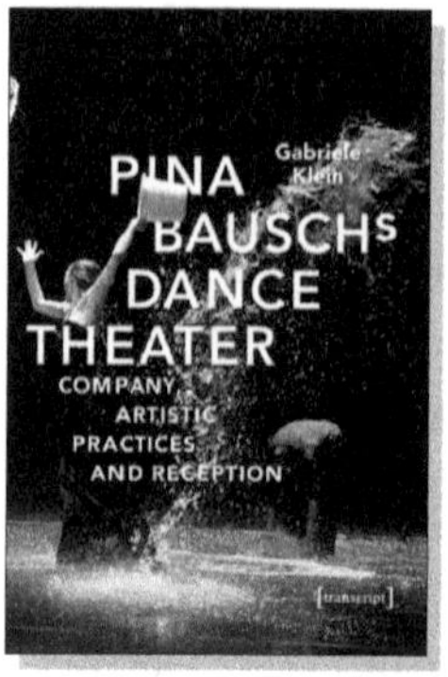

Gabriele Klein
Pina Bausch's Dance Theater
Company, Artistic Practices and Reception

2020, 440 p., pb., col. ill.
29,99 € (DE), 978-3-8376-5055-6
E-Book:
PDF: 29,99 € (DE), ISBN 978-3-8394-5055-0

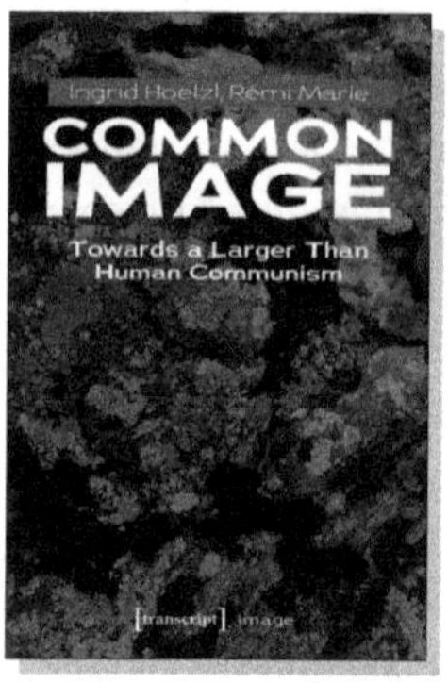

Ingrid Hoelzl, Rémi Marie
Common Image
Towards a Larger Than Human Communism

2021, 156 p., pb., ill.
29,50 € (DE), 978-3-8376-5939-9
E-Book:
PDF: 26,99 € (DE), ISBN 978-3-8394-5939-3

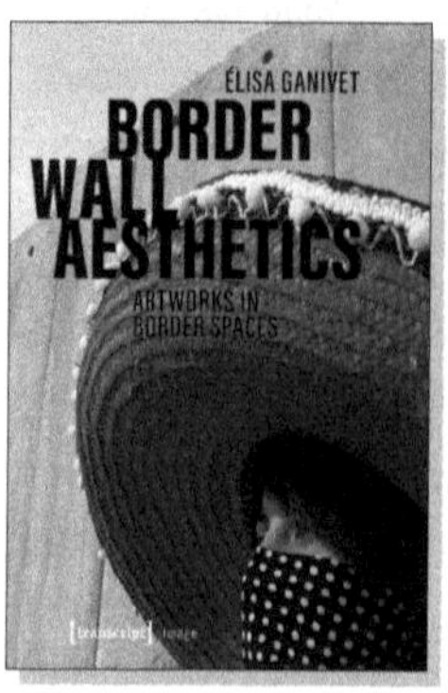

Elisa Ganivet
Border Wall Aesthetics
Artworks in Border Spaces

2019, 250 p., hardcover, ill.
79,99 € (DE), 978-3-8376-4777-8
E-Book:
PDF: 79,99 € (DE), ISBN 978-3-8394-4777-2

All print, e-book and open access versions of the titles in our list are available in our online shop www.transcript-publishing.com